Professional Practice in Learning and Development

Professional Practice in Learning and Development

How to design and deliver
plans for the workplace

Mark Loon

KoganPage

Publisher's note

Every possible effort has been made to ensure that the information contained in this book is accurate at the time of going to press, and the publishers and authors cannot accept responsibility for any errors or omissions, however caused. No responsibility for loss or damage occasioned to any person acting, or refraining from action, as a result of the material in this publication can be accepted by the editor, the publisher or the author.

First published in Great Britain and the United States in 2016 by Kogan Page Limited

2nd Floor, 45 Gee Street	1518 Walnut Street, Suite 1100	4737/23 Ansari Road
London	Philadelphia PA 19102	Daryaganj
EC1V 3RS	USA	New Delhi 110002
United Kingdom		India

© Mark Loon 2016

The right of Mark Loon to be identified as the author of this work has been asserted by him in accordance with the Copyright, Designs and Patents Act 1988.

ISBN   978 0 7494 7742 4
E-ISBN   978 0 7494 7743 1

British Library Cataloguing-in-Publication Data

A CIP record for this book is available from the British Library.

Library of Congress Control Number

2016953255

Typeset by Graphicraft Limited, Hong Kong
Print production managed by Jellyfish
Printed and bound in Great Britain by CPI Group (UK) Ltd, Croydon CR0 4YY

CONTENTS

ABOUT THE AUTHORS

Editor

Dr Mark Loon

Dr Mark Loon is a faculty member at the University of Worcester. He holds a PhD and a DBA. His MBA specialism was Finance. His expertise is in organizational behaviour and his primary research area is in the use of technology in learning and teaching in higher education, learning in the workplace, higher-order thinking dispositions, and leadership development. His secondary research area is within the organizational context that includes organizational learning and change, dynamic capabilities, and business model innovation. He has published in various academic journals such as the *Journal of Managerial Psychology*, as well as practitioner reports and books such as with the CIPD. He is currently the Chair of the British Standards Institute's Human Capital Standard Sub-Committee on Developing International HRM Standards (representing the UK on the International Standard Organization's Technical Committee) and the Deputy Vice Chair of the Programmes and Qualifications committee within the University Forum on Human Resource Development. He is also an associate editor with the *International Journal of HRD Practice, Policy and Research*, and the *Journal of Economic and Administrative Sciences*. Prior to academia, he was in management consulting, working for firms such as Cap Gemini, Ernst & Young and KPMG. He had his own company in Sydney, Australia providing consulting and business analysis services to clients such QBE, AMP, Morgan Stanley and the University of Sydney. He has counted the governments of Malaysia and Indonesia as clients. He is trained in Six Sigma at Black Belt level. In addition to the UK, he has taught in Australia, France and Kazakhstan.

Contributors

Dr Robin Bell

Dr Robin Bell joined the Worcester Business School in 2011. He works as a senior lecturer within the marketing subject group and specializes in entrepreneurial development and enterprise development. He is responsible for coordinating Worcester Business School's activities with international partners, and supervises doctoral candidates exploring enterprise and entrepreneurship development. He is also a visiting professor at Beijing Foreign Studies University, delivering sessions on entrepreneurship and enterprise. His innovative curriculum development and teaching approaches to the field of entrepreneurship and enterprise development have been supported by research and teaching funding from a wide range of institutions, including private multinational organizations, professional bodies, and the European Union. Dr Bell has utilized these awards to develop and encourage the use of active and experiential teaching methods in the field of entrepreneurship, implementing real-world exercises into modules to give students hands-on experience at enterprise creation and fostering their entrepreneurial development. He has a research background in both qualitative and quantitative methodologies. His current research focuses on entrepreneurs, entrepreneurship, small business and international exposure, particularly the utilization of entrepreneurial skills in different sectors and organizations, the development of entrepreneurial skills, and cross-cultural communication within teams.

Dr Ruth Sacks

Ruth Sacks DBA is principal lecturer and business development director at Westminster Business School. As business development director, Ruth has responsibility for the delivery of academic enterprise activities. This includes the design and delivery of a business development strategy for executive programmes and short courses. Ruth is the course leader for MSc Leadership, an innovative post-graduate practice-focused master's for experienced leaders and managers using action learning. Ruth also created and runs the acclaimed Women for the Board Programme, successfully promoting women's development at top levels. Ruth has a background in organization development and change management, having worked both in house in senior consultancy and management roles, and as an external consultant and facilitator for organizations in the professional services, public and not-for-profit sectors. She has contributed at a strategic level to projects designed to enhance organizational effectiveness and improve stakeholder management. Clients have included Cadbury Trebor Bassett, Radiospares, France, Swissport, The Department for Communities and Local Government and the United Nations. Ruth lived and worked in Paris for 14 years and speaks fluent French. When not working, she spends time with friends and family, goes to the theatre, and tries and fails to stay away from e-mail.

Dr Jan Myers

Jan has been a senior lecturer/assistant professor in business and management, organizational behaviour and HR, and leadership and development in both the UK and Canada. She has recently joined the Corporate and Executive Development Centre at Newcastle Business School, Northumbria University (UK) focusing on leadership, individual and organizational development. Before moving into academia, she was a senior manager, trainer and consultant working in and with third sector and public sector organizations, both in the UK and internationally. Jan's research interests include: individual and organizational learning; leadership and sense-making; member-based and member-owned organizations; and participatory mechanisms in and across organizations.

Dr Michael Bagshaw

Mike is currently a senior lecturer at Worcester University Business School. He is chartered psychologist, and management and leadership development professional with over 30 years of consultancy experience in Europe, America and Asia, working in both the private and public sectors. Throughout his career he has designed and delivered the full range of 'soft skills' group programmes and coached individual managers and senior executives from across the professional spectrum using his own coaching process. He worked as a forensic psychologist for 13 years in the UK Prison Service. In 1988 he changed direction and joined the world of commerce. This began at CEPEC, where he developed new programmes for management training, including conflict mediation and dealing with aggressive behaviour. In 1994 he became development director at Coutts Consulting, where he spearheaded the strategic change from redundancy coaching to a focus on employability and career life management. In 1998 Mike started his own consultancy brand from scratch with a business partner, serving a range of small, medium and blue-chip companies including Phizer, Malvern Instruments,

NHS, Royal Mail, Organon, London Fire Brigade, QinetiQ, The National Trust and GlaxoSmithKline. He sold the business in 2007.

Sa'ad Ali

Sa'ad is a lecturer in human resource management with research interests in the field of HR in the Arab Middle East. He is in the final stage of his PhD research, which explores the impact of social networks' 'wasta' (generally meaning cronyism) on employee selection in the Jordanian banking sector, and is being undertaken at Nottingham Trent University. He also holds an MSc in human resource management from Oxford Brookes University and a BA in business management from the University of Jordan. Sa'ad has held a variety of academic and HR roles both in Jordan (Bank of Jordan) and the UK (University of Nottingham, Nottingham Trent University and University of Worcester) which complement his academic experience.

FOREWORD

In the field of understanding organizations and bringing about organizational change, the role of the learning and development professional is much overlooked and seldom explored or explained in the detail given to it by the authors of this volume. That organizations can learn is pretty well established, and in the period since Peter Senge was writing about the learning organization, most leadership and management courses explore this dimension. Less often asked is whether organizations should learn, much less what they should learn, which are essentially moral or ethical questions. The leadership and development professional is, if nothing else, an educator, and education has at its heart a moral purpose – to make a difference, to bring about improvements, to be transformational – therefore, effective leadership and development practice is of necessity rooted in values. This goes much further than an expression of the values and beliefs of the professional themselves. It extends to an institutional ethical direction and purpose, and the working through of this in terms of principles, procedures and actions that govern, shape, regulate and guide transactions, especially with external bodies, collaborators and partners.

One of the most persistent dualities in the field of leadership and development is the extent to which the values of those who lead inevitably complex organizations become uncoupled from the values of the professionals and practitioners they manage. This can arise out of different career patterns and pathways created for an executive tier, be sustained by continued separation of the executive from those who report to them, and validated by a set of working assumptions that support and sustain the status quo without ever seemingly questioning whether such separation is ethically right or practically effective for organizational success. We can recognize the scourge of managerialism in every sector of the economy, private and public. Once marketing, public relations, income generation and financial control take and hold the centre ground in an organization and begin to dominate its discourse, priorities become reoriented and the divide between professionals and managers widened.

Since the beginning of the current millennium we can see beginning to emerge in the theoretical literature a call to build agency and ethicality into leadership education and practice. Business schools for many years inhabited, and to a degree helped to create, an amoral universe of corporate greed, exemplified in the corporate scandals such as Enron and Tyco that rocked the western financial world in the 1990s. The problem with ideologically inspired amoral theories is that they present themselves as predominantly causal or functional, leaving no room for ethics or morality, which are mental phenomena. In other words, research in the field has adopted a naïve and unreflecting empiricism. This determinist direction has been necessary to validate the claim of the field to be a science, with the tragic consequence that leadership is presented in an ethical vacuum, with actions signified as responses to corporate, economic or competitive demands, effectively removing freedom of choice and a sense of individual responsibility for actions.

It is the twin elements of individual agency (the capacity of leaders to choose to resist market forces) together with moral purpose (the ethical aims of business) that have been missing from leadership and leadership research. The question of individual agency, or in our context the ability of leaders to break out of channelled thinking and enacting, is a crucial one for leadership and development studies. In order for a leader to think of acting ethically, there has to be a connection between the ability to make a thoughtful, considered strategic decision and the ability to think and act ethically – the two are inextricably intertwined.

There are two lessons in this for students of business (by which I mean both business students and corporate leaders and all in between). First, organizations are characterized by complexity – they are individual and distinctive. That is not to deny common patterns and trends, but rather to acknowledge that organizational reality is part of a more complex world that cannot be characterized by stereotypical generalization at one pole or dogmatic singularity at the other. In too many studies, it is the assumptive world of the researcher that is laid before us, rather than the actuality of participants' lived experiences.

The second lesson leads on from the first: work-based research should be interpretative. Pre-existing notions of power, leadership and management may or may not apply and be useful in particular business settings. Familiar words like man, woman, strategy, culture, that we use in everyday language, carry a baggage of meanings that can blind us to any one particular reality. A way of seeing is also a way of not seeing. The student of business must develop their own ethical compass and, using that guide, create their own theories of change and test these against more established theories and against their own experience of organizational life. Blindly applying others' theories to work settings is like using the wrong tools or looking in the wrong places.

The contributions that Mark Loon has collected together in this volume do much to ensure that the student of business develops their own critical voice. They exhort the student to be guided by but not blinded by theory; to take responsibility for their own learning, and to recognize their role in helping and supporting their organization and its workforce in adapting to change. Throughout, using real-life case examples and thoughtful reflection, the authors encourage practitioners and professionals to adopt a curious mindset, to refuse to settle for the easy path when the truth may lie elsewhere, and all the time to respect uniqueness and individuality. Asking critical, practical and positional questions is an ethical pursuit around which we are able to build a model of leadership and development which carries moral authority and practical utility.

Dr Geoffrey Elliott
Professor of Post-Compulsory Education
University of Worcester

Introduction

The world is changing! It is volatile, uncertain, complex and ambiguous. As clichéd as it may sound, the evidence of such dynamism in the external environment is growing. Business as usual is more the exception than the norm. Organizational change is the rule, be it to accommodate and adapt to change, or to instigate and lead change. A constantly changing environment is a situation that all organizations have to live with. However, what makes some organizations able to thrive better than others? Many scholars and practitioners believe it is the ability to learn.

Therefore, this book on developing Learning and Development (L&D) professionals is timely, as it explores and discusses trends and practices that impact on organizations, the workforce and L&D professionals. Being able to learn and develop effectively is the cornerstone of motivation, as it helps to address people's need to be competent and to be autonomous (Deci and Ryan, 2002; Loon and Casimir, 2008; Ryan and Deci, 2000). L&D stimulates and empowers people to perform. Organizations that are better at learning at all levels – individual, group and organizational – will always have a better chance of surviving and performing.

Given the new reality of a dynamic external environment and constant change, L&D professionals now play an even more important role in their organizations than ever before. However, L&D professionals themselves are not immune to the turbulent changes, as their practices are also impacted. Therefore, the challenges that L&D professionals face are two-pronged: first, in relation to helping and supporting their organization and its workforce in adapting to the change, and second, developing themselves effectively and efficiently so that they are able to be one step ahead of the workforce they are helping to develop. These challenges are recognized by the CIPD, and they recently launched their new L&D qualification, which has served as an inspiration for this book.

L&D plays a crucial role at both strategic (eg organizational capability) and operational (eg delivery of training) levels. L&D professionals have moved from being reactive (eg following up action after performance appraisals) to being more proactive (eg shaping capability). L&D is increasingly viewed as a driver for organizational performance. The CIPD (2014) suggest that

L&D is increasingly expected to take not only more responsibility but also more accountability for building both individual and organizational knowledge and capability, and to nurture an organizational culture that prizes learning and development.

This book is for L&D professionals. Nonetheless, it is also suited for those studying human resource development (HRD) at intermediate level. The term 'Human Resource Development' is more common in academia, and is largely synonymous with L&D (Stewart and Sambrook, 2012). Stewart (1998) defined HRD:

> the practice of HRD is constituted by the deliberate, purposive and active interventions in the natural learning process. Such interventions can take many forms, most capable of categorizing as education or training or development (p. 9).

In fact, many parts of this book (eg Chapters 5 and 7) are appropriate for anyone who is involved in training and development. This may include a variety of individuals within the L&D community, such as line managers, professional trainers, training solutions vendors, instructional designers, external consultants and mentors (Mayo, 2004). The CIPD (2014) go further as they argue that the role of L&D is broad and plays a significant role in organizational development (OD) and talent management (TM), as well as in human resource management (HRM) in general. OD, TM, HRM and L&D are symbiotic in enabling the 'people management function' to provide organizations with the capabilities that they need.

This book has three themes – *Directions*, *Contributions* and *Solutions* – that underpin the eight chapters. There are specific learning outcomes in each chapter, which are supported by step-by-step exercises that will facilitate professional development. Unique to this book are the case examples involving real people, real experiences, real stories, candid perspectives. These individuals have been interviewed especially for the benefit of the readers of this book. As such special thanks goes to:

- Professor Lamine Bodian, master's programme director, ESDES Lyon Business School, France.
- Pieter Brummer, head of UK HR services and interim head of resourcing, Denmark, LEGO.
- Ashley Callaghan, professional trainer, ACT.
- Barbara Emanuel, training and development manager, Walsall Healthcare NHS Trust.

- Linda Gittings, training officer, Fortis Living.

- Joaquim Gonsalves, HR manager, Bassaka Air.

- Susan Hamilton, senior learning and development manager, Not-for-profit Sector Organization.

- Jason Jestin, financial controller, DBB Worldwide.

- Neil Liddington, area manager, risk reduction, Avon Fire and Rescue Service.

- Abigail Newson, HR business development consultant, IBM.

- Shawn Simpson, training project manager, Agence Iter France.

- Anthonie Versluis, managing partner, Roland Berger Strategy Consultants.

- Flavio Vong, manager, enterprise services, Commonwealth Bank of Australia.

Special thanks also to Lucy Carter, commissioning editor at Kogan Page, for her advice and support throughout the development of this book.

The first theme of the book is *Directions*. This theme concerns the present and potential future expectations that L&D professionals may face in their practice. Chapter 1 is about 'Developing professional practice in L&D'. In the first section, I discuss what 'professionalism' is and what it means for L&D professionals in terms of their development. In this chapter, I argue that expectations of L&D from senior management are growing. L&D professionals need to be able to demonstrate ability to influence decision making by developing new competencies that enable them to provide senior management with new insight, which in turn increases L&D's strategic credibility.

In examining the diverse activities and tasks that L&D professionals currently undertake, and may be expected to undertake in the future, four roles emerge: capacity and capability builders, boundary spanners, consultants, and change agents. Capacity building primarily concerns creating space, time, and cultivating the right environment for the workforce to develop, which can be a challenge, given how fire-fighting appears to be prevalent in many organizations today. Capability building involves enhancing knowledge, and developing the skills and competencies of the workforces, whilst boundary spanning involves networking and growing partnerships within and outside the organization. 'Being a consultant' is briefly touched upon, but it is further discussed in Chapter 5, whilst the role of a change agent involves instigating and managing change. This chapter concludes with a discussion of 12 important knowledge, skill and capability areas that L&D professionals must develop to advance their practice.

Expertise is situated in both the organization and in the professional community (Collins and Evans, 2008). Experts are not just individuals who have specialist knowledge; they also know how and when to apply their expertise by being able to discern between different environments and contexts (Knorr-Cetina, 1999).

Chapter 2, 'Understanding the context of L&D', provides L&D professionals with a number of frameworks, models and examples that will help them to further understand the context of their profession and how this shapes the direction of their organization, and ultimately their practice. This is important for L&D professionals, as their credibility is founded upon their claim to expertise (Pritchard and Fear, 2015).

Chapter 2 recognizes the important role that context plays in shaping the new directions of L&D professionals. In this chapter, Robin Bell and I discuss how L&D's role is significantly influenced by contextual factors such as the external environment, organizational life cycle and size, business/industry of the organization, organizational goals, and senior management's view of strategy. Irrespective of L&D's influence on organizational strategy, which varies amongst organizations, for example, whether L&D is a 'scope maker' (involved in helping to set direction) or 'scope taker' (involved in implementation after the direction has been set), understanding the context it operates in is crucial. This chapter discusses the sources and nature of change and its impact on industry and organizations' business models. We also discuss how this has influenced the general nature of work, the workforce, and ultimately, their learning and development.

The second theme of this book concerns L&D's *Contributions*, specifically how L&D professionals articulate, communicate and demonstrate the value that it brings to the organization. Specifically, Chapter 3, titled 'Using information, metrics and developing business cases for L&D', discusses how L&D professionals can do this using the business case as a vehicle. The business case is a tool that L&D professionals can use to show how new L&D initiatives can benefit the organization and its stakeholders. The value of such benefit can be 'articulated' quantitatively and qualitatively.

Chapter 3 adopts a holistic approach in developing a business case. L&D professionals must be competently knowledgeable about accounting and finance but do not need to be experts – as their expertise lies in L&D. Therefore, to successfully complete a business case, L&D professionals need to form teams comprising the right members (depending on what the business case is about). The political realities that are associated with the development of a business case can be important considerations. How well L&D is able to 'sell' a business case depends on how well it is framed, usually either as a problem or as an opportunity. We then discuss the information, data and metrics required to build a typical business case, specifically in terms of identifying the benefits and costs. The chapter concludes with some suggestions on how the findings from the business case can be presented in infographics-inspired form.

In Chapter 4, 'Developing and using consultancy skills', Ruth Sacks and I discuss what it means to be a consultant and what is it that consultants do. This is presented in the order of stages in a project – starting, 'doing' and ending – with specific sections dedicated to examining each stage. Adopting a consulting approach helps L&D professionals to 'demonstrate' the value they bring, and may be undertaken through projects that have been articulated and justified through a business case.

In this chapter, we stress that whilst there are significant similarities between internal and external consultants, there are also advantages and disadvantages of each that L&D professionals need to consider when playing the role of consultant (and indeed also if L&D professionals are the ones who are doing the hiring of a consultant). There are three 'modes' or styles of how L&D professionals can approach consulting – the expert, the patient/doctor, and that of process consultancy – and each may be required in different circumstances or projects. This chapter also identifies and discusses a number of important aspects of the consulting process, such as relationship building, communication, stakeholder management, managing change, and the project as a whole.

The next theme is *Solutions*. Solutions not only involve programmes and other L&D interventions, but also how L&D professionals cultivate a learning environment. More importantly, the term 'solutions' denotes that what L&D professionals offer does indeed help individuals, groups and organizations to move forward by addressing problems and issues that they are facing, and/or taking advantage of opportunities that present themselves. The next four chapters reflect the 'solutions' that may be designed, developed and implemented by L&D professionals.

In Chapter 5, 'Enhancing participant engagement in the learning process', Jan Myers starts the chapter by highlighting the different orientations to learning. She focuses on the notion of 'deep learning', which is then used as the basis for discussing the focus of the chapter: learner engagement. Jan's discussion in this part of the chapter prompts us to more broadly explore and further consider what really motivates individuals to engage and genuinely learn. In doing so she examines the field of motivation, drawing upon the classic works of Vroom (1964), Herzberg (1968) and McClelland (1985), for example, to help us understand human nature and what drives us to learn. In addition to providing a broad overview of the different approaches to learning, she also explores in depth some of the approaches that are particularly important to enhancing engagement, such as social learning, constructivism and adult learning. In addition to providing some mini case studies to reinforce our understanding of some of the concepts, Jan also suggests a number of processes and tools that L&D professionals can adopt in enhancing leaner engagement.

Chapter 6 concerns 'Designing and developing digital and blended learning solutions'. However, despite its title, it is not aimed at developing L&D professionals to be technologists (just as Chapter 3 is not aimed at developing L&D professionals to be accounting and financial experts). Chapter 6 is about developing L&D professionals to be technology savvy. In doing so, I adopt a culinary analogy in presenting this chapter, where the most important factors in creating a dish (eg blended learning), are the ingredients and the flavours each of them brings.

The chapter first explores the typical technologies and technology products that are available for learning and development, ie the ingredients. I then introduce the data format, interactivity/immersion, timing, content (creation and curation), connectivity and administration (FITCCA) framework, which helps L&D professionals to look beyond the labels of technologies in identifying what the technology offers – its functions and features – which is analogous to the 'flavours' of the ingredients. The next section discusses some multimedia principles that are important for L&D professionals to consider in designing and developing digital learning solutions. Finally, whilst there are innumerable permutations of blended learning, this section focuses on the typical emphasis of blended learning and how technology may support such blends.

In Chapter 7, Michael Bagshaw examines why and how collective and social learning is growing in importance but, equally, how it is important to nurture and facilitate these forms of learning. In this chapter, 'Facilitating collective and social learning', which is organized into seven sections, Michael discusses contemporary perspectives that are underpinned by well-established theories and concepts. In the second section, following the introduction, Michael argues that collective and social learning is a new paradigm, and although the notion has been around for a while, it has taken on a new lease of life, especially given the changing external environment and organizational dynamics. Section three discusses the various forms of such learning, in particular learning in networks, learning in teams, and learning in communities. In the fourth section, we are guided on how to cultivate a more social and collective culture, and why this is crucial given the adaptive and 'wicked' problems that we cannot solve alone as individuals. Section five explores some learning tools such as the communication processes of dialogue, advocacy and inquiry. In the sixth section, social media is explored in detail within the context of collective learning, building upon the basic concepts introduced in Chapter 6. Finally, in section seven, Michael discusses how mentoring, coaching and leadership can play a collective role along with social learning by applying the GROW model that was introduced in Chapter 1.

In Chapter 8, 'Developing and delivering L&D solutions for international markets', Sa'ad Ali and I examine how different dynamics within and between countries can impact the development and delivery of L&D. We build upon the previous chapters, in particular Chapters 5 to 7, that discussed how L&D solutions may be developed in consideration of enhancing engagement, the digital world, and collective and social learning. In doing so, we examine how the effectiveness, and even appropriateness of the concepts discussed in these chapters may be contingent on country-specific factors such as culture.

As there are almost innumerable considerations, we focus on the key factors that impact on L&D in international markets, in particular economic development of countries, economic cycles, technology infrastructure, need for technology in L&D, and perceived importance of technology in L&D, labour markets and educations systems. We also discuss how national culture may shape learners' expectations and preferences in their learning and development. We use Hofstede's cultural dimensions of power distance, uncertainty avoidance, individualism/collectivism and masculinity/femininity as a framework for our discussion. We also explore the capabilities required by global L&D professionals to enable them to develop and deliver L&D solutions for international markets. This chapter also provides three case examples to help demonstrate how both L&D and business professionals have experienced learning and development from an international perspective.

We hope you enjoy reading this book, but more importantly, that you are able to apply what you have learned from each chapter in developing yourself as an L&D professional. As you will observe, the L&D profession is facing many challenges in all areas of its practice. However, we believe the knowledge and skills presented here, as well as the insight provided from our interviewees in the case examples, will provide you with the necessary capabilities to help you support organizations, the organization's workforce and the L&D business unit in the present, whilst putting yourself in a good position to continue to do so in the future.

We wish you the best in your learning and development and career progression.

Support material

You can find multiple choice questions to support this book at www.koganpage.com/ppld

---

References

Chartered Institute of Personnel and Development (2014) The CIPD Profession Map v2.4 [online] http://www.cipd.co.uk/cipd-hr-profession/profession-map/profession-map-download.aspx

Collins, H and Evans, R (2008) *Rethinking Expertise*, University of Chicago Press, Chicago, IL

Deci, E L and Ryan, R M, eds (2002) *Handbook of Self-Determination Research*, University Rochester Press, USA

Herzberg, F (1968) One more time: how do you motivate employees? *Harvard Business Review*, **46**, pp. 53–62

Knorr-Cetina, K (1999) *Epistemic Cultures: How science makes knowledge*, Harvard University Press, Boston, MA

Loon, M and Casimir, G (2008) Job-demand for learning and job-related learning: the moderating effect of need for achievement, *Journal of Managerial Psychology*, **23** (1), pp. 89–102

Mayo, A (2004) *Creating a Learning and Development Strategy*, CIPD, London

McClelland, D C (1985) *Human Motivation*, Scott, Foresman, Glenview, IL

Pritchard, K and Fear, W J (2015) Credibility lost: attempting to reclaim an expert identity in an HR professional context, *Human Resource Management Journal*, **25** (3), pp. 343–63

Ryan, R M and Deci, E L (2000) Self-determination theory and the facilitation of intrinsic motivation, social development, and well-being, *American Psychologist*, **55** (1), pp. 68–78

Stewart, J (1998) Intervention and assessment: the ethics of HRD, *Human Resource Development International*, **1**, 9–12.

Stewart, J and Sambrook, S (2012) The historical development of human resource development in the United Kingdom, *Human Resource Development Review*, **11** (4), pp. 443–62

Vroom, V H (1964) *Work and Motivation*, Wiley New York

Developing professional practice in L&D

01

MARK LOON

1 Introduction

This chapter discusses your development as a learning and development (L&D) professional that will enable you to adapt to the changes in your profession and to better support the learning and development of the workforce and organization. The two learning outcomes in this chapter are:

1 Understand the requirements of being a professional.

2 Identify and develop capabilities for successful L&D practice.

Section 2 contains a discussion on what it means to be a professional. This is a term that is at times taken for granted, and therefore it is important to revisit some of the basic expectations and assumptions that go with being a 'professional'. Prior to discussing the areas for development for L&D, it is important to take stock of what it is that L&D does. However, the development of L&D professionals also needs to reflect the changes impacting an organization, the way it operates and its expectations of its workforce. This evaluation, as discussed in Section 3, is important, as only by knowing what L&D does and understanding what is expected of it, are we in a position to discuss how to develop L&D professionals.

The discussion in Section 3 reveals that there is a plethora of activities and tasks that are expected of L&D professionals, which is anticipated to only grow. Four key roles are identified that comprehensively reflect much of L&D activities, and these are discussed in Section 4. The four roles that L&D professionals play are that of Capacity and Capability Builder, Boundary Spanner, Consultant and Advisor, and Change Agent. Said in another way, L&D professionals are those who 'build' (capacity and capability), 'span' (boundaries), 'solve' (problems, which is the primary purpose of any consultant) and 'change'.

Section 5 examines the knowledge and skills required by L&D to successfully fulfil these roles, and contains a discussion on 12 important areas for development. Whilst many of these capabilities are comprehensively discussed in this section, further discussions of some of them and their contexts are provided in other chapters. Specifically, knowledge of adult learning principles, concepts and theories are presented in Chapters 5 and 7, and how these may differ in different countries in Chapter 8. Context-bound knowledge and competencies are discussed in detail in Chapter 2, some of the principles of project management are discussed in Chapter 4, financial competency is detailed in Chapter 3, whilst technology savviness is outlined in Chapter 6. Finally, Section 6 concludes this chapter.

2 Professionalization

Friedson (1973) states that professionalization is:

> a process by which an organized occupation, usually but not always by virtue of making a claim to special esoteric competence and to concern for the quality of its work and its benefits to society, obtains the exclusive right to perform a particular kind of work, control training for and access to it, and control the right of determining and evaluating the way their work is performed (p. 22).

This means that professionals are those who are considered to be functionally important and valuable to society, require complex skills and qualifications through higher education, have a degree of prestige, and attract higher earnings (Cullen, 1985; Thakor and Kumar, 2000). This is echoed by other scholars such as Pavalko (1971), who argue that professionals are those who have undergone formal, systematic and lengthy training. Professionals are also those who have professional authority that is sanctioned by community, and possess the public's trust and confidence (Greenwood, 1957; Slocum, 1966). In addition, professionals are well-defined occupational groups (Collin, Van der Heijden, and Lewis, 2012) that have their own culture and identity, are self-regulated and are able to exercise expert judgement (Hill and Neeley, 1988; Thakor and Kumar, 2000).

L&D is a profession and is an organized occupation represented by the Chartered Institute of Personnel and Development (CIPD) in the UK. However, the chartership that the CIPD holds is just one of many of the elements that enable HRM and L&D to be proclaimed as a profession in the UK (Stewart and Sambrook, 2012). As indicated by Friedson's definition, professions must make wider contributions to society in addition to those made to their own organization. Given their varied stakeholders and the important role they play, professionals must subscribe to explicitly articulated standards of quality. These standards generally refer to competence and ethics (ethical behaviour) (Rees and French, 2013). These ethical standards usually translate into codes of conduct such as the CIPD's code for HRM professional including L&D practitioners (CIPD, 2012).

Equally important, professionalization also denotes that competency standards have been met through the process of certification and/or qualification. Many professional bodies require their members to pursue continuing professional development (CPD) activities to ensure that they are active in their field and profession, and that their knowledge and skills are regularly updated. Some professional bodies (eg Association for Project Management) even require that their members re-certify themselves after a period of time (eg three years) by passing examinations. Indeed, CPD is one of the cornerstones of professions that require professionals to demonstrate they regularly upkeep their professional knowledge (Collin, Van der Heijden and Lewis, 2012), and are able to at least maintain the threshold standards at any given time. CPD is recognized by the Organisation for Economic Cooperation and Development (OECD) as a significant aspect of life-long learning (OECD, 2000). CPD can be self-directed, by professional bodies and/or employers, and whilst it usually involves formal events/activities, it may also include informal learning opportunities (Collin, Van der Heijden and Lewis, 2012).

There is a debate that effective professional learning should involve the person as a whole (De Weerdt *et al*, 2006); to develop the professional you have to develop the person first. Indeed, Trede, Macklin, and Bridges (2012) argue that technical and interpersonal skills are necessary but insufficient for professional identities to develop. Genuine development of professional identity also requires applying and exercising reason and judgement, self-reflection and evaluation, and self-directed learning and development (Paterson *et al*, 2002). This form of meta-capability is acknowledged and recognized in this chapter in the form of reflective learning and is argued to be the foremost capability that should be gained, maintained and enhanced by L&D professionals.

Professionals recognize that context is important, and this is where the 'practice' plays a role in the term 'professional practice', as individuals need to learn how to apply their professional competencies in their respective unique circumstances. Professional learning is systemic and situated within their immediate context (eg organizational), with a significant component deriving from informal learning (Knight, Tait, and Yorke, 2006). For example, most of management's learning is from doing their jobs (Mintzberg, 2004), and Becher (1999) claims that professionals learn six times more through informal means than through formal interventions. But before we can understand what is it that L&D professionals need to learn, we must first understand what it is that they do.

Exercise

- Reflect upon the term 'professional'. What comes to mind when you come across the term?

- How does L&D as a profession compare to more time-honoured professions such as medical doctors and accountants?

- How does L&D as a profession compare to more contemporary occupations such as occupations in the technology sector?

3 Current practice and expectations

Before we further discuss how to develop the professional practice of L&D professionals, it is perhaps sensible to examine what L&D practitioners do and what is expected of them. The following list is not exhaustive but it provides some ideas of both the traditional and contemporary duties of L&D. The list is divided into three categories: what L&D does (or is generally expected to do) for individuals, groups (eg departments) and the organization as a whole.

3.1 For the individual

At the most granular level, and in keeping with the most basic expectations, L&D is expected to improve the work-related knowledge and skills of individuals within an organization so that they are able to do their jobs efficiently and effectively. Skill enhancement may also extend to soft skills and personal development. Many of the initiatives that L&D undertakes involve direct interventions such as providing training courses and setting up seminars.

Although the enhancement of knowledge and skills to improve job performance is the primary driver of training courses, a secondary driver may involve attaining formal qualifications and certifications. Certification is crucial for some individuals as it may form part of their 'licence' to operate and continue in their role. For example, accountants must be qualified and registered with their respective accounting bodies, and so must trades persons who are involved in electrical work. In addition to attaining qualifications, some professional bodies require individuals to commit to a minimum number of hours in activities related to continuing professional development (CPD). Although CPD is usually undertaken autonomously by the individual and their respective professional bodies, L&D may need to keep check and facilitate this process, especially when there is a need for verification and organizational record keeping. As part of its role in enhancing capability, L&D is also involved in evaluating the effectiveness of its interventions (Kirkpatrick and Kirkpatrick, 2009). Feedback obtained from ongoing evaluation enables L&D professionals to make revisions and improvements.

Whilst some training courses and events may be sourced, curated and/or delivered internally by L&D professionals themselves or by other colleagues, it may be in some cases that L&D will identify and recruit training professionals to deliver programmes. Such an arrangement poses a double challenge for L&D practitioners, who not only need to have some working knowledge of the area but also be able to manage training vendors in terms of content, pedagogic approach (ie how their method will get individuals to genuinely learn), delivery style and costs. However, now that technology and social media have empowered and democratized learning, it appears that UK corporate L&D spending on external services is on a downward trend (Krider, Singaraju, and Carroll, 2016).

Learning and development is also closely related to career advancement, as individuals look to L&D professionals to help them improve their work performances, and ultimately help them progress in their careers. Such support from L&D is usually in conjunction with annual performance appraisal processes (or similar forms) via a learning needs analysis. The learning needs analysis essentially evaluates the learning and training needs of an individual to help them better perform their jobs and/or achieve their career aspirations. In some cases, L&D also plays an important role in helping the human resources department in creating competency profiles (further discussed in the 'for the organization' section later in this chapter). L&D may advise individuals on the requirements of competency profiles of roles that an individual aspires to assume.

In terms of learning in the workplace in general, L&D may also play an important role in assessing and providing input into how jobs are designed to help enhance informal learning and learning on the job. For example,

L&D may provide ideas into how cross-department collaboration may be designed into jobs, to not only facilitate learning but to also improve individuals' effectiveness on the job. The development and implementation of learning and development interventions and environment help L&D promote positive attitudes towards learning and development in the workplace (further discussed in Chapters 5 and 7). Such positive attitudes from staff members are important, as this helps them to see their jobs not only as something 'they do' but as learning opportunities to improve their skills and potentially themselves. Linda Gittings, Training Officer, Fortis Living (not-for-profit housing association based in Worcestershire, UK) shares her view of L&D's role in developing individuals in the workforce for both compliance and capability building.

Linda Gittings, training officer, Fortis Living

L&D practice and function in my organization has changed significantly in the last two to four years, namely in terms of technology, government policy on our sector, the nature of the jobs and training, and the L&D function itself. Technology has impacted the way training and courses are delivered, whilst government regulations (eg welfare reform, universal credit) have had a significant effect on our 'customers', which has in turn required us to provide more legislative training to keep our workforce up to date.

The other challenges relate to the nature of work, which has necessitated new knowledge and skills. Many of these are part of mandatory/regulated qualifications that have to be meticulously planned and delivered. Tracking learners' life cycles and their re-certifications is essential to L&D. Professional traineeships and apprenticeships play an important role in the organization's L&D, as they help to address the organization's skills gap and succession planning. In addition to the trades, we also support professional courses such as those from the Chartered Institute of Management Accountants (CIMA). We are also very keen on seeing more initiatives for personal development as well as development programmes for those who have aspirations to move their career forward (eg talent management).

The L&D unit also plays an important role beyond learning and development. In our organization, L&D helps to promote local housing as a career choice with local schools and colleges, and we also take part in careers events. The organization is strongly recognized but many people do not know what local housing organizations do. We provide insight to prospective employees by showing them that there is more to Fortis, as we have many central services such HR, IT, Finance and Risk Management that offer 'corporate' career opportunities.

As an organization, we have a vast amount of job types requiring very different skills, which is where the variety, challenge and interesting aspects of L&D as a profession come from. One day you are talking to someone doing a very high-level leadership course; the next day you may be talking to a cook and arranging training on a meat slicer. The next day you are discussing L&D with a carpenter and you would be looking at something specific for his/her learning, or you might be having a conversation with an apprentice who has come straight from school and is just starting his/her career. I see L&D as a very interesting career to get into. It is very proactive to what is going on in the whole business; in fact you could say it underpins the whole business.

Fortis Living provides over 15,000 homes, primarily across Worcestershire, Herefordshire and Gloucestershire. With a turnover of over £75 million a year, it is one of the largest housing providers in the West Midlands, UK.

3.2 For the group

In addition to supporting individuals, L&D also contributes to groups such as teams. Such support may be intra-group (between colleagues within a department) or inter-group (between departments). For example, intra-group networking is activities that are held for those from the same department involving, for instance, developing and supporting 'infrastructure' (eg online forum) for communities of practice to take place. Inter-group events, on the other hand, require enterprise-wide cooperation such as that necessitated in product development, for example. In another inter-group example, L&D professionals may also involve external parties as part of internally organized events, for example experts from the accounting profession providing a talk on new legislation. These examples show that there is a growing expectation that L&D is expected to proactively connect people (Overton and Dixon, 2015).

It is not uncommon for L&D to be expected to promote internal networking within an organization through seminars and even job design (as mentioned in the previous section). Networking activities provide learning and development opportunities for individuals, as they are able to extend their reach in recruiting others to collaborate with, and also identify mentors/coaches that they would like to work with. The opportunities for knowledge sharing and partnerships, internally (intra and intergroup) and externally, inevitably provides learning opportunities for individuals to leverage upon and ultimately helps to further foster other important elements (eg trust) for an appropriate organizational learning climate to develop (Casimir, Lee, and Loon, 2012). Susan Hamilton, senior L&D manager in a not-for-profit sector organization, shares her thoughts on how L&D professionals may be more effective in understanding the needs of the workforce.

Susan Hamilton, senior learning and development manager, not-for-profit sector organization

L&D should be getting as close to the business as possible. The days of having a nice brochure of courses which you roll out three times a year are long gone. L&D's role in the past was very narrow, eg running qualifications, but there is a growing recognition even from those outside the profession that L&D has more to offer from both the broader and strategic perspectives. In doing so, L&D has to get closer to directors and managers to understand their challenges and what they need from L&D. This is of course to help the workforce to be more effective in their jobs, but it is also to stretch directors to think about what they need in the future. This is an important point for people who hope to get into L&D – making sure you understand the business you are working in so that you are able to better contribute and add to your own credibility in the eyes of the business.

The profession is moving in a direction whereby the boundaries between L&D and other parts of the business are being blurred. Those getting into the profession are being recruited and developed to recognize that their role is not functional, just working in silos. To be able to meet the expectation of being an L&D professional one has to 'get out there', talk to people and build networks. Therefore, it is important to develop your interpersonal skills. L&D professionals are also integral to improving their internal organizational unit's practices, as they are expected to feed back to L&D units about new/modified approaches, methods and tools.

3.3 For the organization

Perhaps the most significant change in the expectation of L&D's role is with regard to its contribution to the organization as a whole, although this is something that already occurs by default in some sense, as L&D activities at the individual and group levels ultimately contribute to the development of an organization. For example, by maintaining certification of individuals, L&D also supports the maintenance of organizational accreditation. In addition, by increasingly improving the capabilities and competencies of the workforce, L&D helps to enhance people's attitudes towards their jobs and careers, thereby benefitting the organization's reward and retention strategies.

Nonetheless, whilst L&D's contribution to individuals' and groups' learning and development eventually improves organizational capability, this has largely been by chance rather than by design. Senior management now views L&D through a strategic lens, demanding that L&D has more of an input in directly shaping organizational capability. Organizational capability is not merely a collation of the capabilities of individuals in the organization, but a valuable and distinct set of capabilities that provides an organization with the competitive edge over its rivals. Whilst an organization's capability is set by senior management, it must be informed and guided by L&D to help ensure its sustainability.

An example of how L&D may help develop organizational capability is in supporting HR in creating competency frameworks (or similar initiatives). A competency framework is an overarching configuration that guides the identification of competencies required by individuals within clusters, eg job families, occupational groups and organizational levels. Such a framework gives staff and management an idea of the progression and development requirements as they progress in their careers within the organization.

A more contemporary expectation of L&D involves its role in organizational performance. This places responsibility on L&D to ensure that whatever capability it helps the organization to develop must be translated into performance (revenue, profitability and market share growth). Such an expectation shares the responsibility of performance on L&D, thus compelling L&D to be innovative in its approach to individual, group and organizational level learning and development. The link between organizational capability and performance is not new as, Kirkpatrick's model of training evaluation (first published in 1959) posits that learning and development initiatives should ideally be able to be linked to results at the organizational level.

In today's volatile's world (as further discussed in Chapter 2) where organizations have to change, the ability to be agile is becoming more prized. This is not to say that organizations' current capabilities are not valuable, but given the changing nature of the external environment and intensity of competition, it means that being too rooted in one form of capability may hinder an organization's ability to adapt change. Hence, L&D is and will be further expected to help organizations to become agile. However, this should not be at the expense of short-term realities, which means that organizations have to be ambidextrous to enable them to exploit current capabilities to meet short-term goals but also at the same time explore and develop new capabilities for the future (Loon, 2014).

But how does an organization even start to develop agility and ambidexterity when the unpredictability of the external environment and intensity of competition means that organizations are constantly 'firefighting'? There is no easy answer. Nonetheless, as part of its capability-building duties, L&D is also responsible for building capacity within the organization (Loon, 2014; Mayo, 2004). Capacity building is more than just 'making room' for organizations to develop new competencies; it also involves setting the groundwork for new capabilities to develop, whatever they may be. An analogy can be drawn with sports. For example, an athlete can only further develop their skills (eg football) if they remain fit. So they must have the capacity to remain fit and injury free before they can further develop their respective capabilities.

Part of the 'laying the foundation' in capacity building is cultivating a learning-orientated organizational climate such as that usually found in learning organizations (Senge *et al*, 1994). There are many elements that contribute to the development of a learning organization, such as knowledge sharing (as highlighted in the 'for the group' section). It is important for L&D to have already established groundwork through individuals (eg positive attitudes towards learning and development) and groups (eg thriving communities of practices) as this provides an effective platform for a learning-orientated organizational climate to take place.

At the organization level, L&D may be required to collaborate with other business units such as organization development so that organization-level outcomes can come to fruition. For example, although organizational culture and climate tend to be resilient they need active support. Therefore, L&D must work closely with OD to develop strategies to nurture the organization through learning and development programmes and events, and develop the appropriate type of leadership behaviours in the organization's senior managers. In another example, many knowledge management (KM) strategies and initiatives will only be effective if L&D is considered be an integral part. Knowledge can only be created by people, and they do so only if they are effective in their learning and development. Also, tacit knowledge cannot be captured and diffusion may only take place through conversations and collaboration, which can take place via L&D-related events and programmes (Sanchez, 2005). In addition, learning systems such as virtual learning environments and KM systems can be integrated to provide a seamless solution to organizations in developing intellectual capital.

Exercise

The role and expectations of L&D professionals vary greatly amongst organizations for a variety of reasons such as organizational size, strategy and sector. Therefore, it is important to first identify what is it that L&D professionals in a particular organization *do*, and second whether this matches with the present expectations of management (Table 1.1) and the general workforce (Table 1.2). Use the following tables to complete this exercise of an L&D practice and organization that you are familiar with (the first row in each table contains an example).

Table 1.1 What L&D currently does vs what is expected of L&D by management

A What the L&D practice currently does	B What is expected of L&D by management	A vs B What and why differences exist
1. Select trainers.	1. Identify performance issues.	1. L&D assumes managers know solutions to performance and only require help with the delivery of the 'solution' ie more training.
2.	2.	2.
3.	3.	3.
4.	4.	4.

Table 1.2 What L&D currently does vs what is expected of L&D by the general workforce

A **What the L&D practice currently does**	B **What is expected of L&D by general workforce**	A vs B **What and why differences exist**
1. Provide menu of training programmes.	1. Guidance on the 'right' development opportunities for their respective careers.	1. L&D assumes staff are clear about their own career paths and progression pathways and that staff are best positioned to decide which training courses to take up.
2.	2.	2.
3.	3.	3.
4.	4.	4.

This activity can also be extended to include future expectations of management and workforce in the next two to three years. For example (Table 1.3 and 1.4):

Table 1.3 What is expected of L&D by management at present vs what is expected of L&D by management in three years

A **What is expected of L&D by management at present**	B **What is expected of L&D by management in three years**	A vs B **Why do these differences exist?**
1. Identify performance issues.	1. Anticipate and address potential performance issues.	1. Management expect L&D to assume a more proactive role in performance management.
2.	2.	2.
3.	3.	3.
4.	4.	4.

Table 1.4 What is expected of L&D by the general workforce management at present vs what is expected of L&D by general workforce in three years

| A
What is expected of L&D by management at present | B
What is expected of L&D by management in three years | A vs B
Why do these differences exist? |
|---|---|---|
| 1. Guidance on the 'right' development opportunities for their respective careers. | 1. Empower staff to design their own development pathways. | 1. Guidance may still be sought although staff are now more savvy and are able to obtain information and advice from different sources. L&D to develop solutions that enable staff to design their own development pathways for their own careers. |
| 2. | 2. | 2. |
| 3. | 3. | 3. |
| 4. | 4. | 4. |

4 Roles in L&D professional practice

Given the broad activities that L&D undertakes, which will only continue to grow, where do L&D professionals start in developing themselves and what type of qualities, knowledge and skills do they need today and the future? There are many perspectives in terms of what L&D does and what is required of L&D professionals. Indeed, the CIPD in the UK has identified standards for L&D professionals (CIPD, 2014) as part of their HR professional competency map, and divides this into two main parts – L&D activities and knowledge. Each activity and knowledge area has four stages of proficiency (termed as bands by the CIPD).

The CIPD recognizes L&D as a technical area within HRM that contains six key activities: developing learning strategy and plans, designing L&D

solutions, delivery of the solutions, leadership development, talent development, and evaluating the impact of learning initiatives on individuals. In addition, they identify eight knowledge streams for L&D practitioners:

1 approaches and methods in identifying learning and talent development needs;

2 cognisance of the various approaches to enhance learning;

3 understanding the dynamics of organizational learning and how to capture and transfer knowledge within the organization;

4 knowledge of how to implement learning approaches (through various channels);

5 being informed about how to manage information and able to manage vendors and suppliers;

6 able to embed diversity and social inclusion into L&D;

7 knowing how to engage colleagues from other parts of the organization; and finally

8 knowing how to evaluate L&D initiatives and able to demonstrate the value that L&D offers.

Other competency models such as that from the Society for Human Resource Management identify L&D as part of being an HR expert, and deemed it a behaviour reflecting an individuals' working knowledge of function (Society for Human Resource Management, 2012).

Another starting point in terms of understanding where and how L&D professionals should develop themselves is from a role-based perspective. Based upon the discussion in the previous section, four key roles have been identified: Capability and Capacity Builders, Boundary Spanners, Consultants and Advisors, and Change Agents. The discussion of these roles in this section involves the rationale and aims that may be applicable to most L&D professionals in various contexts (eg size and sector of organization). How each of these roles corresponds to examples of what L&D 'does'/ is expected to do is shown in Table 1.5.

4.1 Capacity and capability builders

L&D professionals are capacity and capability builders and this is the essence of any L&D practice. As Table 1.5 shows, building capacity and capability is pervasive across all levels and is a constant goal of L&D. Although the notion of L&D being a builder of capacity and capability may be apparent, it is worthwhile examining what this role entails.

Table 1.5 L&D roles and what L&D professionals do and what is expected of them

What do L&D professionals do and what is expected of them?	Roles			
	Capability and capacity builders	Boundary spanners	Consultant and adviser (solve problems)	Change agents
For the individual:				
Develop work-based skills and know-how, and support individuals' personal development	√			
Support attainment of qualification and certification (including mission-critical CPD)	√			
Identify and source L&D programmes and events		√	√	
Support career advancement	√			
Provide learning needs analysis, eg as part of any performance/ development appraisals	√		√	
Support individuals learning whilst on their jobs and in the workplace, eg input into job design to facilitate informal learning	√	√		
Evaluate learning	√			
Promote positive attitudes towards learning and development in the workplace	√	√		

continues

Table 1.5 *continued*

What do L&D professionals do and what is expected of them?	Roles			
	Capability and capacity builders	Boundary spanners	Consultant and adviser (solve problems)	Change agents
For the group				
Promote networking (internal and external)		√		
Encourage knowledge sharing amongst colleagues (linked with fostering an appropriate organizational climate)	√			
Foster the growth of communities of practice	√		√	
For the organization				
Develop organizational capability	√			√
Support organizational performance			√	√
Drive organizational agility and ambidexterity			√	√

Activity			
Build for the future – capacity building			✓
Cultivate a learning-orientated organizational climate	✓		✓
Support the development and deployment of competency frameworks	✓		
Evaluate results and ROI	✓	✓	
• Strengthen knowledge management systems, eg knowledge capture and diffusion by integrating learning management systems and virtual learning environments	✓	✓	
• Guide/support organizational development	✓		
• Contribute to improving internal organization-wide analytical ability		✓	
• Support the maintenance of organizational accreditation/ certification (through individual maintaining qualifications)	✓		
• Strengthen organizational reward and retention strategies	✓	✓	
• Improve induction/on-boarding processes	✓		

Developing capacity

Developing capacity is usually observed as a precursor to developing capability but what does it mean? Building capacity concerns providing time and space for learning and development. It is about ensuring that individuals (eg staff and management) are given time to learn, reflect, experiment and develop. Focusing only on 'doing' and performing is short-termism and such organizations are not providing time for their staff, and therefore themselves, to develop for the future. Time to learn and develop should be recognized as 'productive' and as part of working hours.

In addition, building capacity is also about providing the space to learn and develop. 'Space' may refer to either physical or virtual space. Physical space includes facilities such as training rooms and amenities. Virtual space is now more common and may refer to organizational intranet sites that contain learning materials. Equally important are 'opportunities' for learning, and these may include prospects for on-the-job training, job rotation, networking and knowledge sharing. 3M is a good example of an innovative company that provides its staff with the time, space and opportunities to learn. Staff are given time (as much as one day per week) to devote to their own projects/initiatives as a form of self-development, and they can do this using the company's existing facilities. In addition, staff are given the opportunity to attend seminars and conferences at 3M locations around the world to facilitate learning, collaboration, knowledge sharing and ultimately innovation (3M, 2012; von Hippel, Thomke, and Sonnack, 1999).

Building capacity also involves developing the appropriate mindset, which is akin to having the right 'attitude' to in turn develop the right aptitude. Of course, providing the time and space for learning inevitably sends the right signal to the workforce that the organization places importance on their development, however, whilst necessary this is insufficient. In addition, L&D must work with other business units within the organization such as HR to ensure that learning and development is observed as part of job performance and career progression. This overlap between the two indicates to the workforce that if they are serious about their work and careers, then they need to put effort into their own learning and development.

Finally, building capacity also involves developing basic and appropriate policies that prioritize and cater for the development of the workforce. These policies should genuinely reflect the values and ethos of the senior management and the organization as a whole. Having the appropriate policies in place also formalizes the L&D practices and helps to ensure that they are sustained. In assessing whether your organization, or one that you are familiar with, builds capacity, please undertake the following activity.

Exercise

Time:

- Are staff provided with the time to undertake learning and development, and if so, how much time have staff taken for L&D courses/events on average in the last 12 months?

Space and opportunities:

- Are there dedicated physical spaces such as classrooms (including facilities) for learning and development?
- Are there virtual spaces for learning and development, eg a repository for learning materials, virtual learning environments, and learning management systems?
- What learning and development opportunities are there for staff to interact, collaborate and to learn informally from one another?

Mindset:

- What do you think staff attitudes are towards their personal learning and development (eg enthusiastic, ambivalent)? How seriously do you think individuals take their own learning and development?
- In what way does the organization motivate/incentivize the workforce to learn and develop?

Policies:

- Do senior management value the long-term development of the organization's workforce? Are there formal policies concerning learning and development that reflect such an ethos?

Alternatively, for those of us who are just starting out and do not have an organization to refer to, try the following exercise:

- What does capacity building mean?
- If you had your own business with a small team, how would you go about 'building capacity'?

Developing capability

Developing capability is to develop 'know how' (aptitude). Whilst most expertise is usually associated with functional or technical capabilities such as accounting or information technology, there are also other important and complementary capabilities such as transferable skills (Cheetham and Chivers, 1998). Transferable skills, which also includes 'soft skills' such as the ability to learn effectively, team-working skills and solving problems, are crucial for people to then better gain functional skills.

In many cases, it is usually assumed that individuals will possess transferable capabilities to some degree, which provides a compelling reason why L&D should have a role in the selection processes. Nonetheless, L&D should not take these for granted, as the nature and dynamics of organizations change, for example with new people with different personalities being introduced into teams, new strategic directions, new ways of working, or adapting to the introduction of new technologies. The importance of developing 'capacity' is further supported in this regard as individuals must feel a sense of the importance of self-development that in turn provides a strong basis for developing other skills.

A crucial meta-capability is learning effectively. This may not at first appear to be a worthwhile endeavour, as surely everyone knows how to learn, otherwise they would not have reached this far in life. However, L&D should not overestimate individuals' learning abilities, as any impediment in learning will in turn hinder the learning of new technical/functional capability (hence why learning is sometimes viewed as a meta-capability as it is a capability of all capabilities). For example, learning something new may at times require us to unlearn what we already know, and to do away with long-held assumptions and beliefs. This unlearning process may be even more difficult than actually learning something new. Learning also requires mental agility in being genuinely open to new ideas, embracing opportunities to learn from change, and being able to do this over and again.

Technical and functional capability generally refers to a set of competencies that are associated with one's job and/or occupation such as those determined by their professional bodies, through their own respective development pathways and certification processes. For example, accountants will have developmental pathways and qualifications set by related professional bodies such as the Association of Chartered Certified Accountants. In addition, functional capabilities also relate to skills that may be specific to the organization and/or its sector. Examples may include organizations' policies and processes. Another example is sets of leadership knowledge and behaviours that an organization has determined to be the most crucial in its context. Whilst there are common leadership behaviours expected of anyone in a leadership role, there may be differences in terms of the nature and priority of certain behaviours. For example, leadership of organizations in the high-technology industry may be very different to leadership in a government agency within the public sector, especially for behaviours related to innovation that are more prized in the former.

Exercise

The following activity is to help us think about L&D's role as builder of capability. In reference to an L&D practice within an organization that is familiar to you, reflect and respond to the following questions.

Meta-capabilities (eg foundation capabilities, ability to learn effectively):

- How does the organization's L&D practice currently develop meta-capabilities? Or in what ways would you suggest this L&D practice develop meta-capabilities in individuals? List three examples. Remember, meta-capabilities are not capabilities to do the work per se but they are underlying capabilities to better help gain technical/functional capabilities. For example, high analytical abilities will help an individual gain the skills of a financial analyst, and highly developed interpersonal skills will help better gain business development skills.

- Reflect on how L&D may improve the development of meta-capabilities.

- Are there other initiatives that L&D could undertake to improve other meta-capabilities?

Technical and functional capabilities (eg engineering):

- Many organizations require a variety of technical and functional capabilities to help contribute to successful operations and performance. Identify two capabilities that you believe are the most important for the organization, and describe how L&D supports the development of these capabilities.

- Reflect on how L&D may improve the development of these two technical/functional capabilities in the future.

Managerial and leadership capabilities:

- Whilst there are universal capabilities that managers and leaders should possess, organizations may value and prioritize these capabilities in a different manner, since each type of organization is unique (with different history, culture, goals, operating environment and needs). Identify three of the most important leadership capabilities required by the organization of its senior managers.

- Reflect on how L&D supports the development of the three capabilities and if the present support is adequate. If not, provide ideas on how L&D may make improvements.

Alternatively, for those of us who are just starting out and do not have an organization to refer to, try the following exercise:

- Think about yourself and your capabilities:
  - What would you say your most developed meta-capabilities are? What aspects of your own meta-capabilities do you think require further development?
  - What technical/functional skills do you have? List these skills and rate them. How would you improve yourself in each of these skills?
  - How would you rate your leadership skills? How would develop your leadership skills?

4.2 Boundary spanners

The second important role that L&D practitioners adopt is that of boundary spanners. Boundary spanning is a term that was initially used to describe individuals who linked an organization's internal systems with the external environment. However, these days the term is used in a variety of contexts to describe an individual who crosses boundaries (Zahra and George, 2002), enabling them to operate in different arenas. Of course, many individuals will undertake some boundary spanning in their day-to-day work. However, to be classed as a boundary spanner means that such individuals (ie L&D professionals) undertake boundary spanning in a deliberate, strategic and sustained manner.

The activity of boundary spanning has long been recognized as a crucial activity for innovation. However, in today's world, boundary spanning is no longer a luxury but a necessity, as individuals and organizations are expected to work across groups and boundaries in working with others. As shown in Table 1.5, L&D practitioners, for example, are required to cross organizational boundaries when sourcing L&D programmes, and work across operational business units in incorporating informal learning in job designs and in developing positive attitudes towards L&D. L&D professionals are also expected to work in partnership with other support units such as OD, and to also orchestrate the networking between groups internal and external to the organization.

The boundary-spanning role played by L&D is varied, as it also involves going beyond sectoral boundaries and even geographic borders, especially in a multinational context. Going beyond the boundaries of the L&D unit is mostly a given in many organizations. The days when L&D professionals just remained within their own departments and organized training as instructed by business managers are almost gone. Many L&D practices are more pro-active as they seek to support business managers in providing learning and development opportunities. Such proactivity is recognized by the business partner model that some L&D functions have adopted, which involves L&D professionals working closely with their respective business units to help improve performance through learning. In such arrangements, L&D practitioners may have dotted line responsibilities to the business manager.

L&D professionals are also spanning boundaries by working beyond their own allocated business unit, as some projects require the management of stakeholders from various parts of the organization. For example, L&D professionals may be required to work with colleagues from knowledge management when implementing new IT systems, have ongoing dialogue with colleagues from the organizational development unit in implementing change, or source expertise from finance colleagues in developing business cases. Internal boundary spanning also includes crossing vertical divisions in terms of levels of hierarchy. L&D practitioners need to be able to engage with colleagues at all levels and be empathetic to their concerns from an L&D perspective. These could be front-line staff (eg training to use a new system), professional staff (eg CPD opportunities, support in studying for professional exams), supervisors (eg soft skills such as negotiation and con-flict resolution), middle managers (eg leadership skills) or senior managers (eg organizational performance issues).

Finally, L&D professionals may need to go beyond organizational boundaries and work with external partners. Such arrangements may be on L&D's own initiative, such as when developing strategic partnerships with universities in delivering a range of educational opportunities and qualifica-tions for their organization's workforce. In other cases, external working arrangements may be a result of the organization's strategic partnership with other firms as part of its new business model. In such a scenario, L&D may be required to work with other L&D units in creating new training programmes to support new operations. Barbara Emmanuel, Training and Development Manager from the Walsall Healthcare NHS Trust, illustrates how partnership with other L&D units in the NHS is growing. L&D may also go beyond sectoral boundaries in obtaining best-in-class best practices and/or ideas from how L&D operates in other industries.

Barbara Emanuel, training and development manager, Walsall Healthcare NHS Trust

L&D used to be seen as a separate entity to the organization, with most of our activity with the business done in a transactional manner. For example, we were given strategic policies to interpret and act upon from the perspective of training and development. But today L&D is now working more in partnership with all areas of the organization such as human resources (HR) and organizational development (OD), as well as externally with other organizations and L&D units.

For example, we are now working more with external partners and also with our regional strategic leaders in the West Midlands to develop a holistic community with a joint agenda. We have now established a Black Country Partnership, where funding is provided from Health Education to Dudley, Walsall, Wolverhampton and Sandwell hospitals, and as a group we decide together how we are going to approach leadership development collectively. Here, funding has been used to obtain resources such as John Adair's Action Centred Leadership (ACL) programme, in which we are all trained, and also in training staff in undertaking 360-degree assessment and using other tools such as Myer-Briggs Type Indicator and Belbin's Team Role Inventories. An innovative practice that has emerged from this partnership involves the training of an associate from each of the Black Country hospitals in the use of each of these tools/ methods, which has enabled the establishment of a development centre that accommodates delegates from all the partner hospitals. I have found this stimulating as I work with new people who have new/complementary skills.

This is a new mindset in how L&D needs to operate, which I have tried to put into practice myself. I always take the initiative to reach out to my colleagues in other departments/functions by saying, 'what are you doing in OD/HR, how can I help?', 'how does this match with what I am doing?' and so on. I would consult and engage with OD and HR on their programmes. HR and OD have the policies and methodology but they may not have all the mechanisms [such as those discussed in Chapters 5 and 7]. OD/HR need L&D to put on the programmes to educate, engage, monitor and evaluate, and to feed this back. L&D is well placed to do this as we have the data and we are skilful in evaluation.

Exercise

- Reflect upon how professionals in an L&D practice have played the role of boundary spanners. As part of this reflection, describe the aims and rationale of the activity (ie what purpose does this boundary spanning serve) and how have (or should have) L&D gone about spanning boundaries?

- Are there other 'areas' (eg business unit, other organizations) that L&D should reach? If so, list two areas and describe why this is important to L&D.

- Describe how L&D may go about their boundary-spanning activity in these two examples.

Alternatively, for those of us who are just starting out and do not have an organization to refer to, try the following exercise:

- Reflect upon a time when you were required to work with someone from another group (eg another class, another community):
  - How did you go about finding someone to work collaboratively with?
  - What was your experience working with someone from another group? Were you able to gain trust and have an effective working relationship quickly?
  - What would you have done differently and why?

4.3 Consultant and advisor

The other role that is important to L&D in today's environment is that of assuming the roles of a consultant and/or advisor. L&D's assumption of the role of consultant and its relevant activities are further discussed in Chapter 4. The role of advisor is generally seen as part of L&D's role as an expert. Fulfilling the role of a trusted advisor means that L&D is not only required to be competent and have a high standard of professionalism but must have the confidence of business managers who are then able to confide in L&D about the issues they may be facing or the aspirations they may have.

4.4 Change agents

The final but equally important role the L&D practitioner assumes is that of a change agent. Change is central to L&D activities, especially at the organizational level. Learning and development inevitably results in change. To learn and develop is to be different and better, be it more efficient, more effective, or both. In addition, to learn and develop also helps organizations to not only adapt but to also initiate change through developing innovation and entrepreneurial skills, for example.

In becoming a better change agent, there are seven key activities that the role should be able to do: articulating need and/or urgency, creating a business case for change, involving others in constructing a plan for change, communication, addressing the concerns of resistors, and identifying indicators of success and continuously evaluating change (Kotter, 1995; Senior and Swailes, 2010). However, whilst it is advisable to socialize any ideas related to change as early as possible, this should be tempered with discretion, as change agents need to be confident of the idea for change.

L&D professionals must be able to translate the urgency for changes such as the need for new capabilities in supporting new ways of working. For example, the organization may develop a new strategy that requires a new business model and therefore different types of capabilities. L&D professionals must be able to help senior managers to translate what this means for departments and individuals from a learning and development perspective. L&D professionals must be able to articulate what these new skills are, and the departments/individuals that are directly impacted. In addition, L&D practitioners also need to convey what type of training and development opportunities will be provided and how managers can best support their workforce. The implementation of a change idea may at times require a business case to be developed, justifying the resources to be committed to the change project, which is discussed in detail in Chapter 3.

In any change initiative, a coalition of supporters of the change must be formed and recruitment of members should be continuous. This is integral to the success of any change, as it helps to give the change momentum and gain critical mass, and also helps to give voice to the advantages of the change. In addition, coalition members should able to feed back concerns of others to L&D practitioners, and this may help alleviate some concerns of their colleagues. For example, as change agents, L&D managers may be able to enlist the help of business managers who are part of the coalition to address concerns that fellow business managers may have.

As mentioned, it is good practice to involve stakeholders in any change initiative as early possible, as this allows people to contribute ideas. Such dialogue allows the change management team to address fears and incorporate ideas in making progress with the change initiative, which may help to gain buy-in from stakeholders. As part of the dialogue with stakeholders, a communications plan must be developed to ensure that individuals have a platform to have their voices heard and for dialogue to take place either on a one-to-one basis or in a collective manner. A range of communication channels should be used with regular intervals. Communication during change is crucial, as people tend to depend on the grapevine, which may carry inaccurate information, stir fear and cause anxiety in the absence of clear and regular communications.

The role of a change agent also means that L&D practitioners may have to deal with resistors. This should be undertaken professionally and tactfully. A force-field analysis may be undertaken (this technique is further explored in Chapter 4), which analyses the forces for and against change. Finally, L&D practitioners should develop indicators to evaluate the success of change and regularly monitor these indicators.

Exercise

- Identify a situation whereby L&D was involved in change. Describe the change situation (eg was it enterprise-wide, was the change technically orientated, such as implementing a new system, or did it involve changes in behaviours?) and what was expected of L&D in the change event (eg was L&D the lead or a supporter of change?).

- Reflect upon situations whereby L&D professionals have/may become change agents by undertaking any of the activities discussed, ie i) articulating need and/or urgency, ii) creating a business case for change, iii) involving others in constructing a plan for change, iv) communication, v) addressing concerns of resistors, vi) identifying indicators of success, and/or vii) continuously evaluating change.

- Reflect upon future situations that would require L&D to play a role in organizational change.

Alternatively, for those of us who are just starting out and do not have an organization to refer to, try the following exercise:

- Making change happen can be a challenge, be it at work or in our own personal life (eg with friends). Think about a time when you had to make a change. This may have been trying to convince someone to change the way they do things. Reflect upon how you went about making this change happen:

- What were the steps that you took?
- What were the challenges?
- What did you think were the most important factors for your success? Or if you were not successful, what were the factors that caused the failure?
- What would you do differently?

5 Developing the L&D professional

This section discusses the specific knowledge, skills and capabilities that L&D professionals need to successfully develop for the four roles. Twelve areas of development are identified and discussed: i) reflective learning, ii) knowledge in adult learning principles, concepts and theories, iii) context-bound knowledge and competencies, iv) practice and experimentation, v) coaching, vi) cognitive skills, vii) project management, viii) emotional intelligence, ix) sensemaking, x) collaborative working and networking, xi) financial competency, and xii) technology savviness.

5.1 Reflective learning

Applying the same notion of meta-capabilities discussed in Section 4 concerning L&D's role in developing capacity and capability, reflectiveness is an important skill to gain if L&D professionals are to be autonomous and effective learners (Cheetham and Chivers, 2001). Reflection is introspection that helps to bring what is in the unconscious to the conscious, questions what we may take for granted, and helps us better make sense of problematic situations, be more articulate in conveying complex ideas, and be better at being candid and tactful.

Reflective learning leads L&D professionals to become reflective practitioners who are mindful in continuously examining the way they practice their expertise. It helps them assess the skills they possess and the new competencies they may need in light of the present and future needs of the workforce and organization. Reflectiveness may also lead to gaining metacognition (ie thinking about thinking), which enables us to better monitor and regulate our thought processes (Georghiades, 2000). Linda Gittings shares her view of the important capabilities of L&D professionals over the next few years.

Linda Gittings, training officer, Fortis Living

In our L&D unit we develop ourselves in a variety of ways, including using the apprenticeship schemes I have mentioned. Apprenticeships are helpful to both individuals and the business units in finding a 'fit'. For example, new starters in HR will spend six months in the L&D team to understand how L&D impacts upon HR, the (business) team and what is involved in the day-to-day running of L&D. These new apprentices may start off with a business administration apprenticeship providing them with the grounding and motivation to stay with housing, but will then move on to other parts of the organization to learn more about the business as a whole.

I think the most important capability that will be most crucial for L&D professionals in my organization in the next three years is that of a reflective learner. L&D professionals need to know and understand how they can complement the organization and they do this by first understanding what and how they can contribute. As an L&D professional, you need to be very self-aware. You need to understand your own strengths and weaknesses so you can identify where your gaps are and support your team, your part of the organization, and help the organization to meet its strategic objectives. L&D professionals need to be able to build upon their weaknesses whilst maintaining their strengths.

It is crucial to have the ability to reflect, because one can go for all the courses there are out there but without really understanding how to contextualize that to one's own situation and knowing what this means, then all the training may come to nought. We can do all the academic learning but we must be given the opportunity to do the work and put it into practice by applying what has been learned (importance of practice and experimentation). So L&D professionals need to find the opportunities to use newly acquired skills and knowledge to further enhance their practice. They should be able to reflect and ask themselves the questions: What does the academic theory 'look like' when I'm back at work? What do the practicalities look like? How will I use it?

If this happens, then the company is getting best from you as you are not only using what you have learned but also growing as a person. L&D practitioners should reflect the things that they try to do with the workforce, which is the transfer of learning. You have to practice what you preach. You have to be prepared to push yourself outside of your comfort zone, and think, 'I will have a go at doing that'. And I think it is important that when you go on a course (even a one-day course) you need to know what is it that you want to get out of it. You need to have at least an idea how you might be able to use it, and you need to know the basics, the grounding. This is where the 'practice' comes into the professional.

To start developing reflective learning as a skill, keep a journal and update on a daily basis of your experiences at work. In addition, briefly describe the key aspects (eg who, what, when, why and how), and highlight critical incidents. Examine and record your thoughts and opinions as well your feelings. Reflect upon the event, and ask yourself what you thought went well and why, and in addition what you thought did not go as well as it could have and why.

Exercise

This activity is to help you get started in learning how to reflect.

- Step 1. Identify a recent situation when you helped someone learn something. This may involve your providing a (quasi) coaching session or helping a colleague in their work.
- Step 2. Describe the situation by writing this down. For example:
  - Who did you help?
  - What assistance was asked for? Was it a specific task or was it a problem that was posed?
  - How did you help? Did you know the solution? Were you not sure but still willing to help figure things out together?
  - Was your help 'successful'? Yes or no, why?
- Step 3. Reflect upon your feelings? For example:
  - If you volunteered help, why?
  - How did helping this person make you feel?
  - Would you do the same for a different colleague?
  - Why did you help? Were you pressed for time when help was asked? Would you do the same if you were pressed for time?
  - Were you confident in solving your colleague's problem? Did you and your colleague work together to solve the problem?
- Step 4. Identify lessons learned and future action. For example:
  - What did you learn from the process?
  - Would you have done things differently?

5.2 Knowledge of adult learning principles, concepts and theories

Clearly, having the knowledge of how people learn is crucial, as this underpins all that L&D professionals do as capacity and capability builders as well as consultants. L&D professionals must of course be critical of their use of such knowledge, as it needs to be contextualized within their sector, organization and the individual learners they are supporting. Chapter 5 and 7, concerning how L&D professionals are able to cultivate a learning environment and develop learning interventions respectively, provides a comprehensive discussion on key concepts and theories on how people learn.

5.3 Context-bound knowledge and competencies

In keeping with the discussion of knowledge, it is also important for L&D practitioners to have insight of their sector (eg who is the competition, what does the supply chain involve), the organization (eg the strategy, the business model, organization structure and hierarchy, life cycle), groups and individuals (eg job families, average age). Such knowledge is crucial in enabling L&D professionals to be critical in how they apply their L&D knowledge, and plays a role in helping them play all four roles successfully. For example, an organization that has a strategy of cost cutting may be best supported by an L&D approach using internal trainers rather than the generally more expensive external vendors.

Competencies that are context specific may also be required. For example, organizations that are charities within the UK must be able to engage and apply guidelines set by the Charities Commission. Also, if an organization is still young, it may mean that its members may be expected to be more entrepreneurial. A comprehensive discussion and a number of exercises related to developing context-specific knowledge is contained in Chapter 2.

5.4 Practice and experimentation

To practise is more than just to 'do'; it is about conscious application and paying attention to what works and what does not, which is a skill that involves employing what has been learned with the purpose of improving and adapting knowledge and skills to one's context and situation. However, to just apply what has been learned may not bring about the innovation in practices that may help the workforce and organization to deal with novel challenges they face in a volatile and turbulent environment (as further discussed in Chapter 2).

As Einstein was quoted as saying, 'madness is when you do the same things over again expecting different results'. Therefore, it is important to continuously try new approaches and methods (Susan Hamilton shares her views on why and how L&D professionals should always be ready to step outside their comfort zone in the next case example). To experiment is to test out ideas in a small-scale manner. Borrowing from ideas from literature involving design thinking, experimenting may also involve prototyping (Brown, 2008). Whilst the concept of prototyping is usually applied to the incremental development of physical models of end products, it may also be applied to ideas and new ways of doing things.

Prototypes are models that one to builds upon and learns from. These may be beliefs, principles and mental models (your understanding of how something 'works'). They can be used, articulated and visualized as part of a reflection process, as prototypes for you to experiment upon, revising your 'prototype' until you have developed a model that works for you (until the situation changes again, necessitating modification of the model). Reflection enables a more considered and managed approach in experimentation. The synergy between the two is also highlighted in Kolb *et al*.'s (2001) experiential model of learning.

Susan Hamilton, senior learning and development manager, not-for-profit sector organization

An important aspect of an L&D practitioner's own development is using informal channels. L&D should take advantage of its position of operating across an organization. For example, I am currently working on a number of initiatives that cut across the organization such as employee engagement, talent management and performance management. I work very closely with colleagues from HR on these projects, as there are many 'people management' processes that link up with L&D – for example performance appraisal and training needs analysis – so I take every opportunity to learn what I can. L&D professionals also need broader HR knowledge to be effective in their role.

My other advice is to be adaptable. L&D practitioners should not see themselves as the gatekeepers of knowledge or as separate from the rest of the organization, but as facilitators, working with the business. There is a time and a place for L&D professionals to play the role of the expert, though this role is becoming less needed. It is important to be adaptable and to listen to those in the business. In learning to be adaptable, take every opportunity to do things that may be outside your comfort zone and to work with the business in terms of facilitating their discussions. For example, if a business area is having a conference, L&D professionals should ask themselves how they can contribute to helping the business so that their expertise can be used and they are able to contribute to what the business is trying to achieve. In such a situation, the business would own the agenda but it would be L&D that supports how the business can deliver the conference (via enhancing skills in presentation, recording the event for future L&D programmes and so on).

L&D can think out of the box and leverage how programmes are delivered by facilitating networking within the organization. For example, our leadership programmes are organized centrally, as people from the business are nominated to come on those programmes. Such centrally organized programmes are helpful, as it is healthy for individuals across the organization to network with other colleagues. This is where the expertise of the L&D partner comes into play through knowing when to organize an event centrally or in a bespoke manner for individual business units. L&D practitioners need to be savvy and entrepreneurial in maximizing the resources and opportunities that are available to them.

Exercise

This activity is to help you get started to practise in your development as an L&D professional, as well as to experiment and try new approaches to improving your practice.

Practice:

- Identify a set of principles or instructions, concept, model or theory that you learned from a course or from your colleagues. For example, how people can learn effectively by modelling behaviours of others (you can also choose something that you may have learned in college or secondary school). These 'lessons' learned should be something that you can apply and practise over a period of time (eg regularly and not just one-off).
- Find opportunities to apply/practise this lesson.
- Keep a record of how well you think you applied/practised this lesson. This record can be kept as part of your journal for reflection.
- Repeat this process for other 'lessons'.

Experimentation:

- Using an example ('lesson') that you identified in the previous 'practice' exercise, identify ways you could improve the practice.

- Identify the status quo, eg what is done and what the current outcomes are.
- Describe the change that you would make. This should be small scale and does not put anyone at risk including you.
- Develop a prototype of this new 'model' of working (it may be helpful for you to also depict visually how the current way works so that you can better picture the similarities and differences between the two).
- Describe what you intend to do. How regular would this experiment be and over what period would it take place? Would each opportunity entail doing something slightly/incrementally different?
- Envisage what new and improved outcome would result.
- Who would this improvement be for; L&D, the learner, the organization?
- It would be advisable for you to consult your supervisor and/or a senior member of staff before you undertake this activity.

5.5 Coaching skills

Coaching is an important area for L&D professionals to be knowledgeable of and also skilled in as it directly contributes to the 'builder' role, as well as that of (problem) solver and change agent. Coaching is a growing approach in helping people to develop, as well as to perform, and L&D is expected to equip, grow and support coaching within the organization. In doing so, L&D may source coaching expertise externally to build internal capability and/or they may develop coaching skills themselves. Coaching is usually a formal, contracted relationship and is generally shorter term – up to a year. Generally, coaching is undertaken to help people learn with a goal of improving performance on their jobs (Passmore, 2007).

Coaches must at least have general business knowledge specifically in terms of the commercial realities that many managers and executives face, and appreciate the broader contexts that their coachees may be part of. Coaches usually have a background in organizational psychology, human resource management, learning and development or a related field, in addition to coaching qualifications. As coaches are in a formal relationship with their coachees, they need to be supported by others in ensuring that the goals of the coaching relationship are met (Wilson, 2011).

L&D professionals need to be aware of the different types of coaching that exist, such as line management coaching, peer coaching, cross-organizational coaching, executive coaching and team-based coaching, as each is different and needs to be supported appropriately. Line coaching is when the coachee also reports directly to the coach. The nature of such coaching may be more performance oriented than learning oriented. However, it is not unusual for this to shift and become more empowerment oriented when this type of coaching involves higher-level executives (CIPD, 2010). Peer coaching tends to be learning and support oriented. This type of coaching requires the coach to have intimate knowledge and insight of the work of the coachee. An extension of this is cross-organizational coaching, which has similar aims, although knowledge of the coachee's work may not be required. In fact, this form of coaching may be appropriate when distance is necessary for the coaching aims to be realized. Executive coaching, as the term denotes, is for executives and usually involves external coaches. Ultimately, L&D professionals need to understand the different needs of coaching so that they are able to develop the right coaching capabilities across the organization and support the different coaching arrangements and relationships.

Nonetheless, another area that is important for L&D professionals to develop is to be a coach themselves. To be successful in this role, L&D professionals must be knowledgeable of the approaches and methods of coaching such as the Goal, Reality, Options and Will (GROW) model. This model that provides a roadmap on how to develop a coachee. As indicated by its name, the first step is to establish goals with the coachee, followed by a candid discussion of the resources available to the coachee to achieve the goal and the constraints that stand in the way. The third step is to develop options available to the coachee in consideration of his/her resources/constraints. Options may be different means and timelines that a coachee may select for reaching the goals established at the start. The fourth and final step is 'will' (also called 'way forward'), which involves identifying action steps that the coachee can take in his/her selected route to attaining the goals (Grant, 2011).

Although process is important, coaching is ultimately a relationship, and is about the coachee. And whilst business knowledge is important, sometimes the most technically proficient and/or most commercially savvy people may not be the best coaches (Ulrich, 2008). Coaches must be candid but also tactful. Being an effective coach requires L&D professionals to gain knowledge from education and learn from experience.

Exercise

The following exercise is to help you develop your coaching skills. This may involve a colleague or friend who is willing to participate and who can observe you in some areas of their work. You may want to ask them for feedback after the exercise.

- Step 1: The first step is to familiarize yourself with a coaching model such as the GROW process.

- Step 2: Build rapport and a relationship with your colleague or friend. No doubt a relationship has already been established by virtue of selecting this person. However, never assume that a good relationship is easily transferable when it involves other areas of the coachee's life. The dynamics of a relationship between two individuals change when their roles change with respect to one another, such as when social friends become work colleagues or when a colleague becomes your supervisor. Therefore, as your roles have changed in this exercise as coach and coachee, you will need to build rapport and a relationship based on your new roles. In doing so:

  - Learn about your coachee professionally and personally (without being intrusive, eg their favourite TV programmes, favourite pastimes, their general goals).

  - Find common ground and use this at the start of your conversations.

  - Get in touch with the coachee beyond the coaching relationship when possible (eg lunch).

- Step 3: Hold your first coaching session. Apply the GROW model (or any other model that you may be more familiar with):

  - Understand the problem that the coachee wants to address or objective they want to attain.

  - Establish the goal(s) with the coachee. If possible, also identify indicators for success.

  - Identify resources and obstacles. Make a list.

  - Establish options in attaining the goal(s).

  - Develop an action plan together that is practical for your coachee to implement.

- Step 4: Be prepared to revisit each of the bullets points in Step 3. As you undertake Steps 2 and 3, it is important to actively listen to your coachee to ensure that you understand where they are coming from. Active listening may involve the following:

  - Be mindful of your body language. Ensure you keep eye contact with your coachee and use posture in a way that communicates that you are interested in what they have to say.

  - Gesture to the coachee intermittently to show that you are indeed listening to them.

- Reiterate and/or rephrase important parts of their dialogue to ensure that your understanding of what they have said is the same and has equivalent meaning.

- Do not hesitate to ask the coachee to repeat themselves if you are not clear on what they have just said.

Another important skill to show in the coaching sessions is questioning. People construct the world based on their past experience, background and assumptions. There is always a reason why people think or behave in a certain way. There will be times when these reasons may not be what we think they are. Hence it is important to ask questions and probe the coachee to genuinely understand them. A helpful tool in questioning is reframing. Reframing helps to put something in a different perspective or context, which may help coachees to understand their own thought processes and behaviours. Ultimately, questioning and reframing should help prompt coachee to self-reflect.

On a final note, in some instances it may be helpful for a coach to observe their coachee at work. Although some coaching aims may necessitate this, it is not always practical. However, if an opportunity arises (eg how a coachee chairs a meeting), L&D professionals should use this occasion to learn how to observe and take notes.

5.6 Cognitive skills: analytical ability, problem solving, decision making and multiple perspective taking

Analytical ability

Cognitive ability is clearly important as it directly contributes to all four roles. Analysis is a basic skill that is used in many L&D activities, as it is in all professional work. Analysis involves breaking something down into smaller constituents to facilitate better understanding of a problem, concept or situation. This is important to do, as some problems and tasks may be too complex and/or broad. Analysis helps L&D professionals to divide the work into more manageable 'chunks' to deal with one at a time.

Being analytical also means that L&D professionals need to be data driven and evidence based as much as possible. Whilst information gained from people (such as their opinions) is equally important, this should be underpinned by hard data and evidence wherever possible. Such a situation enables L&D professionals to then analyse and corroborate the data gained from various sources, which ultimately enhances the accuracy of the analysis and the validity of the results. For example, when analysing an individual's training needs, L&D professionals must not only interview the individual to obtain their view, but they must also review 'hard' data such as indicators of the individual's job performance and achievement scores on courses and tests.

Problem solving and decision making

Effective analytical abilities help to improve problem-solving and decision-making abilities. These capabilities require L&D professionals to adopt a rational and systematic approach, although a degree of creativity is also required in problem solving. Problem-solving and decision-making skills are especially useful when dealing with complex and ill-defined situations that largely relate to people (behaviours, power and politics). Problem solving is a process that involves four main steps: recognizing the problem situation (or finding the problem), identifying the root cause, generating alternative solutions, and solving the problem. The fourth step involves decision making, as the alternatives need to be identified before settling on the option that has the highest chance of solving the problem.

The first stage of the problem-solving process is recognizing that there is an issue. At this stage, especially in complex environments, the problem may be 'felt' and not easy to pinpoint. In 'finding the problem', L&D professionals need to be divergent in their thinking by identifying all the symptoms involved in the problem situation (Lee and Cho, 2007). By listing all the symptoms, L&D professionals should have a better idea of what are merely symptoms of the problem, thereby narrowing down the potential list of root causes. If a problem is complex, it also usually means that there are there are different perspectives on what is the 'problem'. This level of ambiguity is usually best addressed by working in teams and by holding dialogue with people who have knowledge about the situation (eg those impacted by it). The second stage involves examining a problem situation to find its root cause. In most organizational problems, there is usually more than just one source of the problem. Some problems are an outcome of historical events, and exacerbated by various factors (Tallman and Gray, 1990). Nonetheless, there is typically a ranking of root causes in terms of what contributes most to the problem.

The next stage is to generate a number of solutions in consideration of the resources and constraints that an L&D professional faces. It is at this stage that decision-making skills come to the fore. Decision making is about generating a choice of solutions that may be successful in solving the problem by leveraging the resources available whilst mitigating present constraints (Quesada, Kintsch, and Gomez, 2005). Decision making also involves developing a set of criteria that L&D professionals can use as a reference point when deciding which of all the alternatives are most appropriate. Each criterion may be weighted in terms of importance. The final problem-solving stage involves implementing the solution. This step may also require unique skills such as project management (discussed later) that would optimize the deployment of resources in executing the solutions plan.

Multiple perspectives taking

Another important cognitive skill is multiple perspectives taking. Recall how what L&D does and is expected to do takes place at at least three levels: the individual (learners), groups (departments) and the organization. These are, in some respect, different perspectives that L&D has to do adopt. If they cannot adopt the perspective of the individual learners, department managers and organizational leaders, L&D professionals may not be as effective in their role. Also, multiple perspectives taking helps to develops empathy (Hyun and Marshall, 1997), which in turn fosters emotional intelligence (discussed later). For example, multiple perspectives taking will help L&D professionals to better:

- Understand the challenges and needs of learners who may fall within the diversity and social inclusion policies.

- Appreciate that departmental managers have a need to see quick 'return on investment' on L&D, as well as develop their staff for the future. L&D professionals must be able to balance both needs.

- See the big picture from a senior manager's perspective by synthesizing how different parts of the organization work together to realize the strategy.

Exercise: analytical skills

This exercise helps you to decompose a process by analysing the different elements required.

- Find and use an L&D process that you are familiar with or that you can easily research on the internet (eg vendor selection, training needs analysis, competency development).

- Identify the number of steps involved in the process (decide the start and end points of the process).

- Describe the steps involved in the process. In this description, identify i) the task required to be undertaken, ii) who is to complete the task, iii) the resources (eg skills and data/information) required to complete each step, and iv) support required (eg tools, supervisor's input).

- As part of the process, you also need to identify at which stage (eg between steps) decisions may be made, and alternative routes that correspond to each decision (eg if it is a 'yes' decision, what are the steps that follow, and the same if the decision is a 'no').

Exercise: problem solving and decision making

This exercise is to help you reflect on the problem-solving process rather than solve a problem per se.

- Reflect upon a time when you were involved in solving a relatively complex problem (ie when the root cause was far from obvious).

- Think about the approach you adopted in solving that problem. What were the steps you took?

- Were those steps similar to the four-step approach discussed in this section? What are the advantages and disadvantages of both approaches?

- How would you improve your problem-solving and decision-making skills specifically in relation to each stage of the problem-solving process:

  - Problem finding, eg how would you work in teams and work with others in getting a clearer picture of what the problem is?

  - Identifying the root cause, eg what tools and methods could you use in aiding the discovery of the root cause?

  - Generating alternative solutions, eg why is it important to develop a number of alternative means to address the problem? How do you find out what the resources and constraints are?

  - Solution implementation, eg what is involved in a planning process in deploying the solution?

Exercise: multiple perspectives taking

- Identify two stakeholders who play an important role in an L&D professional's work, such as first line supervisor or head of human resources.

- Reflect and describe two important concerns for each role. For example:

- First line supervisors: day-to-day management of work such as troubleshooting daily issues involving absences, managing conflict amongst staff and maintaining good relations with staff members.

- Head of human resources: organizational policies reflect the requirements of legislations and see that procedures are adhered to, and are able to help realize organizational strategy through human resources.

● Identify how L&D may be able to support these two roles and their concerns.

5.7 Project management

Project management skills are important to L&D professionals, especially in the consultant and change agent role, as both typically involve 'solutions' being implemented as projects. Indeed, it would not be uncommon for L&D professionals to be called upon to manage the implementation of a new learning management system for the entire organization, co-lead the role out of a new competency framework with HR to a division, or be a team lead in an organization-wide cultural change management project. Although initiatives vary in scale, project management skills are still important, albeit it applied in varying degrees. This section ties in closely with Chapter 4, as consultants usually implement solutions through projects. In addition, some project management skills are also discussed in Chapter 3. Whilst more detailed discussion can be found in this chapter, this section will cover project management from a broad perspective.

Projects are time-bound initiatives that are given special attention in that resources are specifically committed to ensuring that aims are achieved (Burke, 2013). Projects are not run as part of business as usual (BAU), as the lack of dedicated resources detracts from the successful completion of the tasks. The key skills in project management are stakeholder engagement and reporting, creating logical work breakdown structures (WBS), scheduling, resourcing (roles and skills) and budgeting, managing risks, and monitoring and controlling (Kerzner, 2010).

In defining the project aims and scope, and to gain commitment, it is important to identify and engage with stakeholders. Some of these stakeholders will form the governance team of the project, including the project sponsor, to whom the project manager will be reporting. The project sponsor is there to provide guidance and help with resourcing ('clearing the way'). Engaging with stakeholders is also important, as they are the ones who will have to 'live' with the solution after the project is completed. Therefore, obtaining input from stakeholders and clarifying their expectations is crucial to the success of the project. Chapters 3 and 4 provide further discussion on stakeholders.

Once the aims and scope of a project are known, the next step is to identify the activities and tasks that need to be completed, which can be logically grouped as what is known as work breakdown structures (WBS). WBS is a hierarchical decomposition of work that needs to be executed. Once the work and its dependencies have been determined, the next step is to place a timeline against the WBS in the form of a schedule. The next step is to identify resources (other than time) required to enable the work to be completed. Resources include people, equipment and space (eg meeting rooms). As part of the resourcing plan, the roles and skills assumed and required by individuals should also be established. The completion of the resourcing plan should then allow project managers to create a budget for the project.

All projects, no matter how well planned, will almost certainly face problems. These challenges are considered as a risk to the project, which may prevent it from being completed on time and within budget. Hence it is important for L&D professionals to be able to manage risk. Managing risk involves estimating potential risks to the project, and ranking these risks so that resources and action can be prioritized in addressing them. L&D professionals as project managers must also be able to monitor and control the project by convening regular meetings with team leads, project members and stakeholders.

5.8 Emotional intelligence

Emotional intelligence (EI) is the ability to use information about one's own and others' emotions in guiding thinking and behaviour, and is necessary for all roles. An individual is considered to have emotional intelligence when they are able to recognize and control their own emotions. In addition, such individuals are able to discriminate, recognize and relate to others' emotions. Whilst some researchers recognize EI as a trait, many others have conceptualized it as a skill that can be learned and developed.

The concept of EI was popularized by Goleman (1996), who stated that there are five dimensions of EI: self-awareness, self-regulation, motivation, empathy and social skills. EI starts with self-awareness, as without being self-aware, the other dimensions would not ensue. Self-awareness involves understanding our own emotions and, in general, how they may impact on behaviour, eg mood swings. The skill of reflective learning discussed in the previous section strongly complements this dimension of EI. Being self-aware helps L&D professionals to have more a more realistic self-image, which may help self-confidence, since you know what your strengths and weakness are in navigating different situations.

By being self-aware, L&D professionals are then able to develop skills to monitor and regulate their emotions. Self-regulation is the ability to control and temper extreme emotions, redirecting disruptive impulses, and helps us to think things through thoroughly before acting. Self-regulation enables us to act ethically and with integrity, and to have more control of ourselves, helping us to be more comfortable with ambiguity and open to change. Through self-regulation, the ability to motivate yourself may follow. This is particularly true when faced with daunting and/or tedious tasks, or when you personally feel inert and/or indifferent. Self-motivation is the ability to energize yourself in important moments and to be persistent in achieving goals. Self-motivation enables L&D professionals to have the drive to achieve and be optimistic.

The fourth dimension of EI is empathy, which is understanding and even appreciating the emotional state of others. Indeed, as previously discussed, empathy is usually easier to develop when one has the ability to adopt multiple perspectives. Nonetheless, whilst multiple perspectives taking is primarily cerebral, empathy generally involves the emotional aspect. Empathy enables L&D professionals to be sensitive to others and their needs and circumstances, which helps to develop better working relationships. The fifth and final dimension is social skills; the ability to relate and connect with others. They help us to develop networks and quickly build rapport with others. Effective social skills help us to position ourselves in good stead with others and thus be more influential and effective in collaborative working (discussed later).

Exercise

The following exercise is to help you develop EI specifically in terms of each of its dimensions. Where the development of some of these skills (dimensions) is related to other ex+ercises that have been covered or that will be covered, this will be signposted.

- Self-awareness: the development of self-awareness is covered in the section concerning reflection.
- Self-regulation: in self-regulation, it is important to be able to control and redirect emotions so that your behaviour remains appropriate for a

particular situation (eg in the workplace). Reflect upon a time when your patience was tested, and ask yourself how did you do (could you have done) the following:

- Keeping calm:
  - Employ tactics that would keep yourself calm in such a hostile situation (deep breaths, respond in a measured manner).
- Reframing negative thoughts and believing in positive outcomes:
  - Attempt to understand why the perceived antagonist in the situation is behaving the way he/she is. Why is this issue contentious to this person?
  - Make sense of how such a disagreement may eventually be helpful to surface important issues that may help improve the overall situation.
- Consider the consequences:
  - Identify the consequences of inflaming the situation if you reacted negatively, eg how would this impact on your work and prospects of being seen as a leader?
  - What could be the positive consequences if this issue is dealt with positively and productively?

- Motivation: reflect upon a time when you were demotivated to undertake a task you found uninteresting and wearisome. Reflect upon how you may have better energized yourself to complete the task in a professional manner. You may ask yourself:
  - What are the negative consequences if I did a sloppy job?
  - What skills (even the most minute) could I gain from doing this?
  - Who is the beneficiary of this work? Why is this work important to them?

- Empathy: the development of empathy is partly covered in the section concerning multiple perspectives taking. Try to understand the emotional state of the people in the following situation and reflect on what you would do in trying to help them from an L&D perspective:
  - Staff member: a staff member has just received very poor ratings in the performance appraisal. What do you think would be the emotional state of this person? How would you help this person?
  - Heads of product divisions: you work in a very competitive environment whereby the different product departments are in rivalry to outdo one

another. However, a new strategic initiative means that product departments must now work together. How do you think heads of product divisions would feel? What would you say to them to persuade them to collaborate with one another and share knowledge?

- Social skills: the development of social skills will be covered in the section concerning collaborative working and networking.

5.9 Sensemaking

Sensemaking is about giving meaning to experiences (Weick, 1995). Whilst sensemaking may seem to be an inherent ability, it is becoming more challenging to gain and master. This skill has become more necessary as the world we live and work in becomes more complex and ambiguous. Some of the previous skills discussed, such as cognitive ability, reflection, experimentation and emotional intelligence, all contribute to the enhancement of an L&D professional's sensemaking capability (please refer to the exercises for each of these skills when developing sensemaking skills).

Sensemaking is a balancing act between analysis and synthesis in understanding the elements of a concept but keeping an eye on the 'big picture'. It is an important ability that helps to develop strategic thinking for leadership and also develop the capabilities of an organization's workforce, as highlighted in the next case example from Barbara Emmanuel. Sensemaking also draws a parallel with systems thinking, as it is a skill that attempts to understand the underlying 'structures' in a system such as an organization (Senge *et al.*, 1994). However, the turbulent environment that organizations and L&D operate in means that most things are in a state of flux, as situations change even before we have fully understood them. Therefore, in addition to being a 'skill', sensemaking is also seen as a process of learning (Schwandt, 2005) that enables L&D professionals to continuously learn and shape their mental model as their environment changes.

Sensemaking is important for the builder and (problem) solver roles, although it is especially crucial when L&D professionals adopt the change agent role. A good example is organizational power and politics that tend to override rationality. L&D professionals need to make sense of their environment by interpreting the roles, actions and motives of organizational actors within events that have occurred. Indeed, power and politics are two of the main sources of uncertainty and ambiguity, as they are intangible, concealed and nebulous, operating in a clandestine manner. Power is the ability to influence another to do something that they may not have otherwise wanted to do

(Pinto, 1996). Power creates a degree of dependency; more dependency means there is more power at play. There are many bases of power such as legitimate (eg one's position as a manager), expert (eg special knowledge in L&D) and referent (eg role model). Politics is undertaking tasks and activities that are beyond one's job description. This involves activities that are innocuous, such as buying your boss a drink, or it could be significant, such as lobbying colleagues for support in voting for a decision that is favourable to you. It is not difficult to perceive power, but it can be challenging to perceive the way power is wielded for aims other than that of the organization. What constitutes 'politics' is in the eye of the beholder. Nonetheless, power and politics are major factors that can alter how an organization operates and organizational changes take place, and ultimately put a premium on sensemaking abilities, especially for L&D professionals (Beard, Clegg, and Smith, 2007).

Power and politics are inevitable phenomena in organizations, and not all it is bad, although too much may render an organization dysfunctional. There is no special 'formula' for one to effectively deal with power and politics. The best starting point is to regularly engage in dialogue with individuals in the organization. This will help L&D professionals to understand the people who are most powerful and the type of power they have, and the individuals and groups who are most dependent on the individuals. In addition, L&D professionals will have more clarity about individuals' motives and the dynamics of the relationships between people. This will inform L&D professionals of the appropriate next steps in the context of their goals, for example implementing a new system as part of a consulting project or as a change agent.

Barbara Emanuel, training and development manager, Walsall Healthcare NHS Trust

The most important knowledge/skills/competencies for L&D professionals in my organization in the next few years will be leadership development (within L&D itself), partnership working, and workforce planning (which is traditionally an HR skill). Leadership skills are necessary to help understand the changing NHS landscape. Important leadership qualities required include strategic thinking and thought leadership, as well as being able to make sense of the changes and how they may impact patients, the organization, business units and the workforce, and of course being able to articulate what this means to and for L&D.

Partnership working is growing in significance, as L&D is now collaborating with others within the organization as well as with those outside it (eg regional collaboration and external training providers). Being flexible is important because if you look at the mergers that have occurred involving my organization, and with our staff working across a section of our region, I would now need to be adaptable to work with others. It is important to have a collaborative mindset that relishes working with and learning from others (eg standards and practices in other organizations, as well as their organizational culture).

Finally, whilst workforce planning is generally a remit within Human Resources, and is still so, L&D professionals now need to be well versed with this process, as they need a strategic view of the capabilities that are present and required for the future to be able to be proactive in addressing any potential gaps in securing the organization's future. Workforce planning is no longer just about headcount, but also about present and future capability. In L&D we have statutory responsibilities concerning mandatory delivery, but we also have internal cultural drivers and external drivers around leadership development and organizational change. I think the future is going to be ever-more dynamic and therefore requires L&D professionals to be dynamic themselves.

For people thinking of starting a career in L&D, or those who have just started, my advice would be to 'grab the moment'. L&D has never in its history played a more prominent role in organizations. Take advantage of the opportunities to further develop yourself, as more will be demanded of you. I think now is the best time to grasp and become an L&D professional, and to shape the future.

Exercise

The following exercise is to reflect upon a situation that did not initially make sense to you, but where you ultimately gained new information and insight that made you confident that you now understand how 'things' work.

- Reflect upon a situation where 'things' did not seem to make sense, eg why an organization repeated the same mistake it made two years ago, why your best performing colleague was overlooked to play a role in an important project, or why a small group of your friends tends to snub another friend.

- Describe that situation.
- What was the new information and/or insight (making new links between the information available to you) that helped explain the situation?
- How did you go about finding this new information? How did this insight come about?
- What did you learn from this 'sensemaking' process?
- How would you go about improving this 'process' of sensemaking?

5.10 Collaborative working and networking

Being able to work with others is a fundamental skill that many professionals have to possess and is relevant in all four L&D roles. Literature concerning developing skills related to team working is grounded on possessing effective interpersonal skills (discussed as part of the section concerning emotional intelligence), and understanding the typical roles involved in teams and how they work with one another in developing a balanced composition such as that demonstrated in Belbin's work (2010). Whilst collaborative working or partnership working also involves a group of individuals working towards a common goal, competing goals are usually prevalent. Unlike teams, collaborators are not interdependent and cannot rely on a team leader to address disputes, and they cannot also easily walk away from one another (Campbell, 2011). Collaboration may be used in a variety of situations such as one-to-one coaching, team working in a project, and/or alliance development involving two organizations engaged with one another in scoping new opportunities for a partnership.

Collaborators may be from different divisions or organizations, which may have very different (sub) cultures and systems, and even a different implicit understanding of how people should work with each other. This is important, as people from the same organization, all else being equal, may generally find it more straightforward to work with one another as they draw upon the same principles, organizational culture and systems that may help them to work more effectively with each other. Working with others from a different division or organization may be less straightforward, as the individuals involved have different ways of working shaped by their respective organizational environments. A simple example involves the use of technical terms; individuals may use different terms to mean the same things, or they may use similar terms to mean completely different things.

Collaborative working is growing in importance, as L&D is now required to work more intimately with different departments and divisions. In addition, many organizations are developing more partnerships and alliances, and growing their organizational networks (Harrison, 2009). Inevitably, L&D professionals may be either directly or indirectly involved in working with others intra- and inter-organizationally.

Another aspect of collaborative working involves L&D professionals being proactive in networking within and outside the organization. Whilst networking is important as part of any professional's work, it plays a more significant role in the context of collaboration and partnership working. In some instances, it is L&D that is expected to seek out others and to shape how the different parties can work together to support organizational goals. L&D professionals in such situations may not be given much guidance, and are expected to make sense and scope out matters jointly with other parties.

Negotiation is also a crucial skill to have, as not all parties, even in the most collaborative environment, will have identical needs, goals and expectations (Mazen, 2011). In many cases, there will be differences that will need to be discussed. Although an ideal situation involves all parties holding a dialogue for a win-win situation, inevitably there will be circumstances whereby negotiations are required so that concessions/compromises may be made. However, negotiations must be made in the spirit of long-term partnerships involving trust. Being able to reframe debates is important in the art of negotiation. An example of reframing a debate is viewing the issue through the eyes of a customer rather than from the perspective of what a department wants. Another example is to reframe a debate from a performance evaluation perspective to one that is about coaching and helping.

As with all teams and partnerships, there will be instances whereby conflict may occur (Davidson and Wood, 2004). There are of course actions that L&D professionals can take to prevent conflict from occurring, such as being open and transparent, and holding one-to-one candid conversations with relevant individuals. Inevitably there may also be some conflicts that are almost impossible to genuinely resolve in the workplace, especially those that involve personality clashes.

Exercise

Much of the knowledge and skills that we have discussed contribute directly to the development of collaborative working and networking skills. For example, emotional intelligence, in particular social skills, plays a crucial role in creating a harmonious and amiable work environment, whilst teamworking skills enable the team to gain high performance. Nonetheless, collaborative working also involves a mindset that continuously thinks about how L&D can work with other departments, divisions and partner organizations in a strategic manner. This mindset is not about collaboration for the sake of it, but how to share resources and marry capabilities to achieve goals that may not have been possible alone. There are also other related aptitudes that L&D professionals must gain, specifically negotiation and conflict resolution skills. Reflect upon an organization that you are familiar with in undertaking the exercise below.

Mindset:

- Identify an opportunity for improvement that can be made jointly between L&D and another department, division or an existing partner organization.

- Describe what your L&D unit can contribute (eg in terms of resources or capabilities) and what else may be required that the L&D unit is unable to easily provide.

- Describe what the other department, division or an existing partner organization can contribute that would make up for the limitation identified in the previous point.

- Undertake the steps above for different opportunities.

Negotiation: although negotiation skills can only truly be developed through practice, it also involves preparatory work to make the negotiation successful (for both parties) and more efficient:

- Be clear and explicit about your (eg L&D unit, organizational) assumptions, expectations, goals.

- Reflect and describe what the other party's expectations and goals may be and why.

- Identify potential areas of debate.

- Be prepared to listen to the other partner, make notes and reiterate your understanding of what they have said.

- How would you reframe these debates? What are the different perspectives that could put the debate in a different light and prioritize what may be more important?

Conflict resolution: similar to developing effective negotiation skills, conflict resolution skills can only truly be developed through practice. However, there are a number of actions you can take to help develop them:

- Develop your emotional intelligence, especially in keeping calm (see Section 5.8 on emotional intelligence); be willing to listen.

- Focus on the issue and not the person(s).

- Differentiate between fact and opinion.

- Be willing to collaborate and/or compromise.

- Be solution-oriented.

- Develop a mindset that the conflict is a way to help improve the working relationship.

Alternatively, for those of us who are just starting out and do not have an organization to refer to, try the following exercise:

- Nurturing a mindset: reflect upon a time when you worked well with another person. Think of the positives and how you would have improved the process of working together.

- Negotiation: think of a time when you successfully negotiated with a friend or family member. What did you do right? What would you improve upon?

- Conflict resolution: see previous exercise on conflict resolution.

5.11 Financial and technological savviness

As the expectation of L&D grows, L&D professionals now also have to broaden their skills into other domains, specifically in finance and technology. This is not to say that L&D professionals must become finance and technology experts, far from it (although if you have the interest and can gain such expertise easily it may be pursued as a complementary skill to that of being an L&D professional). However, as a minimum, L&D professionals must be able to understand and interpret financial statements and reports. Being able to read financial statements means that L&D professionals must also be knowledgeable of basic accounting and financial terminologies. In addition, they need to be able to have the basic skills in constructing a business case, which is further discussed in Chapter 3. In addition, as technology is becoming a key enabler in developing and delivering L&D solutions, L&D professionals must also be savvy about technology and media, in particular how it may enhance learning and performance in the workforce. It is important for L&D professionals to be competent in both the financial and technological domains to fulfil the role of a builder, solver and change agent. This is further discussed in Chapter 5. Table 1.6 provides a summary of how these areas for development contribute to successfully fulfilling the four roles.

Table 1.6 Areas for development and the four L&D roles

Developing yourself as an L&D practitioner	Capability and capacity builders	Boundary spanners	Consultant and advisor (solve problems)	Change agents
1 Reflective learning	✓	✓	✓	✓
2 Knowledge of adult learning principles, concepts and theories	✓		✓	
3 Context-bound competencies	✓	✓	✓	✓
4 Practice and experimentation	✓		✓	
5 Coaching skills	✓	✓	✓	✓
6 Cognitive skills: analytical ability, problem solving, decision making and multiple perspective taking	✓		✓	✓
7 Project management	✓		✓	✓
8 Emotional intelligence	✓	✓	✓	✓
9 Sensemaking	✓		✓	✓
10 Collaborative working and networking	✓	✓	✓	✓
11 Finance competency: developing budgets and business cases, interpreting financial statements and reports	✓		✓	✓
12 Technology savviness, eg use of LMS, social media	✓		✓	✓

6 Conclusion

Being a professional means that L&D practitioners must be responsible for their own learning and autonomous in their development. Continuous development is important, as this chapter has demonstrated; what L&D professionals do and what is expected of them is growing, and this helps L&D professionals to stay 'on top of their game'. Given the varied activities and expectations of L&D professionals, this chapter has identified at least four key roles that most, if not all L&D professionals play.

The four roles of capacity and capability builder, boundary spanner, consultant and advisor, and change agent comprehensively encapsulate the key responsibilities of L&D professionals to the individual, group and organization (as shown in Figure 1.1). L&D professionals build individual and organizational capacity and capabilities by spanning boundaries as they solve problems for and with their clients, and by leading and enabling change in their daily work. These responsibilities encompass operational, tactical and strategic levels.

Figure 1.1 Build, span, solve and change L&D role framework

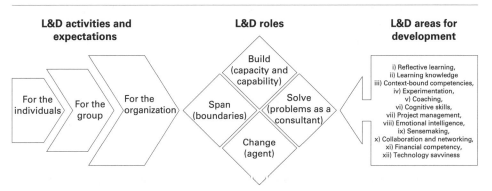

To be successful, L&D professionals need to develop 12 key capabilities of reflective learning, knowledge in adult learning principles, concepts and theories, context-bound knowledge and competencies, practice and experimentation, coaching, cognitive skills, project management, emotional intelligence, sense-making, collaborative working and networking, financial competency, and technology savviness. As Figure 1.1 illustrates, these skills will contribute to the holistic development of L&D professionals to be effective in their work. The discussion in this chapter will have helped you to meet the learning outcomes of understanding the requirements of being a professional, and identifying and developing capabilities for successful L&D practice.

References

3M (2012) A Culture of Innovation, *3M* [online] http://solutions.3m.com/3MContentRetrievalAPI/BlobServlet?lmd=1349327166000&locale=en_WW&assetType=MMM_Image&assetId=1319209959040&blobAttribute=ImageFile

Beard, C, Clegg, S and Smith, K (2007) Acknowledging the affective in higher education, *British Educational Research Journal*, **33** (2), pp. 235–52

Becher, T (1999) *Professional Practices: Commitment and capability in a changing environment*, Transaction, New Brunswick, NJ

Belbin, R M (2010) *Team Roles at Work*, 2nd edn, Routledge, Oxford

Brown, T (2008) Design thinking, *Harvard Business Review*, **86** (6), pp. 84–95

Burke, R (2013) *Project Management, Planning and Control Techniques*, 5th edn, Wiley, Chichester

Campbell, A (2011) Collaboration is misunderstood and overused, *Harvard Business Review* [online] http://blogs.hbr.org/cs/2011/09/collaboration_is_misunderstood.html

Casimir, G, Lee, K and Loon, M (2012) Knowledge sharing: influences of trust, commitment and cost, *Journal of Knowledge Management*, **16** (5), pp. 740–53

Chartered Institute of Personnel and Development (2010) Real-world coaching evaluation: a guide for practitioners, *CIPD* [online] http://www.cipd.co.uk/hr-resources/guides/real-world-coaching-evaluation.aspx

Chartered Institute of Personnel and Development (2012) Code of professional conduct, *CIPD* [online] https://www.cipd.co.uk/binaries/5740CodeofConduct.pdf

Chartered Institute of Personnel and Development (2014) The CIPD Profession Map v2.4, *CIPD* [online] http://www.cipd.co.uk/cipd-hr-profession/profession-map/profession-map-download.aspx

Cheetham, G and Chivers, G (1998) The reflective (and competent) practitioner: a model of professional competence which seeks to harmonise the reflective practitioner and competence-based approaches, *Journal of European Industrial Training*, **22** (7), pp. 267–76

Cheetham, G and Chivers, G (2001) How professionals learn in practice: an investigation of informal learning amongst people working in professions, *Journal of European Industrial Training*, **25** (5), pp. 248–92

Collin, K, Van der Heijden, B and Lewis, P (2012) Continuing professional development, *International Journal of Training and Development*, **16** (3), pp. 155–63

Cullen, J B (1985) Professional differentiation and occupational earnings, *Work and Occupations*, **12**, pp. 351–72

Davidson, J and Wood, C (2004) A conflict resolution model, *Theory into Practice*, **43** (1), pp. 6–13

De Weerdt, S, Bouwen, R, Corthouts, F and Martens, H (2006) Identity transformation as an intercontextual process, *Industry & Higher Education*, 2 (5), pp. 317–26

Friedson, E, ed, (1973) *The Professions and their Prospects*, Sage, London

Georghiades, P (2000) Beyond conceptual change learning in science education: focusing on transfer, durability and metacognition, *Educational Research*, 42 (2), pp. 119–39

Goleman, D (1996) *Emotional Intelligence: Why it can matter more than IQ*, Bloomsbury, London

Grant, A M (2011) Is it time to REGROW the GROW model? Issues related to teaching coaching session structures, *The Coaching Psychologist*, 7 (2), pp. 118–26

Greenwood, E (1957) Elements of professionalization, in *Professionalization*, eds. B M Vollmar and D L Mills, Prentice-Hall, Englewood Cliffs, NJ, pp. 10–19

Harrison, R (2009) *Learning and Development*, 5th edn, Chartered Institute of Personnel and Development, London

Hill, C J and Neeley, S E (1988) Differences in the consumer decision process for professional vs. generic services, *Journal of Services Marketing*, 2 (1), pp. 17–23

Hyun, E and Marshall, J D (1997) Theory of multiple/multiethnic perspective-taking ability for teachers' developmentally and culturally appropriate practice (DCAP), *Journal of Research in Childhood Education*, 11 (2), pp. 188–98

Kerzner, H (2010) *Project Management: Best practices*, 2nd edn, John Wiley & Sons, New York, NY

Kirkpatrick, D L and Kirkpatrick, J D (2009) *Implementing the Four Levels: A practical guide for effective evaluation of training programs*, Berrett-Koehler Publishers, San Fransciso, CA

Knight, P, Tait, J and Yorke, M (2006) The professional learning of teachers in higher education, *Studies in Higher Education*, 31 (03), pp. 319–39

Kolb, D A, Boyatzis, R E and Mainemelis, C (2001) Experiential learning theory: previous research and new directions, in *Perspectives on Thinking, Learning, and Cognitive Style*, eds. R J Sternberg and L F Zhang, Lawrence Erlbaum, NJ, pp. 227–47

Kotter, J P (1995) Leading change: why transformation efforts fail, *Harvard Business Review*, 73 (2), pp. 59–67

Krider, J, Singaraju, R and Carroll, B (2016) *UK Corporate Learning Factbook 2016: Benchmarks, trends and analysis of the UK training market*, [online] https://www.bersin.com/Practice/Detail.aspx?id=19463

Lee, H and Cho, Y (2007) Factors affecting problem finding depending on degree of structure of problem situation, *The Journal of Educational Research*, 101 (2), pp. 113–24

Loon, M (2014) *L&D: New challenges, new approaches*, CIPD, London

Mayo, A (2004) *Creating a Learning and Development Strategy*, CIPD, London

Mazen, A (2011) Transforming the negotiator: the impact of critical learning on teaching and practicing negotiation, *Management Learning*, **43** (1), pp. 113–28

Mintzberg, H (2004) *Managers, Not MBAs: A hard look at the soft practice of managing and management development*, Berrett-Koehler Publishers, San Francisco, CA

OECD (2000) *Where Are the Resources for Lifelong Learning?* OECD Publishing, Paris

Overton, L and Dixon, G (2015) Embracing change: improving performance of business, individuals and the L&D team. 2015-16 Industry Benchmark Report, *Towards Maturity* [online] http://www.towardsmaturity.org/article/2015/11/05/embracing-change-improving-performance-benchmark/

Passmore, J (2007) An integrative model for executive coaching, *Consulting Psychology Journal: Practice and Research*, **59** (1), pp. 68–78

Paterson, M, Higgs, J, Wilcox, S and Villenuve, M (2002) Clinical reasoning and self-directed learning: key dimensions in professional education and professional socialisation, *Focus on Health Professional Education*, **4** (2), pp. 5–21

Pavalko, R M (1971) *Sociology of Occupations and Professions*, F.E. Peacock Publishers, Ithica, IL

Pinto, J K (1996) *Power and Politics in Project Management* Project Management Institute, Newtown Square, PA

Quesada, J, Kintsch, W and Gomez, E (2005) Complex problem-solving: a field in search of a definition? *Theoretical Issues in Ergonomics Science*, **6** (1), pp. 5–33

Rees, G and French, R (2013) *Leading, Managing and Developing People*, CIPD, London

Sanchez, R (2005) 'Tacit knowledge' versus 'explicit knowledge' approaches to knowledge management practice, in *Handbook on the Knowledge Economy*, eds. D Rooney, G Hearn and A Ninan, Edward Elgar, Cheltenham

Schwandt, D R (2005) When managers become philosophers: integrating learning with sensemaking, *Academy of Management Learning & Education*, **4** (2), pp. 176–92

Senge, P, Kleiner, A, Roberts, C, Ross, R and Smith, B (1994) *The Fifth Discipline Fieldbook: Strategies and tools for building a learning organization*, Nicholas Brealey Publishing, London

Senior, B and Swailes, S (2010) *Organizational Change*, 4th edn, FT Prentice Hall, Harlow, Essex

Slocum, W L (1966) *Occupational Careers*, Aldine, Chicago, IL

Society for Human Resource Management (2012) SHRM Competency Model, *SHRM* [online] http://www.shrm.org/HRCompetencies/Documents/Competency%20Model%2010%200%206%203.pdf

Stewart, J and Sambrook, S (2012) The historical development of human resource development in the United Kingdom, *Human Resource Development Review*, **11** (4), pp. 443–62

Tallman, I and Gray, L N (1990) Choices, decisions, and problem-solving, *Annual Review of Sociology*, **16** (1), pp. 405–33

Thakor, M V and Kumar, A (2000) What is a professional service? A conceptual review and bi-national investigation, *Journal of Services Marketing*, **14** (1), pp. 63–82

Trede, F, Macklin, R and Bridges, D (2012) Professional identity development: a review of the higher education literature, *Studies in Higher Education*, **37** (3), pp. 365–84

Ulrich, D (2008) Coaching for results, *Business Strategy Series*, **9** (3), pp. 104–14

von Hippel, E, Thomke, S and Sonnack, M (1999) Creating breakthroughs at 3M, *Harvard Business Review*, **77**, pp. 47–57

Weick, K E (1995) *Sensemaking in Organizations*, Sage, Thousand Oaks, CA

Wilson, C (2011) Developing a coaching culture, *Industrial and Commercial Training*, **43** (7), pp. 407–14

Zahra, S A and George, G (2002) Absorptive capacity: a review, reconceptualization, and extension, *Academy of Management Review*, **27** (2), pp. 185–203

Understanding the context of L&D

02

ROBIN BELL AND MARK LOON

1 Introduction

In this chapter, you will build on the previous chapter's understanding of the requirements of a being a professional as well as the identification and development of key competencies in your practice. This chapter introduces you to a number of concepts and issues that have occurred in the external environment to stimulating your thinking about the context in which L&D operates and what shapes its success. Understanding the role that external factors have on the organization and in turn L&D professionals is crucial in an increasingly interconnected, global world. This chapter looks outward to understand how the outside world affects what is happening inside your organization. What external elements cause change within your organization? What are the main sources of these external forces? Why does an organization need to pay special attention to its context? Organizations that ignore the external world do so at their own peril. Understanding the external environment means L&D can not only react to changing business needs, but can also prepare for them and mitigate any negative impact on the organization. In fact, in some cases, L&D practitioners may be able to leverage these trends and take advantage of opportunities that arise.

There are two learning outcomes in this chapter:

1 Understand L&D's strategic and operating environment.
2 Recognize the implications of L&D's context on its practice.

In addressing the learning outcomes, this chapter will help you understand an organization's context. Section 2 contains a discussion on the sources of change using the Political, Economic, Social, Legal, Technological and Environmental (PESTLE) framework. This section provides various examples of some important trends in each domain of the PESTLE framework. Section 3 then provides a discussion on the nature of change; in particular, it illustrates how the changes in the external environment are Volatile, Uncertain, Complex and Ambiguous (VUCA). Section 4 demonstrates how change has impacted on the nature of competition and cooperation, which is discussed in the context of industry and business models. Section 5 provides an outline of how some of the changes in the external environment have impacted on work and the workforce, in particular the need for new skills and competencies required to deal with the changing external world. Section 6 then discuss L&D's role within a business environment in light of this context. The content in Sections 5 and 6 is only preliminary, as more is further explored in Chapters 5, 6 and 7. Section 7 contains a provocation on how entrepreneurship and intrapreneurship, supported by L&D, are potentially two of the best weapons against an ever-changing world, helping organizations to shape their own future. Section 8 is the conclusion and Section 9 contains some points for reflection. Both learning outcomes are addressed in each section.

2 Sources of change

When examining L&D in an organization, it is not enough to simply evaluate the internal working environment. L&D operates within an organization and that organization must be readily and vigilantly cognisant of its context. This context is shaped by the way the external environment informs both business decisions made by the organization and L&D's decisions with respect to internal operations. Missing out on key opportunities affects all parts of an organization and it is for this reason that L&D must not only be aware of its external environment, it must also be increasingly proactive in acting upon that information.

What is meant by the 'external environment'? When thinking about the external environment, it may be overwhelming to take in all of the factors that may affect a business. Using a logic-based approach in the analysis of the external environment is a good strategy with which to begin. One way to break the external factors down is to use a PESTLE analysis. In a PESTLE analysis, the external factors that have an impact on a business are viewed from the Political, Economic, Social, Technological, Legal, and Environmental perspectives. A PESTLE framework is a useful approach to understanding changes in the external environment. The following discusses each domain in the framework in more detail.

2.1 Political

Politics is the practice of influencing others. Within the PESTLE framework, the political domain concerns the government or public affairs of a country. This includes government decision making at different levels (eg national and local authorities), political parties (ruling, coalitions, and minority), government institutions, government mandates and policies (often in light of which political party is in power).

The political atmosphere at any given point will have an impact on a business. For example, the political party or ruling regime in any country can affect domestic and international commerce and may enact policies that may be more or less business friendly (or employee friendly). Exploring the national level of government is only one piece of the puzzle. While many decisions are made at a national level, some Western countries also 'surrender' some of their sovereignty (through binding agreements) to super-national governing bodies, making some legal, trade, and defence policies beyond the scope of national governments. Examples include the European Union at a regional level, and the United Nations at a world level. There are also bodies that are not geographic-centric but operate for specific purposes, such as the North Atlantic Treaty Organization (NATO), which is defence based in nature, and the World Trade Organization (WTO).

The nature of power sharing within a country is also a consideration. For example, while much of the policy in England comes from the United Kingdom government, in the United States, many decisions are made at a state or even local government level and are outside the jurisdiction of the federal government. While interstate and international commerce is a federal issue, a US company may face different requirements with respect to its responsibilities to its employees, depending on which state it is operating in. One also has to consider the type of government that is involved, which is usually shaped by its historical context. Countries such as the United States and Australia operate within a federal framework, whereby power to the federal government is ceded from the states. The UK, on the other hand, is a unitary government where power is centralized and delegated (eg devolution of power to Scotland and Wales). Although this is only one aspect a system of government, it provides insight to where power lies.

Political parties have a major influence on the decisions that a government may make. The 'philosophy' and principles of a political party are telling of the direction it may take if voted into government and the type of policies it may implement. For example, a Conservative party with the majority in government responds to the global economic crisis with austerity measures, leaving consumers with less money to spend and decreasing demand for goods and services. It may also reduce funding for research and development, and for public–private partnerships, which will have an impact on many businesses that directly or indirectly benefit from these subsidies. A ruling party that is less fiscally conservative may respond by enhancing liquidity into the economy, which generally results in more money for people. Such 'stimulus' is intended to give individuals more disposable income and to 'pump' money into the economy to help consumers make more purchases, thereby increasing demand and improving production. Less direct measures include aid for poor individuals to spend on food, housing, or healthcare, all of which increases demand in these sectors. The political domain is powerful, as it can ultimately have a major impact on other domains in the external environment (eg economic), on organizations and people (eg workforce and consumers) and on sectors such as finance and banking. For example, the UK government's deregulation of the mortgage market in the 1980s completely altered the competitive landscape as the dominance of the market shifted from building societies to banks. The case example by Neil Liddington illustrates the far-reaching impact of government policies on a fire service.

Neil Liddington, area manager, risk reduction, Avon Fire and Rescue Service

The fire service has experienced a lot of changes in the last five to six years due to the austerity measures, as we are asked to do more with less, which is the same in many for public sector organizations trying to gain more efficiency. The activities of the fire service have diversified, as we now help deal with terrorist threats, flood emergencies (including safety training in rescuing people from flood waters), decontamination of chemicals and educating children as part of broader prevention activities (eg traffic safety at various age groups). The diversification of our activities has resulted in significant changes in the learning and development of our staff members.

Even the seemingly straightforward activity of rescuing animals such as horses and livestock requires significant training. The animals we rescue

▶

are not only different, and thus necessitate different techniques, but the act of rescuing animals is also hazardous to firefighters. In addition, the equipment used is unique and highly specialized, so this results in many dimensions for learning and development, such as learning about different animals, health and safety measures for firefighters when rescuing animals, and learning about specialist equipment.

However, I believe the most significant changes that I have witnessed in my career have been over the longer 20-year horizon, in particular from both legislative and social perspectives. In the early years of my career, most of our work would have been more 'reactionary', fighting fires and attending to other emergencies. Over years, things have greatly improved and, thankfully, there are fewer incidents that we need to react to. This reduction in incidents has been largely due to stronger legislation in household health and safety (eg less flammable materials in household furniture and fixtures, better-equipped home safety, and flame retardation mechanisms in homes), and the improvements in people's lifestyles (eg by being more conscious about health and not using deep-frying cooking methods).

However, whilst the reduction in incidents is an absolute positive, this has also meant that firefighters have less opportunity to learn on the job and therefore have to keep up their skills in different ways. Whereas most of their learning used to be on the job, we now have to teach them these skills in contrived environments. The learning cycle used to involve the initial acquirement the skills (eg how to put the fire out) developed off the fire ground, with the maintenance of these skills performed on the fire ground. But now both initial development and maintenance of skills are done off the fire ground. This not only effects front-line staff but is also felt in the management domain, where leadership skills are not tested enough in the field due to the lack of opportunities.

The main issue with off-field training and development is that one cannot completely simulate an incident; for example, a real fire emergency engages all senses such as smell, which sometimes even helps firefighters to develop a kind of 'sixth sense'. As a solution, we simulate major real-life incidents that have happened in the past as closely as possible. Every aspect of these incidents is recorded in detail so that we are able to learn from them and become more successful in dealing with future incidents. Whilst simulations are helpful, they have to be further supported with other learning and development methods to fill the gaps. A challenge that arises in closely simulating real life is that the simulation itself becomes hazardous, and we have to decide how much risk we want to expose our firefighters to in a training and development environment.

Experiential learning is crucial in many cases – if you get on a bike to learn to ride it, then you learn quite quickly. But if I only show you how to ride a bike, show you another person riding a bike, and we talk about it and read books about it, chances are you will still fall off the bike when you first ride it, even after hours of 'learning'

Although the use of technology has been helpful in delivering training content involving standard operating procedures, its application has not always been straightforward. The fire service has members in its workforce who are in their 40s and 50s and are not entirely accustomed to technology-driven modes of training. To address this issue, the fire service has had to first undertake a gap analysis in terms of skill levels in using technology. Second, we then train our workforce in using technology prior to the roll-out of technology-enhanced training programmes. In short, our staff have had to learn about the learning tools before using the tools to learn. Other developments as a result of changes in the external environment include each fire station designing and running their own bespoke learning and development schools and programmes, as we have done here in Avon. Although there is a fire service college, it has become difficult to justify the cost involved in the movement of personnel across the country. An alternative that has been opted for is to have the trainer deliver the training on site.

2.2 Economic

Economic systems include the production, distribution, and consumption of goods and services. Goods and services are not unlimited; in fact, the supply (including the availability in a given geographic region) of goods and services, and demand for those goods and services drives most, if not all, economic decisions. Individuals, organizations, and governments all have an effect on the economy. The health of any economy relates to how well it is balanced. For example, an economy that is growing too fast will result in inflation, whilst an economy that is not growing will experience deflation. An economic crisis may hinder banks' ability to make loans and cause delays in expansion for a business. Not all aspects of an economy within a nation state are in sync. For example, some industries may experience growth, some decline whilst some stagnant. Segments of the population are also key considerations in an economy. For example, growth in the middle-class sector in emerging economies means a new source of consumption and growth.

A country's economy naturally fluctuates between growth and recession (contraction), and is reflected in the Gross Domestic Product (GDP). A GDP includes consumption of goods and services within a country's borders, government spending, investment, and overall net exports, which are exports minus imports. Business and commercial decisions are significantly influenced by where a country lies within a typical economic cycle. When economies are expanding and inflation is still low, investors feel more confident. Investors will place money into technology firms and capital goods, and business inventories, as a result, increase. However, when economic cycles are in contraction and a recession is under way, private investors lose confidence and invest less as inflation increases. Businesses will aim to decrease their inventory as demand drops.

Government spending strategies will differ throughout an economic cycle. Connecting to the above section on political factors, some strategies suggest countercyclical spending philosophies, which encourage governments to spend less during times of expansion, in preparation for the extra capital influx into an economy needed during a recession. Governments may thus spend and invest more during times when investors and businesses are spending less in order to encourage consumers to increase demand. Economic factors are tightly linked to fiscal (eg tax) policies set by governments in the political domain, and both are a major consideration for any organization.

And if balancing an economy within the boundaries of a nation state is not difficult enough, many economies now also have to consider how other economies affect their own. Economies across the world are increasingly becoming integrated. An increasingly interconnected world means the world's economic climate will greatly impact an organization's decisions, as economic slowdowns in any part of the world now have the ability to have a ripple effect on all other countries. Economists were fond of saying, 'when the United States sneezes, the whole world catches a cold' in illustrating knock-on economic effects (however, at present this phrase has changed to 'when China sneezes, the whole world catches a cold'). The new power-house of BRIC nations (Brazil, Russia, India and China) is envisaged to overtake the traditional economic model so long monopolized by the United States and Europe (Roland Berger, 2015). Also, McKinsey & Co state that emerging economies now account for nearly 40 per cent of all global flows (Manyika *et al.*, 2014).

Globalization has increased the focus on the external environment because it has increased the interconnectivity of businesses to suppliers, consumers, governments and other global players. McKinsey & Co has termed this phenomenon 'global flows' (Manyika *et al*, 2014). Global flows include trade routes, internet traffic, and cross-border flows of goods, services, finance, and individuals. As technology and global flows increase, businesses must innovate in order to remain competitive. The key point is that interconnectivity amongst economies has made the management of organizations a lot more complex.

2.3 Social

Social factors involve people. An important trend in this domain is the world's growing population, which is estimated to expand by 18 per cent to 8.4 billion people by 2030 (Roland Berger, 2015). The social domain also refers to changing demographics such as more single parents and the changing composition of rural–urban populations, for example. In addition, the attitudes of people are also considered in this domain, such as growing acceptance of same-sex marriages and same-sex adoption. The social domain also refers to generational issues such as the expectations of different generations (eg Generations X, Y and the millennials) of their jobs, careers and employers. The social domain also extends to cultures such beliefs and values that are founded upon nationality or ethnicity.

The term social also refers to how individuals interact with one another (which can be demographic, generational, and cultural in nature) and these interactions shape how individuals view themselves and their place in the larger world. Social phenomena are crucial as they influence how we perceive the world around us, such as what we deem ethical or otherwise, and ultimately influence our behaviour.

From a marketing perspective, knowing your demographics is an important element in any organization. A business must be cognisant of how they will be perceived by their intended customers and by the public. Preferences and expectations are also different across ages and cultures. From a human resources perspective, millennials have different work and development expectations compared to their parents' generation. For example, millennials may expect to work in many different jobs with different employers across their careers. In fact, some may also expect to have multiple careers, not just jobs, in their lifetime. They also seek a more holistic work–life balance and expect workplace-enabled personal development. L&D will have to respond appropriately not only to millennials but also to those from other generations who may have a slightly different outlook. Monsanto, a global agrochemical and agricultural biotechnology enterprise, has recognized the power of social factors. In 2014 they appointed a 'director of millennial engagement' (who is also a millennial himself) to understand the expectations of this generation (Mueller, 2014).

Cultural aspects, ie individual cultures and multiculturalism, are of increasing importance as well. Global flows of individuals mean many countries are increasingly multicultural. The concept of an individual's identity will be shaped by more than just their nationality, and definitions of what it means to be of a certain culture and ethnicity will change as countries adapt to accommodate more heterogeneous populations. This is exacerbated by the growth of migration across the globe. World cultures will remain in a constant flux. For example, in 2014, the majority of babies born in the United States were to non-white Americans, and it is projected that by 2044 white Americans will be a minority (Smialek and Giroux, 2015). What does this mean culturally? Would the United States be still classified as possessing an Anglo-Saxon culture? Or perhaps it would be better to be classified as having a Latin culture in the future? Multiculturalism is also growing at very fast rates in other countries such as Canada and Australia. L&D must be integrated with the multicultural nature of most organizations and ensure that individuals understand the challenges and sensitivities involved with working amongst and with individuals with different values and backgrounds.

An important growing area of concern for organizations and research is how L&D can play a more influential role in diversity, in addition to training initiatives it provides on working in teams composed of members from diverse racial, ethnic and religious backgrounds. A challenge for L&D is how to maximize the benefits of diversity that are so frequently espoused in research. Another challenge concerns the difference in learning styles of individuals from different cultural backgrounds (Joy and Kolb, 2009), which is an area that is further explored in Chapter 8.

The social domain may also include local communities. For example, when planning construction of a new building, plant, or site, most countries require a public inquiry to take place before a new industrial building can be constructed, allowing the community living in the area to query developers. Petitions, lobbying of the local council and protests can all result from misjudging public perception. Even if there is no reason to oppose new construction, a strong sense of NIMBY, or 'not in my back yard' may prevail.

Supporting this, some studies have found that a simple proposed change in a community can cause opposition regardless of the potential benefits. When considering social aspects, it is helpful to think about who all the stakeholders are before making any decisions. The influence of society is formidable and ignoring this external domain could see an organization faced with unexpected opposition for any of its planned courses of action.

2.4 Technological

Technology refers to methods and processes used to accomplish a goal or produce goods/services. It is often about how scientific research and development breakthroughs are applied. Technology is most often thought of as being embedded within other mechanisms like production machines, computing devices, and software programmes. Technology can also be knowledge based, that is, understanding the techniques and processes used to accomplish a goal. This can be seen in the licensing of goods for export. Certain goods are considered more sensitive than others for either commercial (intellectual property) or security reasons and require a government-issued licence to export them. It is not only objects that may require exports; the knowledge in someone's mind may require a licence too! Scientific experts often require training and understanding of sensitivities before they are allowed to share their knowledge with individuals in another country.

Technological advances occur with increasing frequency. Research and development in science and technology results in innovations that can change the rules in the environment within which a business operates in such a way that a business risks being left behind if it is not tuned into the latest breakthroughs. The abundance of information available and ease of communication have changed the nature of competition and how consumers interact with businesses. Predicting the newest technology is challenging, as is choosing what technology to embrace within an organization.

The 'Internet of Things' (IoT) is an umbrella term for all devices that can be connected to the internet (Manyika *et al.*, 2013). As the IoT grows, so will our ability to connect to one another by text, audio and video, be it synchronously or asynchronously. Data are also ever-increasingly growing, exacerbating the notion of information overload (first recognized about 20 years ago). L&D can embrace technological advances to enhance the L&D experience, but must also respond to the changes that technology makes to everyday workplace operations and adjust its focus. The impact of technology on learning and development is more fully explored in Chapter 6.

2.5 Legal

The law is a system of rules governing behaviour that are enforced through legal institutions. Laws exist in many forms. Statutes are the most common form of law, as they come from legislative governmental bodies. However, other sources of legally binding mechanisms exist and affect business operations. For example, judges making rulings on court cases can establish precedent, in which a court decision is used as the basis for future similar court cases. Individuals and businesses may enter into legally binding contracts that may provide an alternative avenue of dispute settlement (such as arbitration). A government entity may make legally binding decrees outside of the legislative process by issuing regulations. All of these elements contribute to the legal environment in which a business operates. Laws and regulations help make commerce more predictable and transparent.

However, laws are like double-edged swords, as they can be an advantage and a disadvantage. Which laws and regulations enable a business to thrive, and which ones can hinder its growth? The plethora of regulations that any organization must be aware of can make its operations more challenging. Similar to the political domain, laws at various levels must be considered. A good consideration of the court system and law enforcement mechanisms is crucial both domestically and with international stakeholders. Understanding the legal system in a foreign country can inform a business of how to develop contractual arrangements (eg write contracts) to minimize the possibility of litigation in a foreign jurisdiction. With increasingly global flows in the area of employment, employment and visa laws may have an increasing impact on an organization, as can changes in national-level employment policies.

Laws and regulations are not applied evenly to all industries. Newer industries may have fewer (direct) regulations placed upon them because they have not existed long enough for the law to identify what practices need to be regulated. This can put mature industries, which may have long-standing regulations on practice already in place, at a disadvantage. Law making is a traditionally slow process. As technology changes, laws do not always adapt quickly to address the differences enabled by technology. In addition, certain industries have better public images than other industries and thus are regulated differently in response to public demand. It is not a good idea to assume that regulations in one industry apply to others, and a solid understanding of the rules under which any given business operates is crucial.

L&D thus has a role to play in understanding the regulations and laws impacting a business and how a business remains compliant. L&D must ensure standards are maintained, accreditations, certifications, and licences are up to date, and staff are adequately trained and certified in conformance to these rules. By fulfilling this role, L&D helps protect a business from the fallout of a failed inspection, which can be very costly in time, revenue, and public perception. The impact of the regulatory domain is illustrated by Susan Hamilton, a senior learning and development manager in a not-for-profit sector organization.

Susan Hamilton, senior learning and development manager, not-for-profit sector organization

The most significant impact from the external environment is from changes in government direction and policies, in particular the budget cuts that have directly impacted on housing in the not-for-profit sector, eg rent reduction. More recently, the changes in thinking concerning minimum wages and the impending impact of the ruling from the EU that travel to and from work 'is work' (for those with no fixed place of work), will further affect the organization. These changes have ultimately resulted in the need to find significant efficiencies in the organization. Learning and development (L&D) has played a key role in supporting management, which has been a challenge as we have tried to ensure that there is minimal disruption to our present operations and future capabilities.

In terms of our operations, the organization operates in a highly regulated environment and we need to maintain compliance within the regulatory framework. Our operations are also regularly inspected by agencies such as the Care Quality Commission. Therefore, it is imperative that we maintain mandatory delivery of our services by ensuring that our relevant staff are certified and that their competencies are maintained against the respective relevant standards. L&D has contributed to this success at the operational level by reviewing and revising the way training and development is configured and delivered, ensuring that the standards are maintained whilst being more efficient. For example, we were able to find savings through using e-learning in delivering some of our training programmes.

From a future capabilities perspective, it was important that any initiatives in regard to savings were not at the expense of developing future leaders in the organization. In fact, it is actually more important now to ensure that we have a group of promising leaders, as we are now operating in a leaner and more challenging environment. Therefore, it is

▶

crucial that we are able to keep and enhance our talent so that we know we have the leaders in place who are able to successfully steer the organization in this new context.

Indeed, it was quite refreshing in my experience, as L&D is recognized as playing an important role in supporting management in finding efficiencies, rather than as a passive recipient of across-the-board cuts. L&D has played an important role in a strategic sense. Nevertheless, whilst management maintained its trajectory on leadership development, it still meant that our leadership development initiatives had to be reviewed. We are now more focused on behaviours; on what we want our leaders to be throughout the organization at every level. To do this, we have initiated robust L&D programmes at three management levels: first line managers, middle managers and senior managers. We have shifted from classroom learning to more experiential, reflective and individualized forms of learning.

We also use 360-degree feedback process on leadership competencies to inform individuals of their L&D needs and for them to reflect upon these behaviours and how to move forward. In addition, we now also leverage the knowledge of our internal staff members who may have expertise that they can share, by inviting them to contribute to the learning and development of others. In addition, we are shifting our attention to helping future leaders to develop awareness of the external environment in terms of political parties and events by inviting external speakers to present on topical/pressing issues.

Ultimately, our leadership programmes are focused on demonstrating business impact. Those involved in the leadership programme are required to complete a project as part of a group that captures and reports how their participation in the programme has resulted in a positive impact on the organization. This, in part, involves those in the leadership programmes demonstrating how they have applied what they have learned. The focus on business impact supports L&D's approach to demonstrating return on investment (ROI). We use both quantitative and qualitative indicators such as 360-degree feedback to get an idea of positive shifts in behaviour at the individual and group levels. We also review retention and progression indicators, as well as the growth in the scope of individuals' roles. I believe L&D has been context savvy by truly understanding what is going on in the organization and leveraging what the organization has to maximize internal resources in developing leaders, as well as helping the organization to align itself to environment changes.

2.6 Environmental

The environment is a concept that examines how living things interact, and the natural environment includes all living and non-living naturally occurring elements and phenomena on the planet. Elements of the environment include natural resources, temperature, climate and geology. When thinking about how the environment and business relate to each other, it is useful to think about how interaction with the environment can change ecology and nature. Examples include climate change, air and water quality, availability of mineral and water resources, and the threats of species extinction.

Operating in an environmentally friendly manner and being resourcefully frugal is an increasing challenge for businesses. Resources are scarce but at the same time demand worldwide from a growing consumer class is increasing. Examining what is happening outside an organization with respect to the environment is an area for consideration. Environmental and ecological factors may affect which resources are available and how an organization uses energy sources. Changes in the global energy nexus see a trend towards lesser dependence on fossil fuels across the globe and increased incentives for using renewable and 'clean' energy.

Sustainability has become a popular buzz word for many organizations. Originally, sustainability largely applied to environmental matters, but now its definition has expanded to explore the interplay of business operations and the environment such that successful coexistence can continue without damage to either in the long term. Indeed, sustainability now offers a genuine competitive advantage to organizations that embrace the concept in its values, strategic approach and operations (Deloitte Touche Tohmatsu and The World Economic Forum, 2010). The trend in businesses reducing their carbon footprint has implications for organizational operations and may affect how L&D is carried out. For example, the use of e-learning resources may decrease the use of natural resources and make organizational operations more efficient whilst having a positive impact on the environment as people do not need to travel to and from physical locations.

It is important to note that a PESTLE analysis is a starting point, not a 'one-size-fits-all' solution. Online searches will quickly reveal that many approaches to this analysis include additional aspects or a more concise version. For example, some organizations focus on the first four elements and conduct a 'PEST' analysis, while others add an additional 'E' for ethical considerations. What elements are necessary for an organizational L&D analysis will be informed by a number of factors within an organization, but

PESTLE is a good starting framework. Elements may be added and removed as the analysis transpires.

Undertaking a PESTLE analysis may inform you of what problems may be present and give organizations a platform to decide how to best address them, bearing in mind all the external and internal stakeholders involved. Analyses of the external environment should be undertaken on a regular basis. Organizations that undertake regular a PESTLE or similar analyses can identify key trends and changes before other businesses and be at the forefront for what is to come.

None of these trends exist within isolation in each domain. Environmental issues are often aligned with political and legal issues. Consider corporate social responsibility (CSR). This may seem to be a social aspect, but often it is driven by environmental needs and pressures to become more 'green'. CSR can also be a proactive approach to pre-empt regulations being imposed and enable an organization to say that it has undertaken the change before being compelled to by law. Paying attention to these external elements and understanding how they fit together enables an organization and L&D to remain ahead of the curve and identify valuable linkages.

2.7 Undertaking a PESTLE analysis

Before commencing with the next section, it would be helpful to pause to think about how the external environment impacts your organization. In undertaking a PESTLE exercise, please follow the steps below:

- Select an organization that you are familiar with as the focus of your analysis.
- Identify the sources of information. Determine which sources to refer to for information in each domain, for example, newspaper websites, government websites, or the organization's annual reports. In most cases, secondary sources of information will most likely suffice. For example, if you refer to news websites such as the BBC (http://www.bbc.co.uk), the *Guardian* (http://www.theguardian.com/uk) and/or the *Telegraph* (http://www.telegraph.co.uk), each will have headings on its homepage in relation to each of the five domains in the PESTLE framework. However, this is only a starting point; you will most likely need to source information from other credible sources such as the Office for National Statistics (http://www.ons.gov.uk/ons/index) and the Department for Business Innovation and Skills (https://www.gov.uk/government/organizations/department-for-business-innovation-skills).

- Use the following keywords when undertaking a search on websites:
  - the type of industry your organization is in, eg retail;
  - the name of your products/services, eg laptops;
  - customer category, eg online shoppers, high street shoppers, adventure seekers;
  - location of your business, eg London.

- Classify the trend as an opportunity or threat, or both. By virtue of recognizing a trend, it is quite likely, if not certain, that the trend is of some importance and may have an impact on the organization. Environmental scanning not only involves identifying trends in each domain but also requires you to interpret whether or not a trend is an opportunity, threat or both.

- Identify the degree of impact of the trend. For example, this may be in terms of time, whether it is short, medium or long term; is such a trend here to stay? Another way to look at impact is whether it affects the entire industry or is it more local, eg in a particular county? Table 2.1 is a template to give you an idea how to format this analysis.

- Work with others. Interpreting whether a trend is an opportunity or threat, or whether it is short, medium or long term can be quite subjective. In fact, what is short or long term depends on the organization's industry. Long term in the construction industry may be 10 to 20 years, whereas it may be two to three years in the high-technology sector. Thus, it may be helpful to first define what is meant by short, medium or long term in the context of your organization. It would be helpful to gain multiple perspectives and work with a colleague in interpreting the findings. Working with colleagues/in teams can make the data analysis more efficient and can help steer the team members back on track if anyone becomes bogged down in a data trap (eg analysis paralysis).

Table 2.1 helps to analyse the information gathered by breaking it down into more manageable chunks and classifying it into categories that allow us to attach meaning to it in the context of the organization. It is important to take time to analyse the information at hand and understand its implications. Remember, it is the analysis that will inform your decisions, not the raw data. Some interpretation and inference will always be required. You may also start to note additional issues that derive from the findings, such as how will this information be disseminated across to the organization that needs to be informed of the findings? Who besides senior management

Table 2.1 PESTLE exercise template

PESTLE Domain	Describe trend/ event identified	Opportunity, threat or both (with justification)	Degree of impact (with justification)
Political	.....	.....	.....
Economic	.....	.....	.....
Social	.....	.....	.....
Technological	.....	.....	.....
Legal	.....	.....	.....
Environmental	.....	.....	.....

would such information be important to, eg sales and marketing, operations? Which of the trends should be monitored in assessing what further transpires from its development?

Once the findings have been analysed and understood, it is time to understand them from the perspective of learning and development for individual staff members, organizational capability, and, equally as important for the L&D function, L&D practitioners. This is where L&D can support management to interpret the findings from the external environment in order to foster a greater understanding of the organization's context, from both strategic and L&D perspectives. Whilst Section 9 later in this chapter provides a number of reflection points in relation to the learning outcomes, it may be helpful to start thinking about some of the key issues that need to be considered:

- What organizational capability is in place to respond to the findings?
- What capability and competencies need to be developed by L&D?
- What strategic L&D options are available to respond to the PESTLE findings?

3 The nature of change

Change in the external environment is nothing new and is expected. The adage 'the only constant is change' rings true. Indeed, the recognition of the importance of scanning the external environment has always been present, none more so than in the work of Aguilar (1967), who at times is attributed as the initiator of the PESTLE framework. However, the period that we live in is 'special', as it is particularly unsettled. Whereas change in the past has taken a fairly evolutionary path, many of the recent changes have been revolutionary, all taking place within a short period, impacting almost every corner of the world. This makes scanning the external environment particularly important. Today's external environment can be described as Volatile, Uncertain, Complex, and Ambiguous, or VUCA (Bennett and Lemoine, 2014). These are the conditions under which people and organizations plan, make decisions, take action, and manage risk. The terms are outlined in greater detail below.

Volatility: The external environment can be seen as unstable. Unexpected events happen both near and far, can be short or long term in duration and may occur quickly with little or no warning. The external environment is considered volatile when the emergence of a change and the impact of that change cannot be predicted. Many technologies are not just changing the way we work but how whole organizations and industries operate. It is not just new technologies that are disruptive; other innovations such as business models also have far-reaching consequences. Volatility is also experienced when new technologies emerge even before prior changes have had time to settle. A natural disaster or political upheaval in one country may interrupt supply chains and disrupt transportation and communications for an unknown period of time. Interest rates may change wildly in one country upon a decision by another country to devalue its currency. Global volatility is now a consideration for most businesses. However, whilst volatility cannot be fully understood or controlled, one can learn about patterns of change that underpin such volatility.

Uncertainty: The external environment is also unpredictable. Change may occur somewhere unexpected or not occur where it was expected. The future is no longer an extrapolation of the past. Long-term paths are difficult to predict. The volatility in the external environment also gives rise to uncertainty as the actions of organizations, governments and other institutions become unpredictable. The transdisciplinary nature of technologies has also resulted in new trajectories of innovation. How will this play out in the future and what new technologies will be embraced by the public? What technologies will need to be incorporated into a business and which ones will phase out? Tastes and preferences have changed as the internet breaks down walls and exposes consumers to new products and alters expectations. There are also discernible changes in consumer shopping patterns as people prefer to shop more frequently but buy less each time. However, is this trend here to stay? How is this trend commensurate with online shopping habits?

Complexity: Complex situations occur when there is a high degree of interdependence amongst many factors, which can be bewildering. The globalized, interconnected, fast-paced environment means that each decision a firm makes has the potential for unforeseen consequences. Conducting business with a supplier in one country may impact on your business relations with a supplier or client in another country. Ever-changing trade laws and treaties mean that a small change in a product's composition may subject it to trade barriers that significantly impact the profit of each unit. New technology not only emerges at dizzying rates but also impacts us in many ways, eg use of haptic (sense of touch) technologies in mobile, security, and learning and development devices.

Ambiguity: An ambiguous environment is opaque and may contain contradictory signals. An ambiguous environment is one that contains many unknown-unknowns, where the relationships between different factors are unclear (though these relationships are thought of as significant). For example, the UK's bilateral ties with China will inevitably have an impact on both economies but it will also have a derivative impact on other areas such as consumers in the rest of the EU. Will such bilateral ties strengthen China's relationship with the EU as a whole or will it be counterproductive to the rest of the EU? In another example, it is recognized that in the future people will not only have different jobs but also different careers in their lifetimes. This surely will impact on the organizational workforce but the question is how? Who benefits? In retail, one area of ambiguity that is a priority to be addressed is understanding how consumers will want to shop for different goods. The internet and prevalence of online retail means that consumers prefer to buy some goods online while others are still seen as best purchased in a bricks-and-mortar establishment. Changes to these preferences occur often and are often ambiguous to suppliers. Another example is the 'sharing economy'. While services provided by established taxi, hotel, and delivery businesses seemed to be unshakeable, the likes of Uber, Air BnB, and Seamless have changed the way in which consumers interact with these services. How will these new business models affect the more established ones? Are these new business models sustainable?

The nature of change of the external environment is volatile, uncertain, complex and ambiguous. Overall these four factors affect an organization's ability to:

- comprehend the consequences of decisions and actions;
- understand the connections between seemingly autonomous variables;
- anticipate and prepare for issues that may arise;

- identify and appreciate opportunities;

- prepare and adapt quickly to change.

VUCA can seem like a frustrating notion. It may seem like it is impossible to plan in a VUCA environment. However, an organization can strategize carefully with each of the VUCA aspects to mitigate their impacts on operations. Organizations must proactively explore the VUCA environment to improve their ability to generate understanding of the context in which they operate and better position themselves to respond to it. Similarly, L&D can respond to this environment with fresh strategies to help develop human capital within the organization to mitigate negative impact and leverage positive trends. In fact, effective learning is the best weapon against VUCA. Effective learning enables individuals and organizations to be flexible and adaptive.

Whereas the PESTLE analysis helps us to analyse the sources of change, the VUCA perspective provides a different but complementary way of understanding the nature of change. In fact, some of the VUCA principles may have been experienced whilst you were undertaking the PESTLE analysis. For example:

- Whilst you were completing the exercise on undertaking a PESTLE analysis, did you think to yourself, 'Is this a 'trend'? It appears to change month by month'. An example of this is the UK's political relationship with Russia, which has fluctuated between friendly and distant due to various events. The degree of cooperation between the two governments ultimately affects how businesses from the two countries can and may operate in each other's territories. This is an example of volatility, as some parts of the external environment may have a complete change over a short period of time.

- Also, you may have had trouble articulating the impact of a change in the external environment. This may be because there is uncertainty about how a trend will transpire.

- You may have also may have found it a challenge to distinguish whether the source of a trend is political or legal. This is because the external environment is complex as there is a long chain of events (knock-on effect) that crosses PESTLE domains.

- Did you find difficulty in classifying whether a trend is an opportunity or a threat? This may be because some trends are ambiguous.

An important lesson that organizations and L&D practitioners can learn and 'take away' from the principles of VUCA is that it presents a risk. A risk is the juxtaposition between the likelihood of something occurring and the magnitude of its impact. VUCA is a risk because i) given the nature of external environment anything is possible, ii) the impact of many changes is disruptive from various perspectives, eg industry and organizational, and iii) the nature of VUCA dictates that organizations will have very little visibility of these changes, which is a risk in itself. Learning is a key aspect in addressing this issue. Learning helps individuals to be more flexible. The learning process also contributes to organizational adaptiveness and influences innovation in organizations.

Given the VUCA nature of the external environment, one could not be blamed for thinking that it may be a futile exercise to even identify VUCA as a risk, as risks usually connote that something can be contained, eg measuring likelihood and magnitude. VUCA is pervasive and is not containable by any stretch of the imagination. Living with VUCA is now a 'way of life' that is omnipresent. Sections 6 and 7 provide an account of how organizations and L&D can prepare themselves to face the challenges posed by the VUCA environment. The case example provided by Anthonie Versluis below illustrates how VUCA has influenced L&D in a strategy consulting firm.

Anthonie Versluis, managing partner, Roland Berger Strategy Consultants

Roland Berger is a global strategy consulting firm, headquartered in Munich. We have about 50 offices worldwide, in 36 countries, with about 2,400 employees. Over the last two years there has been quite a bit of change in Roland Berger, specifically in the way we view training and development. We are a global firm with global clients, and therefore we need to nurture global capabilities. However, we also need to take a more localized approach to learning and development in recognition of the disparities between national education systems around the world, which influence how equipped a new starter is when he/she joins us. For example, new starters in Germany and Malaysia will have different starting points and therefore will require a more bespoke L&D programme at that level/region.

Consulting is like the army; it is regimented and rank and file is important, in part to ensure that individuals have the right training and experience before moving up to the next level. And it is in such a vein that there has also been a change in the way we are organized, which has had a significant impact on the way we train and develop our staff. In particular, the change has involved expansion of hierarchy and the inclusion of more layers within each level (eg consultants, managers, directors). Part of the reason for this is to reflect the increasing specialism required in our work and also to take advantage of the efficiencies that this hierarchy offers. This change had directly impacted on our learning and development configuration, which now has to cater for more specialist/ narrow roles. Take our operations in South East Asia for example; the disparity between the different countries such as Singapore, Malaysia and Indonesia are quite significant. Hence we have to reflect such realities. As such, our competitive environment has helped to inform us in terms of how best to organize ourselves, how to get the best from our people and how best to develop them. So even for a global firm, regional context is crucial in how we plan and deliver L&D.

Of course, there are certain training and development programmes that have to be approached from a global perspective, such as project management, which is to ensure quality and consistency in the way we manage client engagement and deliver value. Nevertheless, given the different needs of our staff, local clients and the regional firms, many of our L&D programmes are highly customized. Within broad parameters (eg role description and career trajectory), the degree of personalization is quite high, as individuals have a lot of say in how they want to develop. The best person to know what they need is the individual themselves. It is not the be all and end all, but it is a great starting point. In Roland Berger, there is something for everyone at every level where L&D is concerned.

There are also other implications brought about by changes in the external environment, resulting in both 'problems' and opportunities arising. In terms of problems, volatility has meant that keeping up with the pace of change is ever-more challenging. In addition, ambiguity and complexity of change have meant that it is becoming more difficult to predict what will happen even in the near future. However, in terms of opportunities, change has also brought about new technologies that improve the way we work and learn. Also, the advent of new technologies has given rise to the 'crowd', resulting in phenomena such as peer-to-peer learning.

Given the uncertainty in the environmental landscape, be it political, technological or in business, and wherever one may be, the best defence

▶

is learning to be an effective learner. Being an effective learner allows us to adapt to most, if not all, types of change. The democratization of learning has meant that consultants now have the autonomy to decide what is best for themselves and how best to get there. Consultants are informed of their targets and given guidance on the firm's career pathways, and they are given significant flexibility in terms of how they attain those goals.

Of course, this does not mean one takes a laissez-faire attitude to learning and development; on the contrary, it means adopting a different approach, one that involves a portfolio of initiatives and mechanisms. There is a growing emphasis on cultivating a learning climate, and encouraging consultants to leverage the external network. Consultants are supported in growing their network and in doing so they learn from their peers whilst developing a collaborative outlook.

Try the exercise below in Table 2.2 to identify how each domain in the external environment (ie PESTLE) is VUCA. Specifically, provide simple examples in each domain that characterize volatility, uncertainty and complexity and ambiguity. Use the sources of information suggested earlier in this chapter (note: you should show how different domains may link together under the 'complex' column).

Table 2.2 VUCA and PESTLE

PESTLE Domain	Volatile (instability and unexpected changes at speed)	Uncertain (unprecedented trends and unpredictability)	Complex (interconnected parts that can be overwhelming)	Ambiguous (mixed signals, haziness)
Political	.....	.....	.....	.....
Economic	.....	.....	.....	.....
Social	.....	.....	.....	.....
Technological	.....	.....	.....	.....
Legal	.....	.....	.....	.....
Environmental	.....	.....	.....	.....

4 Industry, business models and the nature of competition

Think about the term 'industry'. Industry encompasses the part of the economy that is made up of certain businesses, and it can be categorized in a number of ways. An industry is a grouping of businesses with similar activities. For example, think of all the industries involved in the energy sector (fossil fuels, nuclear, hydroelectric, wind, etc) or in the basic materials sector (precious metals, aluminium, etc). Industries are a helpful way to identify groups of businesses and/or organizations that are similar, eg in terms of activities and/or products and services. This section contains two subsections; the first contains a discussion on industry and business models, whilst the second discusses the changing nature of competition and cooperation.

4.1 Industry and business models

In addition to the external environment, it is also crucially important for L&D practitioners to understand and examine the industry that their organization belongs to. In fact, it is quite likely that the trends you identified that affect your organization will also have an impact on its competitors. In addition, examining an industry also provides more insight on the competitive environment such as the number of competitors in the industry, which of course has an immediate impact on the organization. Porter (2008) suggests the following steps in analysing an industry:

- Define boundaries of an industry:
  - What products and/or services are included?
  - Are these products/services distinct in a way that differentiates them from other products/services?
  - Do these products/services differ greatly? Are they relatively the same across geographic boundaries?
- Identify the participants in the industry:
  - Who produces the goods/provides the services (eg the players who compete with one another)?
  - Who are the buyers/buyer groups?
  - Who are the suppliers/supplier groups?

- Examine the competitiveness of the industry (and therefore its profitability):
  - Are there high barriers of entry, eg infrastructure cost?
  - How are strong are the bargaining powers of suppliers and buyer?
  - Are the products/services easily substituted, eg utility of a car with a train as transport?
  - How intense is rivalry, eg are competitors regularly having price wars with each other?

The analysis above provides L&D practitioners with a better idea of their immediate competitive environment. This insight is crucial, as understanding your industry informs L&D units on how your organization competes, the organization's unique selling proposition, what it does better than all of its competitors and how its customers view the organization (understanding the organization and its context is also crucial for L&D activities such as developing a business case, as discussed in Chapter 3). However, there is a limitation of the 'industry' perspective, as the boundaries of an industry are sometimes blurry. For example, think about Amazon. Is Amazon a retailer? Or is it a technology company, eg Kindle? Is it a service provider with the 'Fulfilment by Amazon' delivery service? Another example is Apple. Is Apple a technology company? Or is it a media company? A different but complementary view to industry is that of the business model.

A business model is a visual depiction of how an organization conducts its business, that is, how it makes its money. A business model also illustrates how an organization allocates resources and implements activities in order to generate revenue (Loon, 2015). The business model is a blueprint that demonstrates how the organization delivers value, and how various parts of an organization are connected, eg activities and markets in generating revenue. A business model is informed by the strategy adopted by the organization to recognize the target consumers, specify outputs and outline operational processes. Whilst there are many components to a business model, Osterwalder and Pigneur (2010) argue that there are essentially three aspects that are most crucial: the value proposition, the value creation process and the value capture process. Figure 2.1 depicts the relationship between the three components of a business model.

Osterwalder and Pigneur argue that a value proposition is the benefit that is derived from purchasing/using the value proposition. They identified 11 types of benefits: i) newness, ii) performance, iii) customization, iv) 'getting the job done', v) design, vi) brand/status, vii) price, viii) cost, ix) risk reduction,

x) accessibility and xi) convenience/usability. They also state that there are essentially three major value creation process: i) production, ii) problem solving and iii) providing access to platform/networking services that may be supported by a variety of resources such as physical (infrastructure), intellectual (software), human (services) and financial (loans). The value capture process concerns how an organization is able to monetize the value it has provided such as i) asset sale, ii) usage fee, iii) subscription fee, iv) brokerage fee, v) advertising, vi) lending/leasing/renting and vii) licensing.

Figure 2.1 The three main elements of a business model

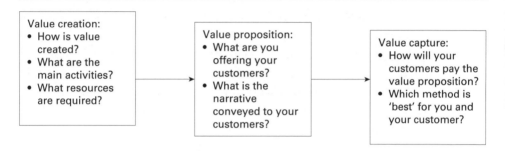

Altering a business model can dramatically change the course of a business, and many senior managers believe that re-evaluating a business model is an important consideration for ensuring future growth and competitiveness (Amit and Zott, 2012). Innovation is often thought of in terms of products or services offered, but it can equally apply to business models, which are often in need of innovation in light of a changing external environment. Innovation is simply the application of a new idea to a design or process that has value (basically what people are willing to part company with their money for).

Business model innovation can take many forms. For example, Amazon first started as an online retailer but as its supply chain operations have grown in sophistication it now allows other business customers (those that do not sell on Amazon's website) to take advantage of its supply chain processes and transport their goods for a fee. This service is called Fulfilment by Amazon. Amazon has also leveraged its advanced computing know-how and now offers computing and storage services (eg cloud) to both business customers and end consumers. Amazon has also ventured into the electronics/smart devices market through the development of Kindle and its own smart phone. Amazon has multiple business models but they all complement one another.

Also, consider how consumers and producers interact for services like hotel rooms and taxi services. While many traditional approaches are still in place, many businesses have changed the nature of business-to-customer relationships (again, think of Uber, Air BnB and Seamless). These changes have allowed for more consumers to have a greater role and say in how products and services are configured and the 'type' of pricing that is involved. Business model innovation may also change what or who performs activities. Take Threadless for example. Threadless is a company that produces t-shirts, but instead of designing its own t-shirts it crowd sources the designs. Its community of designers will create designs and post them on the Threadless website. The community then votes on the designs they like best and Threadless produces the t-shirts with the winning designs, with the creators winning cash prizes.

Take a moment and think about changing business models. Can you think of examples of major firms that have altered their business model in light of a changing external world? Technology firms are often the most readily identifiable, but innovative business models do not necessarily have to do with just technology. Organizations such as Southwest Airlines paved the way for low-cost airline business models, whilst Gillette is often quoted as the originator of the razor/razorblade-type of business model whereby the companies that adopt this model will offer a one-time product (the razor) at a very low price, which is complemented by another product (the razorblade) that customers will buy over and again. It is with this repeat business on razorblades that Gillette makes its money, not the razor. Another example is the 'freemium' business model, whereby the basic version of a product is free but customers must pay to use its more advanced version that contains more functions and features. This business model lures customers in by allowing them to use the free basic version. Once the customers are accustomed to the software they are unlikely to switch and therefore are likely then to pay for the advanced version once their usage of the product becomes more complex (wanting to do more).

4.2 Competition and cooperation

The VUCA environment has changed not only how businesses operate, but also how they view the competition. While traditional business models may view other organizations simply as rivals, it is increasingly the case that VUCA draws would-be competitors together to both cooperate and compete simultaneously (Loon, 2014). This results in 'co-opetition' (Brandenburger and Nalebuff, 1998). Co-opetition is the way senior managers think about their competitors, partners and alliances, and the nature of competition. This change in mindset involves a change from perceiving rival firms as just competitors to perceiving the nature of competition and cooperation as fluid, which is highly dependent on the situation, eg the market and/or product segment in question. Hence, it is not the firm that drives competition or cooperation, it is the event or activity. For example, two organizations may be competitors in one market segment but cooperate together in another market segment. The perspective of the business model is helpful in this regard. Co-opetition is an example of how businesses may innovate in their existing business model to respond to the external environment.

It may initially seem counterintuitive to engage in cooperation with competitors, but there are many instances in which the benefits outweigh the costs and each individual organization benefits as a result. Coordinating on some key features can create a cost advantage and streamline certain operations for all involved businesses. Companies can also share data to foster growth. One example is social media. Sharing logins across multiple social media platforms requires competing businesses to cooperate, but the result will be positive, as there may be increased usage and uptake as seamless logins attract to new users. Using a common login interface does not jeopardize intellectual property of individual businesses but opens up opportunities to attract new users.

Another example is the creation of a joint venture between two companies to respond to changing consumer tastes. Automobile companies have entered into these partnerships to respond to increasing demand for more environmentally friendly vehicles. The pooling of resources reduces research and development costs for all involved parties and speeds up the process. Commercialization of the jointly developed technology is where the companies can separate and decide internally how best to use the technology.

The increase in coopetition does not mean that there are no tensions between organizations. The dual nature of cooperating and competing will naturally be challenging to balance, and best practices are constantly under development. Work by Tidström (2014) provides suggestions for organizations to manage these tensions and argues that these tensions are similar to conflicts, thus using conflict management strategies that may already be in place in an organization is a helpful starting point. Building a culture of trust between businesses working in this way may mitigate some tension. Drafting formal agreements (for example, a Memorandum of Understanding) to describe the nature of the partnership can put all sides at ease. Tensions, when well managed, can be a positive influence on a business.

L&D practitioners are increasingly working in such an environment. Hence they need to help develop attitudes and skills that can adapt not only to a globalized world, but also to an interconnected world where the distinctions between collaborator and competitor are no longer clear cut. The business landscape can no longer be considered a 'zero-sum game' (eg where players win or lose rather than adopting a win-win mentality), and L&D that helps organizations to adapt to the uncertainties of co-opetition creates an environment in which an organization is able to fully reap the benefits of co-opetition via multiple partnerships and alliances. In addition, L&D may cultivate new capabilities and competencies to enable and foster networking in the newly extended enterprise.

5 Work and workforce

Change in the external environment and industry, and how an organization configures its business model to compete and cooperate, ultimately has an impact on the internal aspects of an organization. Changes in the external environment have implications for the skills needed for employees as well as for the nature of careers and work. A business that thrives while operating in this VUCA environment is one that is able to embrace and implement new strategies. It is one that considers its competition to be a source of knowledge as well as rivalry. It is open to technological advances without becoming a slave to newness. It is able to rethink its business model without forgetting its core values. Organizations must be flexible to the need for change in light of the context within which they work and understand how to apply this change in the most efficient and effective manner. This section examines some key aspects of work and the workforce that are most affected by these change from an L&D perspective.

The nature of work is changing in many occupations. The case example presented by Neil Liddington from Avon Fire and Rescue Service shows that even the nature of one of the most time-honoured professions has changed significantly. What more for professions and occupations that are considered more contemporary? As work becomes more interconnected and reactive to the VUCA environment, it becomes less routine and more specialized, adaptive, and spontaneous (Austin, 2010). Organizations that are properly networked can respond to these fast-paced changes by encouraging collaboration and collective work on projects. Individuals both within and external to an organization are increasingly working together to solve complex problems. The changing nature of teamwork that now includes external parties and is more transitory is called swarming by Gartner (Austin, 2010). The notion of swarming also extends to the speed at which individuals come together to work on a problem before dissipating just as quickly.

Knowledge-based work is ever-more important and is an increasing part of global flows, as many manufacturing and low-skilled tasks are automated (even as increasing levels of knowledge-based calculations tasks and activities are becoming automated). The idea of literacy has changed. No longer is literacy limited to the reading and writing of text. The internet has brought about a world where video, animation, visual cues, and interactive features are incorporated into the external environment and into everyday communication. A multimedia literacy is a new competency required in this VUCA environment.

Technology has changed the nature of knowledge workers and 'intelligent' systems have decreased the time necessary to analyse data and make predictions, meaning that the need for specialized training shifts from how to do the operation to how to make a computer perform the operation and how to analyse the results. Understanding information technology is no longer just the remit of colleagues in the IT department, but is now a requirement of many other professions. In fact, CIPD's profession map for L&D requires L&D professionals to manage system vendors and suppliers, which means it is imperative to understand technology.

Also, as machines increasingly take on tasks previously filled by humans, the way an individual adds value to a business is changing. This skill set is based on going beyond what is produced by computers to interpret the meaning behind the data. Adding to this, the ability to think beyond the data and to provide critical analysis in a given situation is increasingly in demand by employers. A new form of cognition is required, one that enables individuals to be more effective in pattern recognition.

The use of technology has also necessitated a change in the way we work. Technology has enabled individuals to work in flexible modes, spatially and temporally. Individuals can now work from home or almost anywhere that has an internet connection. In addition, the nature of some jobs also enables some individuals to undertake their work at any time of the day. Thus the change in the nature of work has an impact on the skills required to work effectively on the job and with one another.

In terms of the workforce, businesses can no longer rely on employees to remain loyal and to build their career in one organization. The concept of a career has taken new form in the VUCA environment. Individuals adapt to the changing and interconnected world before them and thus feel less loyalty to organizations and have a greater desire to align their careers with their own motivations and personal development. Individuals identify less with organizations and more with their personal development and/or profession, meaning they see themselves through the lens of their competencies, skills, and networks.

The reasons for this shift in employee perception are closely linked with the changes in the workplace environment. Fewer full-time permanent employment opportunities are available, and increasingly, businesses utilize contracting staff, part-time staff, consultants, and agency staff to round out their workforce. Even the most skilled individuals find themselves in temporary employment situations and must spend a portion of their time and efforts seeking out new work. Individuals are thus likely to change careers and jobs with increasing alacrity, utilizing their networks to make leaps from one career to another, and are increasingly likely to take the initiative to develop their own learning.

Cross-cultural competencies are also increasingly necessary. Communicating beyond one's own culture within the workplace is not necessarily a function of language ability, but more a result of an individual's cross-cultural competencies, which include open-mindedness, adaptability, empathy, cross-cultural awareness, and cross-cultural mediation (Olson and Kroeger, 2001). These competencies enable an individual to adapt their attitudes and actions in order to learn and accommodate for alternative cultural views, which may be a key element to effective workplace harmony and productivity in an increasingly global workplace. Cross-cultural communication skills are part of overall social intelligence – the ability to connect with and interact with others, either in person or remotely. Individuals with cross-cultural communication skills and social intelligence are also individuals who can effectively work on a team.

L&D must face the challenge of a fluid workforce. L&D must become increasingly proactive and understand the organization's business strategy, using its wide reach within the organization to affect change and steer the organization in the appropriate direction. The next section will briefly discuss how L&D can take on this role.

6 Learning and development

Whilst the impact of such changes is reflected in the contemporary practices of L&D specifically in Chapters 5, 6 and 7, this section briefly discusses the implications of the changes presented in the preceding section on L&D. By paying careful attention to the context in which the business is operating, and factoring in the external environment, L&D practitioners are able to better support senior managers in adapting to changes and thus contribute to the organization's overall performance. L&D is able to contribute in this way because it has the potential to enable a business to remain competitive and to identify and develop new capabilities (Hult, 2003). This is consistent with the findings from the CIPD, who revealed that senior management now expect L&D to play a more prominent role in strategic processes and decision making (CIPD and Cornerstone OnDemand, 2014).

L&D needs to respond to the needs of a workforce with changing work styles, and new and potentially intimidating novel and sophisticated technologies. L&D becomes a core part of affecting change by understanding organization-wide needs and making linkages that inform management of potential issues before they become problems. To take on this challenge, L&D must be connected to the organization and not only understand its needs in the context of the external environment but build a culture that is able to communicate and implement the necessary changes in all areas of the business. L&D must increasingly possess business acumen; it must understand the business model used by the organization. It must be tuned into the organization so that it can identify what new technology is the best fit, what will take the organization furthest, and best develop the organization's capability. L&D must thus be aligned with and tapped into the organization at all levels of the hierarchy.

L&D must engage with different divisions and departments to address both basic and higher-level performance issues. Because L&D crosses departments and divisions, it is thus able to identify systemic problems and help divisions understand if theirs is a local or organizational issue. By aligning the knowledge of the external environment with the holistic needs of an organization, L&D can advance itself and the organization.

Given the increasingly mobile and modern workforce, utilizing the most contemporary means of training and the associated technology is one way in which L&D can keep pace with the changing world. It is also important to consider the motivation of the learner. Learning no longer needs be classroom based, nor is this the most effective way of imparting knowledge. As the workforce becomes more technologically savvy and educated, and as workplace turnover becomes the new norm, new learning techniques will better align personnel with the type of training necessary to prepare them for their business's needs. L&D should thus be learner aligned, meeting the expectations of the learner and accounting for individual differences while still accomplishing the overall goal of L&D within the business.

As shown in all three case examples, on-the-job training is of growing of importance, even more so than it was. This is largely driven by the need for 'ecological validity' (ie the learning is directly applicable because it takes place where work is performed) but also because it is one of the more efficient ways to promote effective learning. Understanding the unique needs of an organization and aligning L&D with them requires a robust knowledge of the ever-changing technological advances and understanding how they fit into a business. L&D can exploit these advances to enhance learning. Active and experiential learning methods are better able to contextualize the subject matter for learners. As a result, learners are better able to retain and fully understand the learning material, as well as apply it to their job tasks.

The use of role playing, simulation-based or game-based learning is increasing in popularity and can better engage learners. These learning approaches do not need to be technology based to challenge learners, as simulation and role-based games can also function as a mechanism to initiate discussions and idea exchange (Loon, Evans and Kerridge, 2015). L&D practitioners must also be innovative in their approach to cultivating a learning environment and developing learning interventions. The lessons from the case example from Susan Hamilton earlier in this chapter show how L&D has had to be more efficient in addressing mandatory L&D initiatives but at the same time 'keep its eye on the ball' in terms of focusing on the development of her organization's future leaders. In addition, she emphasized how they have had to adopt a pioneering approach in developing indicators for evaluating the return on investment of L&D initiatives.

7 Shaping the organization's future

The VUCA nature of the external environment means that nothing will remain the same and that organizations must be ready for anything. Even strategic time horizons, which do differ amongst industries, have nonetheless been shortened across the board in general terms. Scenario planning is growing more in popularity as organizations realize that they have to be more prepared and take into account a broader range of issues.

As Anthonie Versluis from Roland Berger argued, the best form of protection against an ever-changing environment is to be effective in learning. Indeed, learning at the individual, group and organizational levels enables firms to be adaptive and agile, and to stand up to challenges that arise from the external environment. As the popular adage goes, 'offence is always the best defence'. Thus, rather than adopt a wait-and-see approach in a VUCA environment, organizations should be more proactive. Research has shown that organizations that are more entrepreneurial and innovative tend to be in a better position to shape their own futures (Courtney, Kirkland, and Viguerie, 1997; Pohle and Chapman, 2006).

Think about the terms that come to mind when you think of an entrepreneur. In fact, many traits applicable to entrepreneurs mirror the concepts discussed in this chapter, including the ability to be innovative, and the willingness to understand and undertake risk. Entrepreneurial individuals who have these traits are also found in organizations and their skills are a valuable asset. Acting in an entrepreneurial way within an organization is called intrapreneurialism. Intrapreneurship takes entrepreneurial approaches and applies them to improve operations within a business. While an entrepreneur believes in his or her ability to start a business, an intrapreneur believes in his or her team, division, mission, or organization, and its ability to adapt and innovate to accomplish the goals at hand. Intrapreneurship can benefit a business by allowing for creativity in the approaches taken to react to the context shaped by the external environment and identifying new business opportunities.

L&D has a role to play by inculcating an entrepreneurial spirit and developing an entrepreneurial mindset. L&D should think about how it can best encourage employees to take a creative and innovative approach to how the business interacts with the external world. Individuals who can identify and exploit opportunities can give their organization an edge and help it maintain or recapture its competitive advantage (Kuratko and Audretsch, 2009).

L&D can become a catalyst for entrepreneurship by helping individuals and teams to be inventive, resourceful and to take calculated risks in developing new strategies and designing new business models. Entrepreneurial individuals are, generally, driven by achievement. The prospect of setting up and running a successful business is a tangible indicator of success that entices many entrepreneurial individuals to leave their employer in order to undertake enterprise development. L&D has the ability to incorporate these entrepreneurial individuals into the business by giving them a sense of accomplishment through affecting change in an organization.

This is also an area where L&D may need to work with management to ensure that the organizational culture is one that supports the entrepreneurial spirit so that innovation can flourish in guaranteeing the organization's future. Traditional schools of thought often pit managers against entrepreneurs (eg administrators who value stability versus mavericks who thrive on disorder); however, the two increasingly must coexist in order to respond to the many changes needed to survive in a VUCA environment. Managers are typically seen as implementers and enforcers of business practice whereas entrepreneurs are typically seen as challengers to these practices. Management is an important element of any business, and it can create an environment in which the entrepreneurial approaches encouraged by L&D are embraced at higher levels and incorporated into business strategies.

8 Conclusion

In this chapter, we have discussed the context in which a business operates and, in parallel, the context in which L&D must operate. Placing business operations in context requires attention not only to the inner workings of an organization, but also to the external environment and its impact on business operations. The external environment can be thought of in terms of 'sources of change', and in this respect, this chapter has examined the PESTLE analysis as an approach to understanding where the sources of change are present in any business environment. Political, economic, social, technological, legal and environmental factors all create an external context for a business, and should be considered not as isolated domains, but as interconnected elements that can help shape an understanding of the external environment.

Next, the 'nature of change' was considered to help us understand how a business operates in a volatile, uncertain, complex and ambiguous (VUCA) context. Understanding this VUCA environment helps us to understand why it is necessary to re-evaluate existing business models and look again at how the competition is viewed. It also provides context and basis for the changing nature of the workforce. Workers no longer need to remain tethered to a desk but can harness technology to perform their assignments from different locations. In addition, as an organization's employees focus more greatly on their own development and seek multiple jobs and careers in the course of their professional lifetime, so too must an organization adapt its L&D in light of these internal changes.

L&D can add value to a business by understanding the context within which it operates and by acting as a strategic advisor within the organization to identify and break down stovepipes that may be preventing an organization from fully harnessing the wealth of its resources. This chapter has explored in a preliminary manner the ways in which L&D must understand and exploit new technologies. In addition, L&D can help an organization retain competent and entrepreneurial individuals by providing legitimate opportunities for intrapreneurs within the organization and allowing entrepreneurial individuals to be part of the process in helping organizations shape their own future.

9 Points for reflection

Understanding L&D's strategic and operating environment:

1 What are the three levels of in L&D environment?

2 Undertake a Threats, Opportunities, Weakness and Strength analysis of your organization:

   a Identify your organization's strengths and weaknesses, as found from the reflection exercise that you undertook in Chapter 1.

   b Identify the threats and opportunities that the external environment presents to your organization, as found in the PESTLE exercise.

   c Evaluate how your organization's strengths may mitigate the threats, and how the opportunities afforded by the external environment may reduce the impact of your organization's weaknesses.

3 Describe your organization's business model. Specifically:

   a What is its value proposition?

   b How does it create value?

   c How does it capture value?

Recognizing the implications of L&D's context on its practice:

1 Based on an organization known to you, what are the main implications of the opportunities and threats arising from the external environment for the individuals' learning and development and for L&D practitioners?

2 Based on your answer in terms of how your organization creates value (Q3a), describe what capability your organization requires to be able to create this value.

References

Aguilar, F J (1967) *Scanning the Business Environment*, Macmillan, New York

Amit, R and Zott, C (2012) Creating value through business model innovation, *MIT Sloan Management Review*, 53 (3), pp. 41–49

Austin, T (2010) Watchlist: continuing changes in the nature of work, 2010-2020, Gartner [online] https://www.gartner.com/doc/1331623/watchlist-continuing-changes-nature-work

Bennett, N and Lemoine, J (2014) What VUCA really means for you, *Harvard Business Review*, **92** (1/2), pp. 27–42

Brandenburger, A M and Nalebuff, B J (1998) *Co-opetition*, Currency/Doubleday, USA

CIPD and Cornerstone OnDemand (2014) Learning and development: annual survey report 2014, *CIPD* [online] http://www.cipd.co.uk/binaries/6477%20LD_WEB.pdf

Courtney, H, Kirkland, J and Viguerie, P (1997) Strategy under uncertainty, *Harvard Business Review*, **75** (6), pp. 67–79

Deloitte Touche Tohmatsu and The World Economic Forum (2010) Redesigning business value: a roadmap for sustainable consumption, *World Economic Forum* [online] http://www2.deloitte.com/content/dam/Deloitte/ie/Documents/ConsumerBusiness/redesigning_business_value_Deloitte_Ireland_Consumer_Businesss.pdf

Hult, G (2003) The role of entrepreneurship in building cultural competitiveness in different organizational types, *Journal of Management*, **29** (3), pp. 401–26

Joy, S and Kolb, D A (2009) Are there cultural differences in learning style? *International Journal of Intercultural Relations*, **33** (1), pp. 69–85

Kuratko, D F and Audretsch, D B (2009) Strategic entrepreneurship: exploring different perspectives of an emerging concept, *Entrepreneurship Theory and Practice*, **33** (1), pp. 1–17

Loon, M (2014) *L&D: New challenges, new approaches*, CIPD, London

Loon, M (2015) Business model innovation: perspectives and foundations, Paper presented at the Global Business Conference, Tigne, France

Loon, M, Evans, J and Kerridge, C (2015) Learning with a strategic management simulation game: a case study, *The International Journal of Management Education*, **13** (3), pp. 227–36

Manyika, J, Bughin, J, Lund, S, Nottebohm, O, Poulter, D, Jauch, S and Ramaswamy, S (2014) Global flows in a digital age: how trade, finance, people, and data connect the world economy, *McKinsey* [online] http://www.mckinsey.com/business-functions/strategy-and-corporate-finance/our-insights/global-flows-in-a-digital-age

Manyika, J, Chui, M, Bughin, J, Dobbs, R, Bisson, P and Marrs, A (2013) Disruptive technologies: advances that will transform life, business, and the global economy, *McKinsey* [online] http://www.mckinsey.com/business-functions/business-technology/our-insights/disruptive-technologies

Mueller, A (2014) Monsanto names Crowe director of millennial engagement, *St. Louis Business Journal* [online] **Error! Hyperlink reference not valid.** http://www.bizjournals.com/stlouis/blog/2014/07/monsanto-names-crowe-director-of-millennial.html

Olson, C and Kroeger, K R (2001) Global competency and intercultural sensitivity, *Journal of Studies in International Education*, 5 (2), pp. 116–37

Osterwalder, A and Pigneur, (2010) *Business Model Generation*, John Wiley and Sons, New Jersey

Pohle, G and Chapman, M (2006) IBM's global CEO report 2006: business model innovation matters, *Strategy & Leadership*, 34 (5), pp. 34–40

Porter, M E (2008) The five competitive forces that shape strategy, *Harvard Business Review*, January, pp. 78–93

Roland Berger (2015) The Trend Compendium 2030, *Roland Berger* [online] http://www.rolandberger.com/expertise/trend_compendium_2030/

Smialek, J and Giroux, G (2015) The majority of American babies are now minorities: new government data show a changing country, *Bloomberg* [online] http://www.bloomberg.com/news/articles/2015-06-25/american-babies-are-no-longer-mostly-non-hispanic-white

Tidström, A (2014) Managing tensions in coopetition, *Industrial Marketing Management*, 43 (2), pp. 261–71

Using information, metrics and developing business cases for L&D

03

MARK LOON

1 Introduction

A perennial challenge faced by learning and development (L&D) units is in showing the value of their work. The work of L&D is observed as a cost in many organizations, and whilst some senior managers acknowledge the value that L&D brings to their organizations, the hard evidence that supports this belief is not always clear. Indeed, this is a proverbial challenge that faces L&D, and in fact also human resources (HR) in general: demonstrating the link between its activities and organizational outcomes.

It is such challenges that have created an impetus for new trajectories in the development of L&D professionals that focus on demonstrating value and enhancing performance. The second theme of this book, Contributions, aims to demonstrate how to transform L&D from a cost centre to a value-creating hub. Specifically, this chapter focuses on the primary dimension of the theme, demonstrating value, by using the business case as an opportunity to articulate the benefits that will emerge from L&D's activities, and committing to delivering the value as established in the business case.

There are three learning outcomes in this chapter, namely:

1 Appreciate the importance of a business case.

2 Understand how information and data are used in a business case.

3 Be able to present information and metrics in a manner that is easily understood and compelling.

In this chapter the business case is used as a vehicle for demonstrating how information and data can be used effectively. Being able to use information and data 'effectively' is not just about crunching numbers. It is also a process that involves being methodical, clear and transparent in the way information and data are obtained and used. In terms of the business case report, there is also much more than just numbers involved in the creation of a business case. Examples of other important facets of a business case are:

- using the right 'pitch' for the audience, eg urgency;

- framing the solution in the right context, eg problem/opportunity;

- helping the audience to better understand, eg visibility of assumptions;

- articulating the value to gain the right commitment, eg long term.

This chapter takes an L&D perspective in the development of a business case. In particular, this chapter is not about transforming L&D professionals into financial experts. It is, however, about how L&D professionals can lead the design and development of a business case, although in doing so, L&D does need to understand some of the mechanics that underpin typical business cases. By developing a rigorous business case, L&D professionals are able to show the links between training, development and other learning initiatives in driving and/or supporting business goals. This chapter also contains case examples and suggestions from Jason Jestin who is a financial controller at DBB Worldwide London, and a former audit professional with Ernst & Young. In reflecting upon his own experience, Jason shares some relevant examples and practical 'how to' tips for preparing a business case from the perspective of an L&D practitioner.

A business case may include elements that can be used by L&D as a basis to track the benefits of any L&D initiative. For example, such an evaluation may involve addressing Kirkpatrick's Level 4 organizational 'results' evaluation, which is part of Kirkpatrick's framework for evaluating the effectiveness of learning that contains four levels: Level 1 is reactionary in terms of learners' satisfaction and engagement; Level 2 concerns actual learning gained, exemplified by learners' increased knowledge; Level 3 is behavioural and involves changes in learners' application of what has been learned in their day-to-day work where possible; and Level 4 is results, whereby individuals' learning actually translates to some positive outcome for the organization (Kirkpatrick and Kirkpatrick, 2009). A rigorous business case also helps senior leaders and managers to make more informed decisions. A methodical business case provides its audience with a clear visibility of chains of evidence that not only offers a compelling argument but also enhances their confidence in the L&D practitioners who have prepared the business case.

The skills involved in developing a thorough and compelling business case are important to L&D's role as an internal consultant. Internal consultants justify their existence by continuously being able to demonstrate the value they bring to the organization. L&D's contribution via the business case is through generating useful insights in linking learning and development initiatives with organizational goals, supporting effective decision making by senior management through appropriate allocation of scarce resources.

Section 2 provides an overview of a business case outlining the key elements that should be contained in a typical business case and addressing learning outcomes one and two. Section 3 discusses the importance of differentiating between the subject in the business case and purpose of the business case. This section also contains a discussion on the important preliminary work that must be undertaken before the commencement of any business case. Section 4 concerns recruiting team members, as cross-functional teams develop the best business cases. In addition, this section discusses the pre-requisite skills and tools required in developing a business case. Section 5 involves the discussion concerning the design of the business case, in particular the order of the main parts in the report. This section also discusses the points that must be addressed in outlining the business case's method and assumptions. Section 6, in also addressing learning outcome two, concerns the typical steps involved in creating a business case, ie cash flow, metrics, scenarios and the corresponding risk analysis. Section 7 contains some ideas on how best to present information and data based on the idea of 'infographics'. Section 8 contains a case example, and Section 9 concludes the chapter with a summary of the key points.

2 The nature of a business case

How many times have we heard people saying 'show me the business case' or 'the board will only consider this if there is a business case'? What they mean is that they need a justification for a proposal in terms of the financial numbers. Specifically, that the benefits derived outweigh the costs. Therefore, a business case may be defined as a decision support and planning tool (eg to spend or not, and if so, how much and over what length of time) in funding generally non-routine expenditure such as projects, capital assets and special one-off training programmes. A business case report is a collection point that contains all the relevant information, data and assumptions that are interwoven into a cohesive and compelling story.

A business case is a complete decision support tool in that the decision maker should be able to rely on the business case alone to make an informed decision. It is a report that contains an introduction that summarizes all aspects of the business case, in particular the 'what' (subject of the business case and the purpose for the business case in terms of what action you want the audience to take), 'why' (rationale to address a problem or take advantage of an opportunity), 'who' (who developed the business case, who is implicated in the business case, and the stakeholders consulted), 'when' (timeline of actions) and 'how' (an explanation of the benefits envisaged to materialize, the cost expected to be incurred in funding the initiative and the identification of the components of the new project) (Schmidt, 2002).

The business case should include a clear identification of the subject under consideration. A business case is usually warranted when a significant and non-routine expenditure is required. Examples include:

- transformation of the delivery of learning to an online platform;
- a new learning management system is required;
- a substantial change in physical space in the workplace to cultivate collaborative and social learning;
- a complete revision of leadership and management development initiatives.

In terms of the first example, the subject of a business case may involve the procurement of the learning technologies to facilitate the development of a new blended learning strategy. However, given the plethora of learning technologies, L&D practitioners need to identify comparable technologies in light of the L&D curriculum and create a shortlist of technologies to be evaluated. The purpose of a business case is to then identify the options that are available to the audience to decide upon. For example:

- For the subject of 'delivering learning online', the purpose of the business case may be to help the audience make an informed decision involving the options of:
  - only mandatory self-paced curriculum;
  - both self-paced and facilitated mandatory curriculum;
  - all curriculum.
- For the subject of 'a new learning management system', the purpose of the business case may be to help the audience make an informed decision involving the options of:
  - Vendor A;
  - Vendor B;
  - Vendor C.
- For the subject of 'change in physical space in the workplace for learning', the purpose of the business case may be to help the audience make an informed decision involving the options of:
  - incremental approach (starting with headquarters, over 12 months);
  - radical approach (starting with headquarters and other main offices, then other branches, over four months).

The above demonstrates how the subject and purpose of a business case are distinct from one another yet related. A business case is a framework that helps the audience to make better decisions in investing the organization's resources. An effective business case helps to make the decision-making process as straightforward as possible by highlighting the benefits and costs, and the implications of each option (sometimes also called scenario) in terms of risks and contingency plans.

Before a business case is expansively pursued, L&D practitioners should first do some initial evaluation and calculations to assess if the purpose is sensible and reasonable in the first place (also known as a sanity check – further discussed in the next section). The prospective subject of the business case should be sensible, which may relate to the subject being consistent with organizational needs and strategic direction, possessing a general fit with the organization's overall (technical) system and broadly beneficial to the staff members, to name a few examples. 'Reasonable' generally connotes financial feasibility in that the costs are within the bounds of what may be considered reasonable within the context of the organization, eg financial resources and affordability.

The audience of a business case must also have confidence in its content, specifically that it is comprehensive and complete (in producing a 'fair picture'), accurate (numbers are correct) and credible (data and information are from official sources, assumptions are transparent). A business case is read as a stand-alone article and hence it must be comprehensive and complete. This means that the audience of a business case must be able to see the methods of calculation and assumptions made by the authors. In addition, a business case is also informed by a variety of credible sources internal and external to the organization (official sources such as audited accounts). Credible sources are crucial to ensuring that the data and information in the business case are accurate. Developing a business case involves research in identifying evidence and sources that support every piece of data. The level of detail in a business case also extends to the logical links amongst results, data, assumptions and evidence. L&D practitioners must ensure that there is a logical chain of reasoning and that the audience is able to follow this chain.

A key contributor in ensuring that the business case is looked upon favourably in terms of accuracy, credibility and objectivity is the establishment of a cross-functional team in authoring the business case. An obvious example is the recruitment of colleagues from the finance and accounting department. A cross-functional team gives the audience a sense that the numbers are objective, as they are tempered from multiple perspectives, and that there are no inherent biases from the proposer of the business case. In addition, cross-functional teams also help to assure the audience that the right people with the right expertise and access have been recruited to assist in the development of the business case. Accounting and finance colleagues, for example, are able to help L&D practitioners to understand accounting terms and practices and their implications on the business case, for example what items to treat as a capital expenditure (capex) or operational expenditure (opex). In this respect, L&D practitioners must be savvy in knowing where to source information and who they need to ally with to gather the appropriate evidence.

If the particular subject of a business case involves a number of activities and/or actors, as well as dependency on specific resources, then it is crucial for L&D practitioners to identify these critical success factors. Critical success factors (CSFs), as the term suggests, must be present for an initiative to come to fruition. Identifying CSFs is important, as it helps L&D practitioners to bring this to the attention of decision makers. The absence or partial presence of some CSFs may also be classified as a risk. Including such items in the risk register enables L&D practitioners to identify contingency measures in managing these risks. The following sections investigate each of these topics in more detail.

3 Subject, purpose and background

3.1 Framing: problem or opportunity?

As discussed in the previous section, it is crucial that the subject and purpose of the business case are made explicit. Being clear about the subject and purpose of a business case also enables the business case team to identify the individuals who will be involved in evaluating, ratifying and/or accepting it. These individuals should be named as recipients in the business case. Clarity on who the individual members are that make up the audience of the report can be obtained by understanding the business and organizations. Identifying these individuals enables L&D practitioners to specify who actually benefits and who incurs the cost from the project/initiative. In addition, knowing who the individuals are may reveal some helpful insights, as each individual may have a different perspective/view of matters related to the business case subject and purpose. This in turn helps to inform who to include the business case team (discussed in the next section) and the stakeholders to consult.

A business case is assumed to be a rational artefact, which it is of course, primarily. A business case is rational as it involves identifying the benefits and scope of an initiative, involves quantitative estimation of costs, provides metrics and contains clear decision-making thresholds for each metric. However, business cases are also political and emotional artefacts. They are political as they can be used as a vehicle to advance issues. In addition, the success of a business case hinges on the credibility of the authors, although in turn, a successful business case can also enhance the reputation of the individuals who successfully build and deliver on it. Also, as highlighted in the previous section, business cases work best through cross-functional teams who can help to access information and data across the organization more easily. Finally, a business case can also be emotional, as it could be a source of aspiration for organizational direction and its acceptance may depend on how it is framed.

Knowing the identities of the stakeholders and understanding the rational, political and emotional aspects enables L&D practitioners to be in a better position to frame a business case. Typically, this process involves either framing the subject as a problem or an opportunity. Framing has powerful effects on how something is perceived (Tversky and Kahneman, 1981). For example, anti-smoking advocates found in the 1980s that framing smoking as a social problem (causes smokers to be social outcasts) was more effective in convincing smokers to quit than framing it as a health problem. Problems are usually associated with some sense of urgency and may provoke swift action. However, a 'problem' clearly denotes negativity, which may be resented or forcefully argued against by some stakeholders. Alternatively, a subject may be framed as an opportunity. However, unlike a 'problem', taking advantage of an opportunity may be viewed as a luxury and is optional. Framing a subject as an opportunity, nonetheless, is a powerful diplomatic way to put one's message across without implying that there is fault somewhere.

Jason Jestin, financial controller, DBB Worldwide

Success for any business case is to have sufficient buy-in at all stakeholder levels. Irrespective of whether it appears to be a political exercise, it is important to frame things as an opportunity rather than as a problem, as it is more positive and palatable. I cannot emphasize how important this is, not only in terms of determining the success of a business case but also of the eventual project that takes form from the business case. Framing the subject as an opportunity provides a positive tone and uses 'language' that is usually deemed more attractive to people. This stimulates optimism and energy when the initiative is eventually undertaken.

Clearly the activity of framing goes beyond just communicating the perspectives of whether something is an opportunity or a problem, as it is a powerful persuasive tool that can be used in any situation. I once received a proposal to purchase a new communications device. The proposal emphasized the novelty of the device and the new features that went with it. My initial reaction was that this was a luxury item and ultimately the proposal did not get any further. However, it was later communicated to me informally that the new device could also help with cost savings by enabling management to identify non-value-added matters in the communications process. If only the proposal had emphasized these benefits and framed as it a management tool (rather than a new communication tool), the proposal may have been given more consideration. This is an important lesson, not only in knowing how to frame your message but also in understanding your audience and their concerns. Knowing who your audience/stakeholders are will inform you on the perspective to adopt in your business case and what to emphasize.

3.2 Understanding the business

Business cases vary in significance in terms of the funds that are involved and their implications. Nonetheless, understanding the 'business' and operations of the organization will unquestionably contribute to the effective development of a business case irrespective of its funding requirements and scope. Understanding the organization and its 'business' may help L&D practitioners in terms of identifying performance gaps and/or opportunities for improvement that may be a stimulus for a business case. In-depth business and organizational knowledge contributes to the actual development of a business case. These goals can be attained by virtue of the various roles that L&D professionals adopt, as discussed in Chapter 1.

Significant business cases would clearly benefit from a lucid understanding of the organization's operating environment, for example by mapping the implications of the proposals in the business case to stakeholders involved. Nonetheless, business cases that have low or moderate impact will also benefit from L&D's insights into the organization's environment. For example, this enables the L&D professionals to be cognisant of the other activities and/or systems that are in operation that may complement or be an impediment to the proposals in the business case. Knowing 'what is out there' may provide ideas in strengthening the business case and/or preclude any options that may have been initially considered. In understanding the business and environment, some useful questions that L&D professionals may want to address in their research are:

- Industry and competition:
  - Which 'industry' does the organization belong to?
  - Who are the organization's main competitors in the 'industry'?
  - What are the average returns in the industry?
  - What is the organization's business model (ie how does it 'make' money/'earn' revenue)?
  - How distinct is this business model compared to its rivals?
  - How fast is the industry growing, if at all?
  - How has the competitive landscape changed over the last five years?
  - What are the key political/regulatory, economic, social/cultural, technological and/or environmental factors that impact the organization?

- Markets and customers:
  - Who are the key customers and what are their needs?
  - What are the key customer segments?
  - What do customers purchase? What is the organization's value proposition?
  - Why do its customers choose the organization's products/services over those of its competitors?
- Enterprise-wide capabilities:
  - What are the organization's capabilities that enable it to provide value to its customers?
  - How and where can improvements on the organization's capabilities be made?
  - What helps shape these capabilities?
  - Is there a need driving a change in these capabilities?
  - Are these capabilities unique and/or easily replicated by existing competitors and prospective new entrants?
- Goals, objectives, strategy and change:
  - What are the organization's mission and vision?
  - What are its goals and objectives?
  - What are its strategies in meeting these goals/objectives?
  - Has senior management identified key results areas that need to be given special attention?
  - Are there projects that have been identified to be undertaken to help the organization attain its strategy and enable change?

At the heart of the business case are the financial numbers, and therefore it is important to obtain a broad grasp of these as well as general accounting policies and practices in the organization. Financial numbers provide more insight when reviewed over a time period of at least five years (longer-term horizons may be more appropriate for organizations in industries such as construction and shipbuilding due to the longer time scales of their 'production', which can take months and years, and not hours as in other industries). After gaining an understanding of the drivers and sources of revenue, the next natural step involves understanding the cost structure of the organization. A cost structure analysis highlights where the significant costs areas are in the organization. An effective way to help visual information data concerning cost structures is the use of the waterfall diagram as shown in Figure 3.1.

Figure 3.1 Example of a cost structure waterfall for a retail firm in 2016

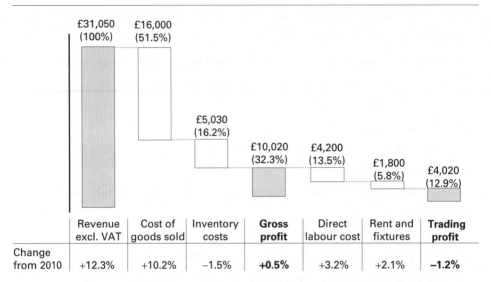

	Revenue excl. VAT	Cost of goods sold	Inventory costs	**Gross profit**	Direct labour cost	Rent and fixtures	**Trading profit**
Change from 2010	+12.3%	+10.2%	−1.5%	**+0.5%**	+3.2%	+2.1%	**−1.2%**

The waterfall cost structure graphically presents the components of the overall costs relative to revenue in descending order. This shows the relative size (and importance) of each cost component. The waterfall cost structure can be used to illustrate the cost structure of an entire organization or it can be stratified to illustrate the cost structure in terms of business units, product family over time and in comparison with one another. A key advantage of such a diagram is that it allows the audience a quick appreciation of trends, comparisons and differences.

In addition, financial ratios are a helpful source of information that may provide insights into how well an organization is doing. Some types of ratio may be more relevant/informative depending on the nature of the organization's activities. There are generally three categories of ratio that may be useful in the context of developing L&D-related business cases: profitability/efficiency ratios, liquidity ratios and solvency ratios. Profitability/efficiency ratios provide an indication of how well an organization utilizes its assets to generate revenue. Liquidity ratios demonstrate an organization's ability to meet its short-term liabilities, whilst solvency ratios indicate the organization's financial strength.

Examples of ratios in each category are:

Profitability/efficiency ratios:

- Return on sales:
  - profit margin;
  - gross margin.

- Return on net assets.
- Return on equity.
- Inventory turnover.
- Days inventory.
- Total asset turnover.
- Days receivable.
- Fixed asset utilization.

Liquidity ratios:

- Current ratio:
  - quick ratio
  - working capital

Solvency ratios:

- Debt equity ratio.
- Interest cover.

Ratios are helpful in transforming financial information into forms that can be used for comparative purposes (to an extent, as different accounting policies adopted by business units located in different countries may skew data). When sourcing and reviewing ratios, L&D practitioners need to ensure that ratios across divisions are comparable and that the nature of activities of business units are similar, with no sharp contrast in accounting practices. In addition, it would be helpful to be cognisant of the different accounting terminologies that may be used in different countries such as the UK and the United States. L&D practitioners should also ensure that the notes that accompany the ratios are meticulously reviewed.

In addition to the financial numbers, important accounting policies should also be examined. Examples of accounting policies that may have an important impact on financial numbers and assumptions in a business case include:

- financial year period;
- policies concerning the recognition and adjustment for capital expenditure (capex);
- operations expenditure (opex) items;
- depreciation rules;
- policies regarding discounting cash flow rate applied within the organization for investment decisions;
- policies regarding leasing versus outright purchase of assets.

In addition, L&D practitioners may also need to interview key stakeholders whose activities have a direct impact on the financial data. For example, L&D practitioners may need to interview the sales director to identify the forecast of business volume, the operations director for forecasted cost and the financial controller for expected margins. Understanding the accounting policies and practices is helpful to inform how the benefits from the business case impact the financial statements. For example, revenue enhancement, cost reduction and avoidance are clearly reflected in the profit and loss statement, whilst capital acquirement or reduction will have an impact on the balance sheet. Any purchases or new investments will have an impact on the organization's cash flow statement.

Jason Jestin, financial controller, DBB Worldwide

In finding out about the business, talk to as many colleagues as possible. This classic approach is the simplest but most effective way to learn about the business. Those who have a lot of experience in either the organization or the industry may provide some invaluable insight. You should leverage social situations, as people tend to be more candid about their area of the business and their own ideas about how to further improve things. Some of these ideas may be hidden gems. People use different metaphors and analogies about how they see the business and this creates a powerful set of perspectives that may help you better understand the business. If you are empathetic, people will be more inclined to share more with you.

In addition, I personally think academic models can be very helpful, for example Porter's Five Forces [which is a model used to analyse the competitive nature of an industry and is usually used in Level 6/7 studies] and the SWOT (Strengths, Weaknesses, Opportunities and Threats) analysis. These models will definitely help L&D practitioners to better understand the business of their organization and competitive nature of their industry.

3.3 Understand how things may work in the organization

Goals and objectives

It is important that L&D practitioners understand the goals and objectives of the organization, relevant business units and at times even some managers. In large organizations, many of these goals and objectives are well known and documented; however, in smaller organizations, enterprise-wide and business unit objectives may be tacit and not documented. In addition, objectives may be quantified in various ways, with some expressed in financial terms. There may be instances where it may be helpful to discover management's aims. They may have different ideas in terms of how they attain their business unit's goals, which may be in conflict with the business case's subject and purpose, such as improving productivity via procuring new machinery rather than enhancing skills.

Funding mode for L&D activities and events

Another important consideration in the development of a business case is the source of funding, as this then informs the L&D practitioner of the potential funding process that may be involved and the stakeholders who will need to be consulted. Whilst every organization differs in terms of its funding mechanism for L&D activities and assets, Mayo (2004) identified four typical modes of funding: centrally funded, funded by business units, a combination of the previous two modes, and a free market mode.

Centrally funded L&D activities are usually characteristic of small- to medium-sized organizations as an overhead cost. L&D activities and events are usually provided 'free' to staff. This mode of funding provides clarity and stability in terms of who holds the purse strings for L&D, which may be the head of the human resource (HR) department. A key advantage of this funding means that the budgeted amount for L&D is usually more predictable.

A business unit mode of funding is in contrast with central funding, as business units have to negotiate their own L&D budgets, typically directly with the finance department and/or with the HR department. An important implication of this mode of funding is that it means L&D professionals must be very clear in terms of who is impacted by the proposed project, as this then informs them on whose (ie business unit heads) buy-in and/or participation is required in the business case. Consequently, L&D professionals also need to determine which business unit benefits most from the project and therefore bears most of the cost. This mode of funding can potentially complicate the business case process. Alternatively, an L&D-related business case may be driven by individual business units, with L&D professionals playing the role of a team member rather than a role driving the business case.

When the mode of funding involves a combination of both central and business unit, the L&D budget is usually shared. Depending on the subject and purpose of the business case, the role and implications on L&D professionals will vary. The final archetype of funding is that of a free market, which results in no specific budget allocated for learning and development. Any business units that would like to undertake such activity and/or event will need to put forth a business case. In such a set-up, the ability to craft a business case becomes even more important, as the existence of an L&D practice is not a given since it has to continuously justify its being through competitive bid funding.

Business planning process and budgeting allocation

L&D practitioners should also understand how an organization plans its business and allocates its resources, specifically how such planning links with the annual budgeting process. For example, an organization may require each business unit to develop a business plan (even for those that are cost centres and serve 'internal' customers). The business unit's activities are to be quantified in financial terms that demonstrate how 'income' (or value) is generated and the costs that are incurred. The business plan therefore informs its budget proposal. These business plans and budgets will help inform L&D professionals of opportunities (or problems) that a business unit may present. In addition, it is important that L&D professionals understand the finance department's budget allocation process (Hope and Fraser, 2003). For example, the budgetary process that is most predictable for L&D practitioners in creating a business case is a fixed budget, which, as the term suggests, means the next budget will be the same as the last. In contrast, a zero-based budgeting approach means an organization essentially revises the entire budget bottom-up. This form of budgetary process generally results in many changes and L&D practitioners should not take anything for granted from the previous year's budget. In addition, a rolling budget occurs when the annual budget is regularly reviewed and revised throughout the financial year on a predetermined interim basis. When an organization adopts such a budgetary process, L&D practitioners will need to obtain the latest version of the budget.

Past successful business cases

It is quite likely that organizations, especially those that are medium to large in size, will have a history of internal staff members developing business cases for various purposes. L&D practitioners should try to obtain copies of successful business cases and have informal discussions with the authors to find the reasons for their success. Nonetheless, one can also learn from business cases that were not successful and talking to those who have experienced disappointment may also be equally informative. In addition, some organizations may have policies, guides and even templates for business case development. It is important to understand what is required if these artefacts are available.

Sanity check

Before pursuing the development of a full business case, it is important for an L&D practitioner to undertake a quick, high-level assessment of the potential benefits of a prospective asset/initiative. Usually called a 'sanity check', this step helps to inform the L&D professional that there is a chance that the benefits will outweigh the costs. A simple way to do this is by creating a list with two columns. The potential benefits are listed in one column and the costs in the other. All benefit and cost items are given some value. All the items in each column are summed and assessed against one another. If the total benefits are more than the costs, then the next logical step is to further pursue this evaluation via the development of a full business case. However, if the costs are substantially more than the benefits, then it may be prudent to identify other opportunities.

Clearly, there is a lot of subjectivity in this exercise. In addition, the quality of information gathered for this exercise may also depend on the nature of subject, in particular whether it is addressing a problem or an opportunity. It is potentially more straightforward to gather information to address a problematic situation if a problem is widely experienced and acknowledged throughout the organization. Stakeholders affected are also able to better tell, based on experience, or estimate the cost of the problem (or on the flipside, the savings that can be achieved by addressing the problem). Opportunities, however, may be more of a challenge as estimates can be perceived as speculative.

This exercise is usually completed by the L&D professional (and perhaps informally with a small group of colleagues), and whilst the accuracy is debatable it is nonetheless helpful and provides L&D practitioners with some confidence in putting forward suggestions in developing a business case. Just imagine if this step was not undertaken and a business case team was formed only for one to find out that it was quite evident that the cost would be greater than the benefits. Such a situation would be awkward for all involved. This step involves doing the obvious; checking that pursuing the project is sensible.

Exercise: articulating the initial part business case

This section provides an opportunity for you to reflect upon the previous section and apply some of the ideas that have been conveyed.

The activity is to identify an organization that is familiar to you, which has information that you can access. Address the questions in Section 3.2 pertaining to the organization's:

- industry and competition;
- market and customers;
- enterprise-wide capabilities;
- goals, objectives, strategy and change.

By addressing most, if not all of the questions in Section 3.2 you will have a good understanding of the organization. Based on this understanding, reflect upon an idea that you may have for a business case in this organization.

1 Think of the 'subject' of the business case. What is it about?

2 Next, ask yourself, how you would frame this subject as:

   – a problem;

   – an opportunity.

3 Next, identify the 'purpose' of the business case (building upon the subject). What are the potential sets of options that you could offer in the business case?

4 Business case team and tools

4.1 Business case team

The development of any major business case is best undertaken in teams. There are primarily three types of reasons: technical, functional and political. First, developing a robust and rigorous business case requires significant skills in finance and accounting, and also understanding of the financial environment of the organization. Developing a business case does not just involve mathematical operations, it also involves understanding current financial policies and having insight into the future investment plans of the organization, which many may not be privy to. Hence, from a technical perspective it is important to recruit a senior colleague from the finance and accounting department into the business case team. However, individuals in finance and accounting, like those in most human resource departments, have different specialisms, and so it is crucial to be specific in one's recruitment based on the subject and purpose of the business case.

Business cases are also functional. Whilst individuals with specialism in finance and accounting are of great assistance in obtaining relevant financial data and interpreting and applying accounting rules and policies, other colleagues from across the organization may be able to help contextualize the financial data and give it more meaning. For example, if the purpose of the business case is to enhance competencies, then managers whose staff may be affected by any new interventions may be able to help estimate how such skill enhancement may translate into financial terms such as productivity and cost savings.

A business case is also political. Whilst the battle to win over others is primarily done through rationality and logic in the form of the business case, sometimes this is insufficient. There may be key decision makers who need to be swayed through other means in addition to a sound business case. The options presented in some business cases may be politically fraught, as the allocation of financial resources to fund a project usually means there is less money to fund projects in other parts of the organization. In a world of limited resources, such a scenario causes a win-lose situation that necessitates political savviness whilst developing a business case. Therefore, the recruitment of individuals who are well networked can be employed as leverage to socialize the benefits of the business case to others who may be opposed to its very idea. These individuals may then, at least, give the business case a fair assessment. Recruiting individuals who have access to the 'right' groups of people, who 'speak their language', and are able to use the 'right channels' is crucial. These individuals will understand the priorities of senior management and know how to position the business case in their communication.

Given the above, the L&D practitioner needs to consider such realities and configure the business case teams in a manner that addresses these issues. A business case team may involve two tiers (Schmidt, 2002). The first tier, the case review team, is made up of individuals who provide advice and steer the overall business case in the right direction, and ensure that the quality of the business case meets the expectation of the audience (usually senior management). The case review team is generally composed of members of the senior management, as well as those in middle management. They also contribute to the 'functional' and 'political' aspects of the business case. The second tier, the case development team, are the individuals who are directly involved in building the business case. The technical aspects of the business case generally rest with this tier. Ideally, members of the overall business case team should be cross-functional to spread a sense of ownership. This helps to improve the success of the business case as no one wants to see something they have been working on fail. In the final report, it is important all team members' names, job titles and roles are listed, as this not only gives them recognition of the work performed but also provides confidence to the audience that the business case is well informed by relevant cross-functional perspectives and has been scrutinized by some members of the senior management team. L&D practitioners may also choose to volunteer in business case teams proposed by other functions to gain experience and also gain goodwill.

4.2 Personal attributes

Developing a business case requires skills and a mindset different to what an L&D professional is accustomed to. The threshold ability involves working knowledge and skills in accounting and finance, eg understanding accounting principles and being able to construct and interpret financial ratios.

L&D professionals also require some project management skills in organizing and coordinating team members, and setting priorities. As part of the role of leading a project team, L&D professionals also need to keep a 'bird's eye view' on the business case and ensure that the overall logic of the business case is coherent, robust and cogent. For example, when an assumption is made for a specific purpose, L&D professionals must also have the foresight to envision potential unintended consequences on other parts of the business case. In some cases, some assumptions may contradict one another. The L&D practitioner needs to keep this in check.

Being business savvy also enables L&D practitioners to see the potential benefits of an initiative and how this may have positive consequences in various parts of the organization. L&D professionals also need to be able to translate soft benefits into tangible, and preferably financial benefits. L&D professionals need also to speak the same 'language' as their colleagues from different parts of the organization when communicating the benefits. Last but not least, L&D professionals need to be able to resolve conflicting interest that may arise from different stakeholders (L&D professionals may also draw upon consulting skills in facilitating discussion amongst stakeholders, which is an area further discussed in the next chapter).

4.3 Business case tools

Spreadsheets are the basic tools for any business case (Pemberton and Robson, 2000). A spreadsheet file is made up of cells in each sheet, and you can create as many sheets as you wish (as much as allowed by the software). Spreadsheets allow for direct input but also may contain formulae to enable automatic computation (Schmidt, 2014). A basic but very important principle in business case development is that data that are inputted (rather than being a result of some calculation) must only be done once. If the data are used elsewhere in the spreadsheet file, then the cell that holds the datum is linked to/referenced to them. This is to essentially ensure that if there is a change to the data then the business case analyst will only have to make the change once. Using a spreadsheet application such Microsoft's Excel program enables L&D practitioners to build the business case progressively using individual sheets (also called tabs) that are linked with one another.

The linking between sheets using formulae is the cornerstone of dynamic modelling of spreadsheets, whereby a change of inputted data and/or assumption will have a subsequent change on relevant data. For example, all assumptions concerning employee pay may be recorded on Sheet 1, and include items such as:

- headcount of all staff by level (eg operational, supervisorial, junior manager, middle and senior manager);
- average compensation per annum by level;
- average salary increase per annum by level;
- average inflation rate per annum in the last five years;
- average training cost per head in the entire organization and by level.

Sheet 2 may include a cash flow statement containing formulae that link and calculate data from Sheet 1. The computed data is for Year 1, with subsequent years eg Year 2 and 3 build upon the preceding year. For example, total salary in Year 2 includes the aggregate sum in Year 1 multiplied by the inflation rate in Sheet 1. Because the sheets are linked, a change in Sheet 1 (assumptions) will result in an automatic change for some of the data in Sheet 2, thereby making this a dynamic model.

Complex business cases layered over multiple sheets can be a challenge, but L&D practitioners can do the following to help themselves keep on top of things:

- Use sheets to categorize data. Each sheet should only contain one set of logically coherent items, and should be named as such. For example, all assumptions, benefits and costs should each be on their own separate sheet.

- These sheets should be ordered in a logical manner wherein they build upon one another. For example, the assumptions sheet is typically the first tab that is built upon, ending with the sheet that contains the cash flow.

- Colour code the cells to reflect different types of inputs or types of data. For example, cells that have a direct input may be coloured, whereas cells that are a result of calculation (have formula in the cells) are left plain (white). A cell may also be coloured if it is used in the cash flow or if it is an assumption that is relevant to the scenarios.

- Spreadsheet programs have text notations functions that should be used generously. These notations may be official, ie to be kept in place when it is time to publish the business case, or may be for personal reference by those developing the business case (one just needs to remember to delete this before publication). Notations help to keep track of what has been done and why, record caveats, signpost future action and so on.

5 Designing the business case

5.1 Start with the end in mind (the structure not the result!)

The management guru Stephen Covey said that one of the key habits of highly effective people is that they begin with the end in mind (Covey, 1989). This assertion could not be any more relevant in the design and development of a business case. The business case team should have an idea of how the content builds upon itself. A well-structured business case report helps audience to 'follow' the rationale and development of the case and thereby enhances the audience's confidence with the business case and the recommendations contained within it. Whilst there may be a number of ways a business case report can be organized, the most common includes the following: i) executive summary, ii) introduction, iii) methodology and, assumptions, iv) business case, v) scenario, risk analysis and contingencies, and vi) recommendations and conclusions. Business cases must be self-contained, which means the audience should not feel compelled to go beyond the business case report for additional information).

Executive summary

An executive summary is essentially a synopsis of the entire report. This section contains the essential information about the business case such as the subject, purpose and rationale, a summary of the methodology adopted, the findings (eg options) and the critical success factors for each, the risks and contingencies involved, and the recommendations. The executive summary echoes the proverbial 'five-second elevator test' in which one imagines oneself having to convince a chief executive of an idea with only enough time for him/her to go from one floor to another in an elevator (eg in five seconds).

Introduction

The introduction is an important part of the business case as it creates a sense of urgency in grabbing the attention of the audience, and hooks them to read more. The introduction must contain the primary message of the business case report. It is vital to bear in mind that some of the audience may be hearing of the business proposal cold, ie for the first time, with little appreciation of the context of the problem/opportunity that the business case report aims to address. Therefore, in addition to initiating the audience to the case, it is important to contextualize the business case report but to do so succinctly (for the sake of those who may be quite familiar with the case). The business case can be logically structured using Minto's (2009) approach. She argues that a comprehensive introduction contains four components: the situation, the complication, the question and the answer (solution), also known as the SCQA structure.

The 'situation' is essentially a story for the audience about what they already know. The situation involves the normal state of, for example, a process and/or organizational relationships. This component of the introduction is about stage setting; providing background to the business case and explaining its importance. The 'complication' is the twist in the tale of the introduction. It is the issue that has made things difficult for any 'normal' situation to remain. The issue may be a problem or an opportunity. The 'question' logically emerges from the complication. It directs attention to the issues that need to be addressed for the complication to be resolved. 'Questions' provide focus in the form of answers (solutions). The 'answer' (or solution), in turn, addresses the questions articulated.

The following is an example.

Bridge Consulting Engineers (BCE) is a local engineering consultancy, with its main office located in Cheltenham and a sales office in Gloucester about nine miles way. Most of BCE's consultants work at their clients' sites where they spend most of their time. This is not an issue, as the clients are located within the local area and commuting between offices is not problematic. This situation has also made organizing and delivering mission-critical training a straightforward matter, which is important given the heavily regulated industry that BCE and its clients operate in that experiences frequent and vital changes in the regulatory environment (situation). However, as BCE grows in reputation it has started to gain clients in other parts of the UK, requiring significant travel time which in turn requires consultants to stay overnight in other counties. This has made organizing and delivering training much more difficult and complicated (complication). The question that BCE has to address is how it is able to continue providing quality service to its new clients by permitting its consultants to be hands on at the clients' sites whilst still being able to provide mission-critical training to its consultants in a timely manner. (question). The answer lies in investing in online learning platforms that enable BCE to deliver training to its consultants in remote locations. Both synchronous and asynchronous formats should be provided so that consultants can learn the materials on demand but also have access to trainers as and when they have queries that require clarification (answer).

Minto (2009) also states that authors are able to change the tone of the introduction by simply reordering each of the SCQA components. The current order of SCQA that was discussed is the most frequently used, as it reflects a typical thinking process that most people engage in when addressing a problem or opportunity. A second order is the Answer-Situation-Complication (ASC), which is generally adopted when it is appropriate to be upfront and the audience is very well aware of the situation and complication (and L&D professionals are sure of this). The third order is Complication-Situation-Answer (CSA), which is best adopted when the audience is concerned about the consequences that the 'complication' poses. The fourth and final order is Question-Situation-Complication-Answer (QSCA), which is an assertive approach that can be adopted to quickly grab the audience's attention. The basic building blocks can be altered based on L&D's needs and the context, such as how well the audience knows about the situation and complication, and whether this communication is read as a report or presented in person. Ultimately, the introduction is crucial as it influences the audience's receptivity to the report. Therefore, the introduction should be constructed in a manner that is not only logical but also persuasive and compelling.

Methodology and assumptions

The methodology and assumptions section identifies the steps that were undertaken in collecting the information and data required in building the business case. Where information and data are not available, assumptions are made. However, the reasons for, and the rationale behind each assumption are articulated. Assumptions may also be made even when data may be available. In such scenarios, assumptions may be used if they simplify understanding and therefore make it easier for the audience, and as long as they do not significantly impact the final figures.

This section identifies the information and data that need to be collected, their purpose and how they will be collected. The sources are also identified as well as the format. Where there may be potential dispute, the business case team must provide reasons why certain sources are favoured over others. For example, market data from the internal marketing team may be favoured over external vendors because of a newly released and niche product that is still 'beyond the radar' of external marketing intelligence vendors. Another important part of this section is specifying the time period and timelines that would be part of the business case. Finally, this section should outline and describe the design of the cash flow and the financial metrics that will be used to help the audience make its decisions.

Business case

The 'business case' section is at the heart of the entire report and is usually presented in the form of a cash flow. The most important element in this section is the identification of the benefits and costs involved. The benefits should be closely aligned with the subject and purpose of the business case. Each benefit in this section should be ideally expressed in monetary terms or if not at least quantified in other terms. Benefits that are qualitatively expressed should be accompanied with a narrative that explains the rationale for their inclusion. In terms of the costs, the section should communicate the format of how they will be presented in the form of cash flow projections, using a dynamic financial model and the metrics that will be utilized.

Scenario and risk analysis, and contingencies

This section should outline the scenarios that are explored in the business case report and the key assumptions that have a significant impact on the scenarios. Typical scenarios are realistic (baseline), optimistic and pessimistic. As part of the scenario analysis, a sensitivity analysis may also be undertaken that shows the impact of change in some assumptions/factors. In any business case, an analysis of the risk must be taken as well as the contingencies that may be adopted to mitigate the occurrence and/or impact of the risks.

Recommendations and conclusion

This section highlights the recommendations made by the business case team for the audience to consider. The recommendations may be a single option or may involve a number of options for the audience to consider. It is important that the recommendations are linked to the subject and purpose of the business case, and that the audience is reminded of this. Last but not least, a conclusion should then proceed after the recommendation that guides the audience through the main points in the case.

5.2 Benefits rationale and cost model

As discussed in Section 4 in regards to undertaking a quick sanity check, to proceed with developing a full business case, L&D practitioners must have some ideas in terms of the benefits that an initiative may bring, and show that these exceed the costs that may be incurred along the way. Once L&D practitioners have decided to proceed, the benefits rationale and cost model is then further developed.

Benefits rationale: benefits impact and benefits contribution

The benefits rationale is composed of two important groups – benefits impact and contribution. Benefits impact is items that have a direct consequence on the cash flow, whilst benefits contribution is items that have an indirect impact but ultimately have some bearing on the organization's objectives. L&D professionals would be well aware of the organization's objectives by first understanding the business (as discussed in Section 3). Indeed, many business cases start life by addressing a problem or opportunity so that an organization objective can be met (Pulliam *et al*, 2008).

Whilst the benefits rationale and cost model is dictated by the subject, and varies along the lines of the purpose (the options presented), there are general benefits that it may help L&D professionals to think about in identifying specific benefits that may relate to their business case:

- Income:
  - increasing availability of services due to more efficient work practices;
  - increasing sales due to increased capacity to produce/service more customers;
  - enhancing reliability thereby attracting more customers;
  - increasing responsiveness of customer service thereby mitigating the probability of losing sales opportunities, eg increasing conversion rate;
  - increasing customer satisfaction thereby increasing return business.
- Direct costs:
  - improving productivity and thereby reducing the need for overtime work and payments;
  - increasing efficiency in workforce planning due to better training interventions;
  - reducing rework through better utilization of inputs and machinery due to enhanced skill levels;
  - improving coordination through better working relationships with partners;
  - lowering the cost of operations by improving work scheduling and rotas as a result of more efficient work practices including more effective use of subcontractors;
  - improved staff morale leading to higher job satisfaction and stabilizing turnover (reducing cost of recruitment and selection).
- Indirect costs:
  - better allocation of resources in critical areas of operations due to more accurate planning (arising from factors listed under 'direct cost').

Benefits also relate to contributions to the organizational objectives that may not be directly reflected in the case flow. For example, the subject of the business case may ultimately contribute to increasing the organization's market share, enhancing the organization's image as an investor in people and improving its brand image as an accessible and friendly organization. Such contributions are difficult to be quantified financially. Nonetheless, it is important that these qualitative benefits are still articulated and recorded.

In addition, whilst some benefits may be intangible and not lend themselves easily to being measured in financial terms, L&D professionals should try to describe the benefits in a manner that can be observed and verified. An example may be enhanced team morale and improved professionalism of front-line staff, which in turn improve customer service efficiency and satisfaction, increasing loyalty and return business/sales.

A source that may helpful in identifying 'typical' business objectives is Deloitte's Enterprise Value Map, which highlights the primary contributors to shareholder value and its antecedents (Deloitte, 2004). For example, the value map identifies revenue growth as a key contributor that can be improved by increasing volume of sales. Volume of sales, in turn, is impacted by customer retention, which can be enhanced by improving account management skills. These 'typical' business objectives can also be part of an organization's strategic direction (Lukac and Frazier, 2012).

Cost model

A cost model is essentially the recognition and pooling of all cost items into a single list, which helps to serve as a definitive record of all cost items. This list helps with consistency and also visibility in ensuring the audience that all cost items have been registered. All scenarios created must draw cost items from the cost model to ensure that all scenarios are comparable.

Schmidt (2002) states that there are essentially two costing models: the resource-based approach and the activity-based costing. The resource-based approach is appropriate when a business case subject involves the procurement of assets, whereas the activity-based costing approach is more appropriate when the most significant cost is labour. The activity-based approach gives a more accurate reflection of the costs absorbed as and when the relevant activities are undertaken. Of course, one could use both, as some projects/initiatives have both components.

It is also helpful to develop some form of cataloguing of the costs that reflects the cost of ownership rather than just upfront cost. The 'cost of ownership' perspective provides a more comprehensive view of the costs involved. An example may involve the cost item for a new learning and development programme over six months that includes the purchase and implementation of a new learning management system (LMS), as depicted in Table 3.1.

Table 3.1 Example of cost model

Cost category	Cost item	Upfront cost	Ongoing cost (per day, week, month, year; over days, weeks, months, years)
Training-related	Instructor/ facilitator	£....	£....
	Direct materials	£....	£....
	Facilities	£....	£....
Systems-related	Software	£....	£....
	Upgrade on existing machines/devices	£....	£....
	System integrator – customization	£....	£....
	System integrator – roll-out	£....	£....
	Support and warranty	£....	£....

Table 3.1 illustrates the cost category and cost item, and the upfront cost and potential ongoing costs associated with the item. It is important to indicate how often payment is required for the ongoing costs and over what period. There is no standard rule as to how a cost model may be formatted as it is highly dependent on the nature of the subject and purpose of the business case. Notes (eg references and assumptions) should be listed with each item as necessary. This helps the audience understand the nature of the numbers, eg formula of calculation.

Translating benefits and costs into cash flow values

Once benefits and cost have been listed and categorized, the next stage is to assign cash flow values to the benefits and costs based on the cash flow intervals (eg monthly, quarterly) that have been determined. Benefits impact tends to have a more direct effect on the cash flow statement, but benefits contribution via addressing business objectives may have a less direct impact on the cash flow. Quantifying and assigning the value of benefits to the cash flow statement is more of an art form than a science, informed by cross-functional experts (a benefit of creating a business case team). As mentioned, it is this deferment in the realization of benefits that plays a role in the time period identified for the cash flow. The shorter the time period the less likelihood that some of the benefits would see the 'light of day' in the cash flow.

5.3 Methods, assumptions and data sources

This section is important, as the audience will surely want to know how the potential benefits were identified and figures for the cost derived. The methods make the case as much as the numbers. In addition, audiences also want to understand the assumptions (eg growth rate of the business), definitions (eg 'effective transfer of learning'), scope (eg time period covered of cash flow) and data sources (eg audited accounts, official quotes from vendors). Validation of data and assumptions are also important, especially for data that are 'unofficial'. Validation can be in many forms, such as a simple confirmation from the officers in charge of the information and data and/or from senior managers who are perceived to be the most well informed in a particular area such as the chief information officer. The methods section should also be explicit in terms of how scenarios are constructed, such as identifying which primary assumptions and data sources are involved. Finally, the methods section should also outline the metrics that will be used to help decision making and the potential thresholds for each metric (as well as the reason behind each metric and the threshold).

Assumptions

Assumptions are stated suppositions. They are important as they help to address any gap in data and also simplify calculations. For example, if a business case is being developed based on data for the present financial year, of which there are three months remaining, then an L&D practitioner may make assumptions about the financial data for these months. In another example, an organization may have a large cohort of part-time workers with a wide range of variability in their hours and working arrangements (eg annualized hours). In such situations, the L&D practitioner can choose to make an assumption about the average hours for all part-time staff to simplify calculations.

Definitions

There may be terms that are ambiguous and that individual members of the audience may not be familiar with. It is therefore important to clarify these terms/phrases by defining each to avoid misunderstanding and to make the business case more accessible. An example of such a term is 'transfer of learning', which in fact is a term that may also be quite ambiguous in the L&D field and in how it is operationalized. Therefore, defining such terms is important.

Scope

Scope may be in terms of the focus of the subject with regard to its impact within the organization and/or the time period that is covered in the business case. In terms of organizational scope, a business case may elect to focus on specific divisions, geographic business units or strategic workforce groups. Whilst there may be sound reasons for articulating these boundaries, there may be implications for data collection. When boundaries are drawn on organizational units such as divisions for example, there may not be much impact on the effort with which financial data is obtained, as each division will usually have their own income, cash flow and even balance sheet statements. However, when boundaries are created on strategic workforce groups, collecting financial data becomes less straightforward, as such data may not have been collected as part of normal operations.

Time periods adopted for data collection must be clearly specified, as with the rationale. There may be cases where the organization has experienced unusual events (that may be advantageous or disadvantageous) that have skewed its financial state and are not representative of 'normal' periods. Given such situations, the business case team may elect to choose different time periods to collect data from and as a basis for the business case. L&D practitioners must then, however, provide a clear reason for doing so, and be consistent in applying this rationale to other aspects of the business case. For example, they should avoid taking an income item from an accounting period whilst recognizing a cost item from the same accounting period.

Timing also plays an important role in showing how benefits may materialize and in reflecting the expenditure of costs in the accounting period. As discussed, it is advisable that the business case adopts a long-term view as some benefits take time for their full effects to take place. A more accurate picture of the magnitude of the benefits may be realized when a longer-term view is taken.

The choice of timing intervals may be important, as there may be a need to identify specific dates in the cash flow analysis. This is especially necessary when there are extraordinary events that may coincide with the business case time period that needs to be recognized. This gives the audience confidence that the business case reflects 'reality'. It is also important that the time period employed is consistent for all data sets. If there are exceptions, this should be clearly indicated, with reasons explaining the departure from the norm.

Data sources

Data are facts with identifiable sources that will not change. Sources of data must be identified and comprehensively listed in the business case. Some data sources may be from official sources such as audited accounts. Whilst some may not be official, they may still have significant credibility, for example the sales director's estimates of sales volumes for the next two years. Other internal sources of data include the enterprise HR system. Sources of data may also be external, coming from institutions/bodies such as the Chartered Institute of Personnel and Development (CIPD) and Office for National Statistics.

If the subject involves the recruitment of external experts and/or procurement of hardware, software and facilities, then of course it is crucial to obtain quotes from vendors in terms of pricing, warranties, guarantees, and terms and conditions. Procurement professionals within the organization will be able to provide more guidance to L&D practitioners in terms of policy and customary practices such as the number of quotes required.

Validation

A supporting process that may be helpful for information and data that may be construed as subjective is validation. Validation, although it can be time consuming, adds credibility to the information and data. This process can be made easier, as validation can be made part of any interview process that L&D practitioners undertake. Examples of validation include:

- Frontline staff: the issues identified do exist and are indeed problematic.
- Supervisors: suggested activity for improving department is justifiable.
- Business managers: benefits and cost to his/her division attributed correctly (type and amount).
- Chief financial officer: the business case adds up and makes sense.

When validating information and data with stakeholders, it is important to present a range as a starting point of discussion. Starting the conversation with a blank sheet of paper may not be very efficient. Also, validation does require interviewees to literally sign off on the interview records. This helps if evidence is required. For each item of validation, do interview a number of people. If the opinions greatly diverge, then L&D practitioners may have to interview more individuals. Validate adopting a bottom-up approach starting with front-line staff, as this adds credibility to the information and data you present to senior managers when it is their turn. Validation is a two-way process; if an interviewer disagrees, then L&D practitioners must work with them to identify the correct information/data.

Construction of scenarios

The identification of scenarios must be consistent with the stated purpose of the business case. In this discussion, the first example of a purpose of a business case as cited in the previous section is 'to help decide on the different approaches to be adopted in improving the delivery of learning and development programmes'. This purpose may involve constructing a scenario based on differing speeds of implementation such as i) within two months, ii) within six months, and iii) within 12 months. The primary factor for each scenario is time, specifically the resources required over each period; the narrower the period the more resources are required. In addition, shorter time periods also carry with them more risks and therefore more contingency resources are required, which may increase the cost.

Using the example in the previous section of 'to support the procurement decision on which system to adopt in enhancing the e-learning systems', the main factors in constructing the scenario may involve the pricing, warranties, implementation cost and time frames proposed by each vendor, as well as the cost of integration and training that may be incurred by the organization. It is important to also create a baseline, business-as-usual (BAU) scenario. This scenario typically involves maintaining the status quo (ie do nothing). BAU scenarios must reflect the impact of not addressing a problem and/or not taking advantage of an opportunity, as this reinforces the incentive to 'do something'.

Exercise: identifying benefits and cost

This activity continues from the activity in Section 3.5. Now that you have identified the 'subject' and 'purpose' of a business case for an organization that you are familiar with:

- List the general benefits of the 'subject'. In doing so, if possible, identify how you would measure these benefits.

- List the potential costs that may be incurred for the business case. Rank the cost items in descending order (costliest item first) based on your best guestimate!

6 Developing the business case

Once the preliminary work is completed, the next step is the actual modelling of the business case. Developing a business case is a reiterative exercise, as information and data may not be available all at once and new events may change some data and assumptions (eg worsening economic conditions, vendor changing pricing).

Identifying the time period and intervals

An important initial task in developing a business case is identifying the time period. Given the nature of most L&D-related projects, the benefits from such projects do take time to materialize. Therefore, it is important to identify a time period that allows for this. However, a lengthy time period needs to be tempered with short-term expectations, especially if the subject relates to fixing a problem.

In addition, whilst not necessarily crucial, time intervals also need to be identified. Usually, the shorter the time period, the more granular the time interval, eg months, weeks, days. However, if there are instances whereby benefits may materialize or costs may be incurred within specific intervals, then this should be considered, as this information may be important to the audience.

Configuring the spreadsheet

The next step is to format the spreadsheet into a cash flow, since most business cases are almost always associated with this format. An example of a cash flow statement is found in Table 3.2, which shows a single scenario. It is important to note that whilst the terms 'income' and 'cost' have been used in preceding sections, neither are necessarily synonymous with cash inflow or outflow. Cash inflow/outflow refers to the actual exchange of cash, whereas 'income' may be on credit and 'cost' may be incurred but not paid. Therefore, it is important to 'convert' items in both income and costs categories into cash, which essentially involves identifying when the exchange of cash actually takes place.

Table 3.2 Example of a business case cash flow statement
(Pie charts build clockwise from largest to smallest; 'other' is always last)

	Year 1				Year 2			
	Q1	Q2	Q3	Q4	Q1	Q2	Q3	Q4
Benefits (cash inflow)								
Item 1	£...	£...	£...	£...	£...	£...	£...	£...
Item 2	£...	£...	£...	£...	£...	£...	£...	£...
Item 3	£...	£...	£...	£...	£...	£...	£...	£...
Gross inflow	£...	£...	£...	£...	£...	£...	£...	£...
Expense (cash outflow)								
Item 1	£...	£...	£...	£...	£...	£...	£...	£...
Item 2	£...	£...	£...	£...	£...	£...	£...	£...
Item 3	£...	£...	£...	£...	£...	£...	£...	£...
Gross (outflow)	£...	£...	£...	£...	£...	£...	£...	£...
Summary								
Total inflows	£...	£...	£...	£...	£...	£...	£...	£...
Total outflow	£...	£...	£...	£...	£...	£...	£...	£...
Net operating inflow/(outflow)	£...	£...	£...	£...	£...	£...	£...	£...
Tax savings/(incurred)	£...	£...	£...	£...	£...	£...	£...	£...
Net cash flow		£...	£...	£...	£...	£...	£...	£...

This step also involves setting up other various sheets such as assumptions in the spreadsheet file. The number of sheets required depends on the complexity of the business and the number of steps in the calculation. The more transparent it is, the more detailed the sheets in the business case.

Inputting data

At this stage, L&D practitioners may start to input the data into the spreadsheet, starting with the assumptions sheets. As assumptions are entered, notes and references to sources should also be inputted at the same time. This helps with clarity for both the audience and the L&D practitioner. Data (eg discount rate) and sources (eg audited accounted) should be used consistently. L&D practitioners should keep to the same source as much as possible for the same set of data/information, as data from different sources are usually not comparable. Unreferenced information and assumptions provide more opportunity for the audience to dispute the contents of the business case. Thus, referencing and explanatory notes are helpful, as the audience may be from different parts of the organization, and not all may understand the data/information. Sheets should be linked via cells where relevant. An important rule of thumb is that a datum should only be entered once, so as to avoid mix-up. In relation to this, another rule is that a cell should contain data, assumption, formula or note, and not a mixture (each should have its own colour code, as discussed in the previous section).

Transforming the data and creating the cash flow

The next step is to transform the data and start shaping the cash flow. The transformation process involves identifying and creating mathematical formulae in the relevant cells and organizing the calculations to flow in a logical manner. L&D practitioners may also choose to annotate the steps as they go along. This is much easier when it comes to retracing/auditing the numbers. Part of the transformation exercise also involves forecasting the size and timing of the future cash flows, which includes the benefits and costs identified.

Identifying and creating metrics

Once the cash flow has been configured and L&D practitioners are confident the data are accurate, the next step is then to identify and develop the metrics. There are a number of metrics that can be used as a decision-making guide (Berk *et al.*, 2013):

- total net cash flow;
- payback period;
- net present value (using discounted cash flow);
- internal rate of return (using discounted cash flow).

The total net cash flow is essentially the final figure that is the result of the cash flow period. In most cases, a positive return is expected and only then will the options be considered. The payback period essentially involves the time taken for the original outlay to be recovered. This is calculated by dividing the initial outlay with the net cash inflow per period. This metric is useful if recovering the outlay is a top priority for the organization. However, it is rather simplistic and may result in the disregard of options where the benefits may take longer to materialize.

The net present value (NPV) is the present (today's) value of the initiative minus the initial outlay. The NPV is the amount of money that one would have if the money was invested at a given discount rate. To calculate this metric, an L&D professional needs to convert the total cash inflow and outflow to the present value using a discounted rate. Most spreadsheets contain this formula. The discounted rate should be obtained from reliable sources and validated by senior finance managers. A decision rule would involve only considering options that provide a positive NPV.

The internal rate of return (IRR) also uses a discounted rate (which should be the same for all metrics for consistency). It is usually expressed in percentages, which makes it easier to compare against projects that are dissimilar. The decision threshold for IRR differs amongst organizations, and will need to be sourced and validated with senior managers. In addition, the business case may also include other important measures to accompany each metric, such as average cost per full-time equivalent (FTE) employee/learner and total cost. It is common practice to use a battery of metrics to inform decision making (CIPD and Cornerstone OnDemand, 2014).

Developing scenarios and undertaking risk analysis

The next step is to develop the scenarios. A scenario is an outcome of a set of assumptions, which is informed by the purpose of the business case (as discussed in Section 1). A scenario may also be created as a result of a sensitivity analysis (discussed further below). Business as usual (BAU) is a typical scenario in most business cases, as it sets the benchmark for comparison with other scenarios. A BAU scenario may involve the projection of the future as a simple extrapolation of the past. For example, if sales over the last five years have been falling on average at 10 per cent per annum, with cost of operations also increasing by 5 per cent per annum, and staff turnover increasing at a rate of 16 per cent annum, then one can assume that the BAU scenario would involve the same trends persisting next year. A BAU scenario does not involve any intervention that may be offered in the business case.

A number of scenarios may be developed to be compared to the BAU scenario. Generally, (as part of the purpose of a business case); the most typical are optimistic versus pessimistic scenarios (eg in realizing benefits), small versus large scale (eg implementation of the solution across the organization), and conservative versus radical (eg commitment of funds for the project). Each scenario would necessitate a change in a number of assumptions (as a set) that would in turn change the results of the business case.

However, at times it may not be appropriate to create scenarios, as the combinations of change in assumptions may be infinite, and it may be more suitable to change only a few assumptions. At this stage, it may be more efficient to then only identify key assumptions that are most important, impactful and/or of interest to the organization (audience). This can be done through sensitivity analysis, which involves identifying key assumptions and inputs that have the most significant impact on the business case analysis. This in turn helps to forecast potential unintended consequences that may occur and informs the risk analysis that is to be undertaken. A sensitivity analysis can be undertaken by changing each key assumption by, for example, 5, 10 or 15 per cent, and then recording its impact on key data points and the final result.

A risk analysis is essentially the process of estimating the likelihood of an event (usually undesirable) occurring. There are a number of tools that help with this analysis, such as the Monte Carlo method (see Rubinstein and Kroese, 2016). This is a 'what if' model that deals with uncertainty and risk by analysing separate sets of assumptions (based on the scenarios). However, this involves advanced knowledge of statistics, which is beyond the scope of this chapter.

In addition, it is important to recognize that contingency plans need to be put place. As part of the contingency planning process, L&D professionals should classify risks into groups: risks that cannot be managed and risks that can be managed. Risks that cannot be managed include natural disasters, government policy and regulation, economic fluctuations and global market prices. Risks that can be managed are recruitment policies, selection of vendors, time to implement software and project team members. Whilst risks that cannot be managed are beyond the influence of the organization, they should still be highlighted to show to the audience where the dependencies are. For risks that can be managed, L&D practitioners should then highlight the actors, teams or departments who are able to help 'control' these risks. The business case's assumptions should then inform and be reflected in the operations and policies of relevant departments for at least the duration of the implementation of the business case.

Checking for errors

Working with numbers requires L&D practitioners to continuously check the accuracy of the data. Some common errors that L&D practitioners may want to look out for include:

- misattributing benefit (eg from increasing inflow to reducing outflow);

- conversion errors, especially when large amounts are involved, eg millions and thousands;

- logical leap by over-extrapolating data and assumptions;

- errors in formulae such as using mean, mode, median casually and interchangeably in calculating the average;

- technical errors such as linking the wrong cells together or having a circular argument misapplication of accounting policy such as not understanding the definition of certain terms and/or how it is calculated and/or applied.

7 Reporting the findings

7.1 Hygiene factors

This section addresses learning outcome three and contains a discussion on how to 'package' and present the business case. In reporting the findings, the business case is no different from any other business document that is presented to busy executives in that it needs to communicate the key message quickly. This section is focused on elements that are unique to the business case that may differ from other reports, in particular the potential use of graphics as a means to help your audience better understand the report and potentially make the arguments presented more compelling.

However, before we discuss the role of graphics, it is important to reiterate that L&D practitioners should include information such as the names of the recipients/audiences at the start of the report, as well as the authoring team, as discussed in Section 4. In addition, it is also key to provide important information on the reporting, in particular i) the date the report is published, ii) the version number of the report, iii) the start and completion dates in the development of the business case, and iv) an expiration date.

The date of publication is important, as it communicates when the business case report was released for 'public' consumption and hence provides some context, such as economic conditions, to some of the assumptions. In addition, given that some business cases are highly reiterative as they are sensitive to time, and that some data may be arbitrary, the publication date and version numbers help the audience to keep track of the changes made. It would be helpful to keep track of all changes made after the first release of the report and provide a summary list in each version. The start and completion dates are also important, as they are background information for the audience. The expiration date is a caveat that the accuracy of the data and findings cannot be assured due to the time sensitivity of some of the information and assumptions. It may also be helpful to draw the audience's attention to any caveats or disclaimers that may be informative to them and/ or protect the business case team.

It is usually better to develop the business case in its entirety before one starts writing the report, as one never knows what the results of the business case will be. The subject may have to be reframed and the purpose (eg options) may have to be revised. In addition, whilst there is a standard structure to the report, it is important to focus on the content in each section to ensure that sections are linked together in a logical manner. Acronyms should be kept to a minimum unless they are well understood throughout the organization, and a glossary may be included if there are many technical terms that may be unfamiliar to any members of the audience.

7.2 Graphic visual presentation

The use of infographics, which are graphic representations of data and information, is growing, especially in light of information overload that people experience, as well as the premium placed on time in the workplace. Infographics are helpful, as they are about presenting information and data in a manner that is easy to understand and quick to grasp. The *Economist* reports that infographics are concerned with presenting information and data in a manner that suits the natural way our brain works (Cukier, 2010). They argue that it is easier for the brain to process information when it is presented graphically as a diagram or image. Presenting information and data in such a manner utilizes both hemispheres of our brains; the right hemisphere helps to process information concerning colour and shapes, whilst the left hemisphere processes numbers and text (Cukier, 2010). By presenting information visually the message can be grasped much more quickly than if it were presented as a table. Information presented as a graphic enables people to identify patterns, relationships and proportions. Infographics not only help with efficient processing of the information/data but also help with storage, which aids recollection. IBM Many Eyes enabled users to upload their own data to be displayed in novel ways to be shared with others. The service is no longer running, but an overview can be found on YouTube (NewsLab, 2011).

Whilst much of the detail in the business case will be in the format of a cash flow statement, graphics can be used in presenting the results (eg metrics), comparing each of the scenarios. This may form part of the report and also the presentation slides if one is required to do a presentation. Graphics and/or images may contain both numerical and visual messages, but it is important not to clutter the image or this will defeat its primary purpose. Sometimes simple really is better. Typically, there are five types of graphics that one may use in a professional environment: pie chart, bar chart, line graphs, ball chart and matrices, which perhaps one could argue are the origin for the current generation of infographics. Each provides unique insights:

- pie charts show portions of a whole;
- bar charts compare data;
- line graphs illustrate trends;
- ball charts illustrate degrees of specified characteristics (eg opinion, level of commitment, etc);
- matrices position data against axes.

The following figures show example of each:

Figure 3.2 Share = pie charts

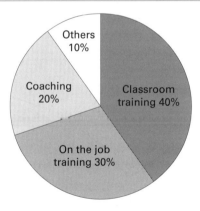

Figure 3.3 Comparisons = bar charts

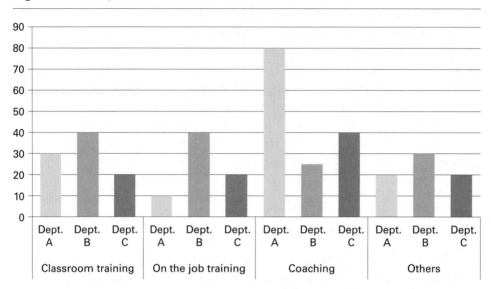

Figure 3.4 Trends = line graphs

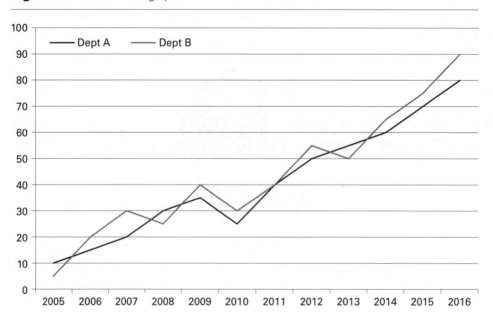

Figure 3.5 Degree = booz balls

L&D Activities	Dept. A	Dept. B	Dept. C
Induction training	●	○	◒
Training needs analysis	○	◒	●
Transfer of learning	◒	●	●
Learning evaluations	●	◒	○
Health & safety training	●	○	○
Leadership training	○	◒	●

Level of Support Required	○ Low	◒ Medium	● High

Figure 3.6 Position = matrices

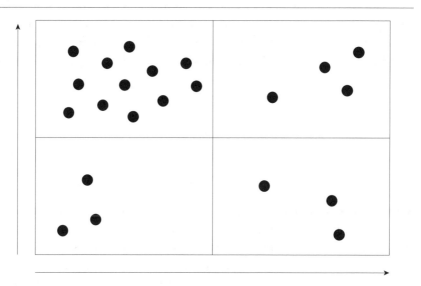

Graphics not only help readers to more quickly grasp the message but also add variety and increase interest. To enhance the effectiveness of graphics, L&D practitioners should omit distracting details. Each graphic should contain one or two key messages. If there are more 'messages' then consider creating another image. Cluttering a graphic is counterproductive. If arrows are used, they should be applied judiciously and not everything needs to have a pointer. If there is crucial information or data, then it should be highlighted in bold, italics or underlined. However, the same rules apply about doing so prudently. 'ALL CAPS' must be used very sparingly and astutely, as it is the equivalent to 'SHOUTING'.

7.3 Writing style

In writing the business case report, it is important to ensure that the style adopts the following principles: write for the audience, keep it simple, evidence all assertions, ensure that each section has a message and role to play, and tell a good story. In writing for your audience, it is important to know who they are, which individuals are decision makers and which individuals are advisers to the decision makers. Adopt an approach that is informative to these individuals and highlight issues that may be of interest to them (rather than what the business case team found informative and/or interesting). In addition, the writing style must accessible to the audience. Avoid jargon that may be specific to L&D or even HR.

The second principle is to keep the text and message simple. This is not to imply that it should be so simplistic that it becomes patronizing. This principle relates to writing in a clear manner that is easy for the audience. Using plain English as a default will be helpful. The main purpose of the business case report is to help the audience to understand the issues and to help them make an informed decision.

The third principle relates to providing evidence for all assertions. This should be easily addressed if all the suggestions from the previous sections are adopted. This also highlights why it is important to keep track of all sources of data and information, as well as validating data that may be perceived as arbitrary. It will be of no surprise that some data/information may be contentious, so it is important to have your references ready to defend the report.

Any report should be as concise as possible. Reports that are verbose and contain unnecessary information are distracting at best, confusing at worst. This is why the fourth principle is important in that every text and section should have a role to play and a message to convey. Finally, the fifth principle is to tell a compelling story. The audience will only act if they are convinced of the arguments. Telling a good story keeps the audience engaged with the report and acts as a stimulus for them to take action.

Jason Jestin, financial controller, DBB Worldwide

The suggestions in this book provide a helpful starting point for L&D practitioners in designing and developing a business case. An important aspect to consider during the design phase is to try to keep the business case as simple as possible in terms of the layout and also computations. From this perspective, it is important to remember how busy executives are, so it is crucial that the business case report can be easily grasped. Clearly, this is not to say that senior management are not able to grasp complex calculations, but this is in relation to the computations being made explicit and the order (or 'flow') being logical (thus previous formats of a business case used in the organization may be helpful, as executives may already be familiar with the format and more easily comprehend it). In terms of the actual findings, do use as many diagrams as feasible to tell the story.

In my experience, the submission of a business case report is not the end of the process. More often than not, one is expected to present the business case, followed by a question-and-answer session. In such situations, I suggest that L&D professionals keep the presentation as simple as possible by, for example, keeping assertions straightforward and avoiding providing too much details on a slide, but do indicate where details are located in the report (so that executives can refer to it if they wish to). Diagrams and graphics are helpful in this regard but the graphics used in the report and in the presentation must be consistent. In the presentation, remember to align the business case to the business objectives and reiterate this almost like a mantra. It is akin to selling a vision, and reminds executives that the vision is achievable only if one of the scenarios in the business case is adopted.

8 Summary

A business case is a decision support tool. In this chapter, the business case has been used as a means to demonstrate how information and data can be used in justifying and showing value in L&D-related projects. This chapter contained three learning outcomes: i) appreciate the importance of a business case, ii) understand how information and data are used in a business case, and iii) be able to present information and metrics in a manner that is easily understood and compelling.

A rigorous business case involves articulating a clear business rationale for the subject matter by explaining the reasons why it is needed and how the proposed initiative will help to achieve this. The subject in the business case relates to the project/initiative that is being proposed. Examples include 'improving the delivery of learning and development programmes', 'enhancing e-learning systems', or 'reinforcing transfer of learning'. The purpose relates to the reason for the business case. Examples include 'to help decide on the different approaches to be adopted in improving the delivery of learning and development programmes', which may involve varying degrees of scope. Another example may include 'to support the procurement decision on which system to adopt in enhancing the e-learning systems'. It is useful to think about how to frame the business case subject in terms of whether it is a problem or an opportunity, as this sets the tone of the 'story' that is being told.

As emphasized, a business case is about more than just numbers. Developing a successful business case requires a lot of preliminary work such as understanding the business of the organization, knowing how things work in an organization, recruiting the right team members across the organization, and possessing the right mindset, skills and tools. Understanding the business and the organization provides a sense of context to the numbers and it also gives the numbers more meaning. In addition, relevant team members such as those from finance are worth their weight in gold, as they provide insight and help to expedite the process of developing the business case. L&D practitioners also need to have effective team-working skills such as regularly communicating with team members, as well as with stakeholders. Developing business cases requires discipline, and perseverance is crucial. In addition, L&D professionals, whilst being fanatical about the accuracy of the data, validation and rational logic, also need to avoid analysis paralysis by knowing when enough is enough.

All successful business cases start off by being well designed. This begins with having the end in mind, specifically about the structure of the report. This step also includes careful analysis of the benefits rationale and the costing model. A useful business case will highlight the benefits, both quantitative and qualitative, and appropriately assign each within the cash flow statement. An effective business case will also contain a comprehensive list of the costs that are associated with attaining the benefit, and similar to the benefits, are appropriately assigned in the cash flow statement. Data should be obtained from credible sources, clearly referenced and validated. Assumptions are sensible, robust and transparent, as with the overall method adopted in developing the business case. Of course, the business case is a reiterative process, but starting on a strong footing with an effective design provides a strong foundation for a successful business case.

In developing the business case itself, the L&D professional and the team need to i) identify the time period and intervals, ii) configure the spreadsheet (eg tabs, sheets), iii) input the data, iv) identify and create metrics, v) develop scenarios and undertake risk analysis, and finally vi) regularly check for errors. The final step involves in writing up the business case report. Graphics may be used to enhance the report in terms of making it easier for the audience to grasp the key messages quickly and to make the report more compelling. It is important to ensure that the numbers (eg benefits, metrics) all link back to the subject in the frame of a problem or an opportunity. It is important that the report is written for the audience, kept simple, all assertions are referenced, the report is concise and to the point, and last but not least, tells a good story.

9 Points for reflection

Appreciating the importance of a business case:

1 How can a business case help advance L&D's aims in improving organizational capability through learning?

2 How does a business case help L&D demonstrate the value of a project/ initiative?

Understanding how information and data are used in a business case:

1 What is the difference between data/information and an assumption?

2 Why are assumptions important in a business case?

3 What is the difference between benefits impact and benefits contribution? How are both important?

4 Which of the two costing models is typically associated with a business case? What is the difference between two?

Being able to present information and metrics in a manner that is easily understood and compelling:

1 What are infographics?

2 How are infographics helpful?

3 What type of graphic would you choose if you wanted to show:

- portions;

- a comparison;

- trends;

- degrees;

- position.

References

Berk, J, DeMarzo, P, Harford, J, Ford, G, Mollica, V and Finch, N (2013) *Fundamentals of Corporate Finance*, 3rd edn, Pearson Higher Education, USA

CIPD and Cornerstone OnDemand (2014) Learning and development: annual survey report 2014, *CIPD* [online] http://www.cipd.co.uk/binaries/6477%20LD_WEB.pdf

Covey, S R (1989) *The 7 Habits of Highly Effective People*, Fireside, New York

Cukier, K (2010) Data, data everywhere: a special report on managing information, *Economist* [online] http://www.economist.com/node/15557443

Deloitte (2004) Deloitte Enterprise Value Map [online] http://public.deloitte.com/media/0268/Enterprise_Value_Map_2_0.pdf

Hope, J and Fraser, R (2003) *Beyond Budgeting*, Harvard Business School Press, Boston

Kirkpatrick, D L and Kirkpatrick, J D (2009) *Implementing the Four Levels: A practical guide for effective evaluation of training programs*, Berrett-Koehler Publishers, San Francisco, CA

Lukac, E G and Frazier, D (2012) Linking strategy to value, *Journal of Business Strategy*, **33** (4), pp. 49–57

Mayo, A (2004) *Creating a Learning and Development Strategy*, CIPD, London

Minto, B (2009) *The Pyramid Principle: Logic in writing and thinking*, 3rd edn, FT Prentice Hall, Harlow, Essex

Newslab (2011) How to Use Many Eyes, *YouTube* [online] https://www.youtube.com/watch?v=aAYDBZt7Xk0

Pemberton, J D and Robson, A J (2000) Spreadsheets in business, *Industrial Management & Data Systems*, **100** (8), pp. 379–88

Pulliam, P P, Phillips, J J, Stone, R D and Burkett, H (2008) *The ROI Field Book: Strategies for implementing ROI in HR and training*, Vol. 16, Emerald, London

Rubinstein, R Y and Kroese, D P (2016) *Simulation and the Monte Carlo Method*, 3rd edn, John Wiley & Sons, Hoboken, NJ

Schmidt, M J (2002) *The Business Case Guide*, 2nd edn, Solution Matrix, Boston

Schmidt, M J (2014) *Business Case Essentials*, 4th edn, Solutions Matrix, Boston

Tversky, A and Kahneman, D (1981) The framing of decisions and the psychology of choice, *Science*, **211** (4481), pp. 453–58

Developing and using consultancy skills

RUTH SACKS AND MARK LOON

1 Introduction

In this chapter, you will build on the previous chapter's understanding of the requirements of a being a professional as well as the identification and development of key competencies in your practice. This chapter helps you to explore how your role may be different when you are working as a consultant.

The chapter will introduce you to the key concepts of consultancy – whether this is a permanent or project-based role – and issues that have an impact on the ways in which you work as a consultant in addressing organizational problems/issues and in managing change. Many managers as well as L&D professionals are now expected to have consultancy skills and be able to design and deliver change initiatives as part of their ongoing workload. This chapter also takes into consideration the differences between internal and external consultancy. It is helpful to be aware of the differences this can make to the understanding and perceptions of your role. This is useful whether you as an L&D professional are employed as an external provider for a specific project or, if within your professional role you have to work with external consultants.

There are two overarching learning outcomes for this chapter:

1 To understand the roles of consultants and what they do.

2 To identify and develop consultancy skills.

This chapter is divided into six sections, and each section has specific learning objectives on which to focus your attention. The first time you read this chapter it is best to work through the sections in the order they are presented, as they follow as far as possible the stages of a consultancy project. Each section builds on the understanding you have acquired in the previous section.

Section 2 introduces the context of consultancy. It includes definitions of consultancy, and suggests reasons why this approach has been taken to help resolve organizational issues. This section also suggests how consultancy projects can support desired organizational outcomes, and it will briefly touch upon the development of a business case for a consultancy project (detailed discussion about building a business case is found in Chapter 3). The rationale for an internal or external consultant will also be considered. We will cover the advantages and opportunities both roles provide and the benefits to the organization of each.

Working through Section 3, you will explore the different ways of 'doing consultancy' and how those differences affect the consultant–client relationship. The management of the consultant–client relationship is key throughout any consultancy project and it is the role of the consultant to manage this. Section 3 will also help you to recognize and differentiate between contact and contract client relationships. This is important so that you as consultant can ensure you focus your attention appropriately, particularly in reporting progress and managing updates and project changes.

The focus of Section 4 is to define and analyse the stakeholder environment. It is vital that as you lead the consultancy project you are aware of and understand your supporters and challengers. You may never be able to change the minds of all of the individuals or groups who oppose or are uncomfortable with the project, but knowing who they are and being aware of their views and feelings is important to managing the project – even more so than keeping your supporters informed.

In Section 5, we present the three overarching stages in 'doing consultancy': getting in, doing the work, and getting out. Although there are overlaps, it is important to get the order right, as this will help your client group understand what is happening and why, and the rationale behind the process you are working through. In this section we focus on 'getting in'. You will also learn about the importance of scoping the project to be clear with your client about what will be included and how you will approach the consultancy project, building upon your understanding of the different approaches to consultancy tasks developed in the previous sections.

We will also discuss what you should take into consideration when working in a consultancy team to support the project. As an L&D professional, team work is likely to be a key aspect of your working style. As a consultant, the roles and expectations are slightly different to 'pure L&D'. Preparing your team for the project is a key task for the project lead. You will need to define the working environment and the ways of working together and managing the client group in ways consistent with demonstrating integrity, trust and openness.

Section 6 will focus on the 'doing the work', the middle stage of the consultancy process. We will present you with a number of tools and techniques to ensure you collect the most relevant data from your client group and to support the consultancy process in which you are engaged. Some of these may be similar to those that you use as an L&D professional, but it is important to remember that in a consultant role, how you facilitate these activities will be different. Section 6 will also explore the ways in which resistance to change shows. We will look at ways of recognizing resistance and how to deal with the different barriers people present. We will also suggest ways of dealing with these barriers. You may not be able to completely break them down but you may well be able to reduce their strength so that the project becomes acceptable to a wider group of people. We will address the issues of those who oppose the project and how you might work with these people or groups so that they do not overwhelm your work and hinder the progress of the change.

The focus of Section 7 is on ending the consultancy project, ie 'getting out'; the completion and evaluation phases of the project. More than ever, the review and feedback stages are important. These phases may link to the release of further funding to support the project on an ongoing basis and, if you are an external consultant, the payment of consultancy fees. This phase often supports the potential of further work. It is also helpful if you are clear in your own mind and can be clear to others when working full time as an L&D professional that you may need to take a different approach when in a consultancy role. Reviewing a consultancy project means demonstrating the success criteria have been met and also defining with the client what, if any, follow-up work is required. Remember, a consultant is only as good as the last project they have worked on. This is the same whether you are an internal or an external consultant. There will be a brief conclusion and summary to this chapter, with a number of points for reflection to support your development as an effective consultant.

2 What is consultancy?

This section contains a discussion of the various definitions of consulting, why a business case is required and the differences between internal and external consultants. By the end of this section you will be able to explain what you understand by consultancy and appreciate why it is relevant in the current organizational situation.

2.1 Defining a consultancy

There is no single definition of consultancy. In fact, it is interesting at the start of any project to ask your client what they understand by this word (Wright, 2008). This will help you define your role. Consultancy is generally described (Block, 2011; Czerniawska and May, 2004; Markham, 1999) as:

- offering independent advice;
- solving problems;
- carrying out an activity or managing a project for which there is not enough internal resource;
- providing skills and knowledge which is lacking inside the company;
- providing training or development activities.

The reasons for using consultancy are as varied as its definitions. Consultants are brought in to offer advice and resolve problems for a number of different reasons (Cope, 2003; Heller, 2002):

- the company wants an independent perspective;
- the team or department needs reorganizing;
- the organization needs new capabilities;
- the company has recognized it is lacking in market awareness;
- a key competitor of the company has made a significant shift in market presence and this is seen as a challenge to be addressed.

2.2 Creating a business case for consultants

Defining the nature of the problem, the people involved, its urgency and its considered importance to organizational performance will all contribute towards the decision to initiate a consultancy project and select internal or external advisors. The following are useful reminders in structuring your business case (which was discussed in detail in Chapter 3):

- Who owns the problem?
- Who is involved in the problem?
- How is the problem defined?
- What are the skills felt to be needed to solve the problem?
- Who needs the solution?
- How quickly does the problem need to be resolved?

Exploring the answers to these questions also clarifies the scope of the consultancy project, which we explore further in Sections 3 and 4.

2.3 Internal or external consultants?

It is often the case that when a problem or issue is identified within an organization, no one wants to be the one to 'point it out'. It may be because it involves particular individuals or a specific incident has taken place and the concern has gradually increased in importance over time. In such situations, where sensitivity may be a concern, an external consultant will often be brought in to sort the problems out. Sometimes a non-partisan view may be the only suggestion that a highly political organization may accept (Newton, 2010).

At times, external consultants may also be used when the organization does not have the required expertise in house (and if they did, they may have then avoided the problems that they are facing, unless of course it is an opportunity that has just arisen) such as in situations such as technical problems relating to marketing, information technology or finance. In addition, external consultants are more often employed when the issue relates to strategy, as they possess the analytical ability, benchmarking data and insights, and fresh perspectives (Markham, 1999). External consultants are also preferred when third-party 'endorsement' is important for senior management in persuading the board of directors to accept a new strategic direction, for example recommendations from prestigious consulting firms such as McKinsey and Co.

In some cases, depending on their size, some organizations may have a dedicated internal consultancy department. Internal consulting departments work on a variety of issues and projects, depending on the need and the resources available. At times, internal consulting departments may recruit individuals from within other parts of the organization on a temporary basis, for the unique knowledge and/or skills they can bring to a specific project. Clearly, members of HR or L&D are often considered the most appropriate people to work on issues of change and development in relation to 'people issues'. Internal consultants may best serve some consulting projects, especially when unique knowledge and insight, and appreciation of the complexities of the organization are imperative (Toppin and Czerniawska, 2005). Therefore, the decision to choose either an external or internal consultant may not be clear cut at times, and this issue is further explored in the next section.

Exercise

You may have come across the term 'consultant' either at work or in your personal life, for example on the phone with a sales consultant. Reflect upon what comes to mind when the term 'consultant' is used, and in what context you came across this term, for example having a meeting with a consultant from the NHS. What do all the 'consultants' that you come across have in common?

3 What exactly do consultants do?

This section will provide you with an understanding of the role of the consultant, and how the role is defined and communicated. It also contains a discussion on the consultant–client relationship. We further discuss the implications of the use of internal and external consultants, and the importance of confidentiality and trust in the consulting relationship, wherever the consultant is from. Finally, this section discusses consultancy styles.

3.1 The role of the consultant

What does 'being a consultant' mean? If you ask six people you will get at least six different answers – and each is likely to be correct. As a consultant you will be:

- giving advice;
- seen as 'independent eyes' on the problem;
- creating and designing change programmes;
- implementing change programmes that others have designed;
- being part of a team providing advice and support in times of change;

- sharing your expertise;
- making suggestions about change programmes;
- solving problems to make the changes work better;
- talking to people to find out what changes should take place;
- talking to people to encourage them to give more support to the changes proposed;
- providing recommendations that you will want people to follow.

Consultants are engaged as independent advisors even if they are part of the same company. They are expected to provide impartial, non-partisan advice (Block, 2011). Before you start the consultancy project itself or even begin defining it, you should find out who you are going to be working with and who you are going to be working for, whether they are external clients that you have never met or colleagues from another part of your organization. Barbara Emmanuel shares her view on consulting in L&D in the following case example.

Barbara Emanuel, training and development manager, Walsall Healthcare NHS Trust

Consulting skills are crucial, as without them an L&D professional could end up commissioning something without understanding/knowing what the internal customer needs specifically. If L&D practitioners are to live up to the 'professional' tag, then they must have the expertise and credibility to have dialogue with clients to understanding their situation and collaborate with them in sharing ideas to help develop 'solutions' to improve performance and other issues.

The days when L&D practitioners were 'order takers' are long gone. L&D now provides professional services. For example, in recommending learning and development solutions to members of the workforce in an organization, L&D has to first gather relevant data and information in undertaking a training needs analysis (TNA). However, this must be followed by a second step, which is a consultation process with the individual himself/herself, in addition to other stakeholders such as the individual's immediate supervisor and human resources, if appropriate. This second step is crucial, as without it, L&D practitioners may not have the full picture to provide the 'right' advice.

▶

The consulting approach can be applied to other activities that we undertake such as delivering training. We are now becoming training consultants as we advance our knowledge and skills in understanding adult learning and how this may best serve to enhance the learning of individuals from diverse backgrounds within the context of varied courses, programmes and organizational outcomes. In addition to understanding how learning and development 'work', as consultants we also need understand the 'technologies' available to help our clients address their needs (technologies may involve information technology and also psychological inventories).

In addition to knowledge about learning and development that helps us in providing diagnostic analyses and expert advice, there are also underlying skills that we need to enhance to help us become better consultants, such as listening and facilitation skills to help clients articulate and identify issues that may be facing. This is important, as the issues that clients think they are facing are just symptoms.

Another area of development that is important to the role of consultant concerns understanding the needs and direction of the sector, in particular how L&D is practised across the sector. This is important, since the context sometimes changes the way how some things are undertaken, eg medical professionals versus corporate managers. Understanding the differences and similarities is important, as it helps L&D professionals to identify the nuances and how they can adapt approaches and methods obtained from other sectors.

3.2 Defining relationships

In any consultancy role you need to consider all the people who will be involved, however briefly:

- The contact clients are the people (or person) who asked you to conduct or take part in the project.
- The contract clients are the people to whom you will be consulting. This group also includes all the people who may or may not be directly affected by the changes to be implemented.

The distinction between contact and contract client groups is a useful one, as it helps you as consultant to be clear about reporting lines, roles and responsibilities. Often your contact client, particularly for an external consultant, may be the person who has introduced the consultant to the company but thereafter has no further need to be informed of the progress of the project. Contract clients are those who need to be regularly updated on the project, as these individuals are those that evaluate the completion of phases within the project and 'sign off' on any intermediate payments (which then goes to finance). It is also possible that the contract client is the senior manager who has overall responsibility for the project and is the person who should have regular updates on the project progress.

3.3 Communicating the consultancy role

At the beginning of the project, you need to work with your client to iden-tify the individuals and groups who will work with you. These will include the people who may be part of your consultancy team, those who are likely to be designing the project with you or perhaps those to whom you will be delegating tasks, for example carrying out interviews to find out more information from the people who will be responsible for implementing your recommendations and setting up the new process or systems.

All of these people need to know from the start of the project who you are, why you are working in the company or department, what your role is and what theirs is expected to be. Do not forget to discuss timescales as well with the contact client. There may be other people acting as intermediaries (members of a steering committee that represent different parts of the organization) to communicate project tasks further. If you are the lead consultant, it is your role to make sure your team understands the project, its objectives and proposed outcomes, the roles and timescale (Wickham, 2004).

3.4 Being an internal consultant

An 'internal' consultant is someone who is permanently employed by the company and who provides consultancy services to different departments as required. He or she is likely to be part of the organization development or human resources (and increasingly from learning and development too) areas of the organization.

People throughout the organization may well know the internal con-sultant, and will know of them in different roles and be familiar with them in a number of contexts. If you are an internal consultant, whether you like it or not your reputation will precede you. One way of finding out how people see you and what they think of you could be to go through a 360-degree feedback exercise. You might also want to review your appraisal feedback, and maintain regular communication with your line manager and colleagues.

Each time you are asked to work with colleagues from a different part of the company you might want to think about the individuals with whom you will be working and what their expectations of the project might be. It is quite possible that they do not have as much information about the proposed change initiative as you have been led to understand. It may well be worth talking to them about their expectations and concerns about the process and outcomes. Some of the questions you might be asked could include:

- Why is this project happening now?
- Who wants it to happen?
- Why do they want it?
- What do they want from me?

3.5 Being an external consultant

As an external consultant, you will probably not be familiar with the company you are about to work with, or alternatively you may be returning to the organization precisely because they have worked with you before and have confidence in you. Known or unknown as an external consultant, you may not have immediate access to the people you need to contact or the formal and informal communication channels that exist. Similarly, you are likely to be unfamiliar with the ways in which the company operates. This, however, can be a real advantage. In order to find your way around you will need to ask many questions which may seem very basic. However, such questions are a very good way to get to know how things work and what people think of the ways they work.

Questions could include:

- What happens if/ when...?
- How do you...?
- Why does...?
- Why can't...?
- Are there exceptions to...?
- Who has responsibility for...?

Knowing how to articulate your questions is important. The right questions will elicit the 'right' answers (Fagley, Coleman and Simon, 2010). The more people get to know you, the more familiar you will become to the client group. This is a very good way to begin to gain trust as they get to know you through answering your questions and giving you useful information. It will of course help you to understand 'what is going on'. Even as an internal consultant it is worth asking these questions. Even though you are familiar with your own company it is best not to make assumptions that everything happens in exactly the same way in all parts of the company (Sturdy and Wright, 2011).

Importantly, each time you ask these questions you have the opportunity to explain the project you are working on. This means you can explain the project personally, which is always better than an e-mail that may or may not be read. It is important to recognize that the concerns and expectations of your client group will be similar, whether you are acting as an internal or external consultant.

Exercise

Both internal and external consultants have advantages and disadvantages. An advantage of being an internal consultant may be a disadvantage for an external consultant and vice versa. Reflect upon situations where internal and external consultants may be required, and situations where it does not matter whether the consultant is internal or external and complete Table 4.1.

Table 4.1 The use of internal or external consultants

Situations: more advantageous to have an internal consultant	Situations: more advantageous to have an external consultant	Situations: does not matter; both internal or external are suitable
1.	1.	1.
2.	2.	2.
3.	3.	3.
4.	4.	4.

3.6 Confidentiality and trust

In order to be viewed as an effective consultant you need to gain the trust and confidence of the people with whom you are consulting (Maister, Green and Galford, 2000). Being trusted in a consultancy role directly influences the ways in which you will be able to manage the relationships of communication, managing and influencing change throughout the project and beyond. Your integrity and ethical stance need to be seen as impeccable. This will include not sharing names and 'gossip' about others at any time. As you know, an aside let slip at a conference to a colleague will be back at work or on social media in a very short time. A damage limitation exercise will take longer than any consultancy project.

It is important to be clear about who you are, your role and how you will use the information you have received for the defined issue. Gaining trust and making sure that your clients are clear about the confidentiality of the information they are giving you needs to be something you should emphasize at key points in the consultancy process. This is equally important whether you are an internal or external consultant.

Key Point 1

When you start collecting information from people about what works and what does not work, you will gain more details, breadth and depth by explaining that although you may use all the information you are given it will not be attributed to individuals. This will also encourage honest feedback about the consultancy activities throughout the project.

Key Point 2

When you give interim reports or updates to managers about the progress of the project, it is worth reiterating the confidentiality that you have agreed with project participants. This helps to manage expectations and maintain your credibility with all concerned and involved groups.

Key Point 3

Final reports should also include the context of the data you have received and state the confidentiality status of the document and its contents.

Exercise

Trust is crucial to any consultant–client relationship. However, building trust takes time (whilst at the same time trust can be easily undermined).

Nonetheless, there are many ways to build trust and there are also practices that we should avoid that could undermine trust building. Reflect and address the following questions:

- How can you build a trusting relationship with your clients and project team members?
- What should you avoid that may undermine the trust-building process?

3.7 Consultancy styles

Although there are various styles to consultancy (Fincham, 2002), there are three fundamental approaches to consultancy. You can work from these styles whether you are an internal or an external consultant. Each style is determined to a large extent by the expectations of the client, their understanding of consultancy and their expectations of the outcome the project. It is therefore very important that at the initial negotiation stages you discuss the scope and outcomes of the project with the contract client to understand what their expectations are of the project. The three styles described here are based on those defined by Schein (1990).

The expert consultant model

Clients who want an expert consultant, want consultants who will solve their problem. The expert consultant is brought in for their knowledge and skill in particular areas, for example marketing, IT infrastructure, communications or strategy. The client will have a clear idea of what the problem is and the resolution they want. The relationship with the consultant is one of supplier and customer. The client is looking for someone to take responsibility for the problem and solve it. The client is only interested in a solution that resolves the issue and takes away the problem. How the solution is found is the choice and decision of the consultant. This type of consultancy project has a clear beginning and a finite end. The scope and boundaries of the project are defined by the client, who also decides the desired outcomes and success criteria.

The doctor/patient model

This doctor/patient approach to consultancy is more collaborative than the expert consultancy model. The consultant spends time with the contact client group in order to define the scope of the problem or issue. This type of consultancy is dependent on the skill of the consultant in identifying the issues and concerns to be addressed. Similar to a visit to the doctor's, the outcome of the doctor's appointment and the resulting 'prescription' is only as effective as the information the doctor has been given to make the diagnosis.

It is up to the consultant to ask a range of questions which will provide a broad view of the situation. Key to the consultancy process is the 'diagnostic phase' in which the consultant explores the problem in order to provide a 'prescription' or report with recommendations that the client group will follow. It is likely that the consultant is asked to provide the diagnosis and the diagnostic report but not to deliver any solutions. The implementation phase of the change will be carried out by the client – very often with no consultant involvement at all. The responsibility for the change activity and the outcomes will be the client's. In this approach the consultant has provided the route to success for the client to follow.

The process consultancy model

This third style is often considered to be the most attractive of the main approaches to consultancy but can, in practice, be the most challenging. A successful process consultancy project fully involves both the consultant and the client from the beginning to the end of the project. Such a project often starts when the client recognizes that there could be improvements or changes in their organization but they are not sure where to start, what the real problems are or how to go about making the required changes. This is when they call in a consultant who they know will work with them in a shared and equitable manner.

In this type of project, there needs to be very close collaboration and trust between the client and consultant. The process becomes one of joint discovery and sharing of the learning and any implemented changes in an ongoing and developmental process. The role of the consultant is to support and challenge the client so that they develop and/or improve their own consultancy skills. In this way the client gains a higher level of competence in change management, which means that they feel confident to manage their own change projects as a result. We will develop these three roles further in Section 4.

Exercise

The three different styles of consultancy are helpful, and each plays a role in contributing to various client problems/needs. Identify situations whereby each style/model of consultancy may be more appropriate in Table 4.1.

Table 4.2 The use of the three consulting styles

The Expert Consultant model	The Doctor/Patient model	Process Consultancy model
1.	1.	1.
2.	2.	2.
3.	3.	3.
4.	4.	4.

4 Managing stakeholder relationships and communication strategies

Stakeholders are crucial to any consultancy project as they can 'make' or 'break' the project. Strong support from stakeholders may result in information being provided easily (eg complete, accurate and timely), provide constructive feedback on the progress of the project and create a positive attitude concerning the project (International Council of Management Consulting Institutes, 2003). Hence it is crucial that you know who your stakeholders are, where they 'stand' in regard to the project, and how you can manage them. This section provides some helpful exercises that will enable you to do this.

A stakeholder is an individual or group who will be affected in some way by the project. Some stakeholders will be very close to the project; they will be involved from the very beginning and will need to know at all times its progress and challenges (Biggs, 2010; Maister *et al.*, 2000). Other stakeholders may be heavily involved in the project at the beginning as it is setting up and then not have any further involvement until it is completed and the process has been 'signed off'.

Some people or groups of people may need to know about the project and what is going on but from 'a distance', as its timeline may have an impact on their work. Once you know that you will be involved in a project and before you start to plan the work and develop the project, you need to identify your stakeholders. The advantage of carrying out a stakeholder analysis is that you can define who you need to communicate with and how often, as well as identify those people who do not need to be included in meetings and so on (Institute of Management Consultants USA, 2005). This can help to make your time management as effective as possible. Working through a stakeholder analysis can support the creation of a clear and structured communications plan for the project.

4.1 Identify your stakeholders

List all the people and groups of people who you think have an (however great or small) interest in or will be affected by this project. Once you have completed this exercise on your own, you should review your list of stakeholders with at least one colleague – even if they are not going to work directly on the project with you. This way you are most likely to make sure you include everyone who should be included. Below is a helpful list of how to categorize individuals or groups based on the impact of the project on them:

- individuals or groups most affected by the project inside the company;
- individuals or groups most affected by the project outside the company;
- individuals or groups somewhat affected by the project inside the company;
- individuals or groups somewhat affected by the project outside the company;
- individuals or groups unaffected by the project inside the company;
- individuals or groups unaffected by the project outside the company.

Whether your project involves a half-day team-building event or a departmental job evaluation, there are likely to be people outside the individuals or groups most concerned who may need to know what is happening. The following is an example of identifying the stakeholders of a marketing team-building event:

- Individuals or groups most affected by the marketing team-building event inside the company:
    - the attending marketing team members;
    - the line manager of the marketing team attending the event;
    - the line manager or other person who signs off the budget for this event;
    - the people who will answer the phones/stand in for the marketing team whilst they are at the event;
    - the catering services, if sourced internally;

- – in-house staff who arrange furniture and other requirements, if sourced internally;
- – the line manager or other person who has decided that this event should take place;
- – the line manager or other person who has sourced/brought you in as consultant to facilitate this event;
- – if you are an internal consultant then your colleagues will be affected by this project you are carrying out.
- Individuals or groups most affected by the marketing team-building event outside the company:
  - – the people who will be providing the location, catering and health and safety if an event is held externally;
  - – the families of the marketing team members whose usual personal arrangements will disrupted buy this event;
  - – external clients of the marketing team;
  - – if you are an external consultant then your colleagues will be affected by this project you are carrying out.
- Individuals or groups somewhat affected by the marketing team-building event inside the company:
  - – the finance team who may need to complete purchase orders, process expenses etc;
  - – other individuals or teams within the same department who are not part of this activity.
- Individuals or groups somewhat affected by the marketing team-building event outside the company:
  - – clients of the marketing team who will not be able to contact them during the time they are at the event;
  - – clients of this team who will be affected by any changes made during this event which may impact on their relationships with the team.
- Individuals or groups unaffected by the marketing team-building event inside the company:
  - – individuals and teams who rarely communicate with or liaise with the marketing team.
- Individuals or groups unaffected by the marketing team-building event outside the company:
  - – future clients of the marketing team.

In another example, the following involves identifying the stakeholders of a job evaluation exercise for the in-house maintenance team:

- Individuals or groups most affected by the project inside the company:
  - all maintenance team members;
  - all individuals who are currently employed in a role on a similar pay scale to the maintenance team members;
  - people whose roles have just been evaluated;
  - the manager of the maintenance team;
  - the line manager of the maintenance team line manager;
  - the line manager or other person who has sourced/brought you in as consultant to facilitate this event;
  - if you are an internal consultant then your colleagues will be affected by this project you are carrying out.
- Individuals or groups most affected by the project outside the company:
  - all individuals, groups or clients who work with members of the maintenance team, eg the cleaning company;
  - if you are an external consultant then your colleagues will be affected by this project you are carrying out.
- Individuals or groups somewhat affected by the project inside the company:
  - all individuals who experience the services of the maintenance team – this is likely to be all other members of staff in the company;
  - other members of staff who expect to have their roles evaluated once the maintenance team job evaluation has taken place.
- Individuals or groups somewhat affected by the project outside the company:
  - all individuals or groups who provide services to the maintenance team, such as uniform suppliers.
- Individuals or groups unaffected by the project – inside the company:
  - NA.
- Individuals or groups unaffected by the project – outside the company
  - NA.

Depending on the project, its size and the number of people directly involved, you may have more or fewer columns completed. Wherever possible and/or appropriate, use the names of the people or team involved. As a result of your stakeholder analysis:

- you should be clear who are the people most affected by your project;
- you will know who you need to get support from;
- you will have a good idea of where challenges may come from;
- you should also have a clear idea of the number of people you may need to communicate with to carry out the various activities involved;
- if you are concerned about the number of stakeholders you have identified, you may need to review the scope of your project to make sure you have clearly set the boundaries of the project so that you know who is and who isn't involved.

The next step is to identify stakeholder support. It is useful to rate each stakeholder in terms of how supportive *you think* they are of the project. If you are working as an internal consultant, you may wish to have each of your team members (ie those who will carry out the consultancy project with you) rate each stakeholder in terms of how supportive they are of the project, without discussion, and then tally individual ratings and discuss obvious differences. While it probably isn't critical to strive for complete consensus, it is usually worthwhile to take the time to generally agree on whether each stakeholder is against, neutral, or supportive. Rank your stakeholders along the following continuum:

Figure 4.1 How supportive are the stakeholders about this project NOW?

Strongly against	Moderately against	Neutral	Moderately supportive	Completely supportive

When there is general agreement about where each stakeholder is currently, the discussion should then turn to where each stakeholder needs to be for the change initiative to be successful:

Figure 4.2 How supportive do you want the stakeholders to be?

Strongly against	Moderately against	Neutral	Moderately supportive	Completely supportive

Remember, some stakeholders may need only be moved from 'strongly against' to 'neutral' (meaning they will no longer be an active blocker), while others may only need to be moderately supportive. Take a moment before concluding this exercise to look for logical relationships between and among these stakeholders in terms of who might assist the team in gaining the support of others. For example, if a key stakeholder who is strongly supportive is also a thought leader for others on your list, it might be useful to enlist his/her support in shaping the thinking of other less supportive stakeholders.

To validate your assessment of stakeholder support, check the team's perceptions by seeking input from individuals outside of the team. In some cases, it may even be appropriate to talk with key stakeholders themselves to validate the team's assessment of their level of commitment. The next step is to summarize the stakeholders' support (or not) for the project. Completing Table 4.3 will help you identify where you will have to work hardest to get buy-in and who you can use to help influence others (the first line is an example).

Table 4.3 Analysing stakeholder support

Stakeholder name	Current level of support	The level of support the project needs from them	Which other stakeholders could influence this individual or group?
John Bridge	Somewhat moderate. Understands the benefits but thinks the costs to gain them are too great.	John may be able to provide important information to the team but this is probably the most that is required from him or his team.	Kathleen Keenan is John's deputy and views the project more positively than John. She could help with convincing him.

The next step is to identify stakeholder expectations. One aspect of defining the levels of support a stakeholder or stakeholder group gives to a project is to understand what their expectations are in terms of what the project can and will offer them. As a consultant, you can conduct this exercise based on your own understanding of each stakeholder group you have identified as important, or you can talk to the individual stakeholder groups. Whichever avenue you decide to follow, it is important that you use the same source of information for all of the groups. For example, if you have a good relationship with some stakeholder groups and feel they have already given you enough information so that you clearly understand their expectations, then you should use the same 'criteria' for all stakeholders (eg impact on their staff, on their work, impact on their annual budget – if they have one). Table 4.4 is a template and the first row is an example.

Table 4.4 Identifying stakeholder expectations

Stakeholder individuals and groups	They want *and* we want	They want but we do not	We want but they do not
	What the stakeholder wants AND what the project sponsor and/or project champion want.	What the stakeholder wants but the project sponsor and/or champion does not.	What the project sponsor and/or project champion want BUT the stakeholder does not.
Procurement	Improved performance.	Procurement wants to further automate systems but based on the project's analysis the issue lies with their staff's capability.	We want to undertake a wholesale competency assessment and provide coaching but procurement think that this will take too much time. They feel they need something to be done urgently and a new system will help.

The next stage is about communications, in particular a communications strategy, which is required by all projects to ensure that there are timely, consistent, accurate and impactful communications. Once you have collected information about the different stakeholder groups from the different analyses carried out above, you will be able to collate this to create a communications strategy. Using Table 4.5, define your communications strategy for the project you are working on. This will then become a useful checklist that can have timings set to it within the project plan and can be updated regularly and easily.

Table 4.5 Thinking through your communications strategy

Who needs to know?	Finance department
Why are we telling them?	They are impacted in two ways. The project will impact their staff and they also need to be informed as we need to make payments to the external consultants based on their successful completion of major milestones identified in the contract.
How do we inform them?	There will be weekly meetings with the head of department as part of the stakeholder meeting. Staff are also communicated via the weekly project newsletter. Change agents will be speaking to staff at least twice a week via informal means.
How often do we communicate with them?	At least once a week.
Who takes responsibility for the communication process?	The communications team in the project, Madison and Alexandra, for the newsletters. The project manager, Jo at the stakeholder meetings, and Derrick the change agent.
Any other information?	Inez and Thirza are change consultants who may change this approach as we enter the next phase.

You should now have a very clear idea of who your key stakeholders are, how you need to communicate with them and how often. It can be helpful for you and your stakeholders if you share the frequency and proposed channels of communication so that they know what to expect and when. Meeting your own deadlines for these updates will also enhance the trust you are developing with these groups.

Exercise

Identifying, understanding and managing stakeholders are crucial to a projects. This section has demonstrated how you can go about assessing stakeholders and their support for the project. Reflect upon how you could convince an important stakeholder who is presently ambivalent to your project to become a supporter.

5 The consultancy project

Many consultancy engagements are undertaken in projects. This section discusses the different stages of the consultancy assignment. As part of this discussion, we emphasize the importance of being able to articulate and define the scope of a project and decide which consultancy approach is appropriate for your client. Finally, this section discusses how you can negotiate with your client and project team in agreeing to how the project will be carried out.

5.1 Starting a consultancy project

All projects are about making changes. It is the size and/or importance of the change that directly relate to the amount of work and the size of the project (Alvesson and Johansson, 2002; Wood, 2002). The three key phases of a project can be summarized as:

- getting in;
- doing the work;
- getting out.

Getting in: being clear about the project starting point:

However you choose to carry out your project there are three basic questions. The answers to these three questions will give you a clear start.

Questions for the client:

- Where are you now?
- Where do you want to be?

Question for you in collaboration with the client:

- How are we going to get there?

Scoping the consultancy project

When you are called in as a consultant, your client or client group want to tell you what the problem is, why it is a problem and very often what they think the answer should be. As you collect this information, which will help you to understand from the very beginning what happened and what needs to be different, you have to clarify if the problem as it is defined is the 'actual problem' or the symptom of a deeper or different problem (Nash, 2003).

Is it a symptom?

- Is the problem linked to something else?
- Is more than one department involved?
- How do people explain the situation to you – do the presenting problems originate in their department or do they say the problems come from a different part of the company or from an external client system?
- Is the problem as it is explained to you about tasks – the 'what' of how things are done – or the how – the relationships, styles or frequency of communication?

The issue may of course be partly a technical problem and partly impacted by the relationships between the individuals concerned. You may also feel that the problem is best defined as several related issues – this may be most useful for the client so that they can see that you have clearly understood the situation and that they can also understand how the approach to improving the situation is likely to be multi-faceted. Whatever your 'hunch', you will need to confirm this with some of the people you have talked to and with others you have not yet spoken to. Such conversations, however brief, will help you to put this issue into a perspective that your clients can relate to.

Where are you now?

Some of the answers to the questions below can help you answer this first question and clarify if the presenting situation is the one on which you need to focus or if you need to explore further:

- What are the team/department/company's recent successes?
- Is there an overall strategy for the team/department/company?
- What has been achieved so far?
- Is everyone in the team/department/company aware of the key strengths?
- Is there consensus about the challenges you face?
- If not, where do you think there are gaps in understanding/awareness?
- Are there recognized people management or leadership issues?
- What issues have been addressed to date? What progress has been made?
- Are there performance issues we the consultants need to be aware of?

Agreeing the scope of the consultancy

It is important that you agree with your client the extent of the work you will carry out as part of this consultancy project. The answers to the previous set of questions will help you and the client to agree what exactly will be covered by the project. It is very important to also agree what will NOT be covered and make sure the client is aware of what is 'out of scope' (Ballock, 2004; Jackson, 2002; Wickham, 2004). It may be that you agree that the 'out of scope' work should form a separate project managed by a different consultant and possibly run in parallel to the one you are currently working on.

Agreeing success and evaluation criteria

If you agree the client's desired outcomes of the project at the start during the scoping process, then the criteria for project evaluation are set. These outcomes will include the data the client requires as 'proof' that the changes have been successful. You will agree a number of goals to achieve, focusing on either quantifiable or qualitative differences or both.

Quantifiable changes are those which can be monitored numerically and include changes to:

- product or process;
- time to market;
- product quality;
- staff numbers;
- resources.

You should be able to clearly define and measure these types of changes. Whilst the delivery of such changes has its own challenges, you should be able to plan for and monitor progress within a defined timescale. *Qualitative changes* relating to differences in behaviours or language, such as increases to staff morale and improvements to service quality, are all much harder to quantify and are not 'quick fixes'.

How you agree to define the success criteria to monitor progress on these types of change management projects will need to be clearly expressed and agreed between you and your client. These criteria will define the 'where are we now', the 'where we want to be' and will help to formulate the interim stages: 'how are we going to get there?' There may be formal and informal mechanisms, which are appropriate in these circumstances according to client requirements. Managing the client's expectations about results for these aspects of organizational life is important and will need constant review. Remember that you need to make sure your project does not grow larger just because the issue is more complex than originally defined by the client.

If you are scoping the project as an *expert consultant*, the clients will be waiting for you to give them a clear definition of the problem and provide a solution that will be precisely defined, with possibly a staged approach they can easily relate to and which will provide evidence of progress that can be easily mapped. If you include some 'technical terms', the client may feel such words demonstrate your knowledge and expertise, and although they may not understand the meaning or exactly the implications they will feel that you have demonstrated your credentials and therefore they will trust your solution.

If you are working in the *doctor mode,* your clients will be expecting a story that they identify as their own problem – you may even use some of the same words that they use to define the problem. It will be clear to your clients that you have understood what they want and need. You may include some 'technical terms', which they feel demonstrates that you know what you are doing, and you will probably give a brief explanation of these terms. The change management plan that you offer will clearly link to the problems you have set out and which the client has agreed with. As you are seen as the person with the consultancy skills, experience and knowledge, your clients will take your solution and work through it as best they can.

If you are developing a joint consultancy approach in *process consultancy mode,* then you will define the problem situation with the client or project champions so that other organization members see you working as a team. You and your client will talk about the project in the same way, using similar words, phrases and questions to identify a route to a solution agreed by most of the people involved in the project.

A learning and development approach may be used with any of the approaches identified above to support a change management programme, which could include coaching, structured training events and programmes. These approaches are designed to promote changes in behaviours, attitudes and culture. They can create different ways of bringing people together through focused learning situations to encourage new or different ways of working.

5.2 Defining or scoping the problem

Working as an *expert consultant*, you will define the problem according to your expertise. Here are the types of questions you might ask if you are working as an expert consultant:

- What do you want to achieve?
- Who should be involved in this project?
- Who don't you want to be involved this project?
- What is the time frame I need to work towards?
- What do you want to achieve as a result of this project?
- Exactly what changes are expected: Processes? Tasks? Behaviours? Attitudes? Skills? Knowledge?

Working in the *doctor/patient mode,* you will scope the project depending on the questions you ask and the answers you are given. Here are some example questions:

- What do you think the problem is?
- What is happening?
- How do you know?
- What is not working well?
- Are some departments or teams working better than others?
- Are there some departments that rarely meet their targets?
- How long has this been going on?
- Are there specific individuals or groups I should be talking to?
- What do you think people are saying about the company?
- Have changes in the customer base been noted?

Working with the *process consultancy mode*, the discussions you might have with your client could include some of the following topics:

- a recognition or awareness of the current issues or problems;
- the current strategic aims;
- the desired aims/outcomes for this project;
- the business aims and people outcomes;
- the links between business and people outcomes and the 'fit';
- stakeholder needs;
- business processes, structures;
- organization culture;
- skill and knowledge levels in the company;
- communication strategies;
- ways to ensure clarity of aims, objectives and outcomes.

Exercise: introducing yourself to a client

Your approach to scoping the consultancy problem is influenced by the approach to consultancy you are taking. Susana, a director at Wilks & Co., a family firm of accountants, wants to contract with a consultancy company in order to increase the SME customers for Wilks & Co. You have been invited to meet with Susana to discuss the project and this potential contract.

What do you want to know from her? What questions will you ask?

Make a note of the questions that first come to mind. Then return to the three approaches and see which style is your preference. It may be that you favour a combination of expert and doctor or indeed doctor and process consultant.

Susana also has questions for you:

- What can we expect from you as a consultant?
- How do you work?
- How often would we see you in the company?
- How often will we receive updates?
- In your experience, what are the key challenges that SME companies are facing?
- Would you be able to design and deliver a training course in social media for our staff?
- Why should we work with you (and your company)?

Thinking through the answers to these questions in advance, whether you are an internal or external consultant, will give you an advantage. You will create a very positive impression if you are able to clearly articulate your approach to consultancy and your style of working. It is just as important as an internal consultant that you are seen to have a professional attitude and understanding of this role. When the project scope has been agreed, you will want to start the project, begin the diagnosis and get to grips with the issues.

5.3 Changing the scope of the project

Managing client expectations is vital to the success criteria of the project. It is important to agree and confirm project boundaries, expectations, timescale and resources. However, the scope may change as your understanding of the issues develops, or indeed because the client changes their mind on a certain aspect.

Remember you have initially agreed a timescale and resources for support for that project. If you are an external consultant you will also have agreed a fee. Changing the size or extent of the project will mean changing other aspects including all resources. The client needs to agree these – do not make assumptions that 'it will be fine'... it may not. Hold a separate meeting with your key client to discuss the changed scope to do this.

Be clear what is 'in scope', ie included in this project, and what will be 'out of scope', ie not part of the propjet. It is a good idea to present the 'out of scope' activities as a separate project that the client could commission or could engage a further internal task force to carry out at the same time as you are working. This would give you ongoing input and support for your work but not take all of your time.

A word of warning. do not make all of the tasks you do not like doing as 'out of scope'.

5.4 Doing the work

Once you have agreed the scope of the project with the client you will have a good idea of what needs to happen and when. Creating a project plan and timeline helps to manage expectations – yours and your client's. It is important to stay on track and inside your project scope. Identifying key tasks and start and finish dates, with some flexibility for contingency, will maintain project focus. Once you have defined your stakeholder communication plan this can be integrated into the project plan as well. Section 6 includes some helpful and useful models that will help you progress the project and collect the data you need to define what needs to happen and how the change process itself should be managed.

5.5 Giving and receiving feedback

One way of making sure you are on track with your project and that the client is satisfied with the progress you are making is to provide your client and key stakeholders with feedback on a regular basis throughout the project. Agreeing what outcomes the client is looking for in advance can give a strong focus to the project, support all your interim reports and also shape the project design and approach. Remember to agree the frequency of the feedback with your client. This is also a helpful strategy to avoid some of the difficult situations that are described in Section 7, where the situation arises where you feel you can no longer work on the project. Why give ongoing feedback?

- You are giving the client your sense of what is happening and why.

- Your perspective will either confirm what the client is concerned about or present issues that you feel will impact on the progress of the project. The feedback will then become meaningful and of value to the client.

- Interim feedback also maintains communication channels with contact clients who remain at a distance from the project.

- Discussing the project and asking for feedback from the client is a good way for you and your client to get to know each other and create a stronger relationship. This leads to a better and more honest sharing of information.

- Receiving feedback on your performance helps you to be sure you are meeting the client's expectations.

- Sharing your comments and views engages the client on a regular basis and may encourage further contributions and time from them.

- Feedback keeps the client informed of what is happening, why and the progress or barriers the project has come up against.

'Getting out' will be discussed in more detail in Section 7. However, being able to close the project in a professional manner that ensures the client has received the agreed outcomes is important. Ongoing, regular feedback to the client group means that the final feedback session once the project is over makes that event more meaningful and constructive.

Exercise

There are numerous advantages to obtaining ongoing feedback from the clients and stakeholders, and also for the project team in providing ongoing feedback. Feedback is also evident in other parts of life – college assignments, work performance, advice from your friends – and can be helpful. Reflect on a time when you received what you thought was good feedback (obtained in any parts of your life such as school, work or personal life). How did you make the most of it? Would you have 'done better' if such feedback was given on a more ongoing basis?

5.6 Working in a consultancy team

Project circumstances may well determine whether you work on a consultancy assignment on your own or as part of a team. These include:

- whether the project demands skills or expertise that you do not have;
- whether or not you have a team of people you can easily draw on as resource;
- whether the team members you would like to include have the necessary skills, experience and consultancy expertise to contribute effectively to the project;
- the size of the project;
- the size of the client group you are working with;
- how available the team members will be over the planned lifetime of the project.

These situations may also help you to agree more resources to support the project than initially agreed.

Working as a member of a team is a role that we all take on regularly during our professional lives. During a consultancy assignment, if you are working as a team it is essential to give the client group confidence that the project is being carried out in a holistic, coherent and cohesive manner. You and your team members need to take time to clarify your approach to the consultancy:

- who will have overall responsibility for the project;
- who will lead particular aspects of the project;
- who will be involved in each of the project activities;
- how and how often you will communicate with the client;

- the development and maintenance of confidentiality and trust throughout the project;
- the approach you will all take to the different phases of the project;
- how you will collaborate and coordinate with all team members;
- what your success criteria are and how you will celebrate the successes;
- how you will manage project problems and challenges.

A meeting to set up and agree your ways of working should help you as a team. A project contract for the consultancy team may well be a useful document, particularly when the team membership may change over the duration of the project. In Section 6, we will look in more detail at the 'doing the work phase'.

Exercise

Working in teams in consulting projects, as with most newly formed teams, can be a challenge but also there are a lot of rewards. What are the advantages of working in teams in a consulting project?

6 Doing the work

This section will focus on the 'doing the work', the middle stage of the consultancy process. We will present you with a number of tools and techniques to help you to collect the information you will need to understand what is happening and how you can help. These tools will support the consultancy process in which you are engaged. Some of these may be similar to those that you use as an L&D professional, but it is important to remember that in a consultant role, how you facilitate these activities will be different. Remember the consultancy approach you are taking and how you are defining your role with the client (as discussed in Section 2).

This section will also explore the ways in which resistance to change is expressed. We will look at ways of recognizing resistance and some ways to deal with the different barriers people present. You may not be able to completely break down resistance but you may well be able to reduce its strength so that the project becomes acceptable to a wider group of people. Not all projects go according to plan and not all client groups are easy to manage. We will look at some of the ways you might handle challenging situations. The topics in this section include clarifying the project, managing resistance to change, understanding the change curve, and tools, tips and techniques for 'doing the work'. By the end of this section you will be able to decide which specific tasks need to be carried out during this consultancy project, and recognize resistance to change and define ways of dealing with it.

It is very easy as a consultant to get involved in the issues you have been asked to explore and start to find answers almost as soon as you start the project; hold on!

6.1 Making sure you are working on the 'right' problem

Key to 'doing the work' is being clear about the nature of the problem and defining what needs to change. To make sure that you are really focusing on the presenting problem – the cause and not just the symptoms – you should spend some time understanding different perspectives and views. To do this, talking to different people who are affected by the project will enable you to get their views and to understand the extent to which they see the importance of the situation as it has been explained to you. You might do this face to face but, depending on the constraints of the resources for the project, you may have phone or Skype conversations or even collect views and opinions through an online questionnaire. Linda Gittings supports the view that is important to listen to clients to ensure that the real problem is discovered so that the right solution can be developed.

Linda Gittings, training officer, Fortis Living

L&D professionals do adopt a consulting role but we may not always use the label consulting. Also, what does consulting mean? There are many conceptualizations and dimensions to it. What consulting means to me may be different to another person. But many of the processes that we undertake in helping our internal clients are similar to those in consulting. For example, we have a big programme running next year and one of the directors believes there are still skills gaps here in this area of work. So we arranged a meeting/workshop on how we can achieve the aim. In such a case I guess you can say they are consulting with me because they see me as the person who has the knowledge regarding L&D. The clients have the technical knowledge, as they are dealing with it on a day-to-day basis, and between the two of us we will come up with a learning programme that will benefit and safeguard our customers and staff. The consulting

▶

process is important, as we do not just book any training programme that our internal clients think they need. It is about having joined-up thinking, and this does epitomize what we mean by consulting, such as facilitation, and being a problem solver.

It is a two-way process; as I am an L&D professional, I need to listen to my internal customer, the business, to understand what they really need, for example a delivery style that will suit the business and the delegates. For example, if I am looking at a course for the workforce to go on, but in fact I know that 80 per cent of staff do not need the whole one as some may just need a shorter reinforcement session, then I will create a bespoke approach to cater for the different needs of the workforce.

Consulting skills are also required to discover needs that may not be obvious. For example, line managers themselves need a bespoke approach to development so that they can more effectively manage staff who have unique job situations such as supporting staff who are involved in lone working and those who work in sensitive areas. These front-line staff need support mechanisms so that they know who to check with to understand if they have done the right thing, to voice any concerns. So the managers need to have the capability to support this. But at times these needs may not be evident unless we talk to the managers.

Exercise

Being able to find out the actual problem depends if you are talking to the right people and if you are asking the right questions. Reflect upon a time when you had to 'interview' people to find out the actual problem (get to the bottom of things) and address the following questions:

- Were you successful in getting to the 'bottom of things'?
- How did you find the people to speak to?
- How did you ask the 'right' questions?

6.2 Collecting information: interviews and questionnaires

As L&D professionals, you know that the quality of the information you receive is dependent on the questions asked. If you send out a questionnaire, you need to remember the response rate may not be what you expect. Whether you are going to use a questionnaire or an interview, it is worthwhile testing out the questions on someone who does not know much about the project – a colleague or a friend who will be a confidential ally to you. Such a piloting exercise can help you to make sure the questions you are asking will give you the information you need. Do not forget that to ensure the validity of the information you gain, the same questions should be asked of all your respondents.

Whatever your consultancy approach, you are unlikely to be in the company or department permanently making sure the situation is completely resolved. It will be the client group who will do that. Your success depends on what you have been asked to achieve in your consultant role and how you define the solution so that it is accepted by the clients and implemented. Remember that you will have negotiated confidentiality agreements with your client and that these should be shared with the people who are contributing to your information-gathering phase. People are often concerned about talking about their opinions of work, its challenges and their opportunities to someone they do not know or to someone who works in a different part of the company (if you are an internal consultant). Explaining how you will manage the confidentiality of the information you receive and how you will ensure anonymity is very important. Remind yourself of the issues on confidentiality by reviewing Section 3.

The data you collect may also be helpful to you when you are compiling the interim and final reports. This makes it even more important to give confidence to your interviewees or questionnaire respondents that their identity is secure and that any comments quoted will be done so in ways that do not reveal or make easily identifiable the names of the individuals who gave the information.

6.3 Organizing the project

As the consultant you will need to define what tasks are needed and how they need to be organized. It is best to take time to be clear about how you are going to work, particularly if this has not already been agreed within the scope of the project. What are your expectations of how people going to work with you? Do you think your clients/colleagues will cooperate with you on delivering the project?

You may not be able to do the entire project on your own. To be clear about the size of the project it is important to review the scope. Refer to the work you carried out in Section 4; this will help. Some consultancy activities have very clear boundaries and definitions, for example, sourcing companies for a new approach to recruitment, or evaluating the most appropriate locations for a company event. These may be termed as consultancy exercises. Remember what is defined as consultancy is done so by your client.

However, other projects may be more complex, for example, merging two separate teams to create a new department in a new building or identifying best practice in learning and development. Each of these could be presented to you as a consultancy project and each would require you as the consultant to take a different approach.

Example 1: merging two separate teams into a new department in a new building

This consultancy exercise is one that will require all of your skills and expertise.

It will be important to define your consultancy role and also the scope of the project and the success criteria required.

Three questions that will get you started in exploring the situation are:

1 Where are we now?

2 Where do we want to be?

3 How are we going to get there?

Questions 1 and 2 will help you to work out the answers to question 3. The members of each team (as far as possible) need the opportunity to talk to you about their understanding of the situation, why the merger is happening and how they feel about it. Some team members will be very excited by the change to a new office, but others may be very worried about the changes of location, role and people they work with. For any or all of these reasons, you will come up against a number of examples of resistance to change.

Example 2: identifying best practice in learning and development

For this type of project, you need to be clear whether this is an internal or external process review. This type of project is one where you may need to rely on secondary information. Secondary information is when you have not been able to collect the details directly yourself. As it may be harder to find out exactly what happens in a range of organizations, your research may take you to industry groups, membership organizations or other already-completed reports or surveys that are readily available. This information-gathering and collection exercise may be labelled as consultancy because in the eyes of your client you are doing the work for them and your L&D knowledge and expertise are important to managing their expectations.

6.4 Reactions to change

Most of us, most of the time, thrive on predictability; knowing what we can expect, what people are likely to say and how quickly or not projects progress. Every time a new project or idea is raised, there will always be people who will be excited by something new and different and others who will see the new 'thing'/change as threatening, upsetting, difficult or even impossible to achieve.

Your skills as a consultant will be to work with all of these reactions and responses, empathizing, encouraging, cajoling and being assertive in managing these emotions. In Section 4, where we explored the stakeholder environment, there was an exercise on understanding the perspective of your stakeholders. Do review this again, as it will help you in this section too. There are a number of typical reactions to change. This is a summarized list which will help you think about how you might understand and manage resistance to change.

The resistors

There are three main types of behaviour you may encounter in resistors of change:

The cynics: 'Oh they tried this before and it didn't work', 'they always get it wrong.' Or 'I've been here 10 years and I've heard this all before. It didn't work then either.'

The 'I don't care'/neutrals: these people will say things such as, 'It doesn't matter what I think, they will do what they want anyway'. Or, 'I can see why they might want to do this, but I'm not sure that it will make any difference to me.'

The troublemakers: these people will say things such as, 'Well, I've already spoken to the unions about this and there are loads of precedents for this not to happen.' Or, 'Can you prove it's been signed off by Head Office? Otherwise there's no reason for us to get involved.'

The supporters

The supporters/champions: these people will say things such as, 'This is a great idea!' 'What can I do to help?' or, 'It's about time the decision was taken to merge us, work will be so much more efficient now.'

Having supporters is wonderful. Talking to them, you know you are on the right track, they agree with you or are very constructive about their feedback. Most of the time this is an honest response to the change. A word of warning: depending on how enthusiastic your supporters are, you may need to consider this delight in the change with a pinch of salt.

6.5 Being realistic about reactions to change

Almost all people have similar reactions to change – we experience them at our own individual pace. The different reactions have been researched and collated into a Grief Cycle model by Elisabeth Kübler-Ross (Kübler-Ross and Kessler, 2014). There are five stages that follow our responses from deep grief to a state of accepting the news and moving forward. Our responses to change in organizations have also been found to follow through the same stages. The time it takes us to work through how we feel about change – whether we are happy about it or not – will be linked to our attitudes about our place of work, the company, how long we have worked there, our feelings about colleagues, our professional role, our successes and challenges, and what we think the new job/team/role will be like.

As you read through the stages I am sure you will recognize some of the responses, attitudes and behaviours described. As you consider people other than yourself, you will also become aware that each stage takes a different time for people to work through – that some people move forward and then slip back but will move forward again. People may choose to wallow in their resistance to change, see only the negative and choose to 'play a victim'. As a consultant and change manager, try not to devote 100 per cent of your attention to them. You need to be firm but fair in sharing your time. Initially the negatives, the resistors will demand and may need much of your time and attention. As other key stakeholders embrace and engage with the change, the resistors may start to recognize they will be left behind. Allocating role-relevant responsibilities can help to shift this perspective. Another way is to have a resistor work with some of the supporters. Do remember that some of the objections presented by your resistors may well be valid, and how you choose to address these is up to you and your team. Managing resistance is hard – but it cannot be ignored. Demonstrating your awareness of it and working with it may be what is needed for the initial steps forward. The following explains Kübler-Ross' Change Curve (Kübler-Ross and Kessler, 2014) in an organizational context.

Denial

Initial reactions to the announcement of change may be very positive and people are encouraged that 'finally something is happening'. There may be lots of conversations about how good it will be and what a difference it will make. However, often, as the reality of the work begins to sink in, morale begins to fall and there is a reluctance to accept that this will go ahead – after all, 'how many other change initiatives have succeeded?' What will it mean to each of the individuals? How will their working lives change? Will there be redundancies? More work? Greater responsibilities?

This is the first in the stages of coming to accept change – it will take different lengths of time for different individuals and teams. Remember that although some people may appear to work through this stage and others very quickly and easily, they may 'fall back', lose confidence and appear to regress and return to a state of negative attitudes towards the change.

Frustration and anger

When you realize that things will change and you may not have the control you would like, or that the change will not address all the issues you think it should, that's when you know you are in Stage 2 of the change curve. People get to this stage and recognize their lack of ability to influence what has gone before and what looks likely to happen. It's difficult to deal with if you are the change agent, but you need to remember that this is only the start, that change strategies may be influenced (a little) and that they can make a difference. It's worth repeating such a message in many different ways, as well as finding some quick wins to show people you really mean what you are saying

Despair

This point in the reactions to change may lead people into a very depressed state. How long they spend in this negative 'there's no hope/here we go again' phase has no real time frame. For some it's a brief moment – a Monday morning moan that by Tuesday or Wednesday has disappeared – but beware, it can return, or even last quite a long time. As change agent and for your team the answer is to be patient, especially if you know that the individuals concerned are not usually this negative. Keep talking about and promoting the benefits of the change

Validation

At this stage, people start to talk about the need for this change. They show their understanding of what's happening and why. These people can help you as your champions. They may not be fully behind the changes but it will give them quite a lot of credibility with their colleagues that they can still be sceptical but recognize there will be advantages. As a consultant you need these people – their support will be invaluable. They are users, potential testers of the change processes. They will be trusted by colleagues and without much interference from you should bring others with them into the 'beginning to support the change' camp.

Acceptance

When you have those concerned being very open about their support, offering ideas and talking about a new future – then you know that the change is becoming embedded into team/department where you are implementing the change. Do not forget that this is still a fragile state and you, as consultant, need to promote the successes you have and ease the progress forward to maintain the momentum. People can still slip back on the curve – this often happens when there is a delay in the process or an unexpected glitch that holds up the implementation time frame.

However, you have, through following this guide, anticipated such events and do have contingency plans. This is why you need them. This may be an opportunity to celebrate the success achieved to date. Rather than wait for the absolute end of the project, a mid-term party or event to promote successes is well placed at this point.

Growth

Once the differences you wanted to see begin to happen then you can project forward. The difference should be much clearer. Those who have been lagging behind in accepting the change often at this point begin to move faster to catch up. They do not want to be left behind. Remember to support them. Their change journey has not really got going yet.

6.6 Why use the change curve?

The change curve is useful for you as a consultant. You may need to refer to it during the 'where are we now?' and then 'how are we going to get there?' phases. During the change process there will be times when you feel that everyone is negative and the changes will never happen. It is likely that these behaviours and attitudes are mostly evidence of resistance. There are no magic recipes to make these negative feelings go away. Time and the support and encouragement of you and your team of consultants will help. So will presenting the successes – however small.

Support from others to this group of resistors is important too – especially if the sponsor can regularly appear and talk. Hold open 'question and answer' sessions – you will be surprised at the questions. It is often concerns that you find very easy to resolve that are raised. Getting these dealt with raises esteem and demonstrates that the change management team are supporting and supportive. Do not waste these opportunities. Try to list all of the tasks and again review your checklist of your priorities and those of the client.

6.7 Managing resistance to change

Many of us have stories about how change does not work and how people have resisted change initiatives. What are the reasons that cause resistance in the first place? Some of the following reasons may well trigger resistance to change. Have a look and consider in your consultancy plan how you might be proactive and try to make sure that these don't happen in the first place:

- Learning and doing things differently has rarely been encouraged. Training has only been about improving what we do – getting faster and smarter.

- The learning and development sessions programmed to support the change programme are few and there do not seem to be enough places or times for all staff to attend.

- The approach of this project is that there is one way only to manage change. There may have been several change projects, each one claiming to have the magic formula which will provide the key to organizational success. Staff may well be fed up and not believe that this is the case.

- Support for the change project from managers and leaders is hardly mentioned by them when they speak to teams and write in company newsletters. This does not encourage the people who must engage with the change to trust those that have initiated the project.

- The change project will be a shift in terms of behaviours and skills. Perceived challenges to individual skills; the change would mean that an individual's set of skills would no longer be as valuable.

- The company believes in getting it right first time. If staff feel there is and always has been a low tolerance of mistakes and a blame culture, they will concerned about how they will be perceived if they don't get the change right first time.

- Creativity, innovation and being entrepreneurial have never been encouraged strongly in this department/team. Creativity may be considered as chaos and disorganization.

- There is low self-esteem in the team because they have been selected to lead the change. They may feel that the reason for this choice is their poor performance.

- Fear of the unknown.

- Loss or changes in responsibility, perceived status and power.

- Restructuring of departments may mean that although job titles may remain the same, management responsibilities may change, which affect the self-esteem and sense of identity of the individual.

6.8 Tools to help with managing change

This section presents some useful tools in managing the various parts of change.

Tool 1: Force field analysis

You may already be familiar with this tool, so you will know how valuable it can be. Here is a brief version. The force field analysis model was originally developed by Kurt Lewin, and will help you and others who are participating in the change process to recognize and understand the factors that will help drive the change forward and those that will pull it back. Lewin was clear that although there are driving forces as well as some forces that hold you back, removing or restraining all of the resisting forces is not the answer. If you do this, the project will go out of control.

Creating a force field analysis helps to understand how the drivers can be strengthened to progress the change and manage the resistors. As its name indicates there is the image of a magnetic tension between the support and the resistance. Working out what the different forces are and how strong they are can help you to develop your strategy for change. You can do this exercise on your own, but if you work with those colleagues who will be involved in the change, you will get much better answers. For the example here, including members of both teams would really improve the quality of the analysis and help to clarify the concerns each of the teams has. The example in Table 4.6 illustrates the case of merging two teams.

Table 4.6 Driving and resisting forces in change

Driving forces	Resisting forces
Each team works well and very efficiently	Team members don't know each other
Each team carries out very different tasks	People might lose their jobs
Each team at different times has received the company team prize for effective team work	The team members don't know why they have to merge
	One team includes very competitive individuals

Tool 2: SWOT (strengths, weaknesses, opportunities and threats) analysis

Using SWOT is a good model to show your findings or to explain why a change initiative needs to take place. The following is for a project organizing an annual awards ceremony.

Figure 4.3 SWOT analysis

Strengths	Weaknesses
• We have done it before and people expect it. • People like a party and an evening to socialize with other people at work – as well as the Christmas party. • It is a good event to invite customers, key clients and potential clients to.	• Last year and the year before it was not seen as successful. • People might not propose others for the awards. • People might not vote or not many people will vote so the awards don't seem to have a value. • It's a really expensive event for the company.
Opportunities	**Threats**
• The event will raise morale. • We can get it right and create meaning to the awards. • Reward some really hard-working people. • Talk about the next change project.	• People are unlikely to participate because the last two years were not seen as successful. • There may be rumours before the event about what might be announced on the night. • People will talk about the company wasting money on this whilst making job cuts and put it on social media.

Tool 3: John Kotter's 8-stage change model

There are many models that propose a number of steps to manage change. All of them are valuable, but none of them are as easy to implement as they seem. If you decide to work with one, remember that the stages may overlap, and just like with the Kübler-Ross model, you can go backwards as well as forwards. There are many articles you can find online that will explain this model (and others) in a lot of detail. Here we will just give you a brief outline. Each stage of Kotter's model is a set of activities that help to manage the change leading to a new state. Here it is explained as a series of tasks and activities that the consultant would need to carry out.

Stage 1: Create urgency

In this first stage, you will need to create an understanding that change is necessary. This may involve a number of different communication activities for the relevant stakeholder groups, depending on their role and contribution to the change. The more the reasons for the change and for it to take place now are made clear, the more you can expect to have some understanding and support for the process.

Stage 2: Form a powerful coalition

As you present the need for change you will need to identify your supporters. As we discussed in Section 4, the role of the stakeholders is crucial to successful change projects. Here this is emphasized. Gaining support from different groups and identifying which groups will support each other will help to progress the activities leading to the change. The key supporting stakeholders will also help to manage the resistors that we discussed earlier in this section.

Stage 3: Create a vision for change

The more you work with the stakeholders, the clearer the vision for the change will become. As consultant you will work with your client group to create the vision of what the desired future state will be. Your role in this activity will be clearly linked to the consultancy role you are taking. Refer again to Section 2 if you need to. Creating the vision may be a joint activity between you and your client, or it may be in 'expert mode', your views of what the client wants.

Stage 4: Communicate the vision

Being able to talk about what the change will bring and how the differences will add value and benefit will also work to create support and engagement in the change process. As change consultant, your role is to 'sell the change' and the activities which will lead to the new state of affairs. The more you tell people what they can expect, the more likely you are to create conversations about the change. These conversations will lead you to Stage 5.

Stage 5: Remove the obstacles

Through talking to people you will hear their views and opinions about the change – some will be supportive and some not. This is where it would be very useful to work on a force field or a SWOT analysis. With the either of these tools you will be able to have a clear and agreed list of views and opinions you can work from. You will have a good idea of what will create support and what you need to work on.

Stage 6: Create short-term wins

Using the results of your force field or SWOT analysis, you will easily identify quick wins. These will be useful to show progress and to create a sense of success. This will help you as consultant to progress the change activities further.

Stage 7: Build on the change

Ensure that you keep up the momentum by keeping track of the schedule in the project plan and making sure that all the other initiatives are maintained. Publicize the news of short-term wins to reinforce the positives of the change and to alleviate fears and concerns about the change.

Stage 8: Find ways to make the change stick

Every success that you create is a step forward and should help you to advance. These steps remind you that the change has to work and people have to know about the successes. Find ways to celebrate the successes even if they seem to be small ones to you. The more people know that the change process is working, the more they will support the process and this helps to embed the change in the culture.

Exercise

Examine Tools 1 to 3. Identify what their advantages are and how they may be used with one another in different parts of a consulting project that involves dealing with change.

Tool 4: Your change management checklist

Here is a checklist to remind you of the different things you should take into consideration as you work through your consultancy project:

1 Remember change is about people. It does not matter what your consultancy project is, whether supporting a department in creating new ways of working, developing a new recruitment strategy or learning how to use social media, you as the consultant are working with people. It sounds obvious, but as you get involved in the change processes, sometimes consulting with the people who are involved or who will be involved gets forgotten, or is only give lip service. If this happens, you will have a lot of resistance to deal with. Take time to talk to people and address their concerns. It will help to smooth the path of the change.

2 Gain senior management support. Once you have the support for the change process from senior managers, you will need to ensure that they support you and you can show their support to other members of the organization. Their endorsement of the project will help to open doors and to give you, as consultant, access to the people you need to speak to. Make sure that whenever possible you have a member of the senior management team at your meetings or a paragraph of support in your newsletter.

3 Change affects all of the organization. Whatever the size of your consultancy project, it will have an impact across the organization. As you promote your project and gain support from your stakeholders, remember to talk to other people in the company so that they know what is going on. In this way you will find out the ways in which your project links to other activities and you can make sure it will work effectively and smoothly.

4 Have a clear vision of the change. As it states in Stage 3 of the Kotter model, you need to be able to tell the story of what the change is, why it is necessary and what difference it will make. The vision, as has been said earlier, needs to be created with (as far as possible) the involvement of your client and any other senior managers who will engage. The more you have an agreed vision that is owned by a number of different people, the easier it will be to gain an understanding and an acceptance of the need for a new state of affairs.

5 Keep your clients involved. Although you are engaged as the consultant to manage the change process, you need to have the involvement of your key clients all the way through the project. This links to the first point on the checklist. Your key clients have asked for you to do the work.

They need to be informed and involved in the progress and process. It may sometimes be hard to have meetings and obtain the responses you need but it is vital you work with them. This support will contribute to making the changes progress and stick as Kotter's Stages 7 and 8 propose.

6 **Communicate, communicate, communicate.** You cannot talk to and inform people enough when you are managing change. Remember that communication is a two-way activity and people need to be able to talk to you too. Make sure you are available, and that you respond to phone messages and e-mails in a timely manner. This will give you credibility and will help to manage resistance.

7 **Understand and work with the culture of the organization.** Different parts of the company will have different cultures or ways of working. You will need to be sensitive to this as you create the processes of change. How people work in the information systems department may well be very different to those in human resources. If you are bringing people together to create a new system, you will have to be aware of how they work and think about what you might do to create ways of working that will be acceptable to all.

8 **Remember to think about risk.** It is very important to create and maintain a risk register. The more you consider what might go wrong and consider the implications in advance, the better prepared you will be.

9 **Review your change plan regularly.** It is important to have a plan of action with dates and activities that you know need to take place. However, as time moves on and the project progresses, the situation can change. Take time to review and reflect on your progress. Some activities may no longer be necessary, others may be more urgent than you had originally thought.

10 **Look after yourself.** As consultant, the responsibility for the change project can be a heavy one. As you start the project, find a mentor or person who you can talk to and will listen to you from an independent perspective. You may feel very confident with your role and your work, but it is useful to be able to 'check in' with someone and take some time to stand back and review.

You should now feel able to use the tools and techniques presented in this section. You should also be able to recognize and understand resistance to change, why it is there and what you can do to manage it. In the next section we will consider how to exit your consultancy project, evaluate and review the activities and move onto the next one.

7 Ending a consultancy project

This section discusses how to end a consultancy project. By the end of this section you will be able to understand the importance of defining and agreeing the end of a consultancy project, review it, ensure success criteria have been met, and identify whether follow-up work is required. It is always helpful to take the time to end a project, either through an evaluation and feedback event or by presenting a summary overview of achievements and next steps for others to take forward. This will leave you free to take on other work and to start from a 'clean sheet of paper'. This is helpful given the different 'hats' or roles that an L&D professional may take, as they are most likely to be an internal consultant.

Why evaluate a project? Although the delivery of the final report (and, if you are an external consultant, submitting your final invoice) is considered as the closing of the project, it is useful to conduct a final and formal evaluation of the whole project with the client and key stakeholders. Such an activity, which may take an hour, half a day or longer, is useful to demonstrate and give evidence in support of:

- the project successes and outcomes;
- the ways in which resources – people and their time – have been well used;
- the ways the challenges have been overcome;
- what has been learnt from the consultancy and what further learning needs to take place; and
- to give the consultant feedback that could be used as recommendations for future projects.

Who gives feedback? The client may decide who needs to contribute to the feedback session. Alternatively, as consultant you may wish to suggest that a selection of project participants and stakeholders contribute to such an event.

We have already mentioned the need to welcome feedback on a regular basis in Sections 2 and 4, hence this signifies an effective start in managing the evaluation process. Any evaluation starts with the definition and the agreed success criteria for a change. When you were scoping the project/consultancy assignment, you will have listed the desired outcomes. The outcomes can be summarized as: what will be different as a result of the consultancy and, importantly, what will be defined as success?

Some of the points on the list below will be more relevant than others, depending on your project, but this is a useful checklist to start with. Depending on the project, you will need to adapt or consider these topics. Two example questions are given for each topic, showing different approaches to gaining feedback to evaluate a particular aspect of the change process.

Supporting the business case:

- Has the change programme supported the initial business case?
- Has senior management support for the business case for change been maintained throughout the project?

Stakeholder communication:

- Have all relevant stakeholders given the project the support it needed?
- Have all the stakeholders been satisfied with the information and communication they have received about the change initiative?

Addressing concerns and reluctance to change:

- Was everyone involved able to talk to a member of the project team about the personal impact of the change?
- Did the change team address the different concerns of those affected by the change in a timely and appropriate manner?

People and processes:

- What were the staff reactions to the change processes?
- Do all of the people who are directly affected by the change understand how they contribute to the change?

Skills and behaviours:

- Have the training sessions to achieve the desired changes to skills and behaviours been well attended and received positive feedback?
- Are people clearly demonstrating the desired behaviours and attitudes? How do you know?

Ways of working and culture:

- Were new ways of working explained and debated during the change process?
- Were people made aware in advance of the proposed changes and how they might impact ways of working?
- Were action plans, progress and goals clearly communicated and shared?

Clear messages that everyone understands:

- Do you agree that wherever you go in the company and/or whoever you speak to is aware of the reasons for the change?
- Can everyone who is affected by the change tell the story of why it has happened and its outcomes/outputs?

Consultancy reports and 'deliverables'

Depending on the length and nature of the project, you may be required to provide interim reports – either verbal or written. Make sure you are clear with your client at the beginning of the project about what their needs are, the frequency of the required reports, and their format and length. There may be a 'house style' for you to follow. Interim reports, although seemingly time consuming, are good ways to manage the feedback process and ensure that the final closing down sessions do not include any surprises.

Providing the final report

Your client may well want to read the report before it is published or distributed and you may need to provide several versions depending on the audience. For example, there may be one report available to the general public and one for internal distribution and/or to investors. Do not forget to include helpful resources and follow-up services that you, your department or company could provide to the client, as well as your contact details such as website, e-mail and/or phone number.

Facilitating feedback

As an L&D professional, you will be familiar with several feedback tools and with different approaches to giving and receiving feedback. The success of your consultancy project may be perceived in different ways by individuals and groups depending on their involvement. It is important to include all views to give a realistic overview of the whole activity. Whatever approach to feedback you select, it should always be framed constructively. For example, a very quick tool can be asking for contributions, as in Table 4.7.

Table 4.7 Feedback at the end of a project

What went well?	What could we do differently next time?
The project team understood our problem and requirements.	The project team could be more flexible in the project plan and in the scope of the project.

Bringing the consultancy to an early close

There are times when you may wish to step away from the consultancy or change project. As an external consultant this is easier than if you are an internal consultant. However, neither role is easy to manage in these circumstances. Consider the following situations: what would you do?

- *Situation 1.* Your client has become more and more difficult to meet face to face, and sends you e-mail messages that strongly direct you to adopt the recommendations that they are suggesting.

- *Situation 2.* Whatever you suggest to key stakeholders in the consultancy as ways forward, they immediately propose challenges or barriers which, they say, are impossible to surmount.

- *Situation 3.* It has been announced in the press that the company you are working with has been engaged in activities that you find unacceptable and unethical.

- *Situation 4.* The company or your client is not providing you with the data/information access or the resources (time or people) that you have been promised.

It is worth discussing these and similar situations with colleagues who are also consultants – even if they are not working on the same projects as you. There is always more than one choice in terms of managing such challenges. The more often you work in a consultancy mode, the more you see. Before you make the decision to walk away from a consultancy project, consider some of these options:

- Having a face-to-face, one-to-one meeting with the client to tell them about your serious concerns.

- Bringing in a new and independent colleague to support and work with you in the project.
- Informing the client there will be a two to three week break to let the situation cool down – you could take a holiday or time out to reflect and review, with no contact at all during that period.
- Reviewing the change strategy to consider different avenues to achieve the desired change.
- Reviewing your consultancy style to become either more structured or more process focused – depending on your original starting point.

It is important that project successes are celebrated. The amount of time, effort and resources that a change project takes are always more than has been planned. As a consultant, you will no doubt have given more time than you had anticipated and your project team and clients will no doubt feel the same. An event, whether coffee and croissants or a meal in a restaurant to celebrate the project for all involved, is positive and affirmative, providing an opportunity to thank all involved and reiterate the achievements. The best outcome from any consultancy project is the feedback after at least six months that the changes you have proposed or implemented are making a difference. As a consultant, don't forget to ask for it! You may then receive an invitation to return for further work or indeed be recommended to other clients.

This chapter has introduced you to the consultancy process and to the role of consultant to help you understand what consultants do and to identify and develop consultancy skills. It has also given you the tools and understanding to be aware of the distinctions between consultancy and L&D. We have explored why consultancy takes place and how a thorough understanding of the company's context will support the business case for a change initiative. We have defined different ways of 'doing consultancy' and how that relates to the ways in which you carry out your consultancy role.

Through a detailed stakeholder analysis, you should now be able to create a clear change communication strategy and focus your attention on the relationship management of key stakeholders. We have demonstrated the importance of scoping a project to ensure it is managed effectively, and we have explored ways of managing resistance to change and addressing the challenges that arise when people don't seem to be supporting the new ways of working. We have also shown the value in project evaluation and the celebration of success, both for the client and for you as a consultant. You should now feel able to clearly explain and define what is meant by consultancy and to design and deliver a change management project.

As you may have noticed, consultants need to have specialist knowledge, but also broad skills sets. In addition, consultants may face very different situations/problems in every project. Flavio Vong, an experienced management consultant, shared his views on how consultants develop themselves.

Flavio Vong, manager, enterprise services, Commonwealth Bank of Australia (formerly a manager in one of the big four auditing and consulting firms)

Consultants (including L&D professionals who play the role as consultants) are there to help their clients to 'solve business problems', and usually find themselves dealing with a number of diverse issues. Whilst there are 'typical' problems that organizations face, there will almost be always some nuance to every issue. Therefore, it is important that consultants are able to learn effectively and quickly so that they can think on their feet and swiftly make sense of things (eg in unfamiliar and/or ambiguous situations).

Other than developing the basic skills in facilitation, stakeholder analysis and so on, as well as advancing expert knowledge in their chosen specialism (ie L&D), there are no strict prescriptions in terms of how consultants should then further develop themselves. Consultants do not have pre-defined or rigid developmental paths as some professions do (although L&D professionals do in some sense, but this is aligned with the overall HR profession). The competencies of some 'traditional' professions such as engineers or solicitors are evident, but it is not the same for consultants. For example, when I say to people that 'I am a consultant', I can tell from their facial expression that they are probably thinking, 'what does that mean?'. Consultants have to determine their own pathways. A consultant's worth is hinged on the value they can articulate and demonstrate to their clients, and this is what gets you as a consultant 'hired' (or, in the case of internal consultants such as L&D, makes you a 'trusted advisor').

I think the most important aspect of developing oneself in the role of a consultant is to be an autonomous and self-directed learner (reflective learning, discussed in Chapter 1, helps to develop autonomous learning). L&D professionals need to identify for themselves what is relevant to them, what they want to achieve down the track, and the capabilities and skills

▶

they need to gain to attain goals that they have identified for themselves. For example, I felt that gaining international experience was crucial to my own development, and so that is when I decided to do my MBA in Beijing (Flavio shares his experience in Beijing in Chapter 8). A self-directed learner seeks out their own L&D resources that provide the knowledge and insights they require. They also need to find their own mentors and even solicit coaching from others. Those in consultant roles need to shape their own personal L&D strategy. This is especially important in consulting, as you need to be constantly selling yourself either directly (knowledge on cutting-edge solutions) or indirectly (by doing a great job and gaining the confidence of your clients).

I believe informal learning is one of the most effective ways for consultants to learn (after they have gained the necessary knowledge and skills through formal education and training). I find that most of the advanced skills and capabilities that I have developed in consulting have been learned and developed whilst on the job. I find that when I learn informally and on the job, the information and knowledge I gain 'sinks in' best, especially when I am able to immediately apply it to my job. I think this is quite typical of adult learners, who learn best from doing and when they need to (on demand and when it can be applied to address an immediate issue they are facing). Learning informally from others can be from a supervisor, a mentor or a colleague, or even research on the internet. I think a 'learning environment' that provides access and enables me to link to the right people and sources may be more helpful than actual learning courses. I think informal learning plays a greater role as you become more senior in a consultant role, as a hands-on, experiential approach grows to be even more important.

Of course, there is a role for formal learning programmes, which provide the cornerstone for those new in the consulting role. When I first joined the firm, there were a number of core courses that new consultants had to attend over a period of time (milestone courses) and most of these were classroom based, which I found very beneficial as a junior. The L&D programmes were very structured to ensure the new consultants received all the necessary training within a time period and that each of the milestones were attained before they moved on to the next. At a more senior level, I think classroom learning is helpful as a form of reinforcement and in providing a framework around what has learned on the job ('bringing it altogether').

8 Points for reflection

In understanding the roles of consultants and what they do, address the following questions:

- What are the differences between approaches and activities for consultants who work in the:
  - expert mode;
  - doctor/patient mode;
  - process consultant mode?
- What are the differences in project outcomes for each of these modes?
- What are the key points to consider when creating a stakeholder communication strategy?

In identifying and developing consultancy skills, address the following questions:

- What are the different stages of a consultancy project?
- What happens at each stage?
- How can you identify resistance to change?
- How can you manage resistance?
- Why is monitoring and evaluating a project on an ongoing basis important?

References

Alvesson, M and Johansson, A W (2002) Professionalism and politics in management consultancy work, in *Critical Consulting: New perspectives on the management advice industry*, ed T Clark and R Fincham, Blackwell, Oxford

Ballock, C (2004) Thought leadership: making sense of what consultants do, in *The Advice Business: Essential tools and models for management consulting*, ed C J Fombrun and M D Nevins, Pearson Prentice Hall, New Jersey

Biggs, D (2010) *Management Consulting: A guide for students*, South-Western Cengage Learning, Hampshire

Block, P (2011) *Flawless Consulting: A guide to getting your expertise used*, 3rd edn, Pfeiffer, San Francisco, CA

Cope, M (2003) *The seven Cs of Consulting: The definitive guide to the consulting process*, FT Prentice Hall, King's Lynn, Norfolk

Czerniawska, F and May, P (2004) *Management Consulting in Practice: Award-winning international case studies*, Kogan Page, London

Fagley, N S, Coleman, J G and Simon, A F (2010) Effects of framing, perspective taking, and perspective (affective focus) on choice, *Personality and Individual Differences*, **48** (3), pp. 264–69

Fincham, R (2002) Charisma versus technique: differentiating the expertise of management gurus and management consultants, in *Critical Consulting: New perspectives on the management advice industry*, ed T Clark and R Fincham, Blackwell, Oxford

Heller, F (2002) What next? More critique of consultants, gurus and managers, in *Critical Consulting: New perspectives on the management advice industry*, ed T Clark and R Fincham, Blackwell, Oxford

Institute of Management Consultants USA (2005) The common body of knowledge, *IMC USA* [online] http://www.imcusa.org/page/IMCBOK/IMC-USA-Common-Body-of-Knowledge.htm

International Council of Management Consulting Institutes (2003) Competency framework [online] *http://www.icmci.org/?page=6972393*

Jackson, B (2002) A fantasy theme analysis of three guru-led management fashions, in *Critical Consulting: New perspectives on the management advice industry*, ed T Clark and R Fincham, Blackwell, Oxford

Kübler-Ross, E and Kessler, D (2014) *On Grief and Grieving: Finding the meaning of grief through the five stages of loss*, Simon and Schuster

Maister, D H, Green, C H and Galford, R M (2000) *The Trusted Advisor*, Simon and Schuster, New York

Markham, C (1999) *Practical Management Consultancy*, 3rd edn, The Institute of Chartered Accountants in England and Wales, Glasgow

Nash, S A (2003) *Be a Successful Consultant: An insider guide to setting up and running a consultancy practice*, How To Books, Oxford

Newton, R (2010) *Management Consultant: Mastering the art of consultancy*, Financial Times, UK

Schein, E H (1990) A general philosophy of helping: process consultation, *Sloan Management Review*, **31** (3), pp. 57–64

Sturdy, A and Wright, C (2011) The active client: the boundary-spanning roles of internal consultants as gatekeepers, brokers and partners of their external counterparts, *Management Learning*, **42** (5), pp. 485–503

Toppin, G and Czerniawska, F (2005) *Business Consulting: A guide to how it works and how to make it work*, Profile Books, London

Wickham, P A (2004) *Management Consulting: Delivering an effective project*, 2nd edn, FT Prentice Hall, Harlow, Essex

Wood, P (2002) The rise of consultancy and the prospect for regions, in *Critical Consulting: New perspectives on the management advice industry*, ed T Clark and R Fincham, Blackwell, Oxford

Wright, C (2008) Inside out? Organizational membership, ambiguity and the ambivalent identity of the internal consultant, *British Journal of Management*, **30** (3), pp. 309–22

Enhancing participant engagement in the learning process

05

JAN MYERS

1 Introduction

The purpose of this chapter is to consider the underlying approaches to learning that underpin and enhance active participation and engagement in the learning process. It is becoming more recognized, particularly in work organizations as well as in training and education institutions, that processes of collaborative learning, active learning, and co-design of learning processes can not only increase interest and engagement levels, support critical thinking skills and creativity, but also link to transferability and sustainability of learning. Active learning strategies that encourage greater partnership between learners create a dynamic learning environment that can promote and 'encourage critical reflection between theoretical aspects of learning and the praxis of everyday life' (Cato and Myers, 2010, p. 51). This approach acknowledges the interconnection between doing, thinking, reflection, feeling and knowing and links with the concepts of social learning (further discussed in Chapter 7), situated learning, and blended approaches to enhancing teaching and learning (Chapter 6). It will also provide support for recognizing the importance of context in learning and development (Chapters 2 and 8). The key objectives of this chapter are to provide an overview of literature and practice to help you to:

1 Understand how people learn and the different perspectives on learning.

2 Be able to enhance engagement in the learning process.

In order to start to understand and explore how people learn, the chapter commences with an overview of learning theory, focusing particularly on experiential and active learning, and exploring concepts of formal, informal, and incidental learning. This discussion, together with those in Chapter 6 and 7, will support an appreciation of the different perspectives on learning. We need an appreciation of theory and its application to practice to start to consider ways in which we can enhance engagement in a variety of learning processes. The chapter then focuses on strategies, processes and tools that move beyond classroom-based approaches to include experiential learning, practice-based learning and work-based learning, drawing on case examples and research stories. Finally, we consider the links between individual, team and organizational learning.

2 Individual orientations to learning

We know that individuals differ in their motives for and preferred ways of learning. A simple perspective on individual orientation to learning and performance can be seen in the continuum between purely transactional approaches to programmed learning and more holistic and intrinsic aspects of self-development and personal accomplishment. The former focuses on gaining credentials, awards, and results. This may result in what is sometimes referred to as surface learning (Biggs, 1987; Biggs, 1999; Kember, Biggs and Leung, 2004; Marton and Säljö, 1976) where individuals focus on balancing the amount of effort with the need to 'pass' or succeed to a satisfactory level – a just-in-time, or just-enough strategy that can often be accompanied by fear of failure, rote learning, focus on assessments requirements, and/or a lack of critical reflection. Where the instrumental focus is on gaining the highest grades or level of achievement and performance, this is often referred to as surface achievement learning.

At the other end of the continuum, deep learning refers to the depth of learning and effort required to engage with and understand the materials, critically assess and reflect on new and previous knowledge, and achieve a relative immersion in the subject. Deep learning can also be associated with a need for achievement; deep achievement learning is about finding the balance between depth and performance. Figure 5.1 illustrates the characteristics and relationships amongst surface, deep, and achievement learning.

Figure 5.1 A learning continuum

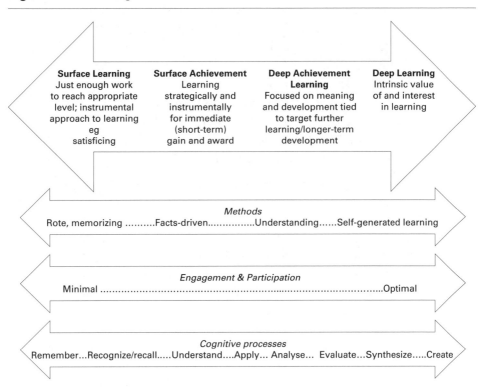

So, the focus of learning can range from the acquisition of skills for job performance or to gain immediate results (surface learning) to learning and development for self and future development (deep learning) and safeguarding of competence (strategic and achievement learning). What is important to remember here is that this typology of learning relates to the learning processes employed rather than to the individual learner. As learners, we may employ one or a combination of learning strategies depending on the situation, context, and our perception of the task/intended output, but in order to obtain optimal results, we need to be aware of our own learning processes – a process referred to as meta-learning. We can also associate different cognitive capabilities (Anderson and Krathwohl, 2001; Krathwohl, 2002) with different levels, which we might link to learning outcomes – for example the ability to identify, interpret, differentiate, critique – all of which signify different levels of learning.

Stop and think. Consider the statement below from a student in their first year of studies. Identify the different elements of surface and deep approaches to learning.

> *On a topic in economics that I do not like I would try to do the absolute minimum possible, whereas for something such as Keynesian economics, which I found reasonably interesting, within the time I set aside for the work, I'd do that [work], whereas for the other one I'd try to find ways around it. Rather than read textbooks and try to understand them I would read textbooks and try to find the bit with the answer and I'd copy it out or paraphrase it or whatever. Whereas if it was something that I like, I'd take a little time to think about it and try to understand it a bit. I'm not very good at doing things I don't like.*
>
> (Oxford Institute for the Advancement of University Learning, nd, pp. 7–8)

Reflect on your own experiences of being a learner and the learning strategies you employed. Can you identify elements of surface learning, deep learning, and or achievement strategies? Jot down the situations in which you used one or more and the results of those approaches. What affected your approach to learning (eg liking for the topic, workload or home-life pressures, previous experience)? Think about when you might have used a different approach more effectively than the one chosen (consciously or unconsciously).

This way of looking at learning is useful because it helps us to think about learners and the learning environment or climate. It connects learning as a variety of processes that we engage with to learning as an outcome of those processes. In turn, this supports thinking around design and development of learning interventions. High levels of participation in learning processes would require a shift towards deep levels of engagement with both content and processes. Learning, however, is a complex concept and it is necessary to look at other approaches that will enable a deeper consideration of the topic. Before doing so, we need to consider other aspects that impact on individual orientations and motivation to learn.

3 Theory and practice of motivation

An additional typology that considers individual orientations to learning is provided by Houle (1981), as cited by Knowles (1990). In his study of adults who engage in continuing education, he suggests three categories similar to the ones discussed above: goal-oriented learners, whose approach may be episodic (eg intermittent) and based on attaining a specific objective; activity-oriented learners, who use the experience of learning for social contact; and individuals who are learning oriented – who engage in learning for its own sake. While an instrumental approach to learning, as described above, may be prompted by a fear of failure, it also links with our desire to succeed or our need for achievement (McClelland, 1976). We can also start to recognize two dimensions of motivation: extrinsic, through awards and external recognition of achievement, and intrinsic, associated more with enthusiasm for and joy of learning, and the pleasure of knowing and performing.

For McClelland, individuals with a high need for achievement appear to be more concerned with personal achievement than with rewards. Even so, such individuals require and seek out feedback about their performance in order to adjust, learn and improve. In this way, McClelland considers achievement motivation as something that can be developed and therefore supported. If as individuals, we believe that with the appropriate resources and support we can reach our own (and organizational) goals, then our motivation to achieve becomes heightened. If as managers or learning and development professionals, we then provide an environment that both encourages and stretches and provides valued feedback and satisfaction (either through intrinsic or extrinsic input), we create a positive association

Figure 5.2 Learning and expectancy theory (adapted from Vroom, 1964)

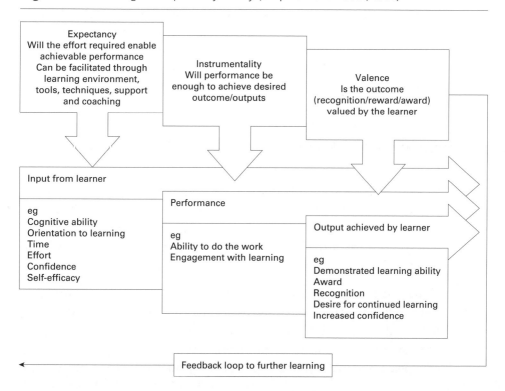

between effort, performance and 'reward'. This fits with the process theory of motivation promoted by Victor Vroom's (1964) expectancy theory.

Vroom's expectancy theory differs from content theories of motivation such as Maslow (1970), Alderfer (1972) and McClelland (1985), in that it 'provides a process of cognitive variables that reflect individual difference' (Lunenburg, 2011, p. 1). In other words, it does not prescribe motivational factors (food, hunger, and safety needs for example), but considers the beliefs and choices that people make in order to undertake a task. It also means that learning and development professionals and managers can intervene at certain points of the process to alter/enhance/support an individual's effort-to-performance expectancy, performance-to-reward expectancy, and the value they place on rewards. We also need to be mindful in some instances that extrinsic motivators can negatively affect intrinsic motivation, eg performance-based monetary rewards (Rock and Cox, 2012).

Stop and think. Think about a time when you have had to undertake a new or difficult task for the first time. What kinds of resources and support do you feel helped you or would have helped you to successfully complete your task? If you can, think about what motivated you when the going got tough and you were faced with obstacles. What personal skills and strengths were you able to draw on?

What we need to consider as managers and learning professionals is how we manage individuals' expectations about their needs, motivations and performance. We also need to consider individuals' past experiences. What are the triggers that might hinder a person's capacity or willingness to engage in learning? Further, successfully accomplishing a task raises self-esteem, it may impact on our sense of calculated risk and certainty of achieving other (related) tasks, and can increase our sense of autonomy, which in turn has a multiplying effect on engagement (Amabile and Kramer, 2010).

Stop and think. Think about these phrases: 'you can't teach an old dog new tricks', 'you're never too old to learn' – what images do they conjure up for you? Which might encourage you to learn? What might be obstacles for you? Can you list other things that might hinder a person's willingness to engage in learning – past experience for example? How might these obstacles be overcome?

If motivation is an internal state, and we know that motivation can be enhanced or decreased according to personal drive and internal and external factors, then managers and learning professionals need to consider how to create an environment that is conducive to learning – a positive learning environment. Herzberg's two-factor theory is often referred to as a content motivational theory, and refers to factors that can influence attitude to work/jobs, namely satisfaction and dissatisfaction. Herzberg (1966) named these hygiene factors and motivators. Drawn from the experience of engineers and accountants, the factors relate to needs (similar to those of Maslow) together with growth and achievement. From his studies, Herzberg concluded that motivators were the prime cause of satisfaction, and hygiene factors the primary cause of unhappiness on the job. While intuitively useful to consider aspects of job design, we might also think about the two factors in relation to developing a learning climate within our organizations, as well as in designing specific learning interventions.

Figure 5.3 Herzberg's Two Factors

Factors that prevent satisfaction (Hygiene factors)	Factors that promote satisfaction (Satisfiers, or motivators)
– Learning environment – Tools – Resources – Administration – Policy, procedures – Relationship with fellow learners	– The learning itself – Sense of achievement – Recognition – Advancement – Growth & development

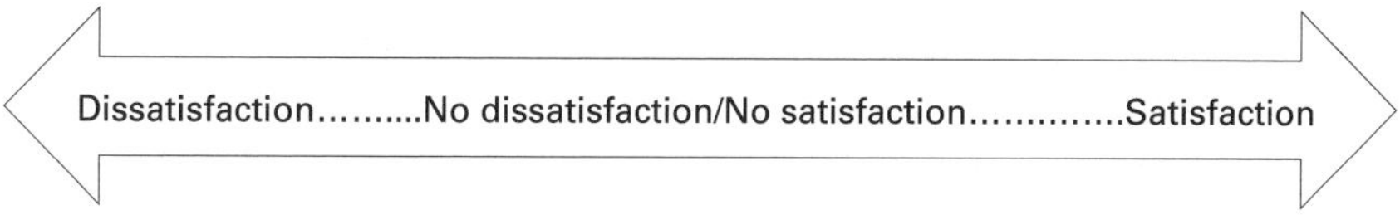

Dissatisfaction..........No dissatisfaction/No satisfaction..............Satisfaction

Our motivation can also be influenced by what we see going on around us in our organizations. We make judgements about ourselves based on our comparisons with others. Concepts of fairness affect our emotional and cognitive commitment to our work. The SCARF model (Rock and Cox, 2012) stands for status, certainty, autonomy, relatedness and fairness. Rock and Cox suggest that the SCARF model has the potential to help individuals to understand, adapt and change their behaviours and therefore become more adept in different situations, with heightened self-awareness and self-efficacy (Bandura, 1971). If we think back to the discussion on surface learning and how to break through some of the obstacles to learning, the model addresses 'social threats' to learning, such as fear of looking bad and potential failure. The model includes emphasis on social rewards – such as acknowledgement for a job well done, or a growing reputation with others for particular aspects of our work – which act as status-confirming triggers, and support learning and change.

People differ in their tolerance of ambiguity and the need for certainty. As Rock and Cox (2012), suggest, ambiguous situations 'can cause a large amount of stress, especially if someone is worried about being negatively evaluated' (p. 5) and can therefore act as a barrier to learning and change. Autonomy, as seen earlier, links to our locus of control and sense of esteem. It is associated with a sense of agency in that we have choice and determination over our actions and behaviours, all of which support engagement and performance and reported higher levels of satisfaction.

Rock and Cox (2012) also recognize the importance, as in other motivation theory models, of relatedness such as the need for affiliation (McClelland, 1976). Being part of group or community of practice supports trust building. Fostering increased social contact across teams and groups can support intergroup relatedness and knowledge and information sharing. Consider how we build this into different learning environments (particularly in virtual learning spaces), as this is important in developing participation and engagement.

Mini Case 5.1: **The singing accountant**

Imagine a group of accountants at a professional branch meeting. They are there to network and to gain input into their continued professional development. The facilitator for the part of the evening asks them to identify their comfort with singing in public. Next, they are asked to line up along the wall and position themselves in relation to their levels of confidence and comfort – those at the far end of the room are the least comfortable; the ones nearest the front of the room are most comfortable. According to stereotype, most walk to the far end of the room and find solidarity and comfort in being one in a crowd.

The facilitator then begins to discuss the idea of creating a choir in 30 minutes. He invites them to try out a simple bassline melody. This seems to work well. If they feel comfortable with that, he tells them, they can try out another line that builds on top of the bassline. They do not have to do anything they feel uncomfortable with and can stay with the bassline if they choose. Given the choice and the reassurance, most choose to continue. They continue building until 30 minutes later they have a four-part harmony and have sung in public. The level of energy in the room is high and one person admits to feeling 'Exhilarated!'.

- What are the key learning stages that you might identify in this example?
- How were the confidence and capacity to perform built by the facilitator?
- How might this impact on other aspects of the accountants' learning?

4 Influences of positive psychology

Recent thinking around individual motivation and engagement has been influenced by the growth of interest in positive psychology and neuropsychology. Much of the language associated with positive psychology is about thriving, flourishing, flow, mindfulness, well-being, authenticity, resilience, and 'valued subjective experience' (Seligman and Csikzentmihalyi, 2000, p. 5), which in many respects resonates with the aims and objectives of engaged learning practice. Despite early critiques, many of the messages have become part of leadership development practice.

There is still, as Luthans (2002) suggests, a need to understand and differentiate between this and what he refers to as 'surface positivity' (p. 695). Drawing on the research and theory offered through the organizational behaviour discipline, he defines micro-level positive organizational behaviour as 'the study and application of positively oriented human strengths and psychological capacities that can be measured, developed, and effectively managed for improvement of performance in today's workplace (p. 699). In both positive psychology literature and in Luthans' work, there is an emphasis on starting from strengths.

This is also echoed by the work of Cooperrider and Srivastva (1987) in their approach to appreciative enquiry, which was developed as part of a change-oriented approach to organizational development. Even so, some of the underlying principles are useful in considering approaches to enhancing participation and engagement in learning and development. For example, instead of focusing on problems, appreciative inquiry starts with the positive aspects of what is and moves onto the possibilities and probabilities of what could be, with an underlying assumption that what is focused on will happen. Citing Ashford and Patkar (2001), Cooperrider, Whitney and Stavros (2003) suggest that individuals and organizations that improve their learning more effectively learn through the process of discovery and valuing, envisioning, having dialogue and co-constructing the future, which is the 'art of the possible' that appreciative inquiry entails (p. 4). We can think of this process, as illustrated in Figure 5.4, in a similar way to the learning and reflective cycles (discussed later). In addition, while it may be discussed at an organizational level, it can also be reframed to help us think about personal and inter-personal relationships and collaboration.

Figure 5.4 The 4D cycle of appreciative enquiry (adapted from Cooperrider, Whitney and Stavros, 2003)

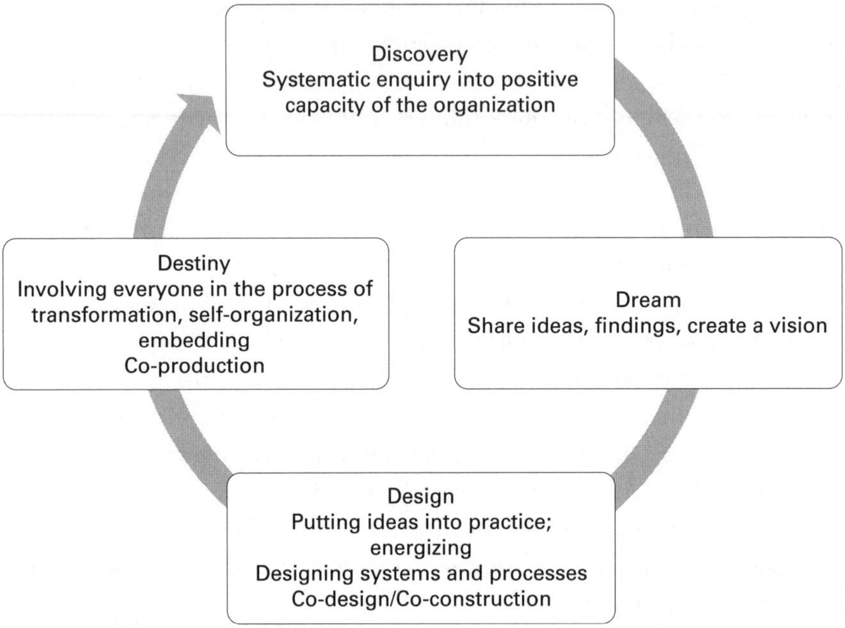

```
                    Discovery
            Systematic enquiry into positive
              capacity of the organization


   Destiny
Involving everyone in the process of
transformation, self-organization,              Dream
           embedding              Share ideas, findings, create a vision
         Co-production


                     Design
             Putting ideas into practice;
                   energizing
            Designing systems and processes
               Co-design/Co-construction
```

Mini case 5.2: Learning in action – citizen leaders programme (sources: Appreciative Inquiry Commons, Imagine Chicago website)

This case will describe how Imagine Chicago applied appreciative inquiry in a community setting to increase civic engagement and help community residents articulate and organize their visions and actions into positive community change.

Imagine Chicago is a non-profit organization, created in 1992. In that year, founder Bliss Browne dedicated nine months to learning Chicago's history and listening to people's concerns and hopes about what might constitute an effective visioning and community regeneration process in Chicago. She visited other cities with emerging citywide initiatives, including Atlanta and Pittsburgh. In 1991, she had begun to question how to stimulate civic imagination on behalf of Chicago's future. She convened a group of 65 experienced community builders actively engaged in civic, corporate, religious, and neighbourhood activities in Chicago for a two-day conference. The highlight of the conference turned out to be an exercise in which people were challenged to imagine visions of Chicago's future considered being ultimately worthy of human commitment, and to identify what would be necessary for those dreams to become reality. In September 1992, 20 of them – educators, corporate and media executives, philanthropists, community organizers, youth developers, economists, religious leaders, social service providers – were convened as a design team for the project, which Browne had already initially conceptualized as 'Imagine Chicago'. The MacArthur Foundation supported Browne in pursuing the work of designing the project's first phase, testing the project's viability, and getting the project organized and institutionalized.

From September 1992 to May 1993, the design team created a process of civic inquiry as the starting point for engaging the city of Chicago in a broad-based conversation about its future. It was hoped from the outset that positive intergenerational civic conversation could provide a bridge between the experience and wisdom of seasoned community builders, and the energy and commitment of youth searching for purpose, yielding deeper insights into the collective future of the community.

Two types of pilot were designed and implemented in 1993–1994: a citywide 'appreciative inquiry' process to gather Chicago stories and commitments, and a series of community-based and led processes. In each case, the intent was to give young adults and community builders in Chicago opportunities to share their hopes and commitments in a setting of mutual respect. The process was designed to use intergenerational teams, led by a young person in the company of an adult mentor, to interview business, civic, and cultural leaders about the future of their communities and of Chicago, using a process of appreciative inquiry.

Interviews were conducted between the summer of 1993 and the spring of 1994. The citywide interview process involved approximately 50 young people who interviewed about 140 Chicago citizens who were recognized by members of Imagine Chicago's design team as 'Chicago glue'. These included artists, media executives, civic and grassroots leaders, politicians, business and professional leaders, and other young people. The interviewees represented over half of Chicago's neighbourhoods.

In the citywide pilot, it became clear that appreciative conversations help broaden the participants' view of what is possible, both within themselves and within the city. In late 1994, a formal evaluation gathered feedback on the effects of Imagine Chicago's appreciative inquiry process on those involved. Interviews and focus groups were conducted in November 1994, with participants from the citywide interview process as well as from

▶

the least extensive community-based pilot. Imagine Chicago's board of directors also did its own evaluation. The board noted two distinct levels of impact: visible outcomes and products (concrete), and 'subterranean' outcomes (less measurable but perhaps more significant). In both tangible and subtle ways, Imagine Chicago has inspired hope and a sense of commitment and dedication to a greater Chicago community.

During 1995, Imagine Chicago continued to work in partnership with local organizations to design and test ways to engage Chicago youth in civic projects that challenge their imaginations, enrich their communities, and build their confidence in a viable future. But Imagine Chicago learned that the appreciative intergenerational interview process would be more effective if it happened within structures that could move more readily to action.

Ten years on, Imagine Chicago has designed its subsequent initiatives to give participants a chance to be city creators in more concrete and sustained ways and move from dialogue to action. That involves working with individuals who are embedded within institutions (eg parents, teachers, young leaders within community organizations, museum staff, etc.) to create programme initiatives designed to be personally engaging and meaningful, building the capacity of the organizations involved around their core mission and leading to visible community outcomes for which individuals are accountable both to the project team and the organizations they represent. This approach involves Imagine Chicago in three interrelated activities:

- designing frameworks for community and organizational innovation with positive and empowering assumptions, which build skills through hands-on experiences and create accountable structures and networks for moving forward key ideas that emerge from the groups;

- developing innovative programmes which test and showcase tools and approaches that can be used by community groups to inspire and sustain civic engagement and action;

- building dynamic collaborations between institutions (represented by interested change agents), which enable them to accomplish their central mission and build their long-term capacity – in addition to creating something of benefit for the city as a whole.

1 What catalysed learning and action in this case?

2 How do you think the process of appreciative inquiry has supported this?

3 What are the core elements that have sustained community-wide engagement and participation in learning?

5 Different approaches to learning

Learning is informed by a number of perspectives, from the purely behaviourist perspective where learning is seen as conditioned responses to external stimuli (remember Pavlov and his dogs, and Skinner's (1968) operant conditioning and reinforcement theory) and where focus is placed on behavioural change, to socio-cultural (constructivist or cognitive approaches to learning) and situational learning (constructionist approaches to learning) to learning. Crucial to behaviour change in the former is continued reinforcement to reward desired behaviour. The learner, however, is often seen as fairly passive within the process, although behaviourist approaches feature in many approaches to instruction and teaching design, including early technology-mediated learning. This is illustrated in Figure 5.5, which presents an order of the types of literature on learning theory.

Figure 5.5 Approaches to learning

Behaviourism (eg Skinner, 1968)	• Stimulus-reward; repeat experience/event to reinforce behaviour/learning • Instructional computer games; computer-assisted instruction
Cognitivism (eg Piaget, 1980)	• Learner able to store, retrieve and use stored information – knowledge • Relate existing and new information for transfer
Social learning and constructed learning (eg Vygotsky, 1978)	• Socio-cultural, participatory ways of learning; socialization, collaborative learning • Active enquiry into issues/experience; action learning
Adult learning (eg Knowles, 1984)	• Learning based on learner needs, interests, and skills levels; collaborative and experiential learning processes; problem-centred and inquiry-based; often self-directed
Connectivism (eg Siemens, 2005)	• Social and or technology enhanced network; connections between people, groups, system; actionable knowledge • Underpinned by complexity and chaos theories
Rhizomatic (eg Cormier, 2008)	• Acknowledges the 'messiness' of learning; looks for suitable pathways to learning and development; learning communities create/co-create the curriculum; problem solving, innovation and change-oriented

Stop and think. Watch this video: https://www.youtube.com/watch?v=jTH3ob1IRFo and consider Skinner's approach to programmed learning and the new teaching machine. Consider your own experience of where you think behaviourism played a role, eg learning for areas such as work-based health and safety programmes.

Similarly, as we have seen above when considering cognitive capability, focus is on the role of the trainer/instructor to develop particular skills and competences. This may focus on surface learning – memorization and adaption – which, as Stewart and Rigg (2011) suggest, 'may not be the most accurate reflector of work-based learning, or the ability of a person to perform competently' (p. 147). In more collaborative, socio-cultural contexts, the learner is central to the learning processes. This puts emphasis on deep learning, where individuals make sense of and engage with new materials and experiences. Emphasis is on enquiry-based learning, problem identification, critical thinking, and reflection. Here, there may also be opportunities for co-design and co-production of learning – ideas that we will return to later in the chapter. For now, this section considers some of the theory and frameworks that support individual and collective approaches to learning, some of which will link to the ideas introduced in Chapter 7.

As mentioned above, context, situation and experience are important ingredients that support (or hinder) learning. Freire (1970), for example, highlighted how critical thinking and learning starts (and then moves beyond) individual experience. Freire, like Dewey (1933) before him, was interested in transformation and change, and the process of active and action learning is, in part, taken from this tradition. He made the distinction between transfer of knowledge from expert to learner as a shift in accumulation of facts by one person, and the curiosity of the engaged learner focused on enquiry into problems.

The focus on interpersonal relationships (collaborative activity), language (discussion and dialogue), and learning by, in and during action is echoed in the works of Vygotsky (1962), Schön (1983), Kolb (1984), and Revans (2011). The social dimension of learning is a central tenet of social learning theory (eg Bandura, 1971) and situated learning and communities of practice eg Lave and Wenger (1991) and Wenger (2000). Similarly, Knowles (1975, 1984, 1990) and Knowles, Holton and Swanson (2012) draw on the humanist approach to psychotherapeutic relations described Rogers (1994), to consider experiential learning and the facilitation of that learning together with the relationship between facilitator and learning, particularly for adult learners. In his approach to andragogy (towards a theory of adult and life-long learning), Knowles (1990) was critical of formal education systems and pedagogic approaches that promoted a focus on achieving (test scores, regular assessments) rather than learning through enquiry, suggesting instead that as learners mature they need to be more self-directing, utilize their own experiences in learning, be able to see the relevance and utility of learning to experience (or problem, or work situation), and have a presumed readiness to learn.

Thinking about how people learn through interpersonal networks and communities, through collaboration and social exchange, informs how active learning environments might be constructed. In some respects, this marks a shift from dependent learner to independent learner, where the learner is supported to carry out tasks or solve a problem to a successful conclusion, until able to branch out on their own – a process Wood, Bruner and Ross (1976) call 'scaffolding'. The growing sense of autonomy in a learning context is also associated with both cognitive and emotional engagement (Hospel and Galand, 2016). For Knowles, for example, this meant moving away from the use of lecturers, canned audio-visual presentations, and assigned reading in favour of discussion, laboratory, simulation, field experience, team projects and other action learning techniques.

Active learning involves learners doing things, reflecting on their actions and learning from this reflection to create or confirm (new) ways of doing things. This, as mentioned above, involves moving from a traditional transfer of information/knowledge to knowledge sharing and creation; a focus on action and change combined with critical reflection. There has been a growing interest in reflective practice as an aid to generative learning and continuous professional development for some time (CIPD, 2016; Francis and Cowan, 2008). The Chartered Institute for Personnel and Development refers to reflective learning as a means of 'thinking about what you learn, how you learn it, and how you can apply it in the real world' (CIPD, nd, p. 6). In this sense, it contains elements of deep learning, especially when considered in the context of single-loop and double-loop learning (Argyris, 1976), where single-loop is learning the 'what', whereas double-loop is questioning 'why', as illustrated in Figure 5.6.

There are a number of recognized tools for supporting the development of reflective thinking and writing, such as using a learning log or reflective journal, applying either Kolb's learning cycle (1984, 2015), or the work of Gibbs (1988) and Honey and Mumford (2000). Although each of the three models uses different terms, there is a lot of similarity, as Figure 5.7 suggest.

Reflection (as discussed in Chapter 1) involves taking a perhaps ignored or unprocessed event and examining it in a way that helps us to make sense of what has occurred. It is particularly useful when thinking about difficult or 'messy' issues, which can be both complex and confusing. While presented as a cycle, learning, action and reflection combine into an iterative process. Different learning styles have been associated with 'stages' of the cycle, with accompanying diagnostics that consider preferred approaches to learning and communicating. Some also link back to neuropsychology, linking thinking processes, emotions and learning styles (see Table 5.1).

Figure 5.6 Single- and double-loop learning

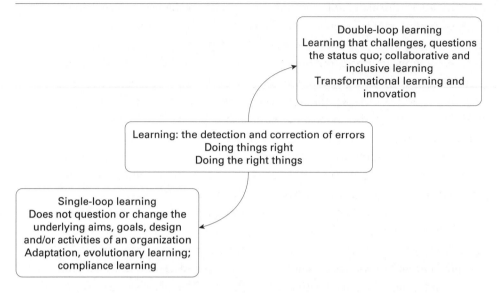

Figure 5.7 Integrating learning cycles and styles: Kolb, Gibbs and Honey & Mumford

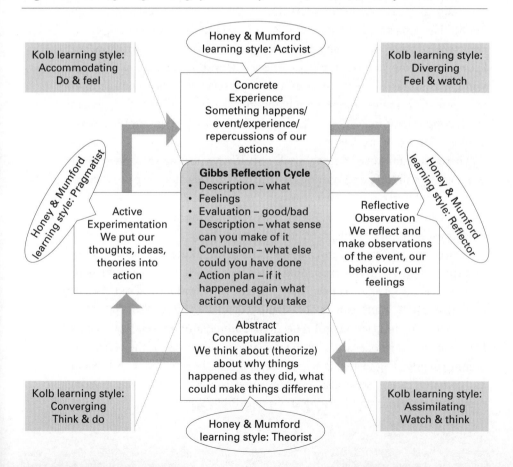

Table 5.1 Engaging learners by anticipating learning styles

We can think about how we might design learning activities that fit different approaches to learning. To help to start to think about this, this table looks at the work of Honey and Mumford (2000) learning styles and sensory learning – visual, auditory and kinaesthetic learners and those who prefer text/the written work (VARK) (Fleming and Mills, 1992). It is not an exhaustive list and many individuals have more than one preferred approach to learning. It is useful, however, to help to think about active and varied activities, as expert learners are aware of which [learning approach] they need to engage in in order to master something new.

Learning approach	Possible activities
Activists – learning by doing; getting involved in the task.	• Group problem solving • Puzzles • Role play
Reflectors – learning by observing, thinking and reflecting; taking time to process information and work to an appropriate solution or action.	• Read, reflection and synthesis of argument • Discussion (asynchronous if online) • Problem-based learning
Theorists – learning by appreciating and knowing the theory that underpins ideas and actions.	• Use of models, theoretical frameworks, and presentation of concepts and theories • Discussion groups • Exploration and application of theories, models, statistical evidence
Pragmatists – learning by exploring how theory works in practice; trying out new ideas to see how they work.	• Problem-based learning and case studies • Consultancy type projects • Integrative learning
Auditory learning: focus on listening, sound.	• Discussions • Podcasts • Web chat • Lectures
Visual learning: focus on sight, visual images.	• Drawing; graphics; diagrams • Posters • Group observation and feedback • Whiteboard
Kinaesthetic learning: focus on touch, feeling, movement.	• Practical tasks • Role play • Case studies
Read/write: focus on words, written information.	• Manuals • Reports • Internet • Books/reading

Stop and think. You are tasked with designing a short learning event for your staff team to introduce a new IT software programme to capture data on customer feedback. Think about how you might incorporate activities that would relate to an anticipated range of learning styles.

While the concept of learning styles has been somewhat contentious (see for example Stewart and Rigg, 2011), thinking about how people approach learning in different ways helps us consider possible tools and techniques for increasing participation and engagement – you may well have identified a number of these in the 'stop and think' exercise above – and we will return to this later in the chapter.

Boud (2001) and Moon (2004) offer various guides to enhancing practice through reflective writing, with Moon articulating different levels/depths of reflection and reflective writing. Schön (1983) too offers different 'types' of reflection – reflection on action and reflection in action. Reflecting on action may take place shortly after the events of the day – a taking stock and reviewing. Reflecting in action is being mindful of our practice as we are directly engaged in it.

Stop and think. Using the Gibbs reflective points, think about an event or critical incident that has happened to you recently. What was it? How did you feel? What did you do? Could there have been different ways to look at the issues? How might you act or respond differently if you were faced with the same or similar situation again?

Gibbs' reflective points:

- Describe the situation/learning event and feelings.
- Evaluate the situation/learning event. Was it good/bad?
- Describe – what sense can you make of it?
- Conclude – what else could you have done?
- Action plan – if it happened again what action would you take?

Reflective thinking and learning may be part of formal programmes but they can also be a bridge between formal and informal learning, and everyday practice. Using learning logs and reflective diaries is often an individual exercise, unless shared with others, and there are examples of reflective blogs using audio blogs or web-based blogs (as discussed in detail in Chapter 6). More collaborative and collective learning building on the process of reflection and action is the action learning set and, if we widen the concept a little to include the concept of action learning spaces, we might also consider communities of practice (Lave and Wenger, 1991).

Action learning involves learning from 'live' problems and derives its theoretical frame (eg principles) from social learning theory (see Chapter 7). It requires commitment to meet and actively participate in regular set meetings over a period of time. This collaborative learning experience aims to support and help individuals to solve problems not through offering advice, but by listening carefully, asking questions that generate insight and avenues for action, and providing space for feedback and reflection. Learning with a group of peers can counteract the isolation one might feel with traditional personal development programmes. It provides an added incentive to act on decisions because each member is accountable both to his/herself and to their fellow group members. As Revans (2011) suggests, this process is built on the premise that '[t]here can be no learning without action and no action without learning (p. 85)'. Key advantages include:

- Personal responsibility for learning – the fact that learning is linked with action supports movement towards individual empowerment. Individuals can let go of the feeling that they are unable to do anything about their own situations – that power and responsibility lie 'out there' in someone else's hands. An action, however small (or indeed a decision to do nothing), opens up choice and the feeling of achievement.

- Learning with intent – the commitment to reflection and action may well lead to significant changes in life experiences as new approaches, ideas and practices occur. This can also affect attitudes and behaviours at work – colleagues may notice an increase in confidence, or engagement in tasks; relationships with supervisors/subordinates may become more positive in surfacing and discussing issues through developed coaching, questioning and listening techniques.

- Commitment to shared leadership and process management – while some sets may be facilitated, each set member must also have a commitment to the leadership and effective process and outcomes of the set. This means learning and reviewing the concepts of collaborative learning and developing fluency in using the process. It also emphasizes a freedom from the constraints of hierarchical relationships, which is an important factor when thinking about the composition of action learning set membership.

- Voluntary – even where collaborative learning and learning sets are initiated by an organization, it is essential that being a member of a set is voluntary. Forced or involuntary membership is likely to lead to disengagement from the process and if a set member feels resentment then this can have an impact on the set performance as a whole. This is different from working with individuals who may be wary or sceptical of joining in. In this instance, it is necessary to fully explain the aims and objectives along with the structure and processes involved. Often an introductory workshop or running facilitated introductory sessions can help to allay fears.

- Confidentiality and trust – when sets work well, the building of swift trust and confidence in each other can be a powerful experience. Part of this is trusting that what is said in the set stays within the set, that disclosure will not compromise an individual, and similarly, individuals will not abuse their colleagues' trust. This allows space for exploration of deeper feelings and emotions or sensitive work issues.

- Support and challenge – set members are not there to offer team sympathy or advice. However, they will develop empathy with an individual's issues, context and emotional response to events. A set member's role is to listen, to support and to question. Support can come through sensitive questioning around an issue, reactions and feelings. However, it is important not to collude with a particular point of view and in these instances, playing the devil's advocate or asking 'what if' can encourage further thinking and challenge unspoken assumptions.

- Non-adversarial – while set members need to be prepared to challenge each other, this needs to be carried out in an empathetic and supportive way. The aim is to work together – collaboratively – to overcome barriers and to work towards new actions and approaches. This cannot be achieved if members feel they are in competition with each other to achieve or to provide the best solutions. It cannot be achieved if we become angry or aggressive with each other.

- Listening with intent – it is important that set members actively listen and pay attention to each other. While it may be a little overwhelming to have each member completely absorbed in one member's presentation, this is a key part of the process in achieving well-formed outcomes for individuals. The interaction within groups – the way we ask questions and approach an issue – is quite specific and not really what we're used to in everyday communications and interactions with each other. Questioning and listening form part of the learning process for all set members. It is a reciprocal process of give and take, and it is also important that set members who are presenting their issue to the group do so in a way that makes this time a valuable experience for all set members. This underlines the need to have a real issue, not one made up for the occasion, or one that where a decision has already been made or cannot be taken.

The effective use of action learning in enhancing teams is crucial; Pedler (2012) argues that well-functioning groups 'maximize... heterogeneity' within the group 'while modelling the proper approach to problem explora-tion... where individuals learn from each other' (p. 419). The proper approach here is in learning to ask the right kinds of questions – to elicit new ways of thinking and fresh insights to a puzzling situation or series of events.

Communities of practice (CoP) also rely on relationships as being central to the learning process. This collaborative learning is founded on both social and situated learning theories where CoPs demonstrate, as Amin and Roberts (2008) stress, 'mutual engagement, sense of joint enterprise, and a shared repertoire of communal resources [ie]... sources of learning and knowing based on individuals doing things together, developing a sense of place, purpose and common identity, and resolving their differences' (p. 354.) Knowledge and learning are therefore created through shared social practice where there is engaged interdependency of activity, meaning, cognition, learning and knowing (Lave and Wenger, 1991).

Mini Case 5.3: Managing to Learn – learning and development of third-sector chief executive officers (adapted from Myers, 2006)

Newell *et al.* (2002, p 107) consider knowledge as 'socially constructed and based on experience' where there is 'exploration through the sharing and synthesis of knowledge among different social groups and communities. Continuous development, learning, and seeking out educational opportunities are not always about promotion and career progression, especially for individuals in senior and executive management positions.

This was observed in a group of third-sector chief executive officers (CEOs) who tended to be more active at the informal end of what might be considered a learning continuum between formal and informal learning activities which takes account of their personal and professional experiences. In this sense, the CEOs could be seen as information seekers who looked towards a range of options to enhance their practice throughout their working lives; there is a deliberate intention in seeking out learning opportunities, as well as a commitment to learn. In order to achieve this, CEOs developed supportive relationships with key individuals outside their employing organizations. For some, this was a formal

▶

arrangement with external supervision and coaching agreed and paid for by the organization. For others, the relationships were more informal ones with peers and former colleagues.

Several CEOs described meeting with other similar CEOs two or three times a year to go through issues of coping and managing their organizations both internally and in negotiating external relationships. This provided ideas, support, and specific information for CEOs to improve their practice, as it also provided opportunities to cross-reference and affirm/disconfirm specific strategic approaches, theories, and actions in relation to, for example, emerging government policies. This supported what one CEO referred to as 'thinking as well as doing'. The formation and development of these networks also allowed inclusion of 'experts' – those with a long-standing experience in the sector/role, and those who might be considered 'novices' – those new or less experienced practitioners.

In thinking about these networks as communities of practice, we can see that individuals learn to function as part of a particular supportive and intentional community. Together they can build a picture of their world – a conceptual framework – that influences, and is influenced by, their actions and behaviours in relation to their working environment and relationships with colleagues. Testing out theories and assumptions, reflecting on and learning from this interactive process is also part of what Brown and Duguid (1991, p. 51) recognize as 'the process of innovating'. This seems particularly relevant if different communities of which they are a part combine multi-sector organizations and coalitions across different organizations. In many instances, CEOs are able to transfer their learning with their external communities of practice back into their organizational strategic and operational planning.

1   What are the benefits of this type of learning for the CEOs concerned?

2   What can you identify in relation to surface learning/deep learning; formal and informal learning; learning theory?

Action learning grew out of the work of Reg Revans (2011) and is seen has having potential impact on supporting strategic planning and decision making, leadership development, and service learning, all of which will be sustained and enabled by technology (Waddill, Banks and Marsh, 2010). Whether by technology or not, issues of sustainability are important in considering learning potential. We need to be mindful of different types of knowing and routes to knowledge acquisition (Cato and Myers, 2011).

6 Strategies, processes and tools to enhance participation and engagement

Scott (2010) makes a forceful and cogent point that effective learning not only have 'tangible and immediately useful outcomes in terms of under-standing, skills, [and] social action... but can also reinforce the capability and motivation for further learning' (p. 3736) at individual, group, and organizational levels. So, how can we develop a meaningful approach to learning and development that encourages and 'rewards' participation and engagement? What we can see from the discussion above is that there seem to be a number of common themes emerging.

As Cato and Myers (2011) suggest, there is a need to challenge the assumption about the way in which individuals learn and acquire knowledge which privileges rational–linear processes to information accumulation and 'calculative thinking'. In these circumstances, 'we are presented with a prob-lem... seek reliable evidence, weigh it rationally [to] arrive at an objective and irrefutable conclusion' rather than, it is suggested, learning as a much more 'complex, open-ended process' (Semetsky, 2005). Learning, or at least deep learning, is thus seen as self-directed, as social and relational, and as a process of critical thinking and reflection. It is both proactive and responsive and based on interaction and engagement. One way of trying to capture these interactive processes is provided by Cunliffe (2008), as seen in Figure 5.8.

From this we can see that we can start to think about some of the processes of active learning by increasing capacity for self- and critical reflection and strengthening the links between knowing and knowledge. We can identify the strategies, tools and process that can start to create meaning, increased participation and engagement in learning processes, which in turn have potential for providing the scaffolding for life-long learning (Nikolaides and Yorks, 2008). Some practical tools, techniques, and resources might include some of the following.

6.1 Learning journals and development portfolios

These tools support engaged and enhanced learning through structured and systematic reflection that enables individuals to review both learning pro-cesses and 'develop the aptitudes, skills, and habits that come from critical reflection' (Zubizaretta, 2004, p. 15). Portfolios also allow for the learning journey to be captured and told through different media – video, photo-graphs, digital recordings, and well as written accounts.

Figure 5.8 Relationally responsive learning (adapted from Cunliffe, 2008 and Cato and Myers, 2011)

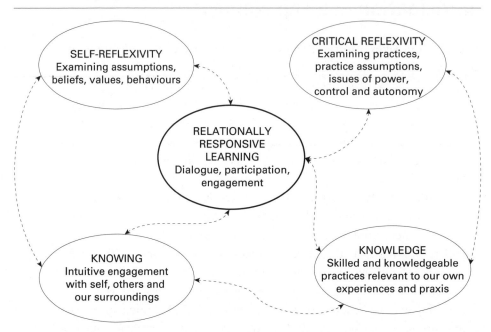

6.2 Discussion boards and groups

These can be included as part of formal training and development through virtual learning environments, or through workplace intranets. It allows for a free flow of interaction, which can be monitored and facilitated or left open, but it is important to set ground rules and ways of working and accepted ways of communicating online. This kind of provision allows individuals to seek clarification, share good practice, inform of updates, provide specialist or specific information, and input suggestions and ideas. It is also useful in bringing together individuals across different locations and time zones.

6.3 Storytelling – use of metaphor, analogies and the role of narrative enquiry.

Storytelling has a long history in community cohesion and learning. Stories are shared and lived experiences; they are a way of helping us to remember information and to convey direct and indirect messages; they are part of our religious, moral, and human development. It is also why we give time to listen to motivational speakers – they provide stories. More than this, stories are a way of making sense of the things around us and, the ability to paint a picture through storytelling, using metaphor and analogies, can remove obstacles to learning (for example making personal or inter-group conflict less personal and more 'objective') and might simply make complex issues more easily accessible (Egan, 1989). Reflective practice also has some of the essential ingredients of storytelling (Ganz, 2010). The Higher Education Authority in the UK sets out some useful questions regarding using storytelling as a learning tool linked to action and collaborative learning (McDrury, 2003):

- Is storytelling the most compelling and memorable way for a group of learners to learn about a topic, and if so, why?
- What form of storytelling best suits the learners' learning needs and objectives?
- What outcomes will learners achieve?
- Will these outcomes be assessed, and if so, how?
- What forms of support are needed?
- How can confidentiality and anonymity issues be addressed?
- Whose story is used? A personal story? A fictional story? A story from practice? The learner's story?
- What is the key lesson that the story will convey?
- Is there time to plan a story or would a spontaneous story fit the time and purposes more effectively?

Stop and think: Hans Rosling's videos try to make meaning from statistics and data through visual imagery and storytelling: https://www.youtube.com/watch?v=jbkSRLYSojo Rosling's work uses technology to enhance statistical information giving and storytelling. Technology-enhanced learning can also support the development of digital storytelling as a deep learning tool. For a longer, more detailed and amusing look at bringing global data to life and challenging pre-conceived (or previously learned) ideas: https://youtu.be/hVimVzgtD6w

> ### Mini Case 5.4: Bangladeshi garment worker seeks better life for daughters
>
> We can use life stories and vignettes to include a number of messages to support critical thinking, reflection and problem enquiry. This short video (three minutes) introduces you to Parul Begum, a 39-year-old garment worker at the Aplus clothing factory in Dhaka, Bangladesh: https://youtu.be/17Uctg_2GPE. In a short space of time, we learn a reasonable amount about the fast fashion industry and Parul's working and family life.
>   Consider the following:
>
> - What is the video about?
>
> - How does it make you feel?
>
> - Does it raise any particular questions for you?
>
> - How might you find out more about the issues raised in the video?
>
> Think about an issue that you would like to raise awareness about in your organization. Find a story (video, news article, photograph) that could act as a basis for your storytelling.

6.4 Using drama in the workplace

Using a combination of work-based research (stories gathered from the organization) and professional actors can help to work through complex and sometimes messy issues in organizations (such as conflict and disengagement). It is an opportunity for organizational members to observe their behaviours from the 'outside'. Some companies who specialize in this type of work use interactive presentations where possible to provide ways forward, actions, and solutions that can be presented as part of the performance by organizational members and become incorporated into the drama as it unfolds, for example re-working the same situation in several ways to see potential consequences of particular courses of action or behaviour. This type of intervention – sometimes referred to as forum theatre – uses real problems in real time, rather than watching actors on video or training films.

Others use carefully scripted scenarios to support learning and development, for example around inter-personal skills (for example difficult conversations, carrying out appraisal and feedback sessions, bullying and harassment).

Actor-led role play can also be substituted with or supplemented by learner-led role play. Using role play can involve learners in practising newly learned skills. It provides an opportunity to both practise and observe others practising skills and ways of communication and negotiating, for example. It also provides an opportunity to reflect on action; to consider thoughts, feelings and reactions to the learning process.

6.5 Multi-sensory resources

Using different sensory sources pulls on individual learning approaches and styles. The Department of Education and Skills (2004) defines multi-sensory as 'using visual, auditory and kinaesthetic modalities, sometimes at the same time'. Using more than one sensory stimulus (often words and pictures, but not limited to this) is seen to lead to deeper learning Moreno and Mayer (2002). Up to now, there has been an emphasis on active engagement rather passive receiving, yet as Moreno and Mayer (2002) explain, multimedia learning (discussed in detail in Chapter 6), particularly instructional media, can be passive in that 'no behavioural or social activity is required on the part of the learner' (p. 110). This gap is closed, they suggest, through stimulating cognitive activity, which includes 'actively' building the connection between words and images. Thus learners presented with narration and animation showing how brakes or pumps work 'learned more deeply' than those receiving just the narration (pp. 112–13).

Stop and think: Have you entered a training room or learning environment where there has been music playing? Has music been played during other activities – for example group work? How was it used? Was the music associated with the topic? Was it energizing or soothing? Did it help to set the tone and tempo for the learning activities? Or help you to concentrate? Think about how music can affect your mood, attention, and concentration. There are suggestions that music can create a positive learning environment that affects engagement and willingness to participate. It is seen as a technique associated with accelerated learning.

6.6 Games-based learning and simulation

A range of games-based technologies is being utilized to enhance learning, and to promote challenge, appeal and engagement in learning. This engages learners in designing and creating games as well as using games as a basis for collaborative learning.

Watch and Think: Kurt Squires, a US-based games-based learning scholar looks at youth education and the impact on broader civic engagement. Watch this video on his experience. How might we take this experience and apply it to different learning environments, for example work organizations or community organizations: http://www.edutopia.org/kurt-squire-games-civic-engagement-video

Simulation and gaming is not a new educational tool and has been around in the business education world since the 1950s, developing more substantially from the early 1970s (Gros, 2007). Simulations have allowed students, for example, to safely set up virtual businesses and/or manage the ravages of the stock exchange. More recently, there are emergency case simulators (eg Royal Veterinary College, University of London), and simulation-based medical education allows learning that is both immersive and experiential (Proserpio and Gioia, 2007).

Gros (2007) tracks the evolution of games-based learning from 'edutainment', focused on behaviour – skills, content, and attitude (behaviourist in approach) – through to third-generation games focused on meaningful social interaction (socio-cultural and situated learning approaches). According Gros (p. 28), games-based learning is still gender biased, and what is required is to have 'critical discourse about the games we encourage and stimulate innovative and alternative images of men and women that do not reinstate doggedly rigid gender stereotypes'. Even so, McFarlane, Sparrowhawk and Heald (2002) suggests a number of areas in which games can contribute to learning in younger learners, including motivation to learn, maintaining attention and concentration, collaborative working, and creative problem solving. Similar results in development of motor skills, improved working memory and attention span have also been found in older players (Anguera *et al*, 2013, Torres, 2011).

6.7 Team-based learning

Team-based learning has been linked with improving communication and teamwork skills as well as improving problem solving and reasoning skills. A study of postgraduate nurses found that team-based learning also improved engagement and overall learning (Currey *et al*, 2015). Team-based learning is also associated with 'flipped' classroom and flipped learning. This is where the content traditionally used in a class-based environment (lecture materials, slides) together with pre-reading or watching a short web lecture or video, takes place before the schedule sessions. This allows for increased discussion and interaction in the session and a focus on application, analysis, evaluation and creation (Bloom and Krathwohl, 1956).

Flipped learning is a flexible approach that allows for a different range of delivery modes and learning environments. It provides a space where learners engage both in the content and the process of learning and where educators or instructors move from being knowledge providers to knowledge facilitators – a move from 'sage on the stage to guide on the side' (King, 1993). This is not a new concept, but has been receiving more attention as developments in technology enhance learning practice. It can involve, for example, the use of mobile technology (Bring Your Own Device/BYOD), technology-facilitated approaches such as online and blended working, and smart tables.

Earlier, in Figure 5.5, the concept of rhizomatic learning was introduced. Dave Cormier, a Canadian academic and online community advocate who has developed a body of work around open online courses and co-construction of learning and knowledge, discusses the concept in a YouTube video (Cormier, 2012). Cormier also has his own educational blog: http://davecormier.com/edblog/whos-dave

6.8 Online virtual learning environments

Whilst this subject is largely explored in Chapter 6, this section focuses on how online and virtual learning environments are used in the context of enhancing learner engagement. With the development of mobile technology, opportunities for learning and reflective practice are not limited to particular times and physical spaces. Personal mobile devices can provide a learning hub to bring together different learning tools to support learning anywhere, anytime, whether that is access to virtual learning environments and company intranets, learning journal software, or virtual/digital classrooms. Learning online with hundreds of others is a feature of the developing scope of massive online courses. Chat rooms allow us to congregate with online communities of practice (Wenger, White and Smith, 2009), and cloud-based software and hosting organizations enable file sharing and collaborative learning and work tools. Open source communities allow for software, research, and publications to be downloaded and shared.

Mobile technology has left its mark in the classroom too, not only with video-based games but also with instant messaging and BOYD. The use of hash tags on Twitter to get instant feedback on lecture content is not common, but it is used in the 'following' of online discussions on Twitter and associated social media sites, and in posting learning materials (Lowe and Laffey, 2011). These, along with webinars, extend the classroom beyond its physical boundaries to include virtual networks, and have reportedly increased student learner interactions and participation (Gao, Luo and Zhang, 2012).

Interestingly, although technology-based information searching and interaction is often seen as the domain of the 'younger generations', online learning – particularly in the form of the massive open online course (MOOC) – has until recently been the domain of employed professionals and graduates, with many aged between 41 and 60 years old (Sacks and Myers, 2014). Learning and creativity are seen to be encouraged through online engagement. For example, Sacks and Myers (2014) report that learner satisfaction is increased through producing something that is perceived to be meaningful (cognitive gain through learning perceived as relevant) and may support the learning of others (through more collaborative and dialogic learning and construction of ideas and practice).

As with any learning environment, but perhaps more so with an online community of learners, the challenge is to find a balance between teaching, social and cognitive presence and to promote a level of cohesion that promotes participation and engagement. This includes promoting and supporting connections and discourse, and providing a safe and inclusive environment to encourage open communication, exchange and collaboration (social presence). Consideration also needs to be given to the content, structure and processes that produce engaged discussion, sharing new ideas and applying theory to practice (cognitive presence) and to promoting a learning climate to direct, focus and facilitate learning (teaching presence).

It is important too to recognize, in some instances, the changing roles and development of both learner and facilitator, something Conrad and Donaldson (2004) refer to as the development phases or phases of engagement. They provide a template for a 'typical' 12–16-week online delivery where learners move from newcomer to initiator and partner in learning activities with a parallel role of facilitator from 'social negotiator' (setting up activities to help learners to interact) to community member and challenger. So here, again, we see the move of instructor from centre to side, as learning becomes more learner centred and in some cases learner led. In summary, activities that support increased engagement and participation include: online study groups; use of wikis and discussion forums, allowing learners their own discussion space and smaller group exchange; and synchronous and asynchronous contact, prompts and exchange.

While it may be a significant challenge to engage learners in design and co-construction of learning, Atkinson (2011) argues that we can make more transparent the learning design process and the relationship to intended learning outcomes. This, he argues, helps to illuminate the ways in which learning is designed and delivered and helps learning providers and facilitators to consider each part of the process (learning materials, contact time and type, assessment, feedback, evaluation) and different approaches required to engage with learners and enhance the learning experience.

7 From individual to organizational learning

The utility and meaning of learning for some learners has been mentioned as a key ingredient to participation and continued engagement with learning. In part, this relates also to transfer of learning to our work environment. The concept of communities of practice and professional learning communities has been introduced and we also need to consider the difference this can make to our work organizations. Much of the focus of this chapter has been on individual and interpersonal learning. As a final part to this chapter we briefly consider the opportunities for organizational learning through keeping people engaged and embedding learning.

Many companies are looking more actively at integrating learning into workflow activities through the use of action learning, coaching and mentoring, micro-blogging, learning portals, online guides, augmented reality, crowd-sourcing tools, apps, as well as task management and workflow systems. For learning to take place and be sustainable, it takes more than provision of tools and technology; it requires a commitment to building an environment that encourages individual, group and whole organization contributions, reflective practice, and innovation. It requires all organizational members to be involved (see BT, 2009)

Mini Case 5.5: Evolving roles, enhancing skills – learning and development at Barnardo's (adapted from Stuart and Overton, 2015)

Barnardo's is one of the UK's largest charities. Its services help children across the UK who are abused, vulnerable, and neglected. The charity employs over 8,000 people and 14,000 volunteers who are committed to working to transform the lives of vulnerable children and young people. Over the last five years, the organization has experienced challenges. There have been a number of changes in senior management over the years, alongside the impact of the economic downturn, which has made fundraising more challenging. The organization has also moved to a new building, resulting in a complete re-architecture of the IT infrastructure.

▶

Barnardo's has a goal to create and embed a learning culture. As Katharine Bollon, head of workforce and organization development, describes:

> By 2025 our CEO, Javed Khan, wants us to be an organization where learning is an innate part of what we do and how we behave. Where we continually embrace and drive learning at all levels, in all spaces, and in all places... [a virtual] university; a community of trusted advisers... this way of thinking strategically, leading and engaging together will fulfil the potential of not just our people but also the potential of the most vulnerable children and young people – our beneficiaries – through the delivery of our innovative services.

One team really driving forward with this agenda is the IT learning and development team who have developed an adaptable way of working and a continual desire to learn. This began with exploring how learning technology could be used to increase reach. E-learning was introduced, followed by virtual classrooms and more recently embedded performance support tools. The team monitor IT helpdesk calls and e-mails, meaning that they can quickly spot trends and the issues that people need support with. Alongside this, they maintain a very strong connection with the business, so that they can respond quickly to needs.

What's helped throughout this time is the team's willingness to try new things and continually develop their own skills. This has ranged from attending formal training to learning on the job through each other, attending conferences and immersing themselves in new techniques and technologies. The team have also recently introduced development days once a month, which are designed to boost creativity and innovation. This might mean attending training or a webinar, conducting research or creating something new. These days are an effective way of exploring new ideas and either adopting or discarding them.

Alongside this continual self-development, getting the L&D operating model right across the organization is critical, especially in relation to Barnardo's goal for a learning culture. Back in 2008, along with many other organizations in the recession, Barnardo's needed to increase efficiencies while still delivering effectively. The decision was made to move L&D management responsibility into local HR teams.

Reflecting on the current operating model and the goal to realize a learning culture, it was felt that central L&D adds greatest value and sustainable impact when it works in partnership with the strategy function in order to truly meet the needs of the workforce in a timely way. As L&D sits within the IT function and has experience in the business, it is seen as a business service, rather than a traditional L&D function. This has been conducive to introducing new technologies to drive change.

Outside of IT, many learners still tend to associate L&D with the use of more formal training programmes. Therefore, one of the challenges in transitioning to a learning organization will be shifting perceptions about what learning really is. Part of the solution to shifting learner perceptions is in recognizing and leveraging the great L&D already happening within the organization. This shift in perspective will also involve approaching learning delivery differently. Katharine has aspirations to introduce 'leader-led development', which will involve 'our own leaders facilitating development of performance management or how to coach effectively. In effect, role-modelling effective leadership with our people face to face.'

Katharine is clear on the challenges, the journey the organization needs to go on and the role L&D will play. L&D is at its best when it's being the conscience of the organization and thinking ahead about 'Actually, what are we going to need to do more of? What are we going to need to do less of?... We're going to have to up our game. We're going to have to look at ways to increase learning capacity and be more effective around when and how we deliver and integrate learning. We're going to have to do lots of continuous improvement, be innovative, and make some tough decisions.'

Whilst driving change at a corporate L&D level may be more challenging, Katharine recognizes the value of finding 'pockets of excellence' in the business, which can then be shared and showcased in a really collaborative way to instigate wider change and performance improvement. In this respect, having an established and forward-thinking IT L&D team is a substantial benefit to the achievement of the wider L&D vision.

1   How has the organization used IT to build a sense of a learning community?

2   How is this supported and encouraged?

3   What challenges might the organization face in sustaining learning and development? What strengths does it have to build on?

8.0 Summary and reflection

Atkinson (2011) cites Knight, Tait and York (2006, p. 332) in thinking about how we make workplaces 'evoke learning'. They suggest that 'Firstly, spaces need to be found for this activity, for the creation of shared meaning. Secondly, power relationships within activity systems need to encourage collegiality and participation. Thirdly, appropriate procedures and practices are needed' (p. 1).

This echoes the themes that have been emerging when considering the ways in which participation and engagement in learning can be enhanced. There is a strong sense of the need for some level of growing autonomy, of action learning and reflective practice, and feedback/feed forward to deepen and sustain learning. There is a sense, particularly in relation to work-based learning and transfer of learning back into work, that meaningful theory-practice links should be made, and applied and practised. Building interaction, networks, and learning communities widens the scope and longevity of the practice of learning and development. It also supports increased self-direction and motivation to learn.

These fundamental aspects provide cues to think about the design and development of learning interventions and learning spaces. The context of learning is also important. Increased technology also increases the opportunity for a wider variety of modes of learning. Technology can meet basic task and behavioural skills development and develop increased engagement with tasks. It can also promote higher levels of cognitive, socio-cultural and networked learning, which through increased levels of interpersonal engagement and interaction promotes engagement at cognitive and emotional levels and has potential to provide opportunities for increased participation in the design, delivery and experience of learning.

Further reading

If you would like to find out more about some of the concepts and ideas discussed in this chapter, you can access these recommended links and materials.

Appreciative Inquiry Commons: https://appreciativeinquiry.case.edu. Hosted by Case Western Reserve University's Weatherhead School of Management, this is a web portal for sharing academic resources and tools on AI and positive change

Freire Institute: http://www.freire.org. A community-based learning website based on Paulo Freire's critical pedagogy.

Imagine Chicago website: www.imaginechicago.org

Infed: www.infed.org. A non-profit site that specializes in the theory and practice of informal education, social pedagogy, lifelong learning, social action, and community learning and development.

International Foundation for Action Learning: www.ifal.org.uk. A charity focused on creating, supporting and encouraging networks of action learning enthusiasts and practitioners.

Glossary of terms

Action learning – learning based on the work of Reg Revans. Learners work in small learning sets and work on 'real' issues to reflect on action and behaviour with a view to taking subsequent action and review.

Active learning – a process to engage learners in activities that promote discussion and problem solving; includes the use of information communication technologies, group work and team-based activities.

Asynchronous learning – usually online learning where communication or learning activities are not delivered in real time; use of, for example, pre-recorded web lectures, discussion boards, and e-mail.

Collaborative learning – working in peer-to-peer or larger groups and often incorporates active learning technologies.

Community of practice – formed by people involved in a process of collaborative or co-operative learning, who share a common concern and are looking to learn and develop enquiry- or inquiry-based learning – focuses on exploring and researching an issue/problem where learners take responsibility for enquiry and learning.

Learning environment or climate – the range and type of space, context and learning culture focused on enhancing the learning experience.

Meta-learning – the process of being aware of and taking responsibility for one's own learning.

Problem-based learning – focuses on open-ended problem exploration and solution.

Scaffolding – techniques to move learners towards increased understanding, with support gradually being removed to allow increased independence in the learning process.

Situated learning – the concept that learning is located in interpersonal relationships – an 'integral part of generative social practice in the lived world' (Lave and Wenger, 1991, p 35)

10 References

Alderfer, C P (1972) *Existence, Relatedness, and Growth*, Free Press, New York, NY

Amabile, T M and Kramer, S J (2010) What really motivates workers? *Harvard Business Review*, **88**, pp. 44–45

Amin, A and Roberts, J (2008) Knowing in action: beyond communities of practice, *Research Policy*, **37**, pp. 353–369.

Anderson, W and Krathwohl, D R, eds (2001) *A Taxonomy for Learning, Teaching, and Assessing: A revision of bloom's taxonomy of educational objectives*, Longman, New York

Anguera, J A, Boccanfuso, J, Rintoul, J L, Al-Hashimi, O, Faraji, F, Janowich, J, Yong, E, Larraburi, Y, Rolle, C, Johnston, E and Gazzaley, A (2013) Video game training enhances cognitive control in older adults, *Nature*, **501**, pp. 97–101

Argyris, C (1976) Single-loop and double-loop models in research on decision-making, *Administrative Science Quarterly*, **21**, pp. 363–375

Ashford, G and Patkar, S (2001) The positive path: using appreciative inquiry in rural Indian communities, International Institute for Sustainable Development, Winnipeg, Manitoba

Atkinson, S (2011) Embodied and embedded theory in practice: the student-owned learning engagement (SOLE) model, *The International Review of Research in Open and Distributed Learning*, **12**, pp. 1–10

Bandura, A (1971) *Social Learning Theory*, General Learning Press, New York

Biggs, J (1999) *Teaching for Quality Learning at University*, Open University Press Buckingham

Biggs, J B (1987) Learning process questionnaire manual: student approaches to learning and studying, Australian Council for Educational Research, Hawthorn, Australia

Bloom, B S and Krathwohl, D R (1956) *Taxonomy of Educational Objectives: The classification of educational goals. Handbook I: Cognitive domain*, Longmans, New York, NY

Boud, D (2001) Using journal writing to enhance reflective practice, *New directions for Adult and Continuing Education*, **90**, pp. 9–18

Brown, J S and Duguid, P (1991) Organizational learning and communities-of-practice: toward a unified view of working, learning, and innovation, *Organization Science*, **2** (1), pp. 40–57

BT (2009) Dare2Share podcast, *YouTube* [online] https://www.youtube.com/watch?v=gtVYkEdGtfo&feature=youtu.be

Cato, M S and Myers, J (2011) Education as re-embedding: Stroud Communiversity, walking the land and the enduring spell of the sensuous, *Sustainability*, 3, pp. 51–66

CIPD (2016) What is reflective learning? CIPD [online] http://www.cipd.co.uk/cpd/reflective-learning.aspx

CIPD (nd) Guide 8: Continuing Professional Development, *CIPD* [online]: http://www.cipd.co.uk/NR/rdonlyres/3F6D3423-3463-4638-A590-7C1A99FDD418/0/student_guide_8_cpd.pdf

Conrad, R and Donaldson, J A (2004) *Engaging the Online Learner: Activities and resources for creative learning*, Jossey-Bass, San Francisco

Cooperrider, D L and Srivastva, S (1987) Appreciative inquiry in organizational life, *Research in Organizational Change and Development*, 1, pp. 129–69

Cooperrider, D L, Whitney, D and Stavros, J M (2003) *Appreciative Inquiry Handbook: The first in a series of AI workbooks for leaders of change*, Berrett-Koehler, San Francisco

Cormier, D (2008) Rhizomatic education: community as curriculum, *Innovate: Journal of Online Education*, 4 (2)

Cormier, D (2012) Embracing uncertainty: Rhizomatic learning, *YouTube* [online] https://youtu.be/VJIWyiLyBpQ

Cunliffe, A L (2008) Orientations to social constructionism: relationally responsive social constructionism and its implications for knowledge and learning, *Management Learning*, 39, pp. 123–39

Currey, J, Oldland, E, Considine, J, Glanville, D and Story, I (2015) Evaluation of postgraduate critical care nurses' attitudes to, and engagement with, team-based learning: a descriptive study, *Intensive and Critical Care Nursing*, 31, pp. 19–28

Department of Education and Skills (2004) A framework for understanding dyslexia [online] http://www.achieveability.org.uk/files/1270740075/dfes-framework-for-understanding-dyslexia.pdf

Dewey, J (1933) *How We Think: A restatement of the relation of reflective thinking to the education process*, D. C. Health, Boston

Egan, K (1989) Memory, imagination, and learning: connected by the story, *Phi Delta Kappan*, 70, pp. 455–59

Fleming, N D and Mills, C (1992) Not another inventory, rather a catalyst for reflection, *To Improve the Academy*, Paper 246

Francis, H and Cowan, J (2008) Fostering an action-research dynamic amongst student practitioners, *Journal of European Industrial Training*, 32, pp. 336–46

Freire, P (1970) *Pedagogy of the Oppressed*, Herder & Herder, New York

Ganz, M (2010) Leading change: leadership, organization and social movements, in *The Handbook of Leadership Theory and Practice*, ed N Nohria and R Khurana, Harvard Business School Press, Boston

Gao, F, Luo, T and Zhang, K (2012) Tweeting for learning: a critical analysis of research on microblogging in education published 2008–2011, *British Journal of Educational Technology*, 43 (5), pp. 783–801

Gibbs, G (1988) *Learning by Doing: A guide to teaching and learning methods*, Oxford Further Education Unit, Oxford

Gros, B (2007) Digital games in education: the design of game-based learning, *Journal of Research on Technology in Education*, **40**, pp. 23–38

Herzberg, F (1966) *Work and the Nature of Man*, Harper, New York

Herzberg, F (1968) One more time: how do you motivate employees? *Harvard Business Review*, **46**, pp. 53–62

Honey, P and Mumford, A (2000) *The Learning Styles Helper's Guide* Peter Honey Publications, Maidenhead, Berkshire

Hospel, V and Galand, B (2016) Are both classroom autonomy support and structure equally important for students' engagement? A multilevel analysis. *Learning and Instruction*, **41**, pp. 1–10

Houle, C O (1981) Continuing learning in the professions *Journal of Continuing Education in the Health Professions*, **1**, pp. 76–80

Kember, D, Biggs, J and Leung, D Y (2004) Examining the multidimensionality of approaches to learning through the development of a revised version of the Learning Process Questionnaire, *British Journal of Educational Psychology*, **74**, pp. 261–79

King, A (1993) From sage-on-the-stage to guide-on-the-side, *College Teaching*, **41**, pp. 30–35

Knight, P, Tait, J and Yorke, M (2006) The professional learnings of teachers in higher education, *Studies in Higher Education*, **31** (3) pp. 319–39

Knowles, M (1975) *Self-Directed Learning*, Follet, Chicago

Knowles, M (1990) *The Adult Learner: A neglected species*, Gulf Publisher, Houston

Knowles, M, Holton, E F and Swanson, R A (2012) *The Adult Learner: The definitive classic in adult education and human resource development*, Elsevier, Burlington, MA

Knowles, M S (1984) *Andragogy in Action*, Jossey-Bass, San Francisco

Kolb, D A (1984) *Experiential Learning: Experience as the source of learning and development*, Prentice-Hall, Englewood Cliffs, NJ

Kolb, D A (2015) *Experiential Learning: Experience as the source of learning and development*, Prentice-Hall, London

Krathwohl, D R (2002) A revision of Bloom's taxonomy: an overview, *Theory into Practice*, **41**, pp. 212–18

Lave, J and Wenger, E (1991) *Situated Learning: Legitimate peripheral participation*, Cambridge University Press, Cambridge, UK

Lowe, B and Laffey, D (2011) Is Twitter for the birds? Using Twitter to enhance student learning in marketing course, *Journal of Marketing Education*, **33**, pp. 183–92

Lunenburg, F C (2001) Goal-setting theory of motivation, *International Journal of Management, Business and Administration*, **15**, pp. 1–6

Luthans, F (2002) The need for and meaning of positive organizational behavior, *Journal of Organizational Behavior*, **23**, pp. 695–706

Marton, F and Säljö, R (1976) On qualitative differences in learning: outcome and process. *British Journal of Educational Psychology*, **46**, pp. 4–11

Maslow, A H (1970) *Motivation and Personality*, Addison-Wesley, Reading, MA

Mcclelland, D C (1976) *The Achieving Society*, Irvington Publishers New York, NY

Mcclelland, D C (1985) *Human Motivation*, Scott, Foresman, Glenview, IL

McDrury, J A M (2003) *Learning through Storytelling in Higher Education*, Routledge, London

Mcfarlane, A, Sparrowhawk, A and Heald, Y (2002) Report on the educational use of games: an exploration by TEEM of the contribution which games make to the education process, available at Cambridge

Moon, J (2004) *A Handbook of Reflective and Experiential Learning: Theory and practice*, Routledge, Abingdon

Moreno, R and Mayer, R E (2002) Learning science in virtual reality multimedia environments: role of methods and media, *Journal of Educational Psychology*, **94**, pp. 598–610

Myers, J (2006) 'Making a difference', A study of experiential learning and practiced development of non-profit managers, unpublished thesis, Nottingham Trent University

Nikolaides, A and Yorks, L (2008) An epistemology of learning through, *Emergence: Complexity and Organization*, **10**, pp. 50–61

Oxford Institute for the Advancement of University Learning (nd) *Student Approaches to Learning* [online] https://www.learning.ox.ac.uk/media/global/wwwadminoxacuk/localsites/oxfordlearninginstitute/documents/supportresources/lecturersteachingstaff/resources/resources/Student_Approaches_to_Learning.pdf.

Pavlov, I P (1927) *Conditioned Reflexes*, Clarendon Press, London

Pedler, M (2012) *Action Learning in Practice*, Gower, Farnham

Piaget, J (1980) *The Equilibrium of Cognitive Processes: The central problem of intellectual development*, Basic Books, New York

Proserpio, L and Gioia, D (2007) Teaching the virtual generation, *Academy of Management Learning & Education*, **6**, pp. 69–80

Revans, R (2011) *The ABC of Action Learning*, Gower, London,

Rock, D and Cox, C (2012) SCARF in 2012: updating the social neuroscience of collaborating with others, *NeuroLeadership Journal*, **4**, pp. 1–16

Rogers, C R (1994) *Freedom to Learn*, Merrill, New York

Sacks, R and Myers, J (2014) Teaching in the Open: Widening access of homogenizing learning opportunities, *HETL* [Online] https://www.hetl.org/teaching-in-the-open-widening-access-or-homogenizing-learning-opportunities/.

Schön, D (1983) *The Reflective Practitioner: How professionals think in action*, Arean Publishing, Boston

Scott, S G (2010) Enhancing reflection skills through learning portfolios: an empirical test. *Journal of Management Education*, **34**, 430–57

Seligman, M E P and Csikszentmihalyi, M (2000) Positive psychology: an introduction, *American Psychologist*, **55**, pp. 5–14

Semetsky, I (2005) Not by breadth alone: imagining a self-organized classroom, *Complicity: An International Journal of Complexity and Education*, **2** (1) pp. 19–36

Siemens, G (2005) Connectivism: Learning theory for a digital age, *International Journal of Instructional Technology and Distance Learning* [online] http://www.itdl.org/journal/jan_05/article01.htm

Skinner, B F (1968) *The Technology of Teaching*, Appleton-Century-Crofts, New York

Stewart, J and Rigg, C (2011) *Learning and Talent Development*, CIPD, London

Stuart, R and Overton, L (2015) *L&D: Evolving roles, enhancing skills*, CIPD, London

Torres, A C S (2011) Cognitive effects of video games on old people, *International Journal on Disability and Human Development*, **10**, pp. 55–58

Vroom, V H (1964) *Work and Motivation*, Wiley, New York

Vygotsky, L S (1962) *Thought and Language*, MIT Press, Cambridge

Vygotsky, L S (1978) *Mind in Society: The development of higher psychological processes*, Harvard University Press, Cambridge, MA

Waddill, D, Banks, S and Marsh, C (2010) The future of action learning, *Advances in Developing Human Resources*, **12**, pp. 260–79

Wenger, E (2000) *Communities of Practice: Learning, meaning, and identity*, Cambridge University Press, Cambridge

Wenger, E, White, N and Smith, J D (2009) *Digital Habitats: Stewarding technology for communities*, CPsquare, Portland, OR

Wood, D J, Bruner, J S and Ross, G (1976) The role of tutoring in problem solving. *Journal of Child Psychiatry and Psychology*, **17**, pp. 89–100

Zhang, C Kyriakidou, N and Chesley, D (2013) Learning theories and principles, in *Human Resource Development Theory and Practice*, 2nd edition, ed J Gold, R Holden, J Stewart, P Iles and J Beardwell, Palgrave, Basingstoke

Zubizarreta, J (2004) *The Learning Portfolio: Reflective practice for improving student learning*, Anker, Bolton

Designing and developing digital and blended learning solutions

06

MARK LOON

1 Introduction

This chapter will discuss a number of key learning technologies that are relevant for learners, instructors and L&D professionals. The learning outcomes of the chapter are:

1 Identify technologies available for blended learning.

2 Be able to discern the appropriateness of technologies in designing and developing digital and blended learning solutions.

It is a cliché that technology has changed our lives – the way we work and learn – but to a large degree this is true. Technology opens new possibilities, as it allows L&D professionals to deliver programmes and events in ways that would not have been possible without it. Intelligence that can be gained from data generated by technologies can provide fresh and even unexpected insights that could improve learning by leaps and bounds. However, traditional approaches such as face-to-face learning and on-the-job-training are still much valued and still have their place in L&D. Technology has made learning and development more effective and efficient but it must be applied with some nous.

Technology can be used in various ways and the permutations are endless. The opportunity to use learning technologies should always be balanced with the overriding learning aims and objectives. In some cases, this may involve using technology to support L&D interventions and environments. However, in other circumstances, technology may be the main driver in leading the development and delivery of learning programmes.

L&D professionals need to be technology savvy in not just knowing what technologies are out there but also being aware of the functionalities and features that are available, and how they can be applied to a variety of learning settings. A technology-savvy L&D professional is also one that is pragmatic. They are aware that any learning and development intervention is usually informed by the objectives of the L&D initiative (informed by learning theories such as those discussed in detail in Chapter 5), situational factors (eg time constraints) and available technologies, and therefore know that they can only work with what they have and are able to make the best of it.

The use of technology in learning and development in some ways is similar to cooking, to use a culinary analogy. The two most important factors are the ingredients (ie the technologies) and the recipe (the digital and blended learning solution). To be able to prepare a dish you need to know the ingredients that are available to you or are out there. Section 2 does this, as it contains a discussion on the typical learning and development technologies that are available to L&D professionals (however, given the plethora of technologies available and the speed at which they evolve, it may not be possible to list all the technologies and their functionalities and features).

In addition, L&D professionals also need to know how the flavours of the 'ingredients' may affect the 'palate'. In L&D terms, this means how the functions and features of a learning technology may impact the blended learning solution. This is discussed in Section 3, which goes beyond the label that accompanies the technologies and discusses their 'utility' instead using the data Format, Interactivity/Immersion/Timing/Content, Connectivity and Administration (FITCCA) framework.

The 'ingredients' and the 'flavours' they create then help to inform the 'recipe' in terms of what digital and blended learning solutions L&D professionals can provide to learners. This discussion is contained in Section 4, and covers some important digital and multimedia principles that L&D professionals should bear in mind in developing learning solutions. Section 5 is an extension of the discussion of 'recipes', as it examines the different emphases of blended learning solutions and how technology can support them. Finally, Section 6 concludes the chapter.

2 Digital technologies

This section discusses some technologies used in learning and development. It is not exhaustive and is intended to give L&D professionals an idea of the present technologies available to them. A broad meaning of the term 'learning technology' is adopted to also include classes of products. This section discusses 21 types of technologies, with an exercise from an L&D perspective following most discussions.

2.1 Blogs/vlogs

Blogs are informational sites on the internet that contain the views and opinions of an author. Blogs (which is the truncation of the word weblog) are generally used as a means to express thoughts and/or reflections. The length of a blog entry can vary significantly, as can the frequency of the entries. Donald H. Taylor (who is the chairman of the Learning and Performance Institute, based in the UK) provides a list of learning and development blogs that may be noteworthy (see Further Reading, p. 296).

Vlog (or video logs) are similar to blogs, but they are captured in video form rather than text. The purpose of vlogs is similar to that of blogs, as they also may be created to capture individuals' thoughts and feelings, although many are for entertainment purposes. Nonetheless, blogs and vlogs can also be used for learning and development, for example, as a tool to capture learners' reflections as they complete different stages of a course. The capture of a learner's reflections in an electronic form helps instructors and/or L&D professionals, as well as other learners, to easily access and read them. Blogs may be used to facilitate individuals' learning (eg understand why something may have gone right or wrong, and how they may plan for the future if similar tasks arise), or it may even be part of a course assessment.

In addition to blogs and vlogs, there are other platforms that allow multiple parties to write and respond to one another asynchronously. Such tools are for L&D as well as for other work-related purposes. These forums may be available to the public at large or reserved for access by certain communities. The following case example is from Abigail Newson, an HR business development consultant with IBM, who shares her experience in using technology for L&D in an organization that epitomizes high technology (note: Abigail refers to IBM's own bespoke online community system, which may not be comparable with other publicly accessible systems).

Abigail Newson, HR business development consultant, IBM UK

Digital technologies are vital, as a large part of my day-to-day work is undertaken in the virtual world, which of course is necessary given that IBM is a global company with the HR team spread all over the UK. We use a variety of platforms for diverse purposes, and it is quite difficult to be categorical in terms of when it is used to learn, for news, as a productivity tool that directly helps us in our work, or to communicate and interact with others. Why, how and when we use digital technologies is all very fluid and organic, which is great.

In terms of the most regularly used tools, we use a lot of blogs and internal collaboration tools (called online communities), with videos being increasingly used in a variety of ways. Where blogs are concerned, individuals will create and maintain their own blogs and you can communicate with them and have a discussion on anything. From a learning perspective, this is stimulating and lively, as the content is user generated, with many others joining in. Sometimes participants will also share materials (eg by providing links) that they found interesting online.

In terms of online communities, most parts of the business, for example HR, will have their own communities. I frequently use the UK HR online community, which is very helpful for all the different teams in HR to stay in tune with current news and in touch with one another. This is great, as you are not always stuck in your team bubble, so to speak, and can explore what other parts of the organization are doing and interact with other colleagues. For example, although I am not in recruitment, I am able to learn about the recruitment function and keep myself updated on what is happening in that part of HR. If there are new projects that they are working on, I can learn about this through the online communities. We not only learn about new developments in our HR practice, but we also keep updated with any news that could be important to our work, such as changes in policies regarding compensation.

The online communities also of course extend globally. I am able to access and learn about the global HR strategy, and how this is implemented in regions and at country levels. The communities are helpful as they provide both macro and micro views of an area such as HR, which means it can be high-level strategies or local practices. The online communities provide real-time, bite-size, incremental learning, which supports us to be productive in our work.

In addition, the online communities are also useful for knowledge capture and sharing. For example, community members will share their work such as reports or templates that they have used in their business-as-usual work and/or in projects. This enables us to learn what others have done in the past, learning good and best practices. In addition, you can also get in touch with the creators of the documents and/or project members to better learn from them about their experiences and ask for their thoughts and suggestions. I have used online communities to ask questions in obtaining assistance from colleagues who may have come across similar situations. The histories of discussions are stored and are easily accessible, which is helpful, as some issues may have been discussed and 'dealt' with in the past, and I can then quickly look them up without the need to revisit this with colleagues. This is of course much better than e-mail, as information and knowledge are shared in online communities, rather than being kept away in someone's inbox.

As mentioned, the use of videos is increasingly growing. Videos are also used a great deal to stimulate learning and development. For example, teams may have a hot topic or area that they want to share or spur others to also look into, and they do this by creating a video to be shared with others to communicate the ideas and details for a new initiative. For example, if there is a hot new topic that the CEO is focusing on, she would start her communications using a video, with the details captured in a self-paced learning solution helping to explain the idea further and suggesting how it can be taken up or 'implemented'. The CEO also uses videos as part of her annual address to the organization. In these videos, she informs us of the focus of the organization, new directions, congratulates teams/individuals for their success and so on. This is helpful for us in learning about the changing context of the organization, how this has impacted strategy and so on (this is a source of learning that is related to Chapter 2 concerning the organizational context). I find it helpful and it gets you engaged to learn about the wider company.

Learning in IBM is almost all online, except for a few instances, and therefore any blended learning would be a combination of technologies and media (as discussed in Section 5). This is because of the size of IBM and how it is spread over wide geographies. We are not just located in different parts of UK; we also travel to different locations, as this is regularly required by most of our work. Hence, mobile technologies are also important and frequently used, not just for communications but also for learning and development that can be used on almost any portable device, eg smartphones and laptops. But of course there are times when we are required to meet in person for learning and development. For example, every quarter there is an HR team meeting for L&D where different speakers attend to share insights and information on key topics.

Exercise

This exercise is to help you to get some ideas on how blogs/vlogs may be useful as an L&D tool. Find three to four blogs and/or vlogs that are publicly accessible. The blog/vlog should contain an element of learning and development such as a person reflecting on what they have learned, and address the following questions:

- What guidance would you provide in helping someone create a better blog with respect to:
  - their reflection;
  - maximizing the use of blogs, eg creating hyperlinks to other websites.
- How could blogs/vlogs play a role in a course that you are familiar with?

2.2 Collaboration tools

Collaboration tools are technologies that enable more than one person to create and edit a piece of work, such as a document, in a simultaneous manner. These types of tools are useful to enable individuals who are located remotely from one another to come together and collaborate. For example, individuals can use Google Docs to concurrently compose and annotate the same document. This not only saves time, as the document does not have to be e-mailed to each individual one after another, but also facilitates better understanding amongst the collaborators. In addition to text, collaboration tools such as whiteboards (see Further Reading, p. 296) allow participants to draw and visually depict their ideas and thoughts. This is similar to what happens in a workshop, but this is done virtually.

In addition to being used as a productivity tool in helping people work more efficiently and effectively with one another, collaboration tools can also be used for learning and development purposes. For example, L&D professionals and/or instructors can embed these technologies within VLEs for learners to use as part of a problem-solving activity. Collaboration tools can also be used as a knowledge-sharing tool that forms part of an informal learning environment that individuals can use as and when required.

Exercise

Identify and describe three L&D activities that at least two individuals can undertake using a collaboration tool. As part of the description, highlight the purpose of the activity and why collaborating synchronously would be more beneficial (than in turns).

2.3 Content management system

Content management systems (CMS) are technologies that enable L&D professionals to collate, inventorize, modify, transform and reuse learning content. Content is usually in the form of learning objects, which are multimedia, eg a short video that has been converted for the purpose of learning. For example, a learning object may involve a standalone video that includes a description of how it can be used for learning and development, in what way, and suggestions for potential activities that may be provided for learners or other materials to be used as an 'extension' of the existing learning object.

As you probably can tell, a CMS is an administrative tool that works 'behind the scenes' rather being a learning technology per se that learners engage with in their learning. An important feature of learning objects is their reusability, which is helped by the ability to disaggregate the various elements in a learning object, such as the multimedia (ie the content), how it is presented, its structure (eg the order of when the content is presented) and the pedagogy (ie how to understand, apply, analyse and/or synthesize). A CMS enables organizations to house these learning objects all in one system so that L&D professionals can maximize their use of existing learning objects to help develop new courses.

Exercise

- Do a search on the internet for publicly accessible and available learning objects, for example https://www.merlot.org/merlot/index.htm and http://www.careo.org/.
  - Identify three learning objects, analyse the different elements of these learning objects.
- Reflect on how learning objects can support L&D professionals in developing learning solutions.
  - Whilst using learning objects within a CMS is helpful, L&D professionals must monitor where and when they have been used so that the same learners do not come across the same elements too frequently. What other drawbacks may there be in using learning objects and how can L&D professionals mitigate this?

2.4 Curation

Curation involves bringing together learning materials (eg content and learning objects) for a particular purpose. With the advent of the internet, L&D professionals, as with other professionals and the workforce in general, face an unprecedented problem of information overload. However, the corollary of this also means that there is almost 'something out there' for most purposes. For example, if you wanted to find material related to different leadership behaviour types in sub-sectors of the voluntary/third sector, it is quite likely that you will be able to locate something that relates to that topic, usually in more than one format, eg text and video.

In addition to navigating materials in a dense jungle of information in an efficient manner, L&D professionals also need to catalogue and organize materials curated. There are a number of free-to-use sites such as Learnist, Pinterest and Scoop.it, as well as Curatr. Curation of learning technologies benefits both learners and learning administrators (eg L&D professionals). The democratization of learning through the internet means that people now have access to information, knowledge and learning materials (many of which are for free). Hence, curation of learning technologies helps individuals to collate and organize materials for their own personal learning. Curation is also helpful for L&D professionals as they then do not have to 'reinvent the wheel' in terms of content.

Exercise

This exercise is to help you get started in curating content for either your own learning or for a particular topic. The first thing is to decide whether you are doing this for your own learning or playing the role of an L&D professional curating materials for learners in a short course.

- Your own learning:
  - If you are curating for your own learning, identify one of your most important learning needs, eg negotiation skills and conflict resolution.
  - Identify and use a curation tool to collate your materials.
  - Organize the curated materials in some logical manner, such as degree of difficulty, that you will find easy to follow.
- As an L&D professional:
  - If you curating for a short course, identify a topic that is narrow enough to be taught as a short course (eg a few hours of study) such as time management or how to create a pivot table in MS Excel.

- Do some research to identify the steps required to develop such a course.
- Identify and use a curation tool to collate learning materials.
- Organize the curated materials in some logical manner, eg degree of difficulty, which includes exercises after each major step to reinforce learning.

2.5 Digital/video games

The use of digital and video games as a learning tool have been met with suspicion. Indeed, research into the use of technology such as video games in learning is affected by a phenomenon called the *third-person effect* (Perloff, 1999). This means people believe that media affects the 'unknown others' more than it affect themselves. An implication of this phenomenon on the perception of video games is that people who are the least familiar with video games tend to believe they pose a threat (Ferreira and Ribeiro, 2001).

Digital/video games may include simple electronic versions of Sudoku and crossword puzzles as well as more complex games such as Game Dev Story (playing the role of a software development entrepreneur) and Bridge Constructor (challenge in building bridges with real-life constraints and limited resources) (both are paid-for services). Electronic games are an attractive method of education and learning, as they provide real-time feedback, help to stimulate and develop problem-solving strategies, allow people to experience consequences of action in a safe environment, improve hand–eye coordination (in some games), and improve memory and the ability to recall information and stimulate cooperation (when games are designed for team working) (Goldstein, 2003; Loon, Evans, and Kerridge, 2015).

Indeed, games have an effect on players' physiological state, as many studies reported participants playing games having significantly increased heart rate, increased oxygen consumption and an increase in dopamine levels (dopamine is natural neurotransmitters released by the brain that make us feel reward and pleasure) (Scott, 1995). However, whilst games are increasingly being used in education and learning, as they are fun and engaging, interactive, challenging, novel and stimulate curiosity, they must be supported by a clear instructional design that integrates game playing with other aspects of a course.

Exercise

Watch the following videos and address the following questions.

Watch the videos:

http://www.bbc.co.uk/news/technology-34255492 and
https://www.coursera.org/course/videogameslearning (you may even
want to sign up for this course on Coursera offered by the University of
Wisconsin–Madison).

Address the questions:

- How important are video games becoming for learning and development today?
- Identify a group of people or professions who may benefit from game playing (describe the kind of game that they would play).
- How would this game playing help/develop them?

2.6 Digital resources repositories/portals (e-library)

Digital resources repositories/portals are systems that house learning content such as reports or articles and/or act as a gateway to other secured sites that contain copyright materials. Digital resources repositories/portals usually pertain to materials that are not obtainable for free on the World Wide Web, and hence require the security and tracking features that usually accompany it. Such systems may contain specialist materials such as academic journal articles, or reports on technology and the markets.

Digital resources repositories, sometimes known as e-libraries, support learning as they contain materials that may be essential for learners to further their knowledge about a particular topic and which may have only been highlighted in the main learning material (see Further Reading, p. 296). The copyright for such content may be owned by the organization or at times may have Open Access copyrights that allow users to copy and reproduce materials as long as they are attributed (but in this case the materials can also be found on the World Wide Web). However, in some instances, these digital resources are not contained within the virtual boundaries of an organization's network but are retained by owners of the copyright such as publishers who house the materials in their own systems, only accessible via a link that authenticates the user (and users' organization). A key feature that some digital resources repositories/portals (e-libraries) have is the function that enables users to undertake federated searches across multiple databases, which is valuable in making the research process more efficient.

Many of these systems may be used in a workforce's day-to-day work, such as those in consultancies that may access internally generated reports as well as those from specialist information brokers and research from companies such as the *Economist* and Frost and Sullivan (a market research company). In addition, they can also be used for learning and development programmes that use digital resources repositories/portals for learners to undertake research as part of their course and their assessment. Many of the materials accessible via such systems hold information that is credible and considered generally reliable, which is important for professionals in science and technology fields, for example.

Exercise

You may have come across digital resources repositories/portals as part of your studies at a college or university. Reflect upon how materials in a digital resources repository/portal may enhance a course that you are familiar with.

2.7 Document repositories and sharing tools

Document repositories and sharing tools are learning technologies that are created to store materials/working documents generated by users (eg the workforce in an organization). These repositories and sharing tools are used when various individuals need to access and edit 'living' documents remotely. The systems record all work done on documents (and folders), such as their creation and subsequent editing, to help users to track and monitor their development. These systems come in different forms and vary in sophistication. For example, Microsoft's Sharepoint is a dedicated system that performs the functions discussed (and more), but these systems may sometimes be integrated with other systems such VLEs. Sharepoint can even be used as a platform to develop in-house learning management systems.

As indicated, document repositories and sharing tools support learning and development. Whilst this technology is not a learning tool per se, it does offer learners a facility to store work that they may have created during the length of a course. This is helpful, as learners can refer to previous versions as and when required. In addition, these versions can be shared with other learners when they need to work together as part of their coursework. These systems are similar to the collaborative tools discussed earlier, although some may not allow for synchronous working.

Exercise

Document repositories and sharing tools are basic learning and development (as well as productivity) technologies that are usually taken for granted. Their presence does not significantly enhance the learning experience but its absence is usually felt. Undertake research on the internet and identify at least two document repositories and sharing tools that can be used for learning and development. Describe the function/features of both technologies.

2.8 e-portfolio

E-portfolios (also known as digital portfolios) may be viewed as a collection point for L&D evidence, for example, that is in electronic form. E-portfolios may be used to collect any multimedia files (eg text, audio and video), and contain hyperlinks to other people's blogs and materials. E-portfolios share similar purposes with curation technologies and can be used as part of an individual's personal learning environments (PLEs – further discussed later). A key difference unique to e-portfolios is their use as a tool to capture people's reflection and to enrich the reflection with the inclusion and links to other content (see Further Reading, p. 296).

Whilst digital portfolios can be used for work-related purposes such as collecting evidence for performance appraisals and promotion applications, they are typically used in learning and development. For example, e-portfolios many be used in work-based learning programmes that require learners to collect evidence of what they have learned and organize it in a manner that supports their claim for attainment. In addition, e-portfolios may also be used in formal education settings, with students collating the work they have completed throughout their course to support their reflection, which may form part of their overall assessment. Another example is the use of e-portfolios in personal learning environments (PLEs). Personal learning environments is an umbrella term that refers to environments created by individuals for the purpose of their own learning, which may include their professional work (eg as a health and safety officer), hobbies (eg gardening) and personal development (eg meditation). E-portfolios, as well as other technologies such as curation tools, may be used by individuals to organize their own resources for learning.

Exercise

This activity requires you to undertake research to find out more about e-portfolios, and the various products available.

- Do a search on the internet to identify at least three e-portfolio products that are available for free to use or at least have a trial period. You may want to start with Weebly: http://www.weebly.com/.

- Access and download each of the three products.

- Explore each product and list the functionalities and features of each. Which would you recommend for use and why?

2.9 Learning badges

As part of a person's continuing professional development (CPD), any recognized form of activity undertaken (including seminars attended) may count towards their CPD, usually recorded in some form of registry that is maintained by the individual, their respective professional association and/or their employers. The technology of learning badges builds upon the notion of CPD; specifically it enables individuals to have their learning recognized and verified.

Learning badges are a borrowed concept from scouting/guiding, where a boy scout or girl guide is awarded a badge when they are able to demonstrate some competency such as tying knots. In the case of learning badges, a professional will be able to gain a 'badge' from the 'awarding body' when they have shown that they have 'learned'. Learning badges recognize a variety of activities and attainments, such as attending a seminar or passing an examination, and reflect this in their records.

There are a variety of digital learning badges such as Mozilla and Badgecraft's learning badges (see Further Reading for links to both products). Digital badges have a number of advantages over traditional record keeping. The first is because it is now in electronic form, it is portable and helps learners to be even more mobile. This is important, especially when many people now change jobs and even careers more frequently than they used to in the past, and at times this may even mean emigrating to different countries. Digital badges also allow for easier verification from the 'awarding body'. Learning badges do not help learning per se but they help with 'administration', as the information contained can be exported (with relative ease) to enterprise learning and HR systems.

Exercise

This exercise is intended to help you get started in creating your own portfolio of learning badges using a digital platform. Similar to the e-portfolio exercise, identify three free-to-use learning badges products (or at least ones that have a free version), evaluate each and decide on one to use. Set up your learning badges. You may use your most up-to-date curriculum vitae (CV) as a reference to record education qualifications, training courses completed and other attainments and achievements.

2.10 Learning management systems

Learning management system (LMS) is a generic term describing systems used to administrate learning by maintaining, tracking and reporting on learners' progress and also to deliver courses (sometimes used interchangeably with VLEs, as they both may overlap considerably in functionality for some products). LMSs are used to manage learners, as they contain the relevant personal details of learners, eg name, title of position, and of course, their learning history – education qualifications and training courses attended. LMSs may also contain information concerning an individual's career pathway, training needs analysis, future learning and development requirements, and any certification and accreditation needed.

One may view an LMS as a system that helps manage individuals' learning cycles, as it keeps track of their learning and development relevant to their career, and their up-to-date certification that may be relevant for their jobs. Sometimes courses may be offered from LMS, which is what a VLE does. Nonetheless, generally an LMS is used to manage the needs of learners, whilst a VLE helps learners to meet the learning outcomes of courses contained within it.

Whilst an LMS may be used directly to help individuals (if there are functions and features within the product to do this), it may be typically used as an administrative system to manage learners. This is an important role nevertheless, as data from LMS can be used across other systems (if it is technically possible to do so) to better facilitate learning, eg recognize individuals' prior learning to better inform instructors about the participants in their class. To learn more about the variety of LMSs in the marketplace, please see Further Reading, p. 296.

Exercise

LMS should be able to manage learners' needs and life cycle whilst they are part of an organization. Examine how possessing data and information about the learners themselves can help enrich their learning experience as well as support L&D professionals.

2.11 Mobile learning

The early uses and versions of mobile learning were essentially to mirror content that was consumed on personal computers. This narrow view of mobile learning meant that it always followed PC-based learning in the same trajectory. However, as smartphones have become more powerful and developers more innovative, mobile learning now offers a different experience for learners (OUP, 2016).

Mobile learning is best designed for learners who are 'on the move' and who may best consume materials in bite-size pieces. An area of learning where mobile learning can be most advantageous is improving the ability to recall. Learners using their mobile phone are able to consume, memorize and learn to recall specific information. This information can be timed and relayed to learners over a specific interval. Given the exponential growth of computing power, many mobile devices and 'phablets' (a device that is somewhere between a phone and a tablet) are more able to process more resource-intensive applications. As the size of the hardware increases, it is also more ergonomic for individuals to use the phones for longer periods, therefore broadening the types of L&D applications that they can use comfortably.

Exercise

Learning on a personal computer or laptop is generally considered more comfortable and hence given a choice and the opportunity many people may choose to learn using this method. Under what circumstances would mobile learning be more advantageous for people?

2.12 Media streaming/video learning

Media streaming technologies enable data-intensive multimedia such as audio, video and even games to be played over electronic devices. Media streaming technologies are crucial to the service that companies such as Netflix provide, as streaming allows videos to be consumed (watched), but not retained by the consumer due to copyright. Videos are also useful in learning and development, as they present information in a richer manner and may be more action orientated. This form of learning technology enables L&D professionals to 'show' rather than tell. Whilst L&D professionals can create their own videos, the cost of this may be discouraging. However, there are firms that specialize in developing bespoke videos for learning and development. These firms use professional actors in their role playing. However, with the plethora of videos available over the internet, there is always a fair chance that L&D professionals will find a video that suits their needs (this then relates to curation and the use of curation tools as discussed).

Exercise

The CIPD provides a number of bespoke videos for HR professionals (http://www.videoarts.com/cipd/). Whilst these are paid for, each video contains free-to-view trailers. Select and watch two video trailers, and reflect upon the following:

- If you were a junior HR professional or a first-time line manager (implementing HR policy), how helpful would these videos be to you?

- If you were an L&D professional, how could you make use of these videos?

2.13 Personal response system/software

Personal response systems (PRS) are devices that are typically used by learners in physical classroom environments to interact with the instructor or sometimes with one another (eg classroom activity). A simple example involves polling. An instructor may ask the class a question and the students respond using the PRS; the results are shown on the instructor's screen in the front of the class. However, PRS can also be used in a variety of ways to stimulate learning through in-class collaboration and even competition. Whilst the term PRS refers to a broad range of hardware products that have a similar function, these learning technologies do differ significantly in terms of their capabilities (eg software in the system) and usage.

Indeed, the software that enables PRS devices can also be used on personal devices such as smartphones, tablets and laptops. These applications can also be used online and as part of gamification. An example can be explored on this webpage about how a product called Kahoot can be used: https://getkahoot.com/how-it-works

Exercise

Watch the following video that contains an example of how an instructor used personal response system software in his class to enhance his students' learning experience and then address the following task.

Watch this TEDTalk video about a lecturer, Matthew Stoltzfus, using PRS (note: the video is 14 minutes 13 seconds long. The part that discusses the use of PRS technology starts about 7 minutes into the video): https://www.youtube.com/watch?v=o8a1dsv5IXo&feature=youtu.be

Address the following the questions:

- How was such a personal response software used in the video?
- In what other ways could PRS technology be used to stimulate learning?
- Can PRS be linked to other learning technologies to enhance learners' experience and/or improve the administration of learning (from an L&D professional's perspective)?

2.14 Podcasts

Podcasts are audio recordings made by an individual talking about a particular topic; it may also be a live discussion amongst individuals. Even snippets of radio shows can be recorded as podcasts. These audio recordings provide an extra and different dimension compared to content such as text. Audio recordings enable the people to be more lively and creative when developing the podcast. Indeed, the ability to alter tone and speed helps to keep the content from being monotonous. A podcast can be one-off or created as a series of episodes.

Podcasts have been used as a learning tool as much as they have for entertainment. Podcasts are portable and can be saved and played over again by the learner. Similar to mobile learning, podcasts are handy as learners can save the files into their phones to be played whilst they are commuting, waiting in a queue, etc. Podcasts also add variety to other content formats that a learner may already be using, such as text.

Podcasts also present an opportunity for L&D professionals, as they are generally easy to create, especially when the equipment (eg audio recording devices) and facilities (eg a conducive room) are available. For example, as an L&D professional creating course content, you may want highly regarded individuals in the field to contribute insights to the course. Podcasts allow L&D professional to capture such knowledge and build it into learning content quickly, without the need to transcribe interview notes. Also, people tend to have less of a problem with making a voice recording than with appearing in a video.

Exercise

Identify two or three podcasts related to learning and development. Listen to these podcasts and reflect on the following (you may start with Apple's podcast on their iTunes platform: https://itunes.apple.com, and search for 'podcasts', some of which are free).

As a learner:

- Are podcasts more interesting than having the information in text format? Why or why not?

- Do you think you would learn 'better' from podcasts compared to if the information was in text format? Why or why not?

As an L&D professional:

- How would you improve some of the podcasts that you have just listened to?

2.15 Screen casting and lecture capture

Screen casting, as the term suggests, concerns recording what goes on your computer screen, to the level of detail in terms of keystroke and the movement of the cursor. A common example of screen casting is recording how to install a software application on your computer, or how to use some feature/functionality of a software application. In addition to capturing keystroke movements, screen casting also allows audio narratives to be recorded.

Lecture capture is similar to screen casting, but instead of capturing the instructor's computer screen, it records instructors teaching a class. The two are not mutually exclusive. For example, the University of Michigan in the United States offers Six Sigma (a statistical method for quality management) programmes online. The presentation of the video recordings can be described as containing elements that you would expect from a screen cast and lecture. As the video plays, one part of your screen shows the instructor's screen as he/she performs the statistical calculations (See Figure 6.1). Another part of your screen contains a video of the instructor as he/she explains the concepts while performing the calculations (both parts are in sync).

Figure 6.1 Example of screen casting and lecture capture

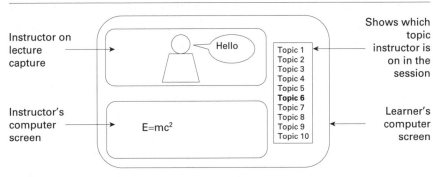

The advantages of screen casting and lecture capture for learners are similar to those of video learning. Learners are able to play the video at their own convenience and at their own pace. For instructors and L&D professionals, screen casting and lecture capture offer consistency in delivery and enable them incrementally improve their lectures. Indeed, screen casting and lecture capture can also be recorded in bite-sized chunks and put together in modularized form. To find out more about these technologies, please see Further Reading, p. 296.

Exercise

There are a number of suggestions (eg http://www.mediacore.com/blog/how-to-record-your-screen-and-create-engaging-screencasts) on how to develop a screen casting video on the internet. Do a search and construct a mini guide (half an A4 piece of paper) on how to create a screen cast.

2.16 Social media and enterprise social networks

Social media is a family of products that enable people to link up with one another. These products can vary a great deal in terms of their functionality and also purpose. For example, Facebook has many features (eg friends can tag one another's photos), whilst Twitter primarily allows users to only use text and photos or graphics. Other websites such as LinkedIn are primarily used for professional networking rather than for purely social purposes.

Social media has great potential for enhancing the way people interact, collaborate, share ideas and ultimately become more productive in their work. However, social media also has drawbacks, especially concerning security and confidentiality of organizational data and information. In recognition of this, enterprise social networks, which build upon the advantages of social media whilst attempting to mitigate its shortcomings, have emerged. Companies such as Yammer offer organizations more control in terms of security of information shared amongst their workforce. Examples of other providers can be found in Further Reading, p. 296.

Social media and enterprise social networks, in addition to facilitating work, can also be used for learning and development. As the adage goes, 'it's not what you know, it's who you know'. These technologies link people together so that working relationships develop and ultimately people are able to help one another in different aspects of their professional lives, including learning and development. As Cheetham and Chivers (2001) argue, adults learn best informally, and when they need to (eg when faced with a present problem).

Exercise

This exercise will involve reflecting upon your use of any social media that you are registered with, for example Facebook or LinkedIn. Reflect upon a time when you felt social media provided you the opportunity to learn, for example, provide information that was sought, or introduced you to another person who was able to provide the information/knowledge. What was it that you learned? Did social media make this process of learning more 'efficient'? Is this form of learning impactful from an organizational perspective?

2.17 Simulation games

Simulation games are similar to video games in many respects, as both provide feedback to players, offer an element of competition and are stimulating. However, there are differences. Realism is an important aspect of simulation games (they simulate reality) and although it is impossible to completely reflect reality, key elements of reality (or at least those that are part of learning outcomes) need to be present. High-quality and sophisticated simulation games also tend to provide richer feedback to players, especially those that are used for learning and development. Such simulation games are also more complex, compel players to be more thoughtful in the way they approach and play the game, and enable players to make risky decisions in a safe environment.

There are many off-the-shelf simulation games available for different subject fields such as change management, leadership development and operations management, and they come in formats such as 'client' installation or via the internet, for example. A crucial aspect of simulation games is their ability to attract and induce players so that they become immersed in the game (Loon, Evans and Kerridge, 2015). Immersion is important and is a key differentiator amongst simulation game products; the more immersive a simulation game is, the more likely it is to provide a better learning experience. Immersion requires a rich and detailed story to be set as a background.

However, many scholars, for example Landers and Landers (2014) and Loon (2014) argue that learning does not occur automatically by playing a simulation game. Instructors and/or L&D professionals must support and integrate the game with appropriate instructional design. For example, learners need to be invited to reflect on key learning elements during game play, reinforce the concepts learned, and integrate lessons from the game with those learned in a classroom.

Indeed, many high-quality simulation games provide suggestions on how to support student learning using their respective simulation game. Proserpio and Gioia (2007) argue that L&D and teaching professionals should ensure that any simulation game procured has sound pedagogical underpinnings (supported and integrated with instructional design). It should possess an engaging and potentially immersive storyline and background, and contain mystery and opportunities for learners to discover. The case example below from Professor Bodian illustrates why and how he uses simulation games in his postgraduate courses.

Professor Lamine Bodian, master's programmes director, École supérieure pour le développement économique et social (ESDES Lyon Business School, France)

I've always been attracted to business games, as they help students figure out the theories taught by their teachers. From a practice perspective, business games help students comprehend the business world, notably the strategies deployed by firms, the costs incurred by different operations, the financial outcomes, the risks, international transactions, supply chain issues, currency fluctuations, self-production versus outsourcing, and HR issues as well.

One of the reasons my students love the business games is that the games seem very close to the real business world, whilst theory sometimes appears very remote. I do, then, use business games to illustrate what my students have learned in concrete terms. Therefore, students themselves become part of the game as they have to figure out all the details.

▶

> I use three business games, all from Cesim: 'Global Challenge' for global strategic management; 'SimPower' for my master's students in international purchasing, about how to purchase electricity and the complexities and technical aspects of the sector; and SimBank, based on credit and liquidity risks management within a bank for my master's students in international risk management.
>
> In terms of instructional design, the games are organized at the end of each programme as a capstone activity to 'wrap up' what has been learned during the semester. The games are played over the course of a week, within teams of five, with each member playing specific roles, eg CEO, CFO, HR Director etc. Once the game is completed, the teams have to present their results to the General Assembly of Shareholders and address any questions in regard to their performance.

Exercise

This exercise requires you to play a simulation game on entrepreneurship, Simventure. This website allows you to trial its product. Access the game via http://simventure.co.uk/classic/the-product/free-demo Evaluate the game against the criteria set by Proserpio and Gioia (2007), and reflect how this simulation game would help learners in developing entrepreneurship capabilities.

2.18 Talent management system/HR enterprise system

Talent management and/or HR enterprise systems are technologies that are generally used to store and manage information about the organization's workforce. The data stored generally include people's personal details, work-related information such as date of commencement of employment, job title, compensation and so on. In terms of learning and development, these systems play an indirect but important role, although this does vary by a significant degree amongst organizations.

For example, these systems can feed data into an LMS (discussed previously) concerning some of an individual's personal details so that this can be matched and further processed for learning and development purposes. It is considered good practice that when a system requires data that is already stored in another system, then the data needs to be imported rather than directly entered, so as to maintain data integrity by ensuring that there is only one source for the data. Alternatively, if organizations do not have an LMS then these or similar systems may fulfil the role played by an LMS (which talent management systems should be able to do – please refer to the exercise concerning LMS).

2.19 Virtual learning environments and massive open online courses (MOOCs)

Virtual learning environments (VLEs) is a generic term referring to web-based platforms used to deliver learning and development programmes. For instance, a VLE can be used to store materials for a programme, organize weekly tutorial sessions, and contain quizzes and tests. Although there are off-the-shelf VLE products such as Blackboard (also known as an LMS, see Further Reading, p. 296), and open-source software such Moodle (popular amongst universities) which allows users to further adapt the software for their specific needs, VLEs can vary significantly from one another, especially those developed in-house, as VLEs themselves are made up of various technologies such as repository tools. What technology is incorporated depends on the organization and L&D units. VLEs may also be part of an LMS and other similar technologies and platforms.

Massive open online courses (MOOCs) are a form of VLE that already have content (developed and managed by the respective universities and other providers). MOOCs are grouped according to providers such as FutureLearn (UK-based), Udacity and edX, which themselves are made up of universities and other education providers (see list of MOOCs in Further Reading, p. 296). However, there are also other independent providers such as Khan Academy. Many courses on MOOCs are free, although not all are credit bearing. Courses on MOOCs can be curated by L&D professionals as part of the design and content of a learning and development programme.

VLEs provide many advantages to both learners and L&D professionals. For example, they are easily scalable and are not limited by physical constraints such as the size of a classroom. If the course on the VLE has more self-paced components (more akin to a do-it-yourself mode of learning, which is discussed in Section 5.2), it is more scalable, as dependency on an instructor becomes minimal. Even if there is a dependency on an instructor, the asynchronous nature of some communications technologies within VLEs allows for larger cohorts of learners to be more easily managed. VLEs also allow for consistency, as they can be delivered to more people using the same materials and approach. Also, VLEs allow L&D professionals to reach out to learners who are a far distance away and in different time zones.

Exercise

Watch this YouTube video about VLE, specifically on its use and general advantages and disadvantages: https://www.youtube.com/watch?v=hltvryZ-Llc

The video discusses the advantages and disadvantages of VLEs. Reflect upon how a VLE may have better supported a course that you were on. Did the course that you attended maximize the features of the VLE? Could the course have used the VLE more effectively? If so, how?

2.20 Virtual worlds

Virtual worlds (or sometimes referred to massively multiplayer online world) are simulated online environments that allow people to create their own 'worlds'. Virtual worlds are also aptly called 'collaborative virtual environments', as they enable many people to not only access and play at the same time but also to communicate, interact and collaborate with one another. Virtual worlds can be 'stand-alone' in that players establish their own goals and rules, or as part of simulation game such as an auditing game developed by the University of West of England (UWE, nd) This learning technology is foremost a simulation game, but some of its more interesting features are the avatars and the virtual world that is part of the game. There are many virtual worlds available on the internet, for example Second Life, which is free, and the popular Minecraft, which is a paid-for service (see Further Reading, p. 296).

Amongst its various uses are entertainment, as well as learning and development. There are a variety of ways to design learning and development programmes using virtual worlds. For example, the setting may be created by an instructor who also establishes the rules of the game for the learners. In another example, instructors may be less prescriptive and provide just a framework (with the objective and roles to be adopted by learners) and let the learners decide on how they are to reach the goals. Virtual worlds can and have been used for learning and development in many contexts and subject matters.

Exercise

SecondLife (http://secondlife.com/) has been used as an educational tool and both the developers and users have contributed to providing guidance in developing educational programmes to those new to SecondLife. Some of the guidance can be found here: http://wiki.secondlife.com/wiki/Second_Life_Education

This exercise requires you to explore the pages in the website above, including watching the videos, to get an idea of how you can create an L&D programme. Once you have done this research, develop a task for learners to undertake. To keep this exercise light, identify a task that is not too onerous and only requires you as the L&D professional to provide simple guidance (eg objective and bullet-pointed steps, and give learners the autonomy to decide things for themselves) rather than detailed rules.

As part of this task you may want to include the following:

- establish the objective of the game;
- identify the rules (short and simple is recommended for this exercise);
- describe what you would expect learners to do;
- describe what you expect learners to learn from this virtual world activity.

2.21 Wiki

Wiki is a Hawaiian word for 'quick', and from the view of a learning technology it allows people to collaboratively build and construct knowledge. One of the most popular wikis is Wikipedia. Wiki allow people to access and edit each other's work. The open philosophy of wiki has many benefits, as it encourages people to share their knowledge, and the exchange of ideas sometimes helps make the knowledge created more robust as it includes multiple perspectives. Of course, the use of wikis is not without its problems, as the accuracy of people's work cannot always be guaranteed, nor will everyone keep to the basic etiquette.

The open philosophy also encourages the concept of 'crowd-sourcing', as people pull together their expertise to help one another. An example is an Oxford academic who created a 'crowd-source' website to gain help from the public to help decipher some ancient text (Coughlan, 2012). Whilst this is not a wiki, it reflects the same principles as a wiki – large groups of people sharing knowledge and collaborating.

In a learning and development environment, wikis can be used to a great extent and are especially useful when a particular topic is subjective and there is no one single perspective. There are multiple views that are just as valid as the next. Also, wikis are helpful in encouraging learners to interact with one another, especially when developing teamwork is one of the objectives of the programme.

Exercise

Explore and read the following guidance on how to create a wiki and the ideas of its uses: https://ipark.hud.ac.uk/content/wikis The next step is to identify an activity that learners (eg five learners) can collaborate on using a wiki, for example, define 'leadership'. How would you guide learners in sharing a wiki (eg draw upon their personal experience from the viewpoint of a woman, a student, a member of an ethnic minority group), and what do you envisage as the final 'product' at the end of the exercise?

3 A framework to guide the use of digital technologies for learning

There are a plethora of technology types available (eg social media, curation), and even within each type there are also a host of providers (eg Twitter and Facebook) that vary greatly in terms of features and usage (eg free or subscription based). Learning technologies can also be used for other purposes than they were initially designed for. For example, a technology used for friends to keep in touch with one another can also be used as a collaboration tool for work. In many cases, it is not the learning technology itself but what it enables that it is important (although the popularity of a certain technology is important, as it means that there is already existing uptake, and this makes further adoption easier and more rapid).

L&D professionals need to be savvy about the attributes of various learning technologies so they are able to make discerning decisions about which to adopt for their respective learners and organizations. By understanding the attributes of each technology and what they offer, L&D professionals will also be more informed about how best to combine the different learning technologies to optimize learning. A helpful way to evaluate learning technologies is to examine it from the attributes of data Format, degree of Interactivity, Timing, Content creation and curation and Administration (FITCCA) as shown in Figure 6.2.

3.1 Format

Data format includes text, graphics, audio and video. Some learning technologies may include all different formats (eg mobile learning), whilst some may only cater for a limited number of types. The more types of data format

Figure 6.2 The data Format, degree of Interactivity, Timing, Content creation and curation, Connectivity and Administration (FITCCA) framework for assessing the attributes of learning technologies

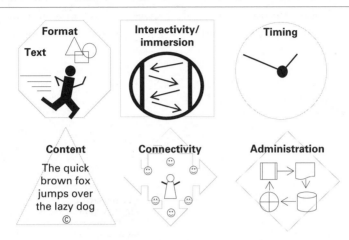

that learning technologies can accommodate, the richer and therefore more appealing they will be.

For example, virtual learning environments (VLEs) are considered rich, as they are multifaceted and may be able to contain various types of data formats. Off-the-shelf VLEs such as Blackboard provide more flexibility to L&D professionals in terms of content development (although there is a cost to it). Screen casting and lecture capture technologies are also a good example in terms of the type of data format that are used and how well they allow L&D professionals to synchronize video/audio with graphics and text. Data formats may also come in the form of avatars that are created in virtual worlds that contain text, graphics and audio.

3.2 Interactivity/immersion

Interactivity is the degree to which a learning technology allows for feedback and participation of different individuals. For example, blogs may be considered more of a one-way form of communication, as the content is usually to be read by learners unless of course there is a facility for readers to comment on each blog entry. However, readers are generally not able to 'co-create' content. Wikis, on the other hand, allow participants in a learning environment to build upon each other's work in co-creating content. Similarly, collaborative tools such as 'whiteboards' allow learners to visually create diagrams and illustrations.

Simulation games also usually rate highly in terms of interactivity, as the simulation games take into consideration the learners' actions and provide them feedback in the form of a score and change of events in the game (Figure 6.3 illustrates the relationship between the richness of information typically afforded by each technology and its potential in engaging learners).

Figure 6.3 Types of digital content in terms of richness of information exchanged and learner engagement

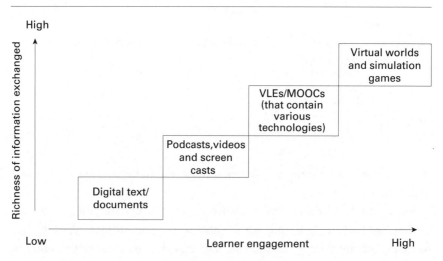

Some simulation games that allow for different players to participate are even more interactive. Multiplayer games may involve competition or cooperation whereby players may cooperate to compete against the computer or against one another and the computer. The high interactivity in some simulation games and virtual worlds (designed for L&D) should allow for learners to immerse themselves in game playing and therefore, potentially, in learning (Overton and Dixon, 2015).

3.3 Timing

Timing is another important element for L&D professionals to consider when evaluating learning technologies. Timing primarily relates to whether a learning technology allows for synchronous or asynchronous communications or both. Synchronous communications take place in real time, and the parties involved have to be operating the learning technology at the same time. Examples include Skype, which allows people to contact one another via text (text messaging), audio or video concurrently.

Asynchronous communication is the opposite, and the participants involved do not need to be operating the learning technology at the same time. Skype also allows for asynchronous communications, as text messages are kept in the recipient's account until they access it. Users are also able to make audio and video recordings for others to listen to/watch. Many learning technologies these days allow for both. The attribute of timing generally relates to the goals that L&D professionals want learners to attain. For example, wikis are useful if L&D professionals want participants to take their time to deliberate and contribute in their own time. However, collaborative tools such as 'whiteboards' are generally more suited if used synchronously, and this would be appropriate if it is crucial to complete an exercise at a particular point in time simultaneously.

3.4 Content (creation and curation)

The discussion concerning collaboration also raises an important point concerning content creation. Who creates content and to what degree? The traditional approach involved only, or at least most of the time, the instructor being allowed to create content for learners to consume. However, in the present day, content creation is no longer the preserve of instructors but has now extended to participants. This approach to knowledge building is especially appropriate for subjective fields such as leadership, for example, since the ways people 'construct' reality are also important and valid perspectives.

Technology is able to cater for different types of knowledge building and dialogue. For example, wikis are great for knowledge building, as learners are able to contribute to developing a concept in a more holistic manner that encompasses many perspectives. In addition, some VLEs such as Blackboard allow learners to be segregated into groups and allocated a virtual room for them to hold dialogue and create content that is work in progress before presenting it as a collective as part of a knowledge-building exercise.

Another aspect of content creation is curation. Curation is taking content from other sources and organizing it in a manner that is relevant for and suits a particular purpose. Curation is especially important in today's world of information overload, and it may be better for L&D professionals to curate content rather than 'reinventing the wheel', especially if originality is not important (although attribution is still given). For example, L&D professionals or learners themselves may curate content concerning how to develop professionalism, drawing upon examples from other various professionals such as medical doctors and accountants and their codes of ethics and pathways for development.

3.5 Connectivity

A related but distinct consideration with interactivity/immersion is connectivity. Whilst interactivity is mostly about the richness of 'feedback', be it from a person or system, connectivity concerns the number of people a system allows you to connect with (as well as other systems and devices). Connectivity plays on the phenomenon called 'network externality', which basically means the value of something increases as more people have or use it (Katz and Shapiro, 1986). An example is the telephone. If you were the only person on the planet that had a telephone, it would not be much good to you. But as more people have a phone, your phone becomes more useful. In a more recent example, social media allows for high connectivity (indeed it is central to the concept – again Facebook would have very little value if you were the only one on it).

The connectivity within technologies is also growing, as many can now cater for different devices (eg smartphones). Connectivity also relates to other devices in addition to people. The concept of the 'Internet of Things' is a term used to describe all the types of devices that are connected to the internet, from personal computers, tablets, smartphones, to even kitchen appliances and home heaters that can be controlled via the internet (Manyika, Chui and Bughin, 2013).

3.6 Administration

The final factor for consideration in the FITCCA framework is administration. Administration concerns the degree of control that the learning technology makes available to the user, the L&D unit and/or the organization. All learning technologies provide users (learners) with some control, such as the visibility of their presence on the system to other users. Other examples of user-controlled features may involve how often they are notified of message postings on VLEs, eg whether they are notified of every message that is posted as and when, or are notified on a weekly basis that collates all messages that have been posted throughout the week. Allowing learners some degree of control over the learning system is helpful and allows learners to personalize the system in a manner that is suited to their preferences/circumstances.

Nonetheless, a more crucial aspect of administration is from the perspective of the administrator/L&D professionals. Administration may be for various purposes such as the administration of learning content that can have various uses such as a programme/course, administration of a class, or administration of the workforce's learning and development pathways.

The administration of content allows L&D professionals to enhance, remove, amalgamate, organize, monitor and evaluate the content's usage.

Content management systems are usually used for such purposes as they help L&D professionals to monitor the usability and currency of content and ensure that all materials available for use in the development of digital learning technologies are relevant and appropriate. The administration of classes is also important, as it enables L&D professionals to organize learning materials in a coherent and logical (eg incremental in complexity) manner, and, equally importantly, to manage the learners in the class, for example, assisting learners with queries, helping resolve issues regarding participation, and assessment, if relevant.

Learner administration systems help L&D professionals to manage learners' development pathways throughout their careers within the organization. They may even help track a learner's attainment in formal education programmes as well as those that are experientially based. Talent management systems, HR enterprise systems and learning management systems are typical systems that help L&D professionals manage their workforce's learning and development.

Although it may seem that the monitoring and tracking appears to make L&D out to be 'big brother', this is hardly the case. Administrative functions within systems help L&D professionals to evaluate how effective or even popular a particular learning technology is. Most third-party technologies have strong privacy and confidential policies, and will not allow other parties such as L&D to access users' data (even if it is metadata such as frequency of login rather than the content itself). However, enterprise systems that are procured by the organization such as Yammer, an enterprise social network system, allow administrators such as L&D to access data that may be helpful for them to evaluate the usefulness of the particular learning technology.

The FITCCA framework is a helpful way to assess learning technologies, as it compels L&D professionals to view learning technologies from the perspective of their utility. This is important as these attributes/utilities change over time as companies enhance their products in light of new and more cost-efficient technologies. L&D professionals also need to be aware of the evolving functionalities and features.

Exercise

Complete Table 6.1 by evaluating each technology using the FITCCA framework. In addition to the attributes identified in the FITCCA framework, reflect if there are there other distinctive types of attributes that may be helpful in the comparison and evaluation of digital learning technologies. You may also include other learning and development technologies. The first row involving blogs/vlogs is an example of how you may undertake the activity for each 'technology'.

Table 6.1 Examples of digital learning technologies/solutions and their purpose/characteristics

Example of digital learning technologies/ solutions	Format Text	Interactivity/ immersion	Timing	Content The quick brown fox jumps over the lazy dog	Connectivity	Administration	Others?
	What type of format does this technology allow for, eg text, graphics, audio, video, combinations?	What is the degree of interactivity that this technology allows for amongst learners and instructor(s) and for immersion?	Does the technology allow for synchronous, asynchronous or a combination of both communications?	• Who generates content? ○ Instructor/ L&D generated/ curated ○ User peer user generated	How and to what degree does this technology allow for learners to connect to people and/or integrate with other technologies?	How does this technology help to support learning by managing content, class/ course and/or learner?	
1. Blogs/vlogs	A combination, depends on learners' access to media devices.	Limited interactivity. Others are able to provide feedback but not a communication tool per se.	Asynchronous.	Content usually created by learner. Peers can provide feedback to blog/ vlog.	Allows blogger/ vlogger to 'connect' to others as long as access is provided. Blogs/vlogs can be easily integrated with other technologies, eg VLEs	Limited administrative functionality for L&D professionals.	-NA-
2. Collaboration tools							
3. Content management system							
4. Curation							

continues

Table 6.1 *continued*

Example of digital learning technologies/ solutions	Format Text	Interactivity/ immersion	Timing	Content The quick brown fox jumps over the lazy dog	Connectivity	Administration	Others?
	What type of format does this technology allow for, eg text, graphics, audio, video, combinations?	What is the degree of interactivity that this technology allows for amongst learners and instructor(s) and for immersion?	Does the technology allow for synchronous, asynchronous or a combination of both communications?	• Who generates content? ○ Instructor/ L&D generated/ curated ○ User peer user generated	How and to what degree does this technology allow for learners to connect to people and/or integrate with other technologies?	How does this technology help to support learning by managing content, class/ course and/or learner?	
18. Talent management system/HR enterprise system							
19. Virtual learning environments (VLE) including MOOCS							
20. Virtual worlds							
21. Wikis							
22. Others							
23. Others							
24. Others							
25. Others							

4 Principles in the design and development of digital learning

This section discusses some principles derived from research in the field of cognition and how it can inform ideas in designing and developing digital learning. The term used, 'designing and developing digital learning', does not mean programming or developing new learning technologies from codes or anything that requires technical information systems competencies. The term, instead, refers to using and applying existing technologies such as those discussed in Section 2. In addition, this also involves knowing how to use specific elements in a technology, such as when and how to use text and video.

As in Chapter 3, where we stated that L&D professionals are not expected to be finance and accounting experts, this chapter does not expect them to be technologists. The aim of this chapter, as mentioned, is to develop L&D professionals to be technology savvy; to know what is out there, to be able to look beyond the product and understand the functions and features that technology may offer for specific learning and development opportunities, to be able to make trade-offs (eg use the free version and be able to make do with basic functions for a narrow application or spend and gain more functionality), to be capable of 'putting it all together' (different technologies) and to know what 'works'.

4.1 Digital and multimedia learning

Cognitive science tells us that the advent of multimedia and digital technologies for learning and development, as well as in day-to-day work, does influence us cognitively. Multimedia and digital technologies are a double-edged sword. First, it means that people's learning and cognitive strategies have had to change, for example in how to better select and to store more information in their memory (Van Oostendorp, 2003). In addition, people are more 'stretched', as multimedia and digital learning is more cognitively demanding.

Second, multimedia and digital learning over time does help learners, as multimedia learning can be used as a cognitive exercise to help learners to better integrate information. Richard Mayer (1997), in his multimedia learning theory, argued that multimedia learning has 'caused' learners to be 'constructors of knowledge', as they are required to integrate verbal and visual information. Clark and Mayer (2011) argue that because of this, multimedia learning should be encouraged, and state that learners learn better when optimum use of a range of media is present. This may typically involve a combination of text with video, or text with a graphic. The combination of different data formats can also help with retention of information. As the different data formats are presented with one another, the learners learn to make associations, which may help them to better hold and retain the information.

Ultimately, digital and multimedia enable rich information to be conveyed, which can be stimulating. However, such rich information can be complex and even more so if it is delivered at speed. In such situations, the modality principle informs us that it is best to have audio information to accompany graphics, rather than text (Low and Sweller, 2010). By presenting information in such a manner, L&D professionals may enable learners to not merely adapt and just be able to consume the information they are presented with, but in addition, to expand their working memory (Low and Sweller, 2010).

However, there will be times when information may be overly complex. The most obvious action is to then break the information into smaller and more manageable components for learners to learn from, which is termed as the segmenting principle (Mayer, 2010). Long videos (such as interviews) may be segmented into smaller parts, and each segment is accessible by tabs located either at the top or bottom of the video. Segmenting a long video is an effective way of breaking the information into smaller chunks so that learners can retain information in a gradual manner by allowing them to easily revisit each segment, as the case example from Pieter Brummer illustrates.

Pieter Brummer, head of UK HR services and interim head of resourcing, Denmark, LEGO

One of my responsibilities is to act as a company-nominated trustee for one of our company pension schemes. I have to use e-learning as part of the pensions trust toolkit to keep my personal development going. E-learning is an easy and practical way to remind and educate people about important things, especially company policies, and then test their understanding of how they would apply that knowledge in practice.

E-learning is the primary technology I gained most from, but podcasts are also useful just to catch up on the latest thinking on this or that... My advice to L&D practitioners using technology to develop learning opportunities is to keep the content as concise as possible, to the point and in small parts. I once had to do an e-learning piece about code of conduct and it lasted almost two hours! Too long for me, especially as people seem to be getting busier and bombarded with information on a daily basis. I try to limit my own meetings to between 40 mins and an hour, and I would prefer using e-learning for a similar amount of time.

Exercise

Identify a digital and/or multimedia learning 'solution' on the internet. This may be a video, a game or even just a webpage. Referring to any or all three principles of multimedia, modality and segmenting, how would you improve this digital/multimedia solution?

4.2 Contiguity in digital and multimedia learning

The demands of digital and multimedia technologies on people's cognition are an important consideration. Cognitive load theory states that the human brain is inherently limited in the information that it can maintain at any one time (Sweller, 1994). There are two types of cognitive load: intrinsic and extraneous (Goldstein, 2003). Intrinsic loads are the demands placed by the material due to its inherent nature (complexity of the information) and not the way it is presented. Extraneous cognitive load is determined by how materials are presented, irrespective of the inherent nature of the material. Extraneous cognitive load is alleviated by how content is presented, such as those in infographic format (discussed in Chapter 4).

Extraneous cognitive load informs us on how digital learning materials should be presented, especially when multimedia content includes different formats, and people's minds have to work extra hard to integrate the different sources of information. The dual-coding theory (Paivio, 1986) states that different formats mean that people have to code information using different processes. Also, demands on cognition are high when integration is necessary, especially when text and diagrams are only intelligible together (if each does not make sense when viewed in isolation). This is called the split-half effect (Mayer and Davis, 1999). The split-half effect can be eliminated when the information is presented together.

There are two important principles to consider when different types of information are presented: spatial and temporal contiguity. Spatial contiguity, as the term suggests, states that when presenting related information, formats such as text and graphics should be presented together (Clark and Mayer, 2011). An example is the presentation of a four-bar chart, with an explanation for each bar located next to each respective bar. The spatial contiguity principle argues that when possible, the design and development of learning solutions should involve the parallel presentation of information. Of course, there is an optimum level, as too much information shown at once will be counterproductive, as it clutters the presentation and learners will find it more confusing than helpful.

The advent of infographics takes advantage of what spatial contiguity teaches us – that the mind has the ability to manipulate visual images to better help pattern recognition. This ability can be facilitated if graphics can be designed to complement the text. For example, if a survey concerning the views of men and women is presented, then in addition to the bar charts and explanation, a silhouette of each gender in the background of the respective data sets helps people to more efficiently process the information, as shown in Figure 6.4:

Figure 6.4 Example of infographic and spatial contiguity

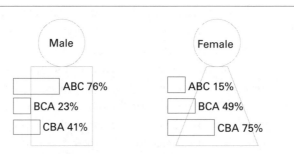

A related principle is temporal contiguity, which refers to the appropriate timing of presenting of formats. For example, the audio in a video should be presented at the same time as the visuals. Simulation games also reflect the contiguity effect where action and feedback occur together continuously.

Exercise

There are vast numbers of examples of how both spatial and temporal contiguity are used to good effect on the internet. Undertake research on the internet to find such examples, and reflect on how each of the examples reflects the principles.

4.3 Coherence and redundancy of information in digital and multimedia content

As with traditional pen-and-paper learning approaches, coherence is just as important in digital and multimedia learning, although there are more dimensions to coherence than just the content making sense. Similar to traditional learning methods, a logical structure and pattern must be provided to learners that builds upon previous lessons.

However, with multimedia, there is always a temptation to provide too many types of media for similar purposes. More is not always best. For example, for the same content text, audio and video formats for the same material are not always necessary. Nonetheless, there are exceptions, such as when L&D professionals are catering for learners with disabilities, or learners whose native language is not the language used to deliver the course. Another exception is when you want to accommodate learners who may be using different devices or are limited in terms of the type of software they use. For example, some universities provide various text formats of their online materials, eg MS Word, Portable Document Format (PDF) and Kindle.

As Sections 4.1 and 4.2 indicated, whilst multimedia learning can enhance memory, it is inherently more demanding. Hence it is important that design of digital learning solutions is optimized so that the technologies, media and content used complement one another and are coherent. Superfluous material should be removed as it can be distracting.

Exercise

Undertake research on the internet, including signing up for a short MOOCs course, to identify a learning material that you believe observes the coherence and redundancy principles. This may involve the effectual use of different but optimum numbers of technologies (such as those discussed in Section 2), media (eg text, audio, graphic and/or video), and content (eg length).

4.4 Considering individual differences and user experience

We know that people are unique from one another. A common example is our personalities, which not just differentiate us in terms of our behaviours but also the way we think. Indeed, research such as Ackerman and Kanfer (2004) and Perkins, Jay, and Tishman (1993), show that our personalities can influence how we process things such as the type of information we are sensitive to and therefore 'pick up', and our natural inclinations in the perspective that we adopt when evaluating information. Of course, the way we seek input and process information is also influenced by external factors such as experience. Therefore, L&D professionals have to bear in mind that learners are different, and whilst it is impossible to cater to every minute difference amongst a large group of people, there are some significant differences amongst learners that are directly relevant and have an impact on their learning.

An important factor that L&D professionals have to bear in mind is that the effective use of learning technologies by individuals may significantly vary depending age, familiarity with and ability to use technology, and the subject matter. The use of graphics may be helpful for learners who are novices in a particular subject (or when the programme delivered is for beginners) as they are more impactful and helps with retention, as well as those who are naturally high spatial learners. However, too many graphics can be redundant or distracting for expert-level learners.

Whilst the recognition of differences amongst learners and being prepared for these differences is important, L&D professionals must also be always prepared to provide pre-training for learners before the start of any learning programmes using technology. As with the use of any form of technology, eg for productivity purposes, users must be provided some 'pre-training' so that they are able to familiarize themselves with the system. User/learner experience is important, as any frustration on the part of the learner regarding the digital solution may discourage them from further use in the future (Lazar and Preece, 2003). Therefore, users and learners must know, at least, the fundamental aspects of the systems (eg navigation) and know who they can contact if they have an issue.

Exercise

This exercise is to help you assess the typical design of digital and multimedia learning solutions on the internet (eg MOOC). However, if you are unable to do so, then a website can also be used (although not all the evaluation criteria below may be relevant). Use the criteria in the table below to evaluate the design of a digital and multimedia learning solution. You can rate the learning solution from a score of 1 to 10 (10 being the best), and provide a reason for your rating. You can repeat this exercise on a second learning solution, and compare both. This exercise should help you be more cognizant of the important principles in designing digital and multimedia learning solutions, in addition to the FITCCA attributes discussed in Section 3.

Table 6.2 Evaluating the design of a digital and multimedia learning solution

Criteria		System 1	System 2
Usability	Consistency (eg layout, fonts)		
	Control (for users). The more control users have the better, eg background colour that is available in Gmail.		
	Predictability (of how function and features work). For example, the volume control for embedded videos should work the same in every other page.		
Navigation	Frames within page should be avoided (as this prevents bookmarking).		
	Long pages to be avoided.		
	Navigational support is to be provided.		
	Narrow and deep hierarchies to be avoided.		
	Consistent look and feel.		
Access	Complex URLs should be avoided (if the website address were to be written, it should be relatively short, and just contain letters and numbers).		
	Short download times (if the file is big, then it may be best to be disaggregated into smaller files).		
Information design	Accuracy and completeness of information.		
	Good graphical design (such as the principles discussed concerning spatial contiguity).		
	Excessive use of colour should be avoided, as should gratuitous animations.		
	Consistency within pages and within site.		

5 Designing and developing blended learning

A blended approach to learning is on the rise (Overton and Dixon, 2015), as it provides flexibility and genuinely enhances learning and development. Blended learning is not an entirely new concept, as L&D and education professionals have been using varied and diverse approaches and methods in delivering learning and training programmes for decades. However, this term has gained more prominence with the growing development and use of learning technologies. Hence, blended learning is usually associated with the use of digital technology (many universities in the UK use the term 'technology-enhanced learning').

Indeed, technology can and usually does play a significant role, but strictly speaking, blended learning does not necessarily have to include technology (but of course, given that this topic is situated within the chapter, the blends discussed should feature technology). For example, the Open University in the UK offers courses that can be undertaken via distance learning and attending classes. What technology has done is provide L&D professionals with more options in addition to genuinely enhancing learning and development.

Exercise

There are many advantages to adopting a blended learning approach, some of which include working with resources available to L&D professionals, as they are not restricted to just 'one way', and being able to leverage upon new and existing technologies. A blended approach also gives L&D professionals the freedom to experiment with applying technology in a different manner. In addition, scalability also enables L&D professionals to easily cater for a wide number of learners, where quorums are no longer required. What other advantages are there from adopting a blended learning approach?

5.1 Types of Blends

The combinations and different permutations of what would be part of a blend are almost innumerable. But in many cases, blended learning usually refers to the mix within and between formats, technologies and media. This provides us with a basis to discuss and understand what 'types' of blends people usually refer to when they use the term blended learning. Some blends involve the mode of delivery, work-based learning, technology and media, with varying degrees of each in every combination.

The mode of delivery blend involves the different approaches in providing learning and development programmes. For example, this may involve face-to-face classroom delivery and e-learning. To what degree each component plays a role varies. In some cases, the classroom may play a major component, with e-learning technologies such as VLEs used to support what has been taught in the classroom and as a repository for electronic materials. On the other hand, the VLE may be the most significant component, with learners only meeting one another and the instructor in person once or twice in the entire course. Modes of delivery may also involve outdoor training. In such a scenario, learners are provided with the 'theoretical' knowledge in a classroom environment but the practical component is all undertaken outdoors or 'on the field'. This also includes adventure (outdoor) team activities that some companies organize for their staff.

Another blend is work-based learning and apprenticeships. This blend may involve the attainment of a qualification, in which case there may be a significant component involving classroom learning as well as learning at work. Learning at work may require a learning contract to be developed and agreed upon between the learner and supervisor to ensure that the learner's activities will help them attain the learning outcomes that are a part of the course. Work-based learning and apprenticeship may also involve various on-the-job training schemes such as job rotation. In such situations, document repositories and sharing tools may help learners to access important learning content about their training for new roles, wherever they are. E-portfolios may also help to capture learners' reflections and evidence of learning and development throughout their entire programme.

The blend involving digital and multimedia technologies may involve the use of various technologies within a course. For example, in addition to the use of VLEs, a significant part of the course may also involve using enterprise social networks to learn from others, as well as simulation games. A blend involving media may include the use of text, audio and video within a course. The blend of technologies and media is especially useful when a course has minimal input from an instructor, as it helps to vary the content and negate monotony.

Of course these three 'groups' of blends – modes of delivery, work-based learning, and technologies and multimedia – are just examples, and there are many more. In fact, the labels given to these groups should not matter when designing and developing a blend. It is more important that a blend (whatever its components are or whichever 'group' it belongs to) suits the learning outcomes, the learners and the organization. For example, an e-learning course undertaken via a VLE may be used to support on-the-job-training (instead of supporting a qualification course), using a variety of media and technologies that include virtual worlds. The types and degrees of blends can be endless.

Exercise

The flexibility that blended learning brings is a double-edged sword. It gives L&D professionals room to be creative but at the same time it does not provide a lot of structure or guidance on how to design blended learning. This exercise is to help provide some guidance in designing blend, and you can practise its application by designing your own learning programme. Address each item in the table, and as you do so make sure each follows another (is consistent with another as though these actions are being undertaken in one class for the same group of students).

Table 6.3 Designing a learning programme

Guidance	Response
Learning objectives: • What are the learning objectives? • What knowledge do they need to have? • What 'skills' (ability) must they be able to demonstrate (include cognitive skills such as critical thinking as well as overt skill such as negotiation)?	
What level of proficiency would you describe the learning objectives to be at? • Entry level. • Intermediate (someone with 3–6 years working experience). • Expert (more than 7 years of working experience in this area).	
What should the curricula involve? • What are the content, activities and resources required for them to read and do to attain the learning objectives? • How would you break down each learning 'session' in a logical manner? • How much time would each 'session' require?	

Table 6.3 *continued*

Guidance	Response
Who are your learners? • What are their qualifications and prior learning? • What demographic information do you have of them, eg age, gender? • Where are they located? • How many of them are they? How are they distributed in terms of location? What resources would be required? • Are instructors easily accessible (internally and externally to the organization)? • What resources and technologies are available to you to design, develop, deliver, maintain and implement the content, activities and resources? • What facilities and amenities are available to you? • How can you use resources optimally? What are the organizational needs? • How important is this course to the organization? • Does it need to be delivered frequently? • How much is the organization willing to invest in this course?	

5.2 Learning on your own

Blended learning can suit a variety of learning objectives, which of course can be too diverse to generalize. However, in some cases there may be certain emphasis in the learning programme. This section provides three examples of such emphasis in blended learning. The three are: learning on your own, learning through practice, and learning from and with others.

'Learning on your own' refers to situations where learners are expected to complete a course or programme on their own, with minimal or no contact with an instructor. In such cases the contact with the instructor is by exception, helping learners when a problem arises. However, other than that, the course is designed in such a way that the learners do not need to engage with the instructor or anyone else.

'Learning on your own' programmes are self-paced and come in many forms such as short courses for the purpose of induction, and health and safety. The duration of these courses can range greatly from one hour to a few days. Many of these courses are self-paced in that learners can do as much as they want in one sitting, or they can start and stop as often as they wish as long as they complete the course within a specified time.

These self-paced environments largely depend on a blend of technologies and media. For example, VLEs are usually used to house a number of other technologies such as video, repositories and even act as a gateway to other digital resources. Such environments may even allow for learners to complete their assessments, which may involve multiple-choice questions for mandatory courses such as security on user information technology in sectors such as banking. Of course, self-paced learning may be offered for more advanced courses such as statistics. Video learning, developed using screen casting and lecture capture, is an important tool. Although instructors do play a role here, it is usually in preparation of the course through recording of the video, which can then be used multiple times without the instructor's further involvement.

5.3 Learning through practice

Technology may also be used to support blends that contain an emphasis on 'practice'. Of course, not all types and forms of work can be practised and mastered by just using technology. However, there are technologies that are being used in innovative ways to enable professionals to practise their craft whilst learning. For example, hospitals are now using video learning and simulations to train doctors, nurses and other emergency personnel to deal with major burns surgery (Sadideen *et al*, 2016), which is similar to the training that fire and rescue personnel undergo as highlighted in Chapter 2.

The flexibility that virtual worlds offer provides L&D professionals with an opportunity to create any type of environment for any profession or occupational groups that they intend to develop through practice. Virtual worlds allow learners to 'do' and be active learners. Simulation games are very useful in enabling learners to apply what they have learned conceptually and theoretically. For example, a number of off-the-shelf (where rules of the game are pre-determined) providers of simulation games such as Harvard Business Publishing offer games for the development of change management, leadership, operations management and financial skills. Simulation games provide an immersive environment by providing rich and detailed background information concerning roles and situations to create a real-as-possible scenario for learners to make decisions and 'experience' the implications of those decisions.

However, a significant area of 'practice' is the practice of 'learning to learn', which is relevant to everyone. Technology can offer genuine opportunities for learners to develop their learning skills. As discussed in Chapter 1, reflective skills and learning to learn are crucial in anyone's personal development. Being self-directed and autonomous in one's own learning is crucial in today's dynamic world. Technologies such as blogs and vlogs are helpful to enable one to capture one's own learning. Curation tools are also helpful for learners to create their own personal learning environment (PLE), which is an individual's own collection of content, materials, tools and systems used for their own development.

Exercise

This exercise is aimed at helping you learn to identify and describe how two learning technologies can help learners to practise their craft.

- Identify a profession or occupational group.
- Describe a task or activity that is required from a person in this profession or occupation (it can even be an L&D profession).
- Research and identify a learning technology that may enable this learner to 'practise' this task or activity.
- Finally, create a reflective learning activity that enables the learner to capture and improve how they learn and ultimately improve their practice.

5.4 Learning from and with others

Many scholars and practitioners such as Marsick and Watkins (2001), have long recognized the importance of people learning from one another. Indeed, whilst formal learning (eg courses) is important, people also, arguably, learn more effectively informally and incidentally. Many informal and incidental learning opportunities occur when we network with others, whether it be for knowledge sharing or just plain socializing.

Technologies play an important role here in being used either as part of an intervention such as a training programme or as a tool to create an environment for learners (as discussed in Part 2 of this chapter). Technologies can be used for people to connect and collaborate as part of their course. For example, forums can be accessed and used by learners to discuss what they have learned from one another, as can other social networking and/or enterprise social networking platforms.

However, the success of learning through asynchronous communication cannot be taken for granted. It is important that L&D professionals are able to understand how learning through asynchronous communication takes place by participating and monitoring the pattern of dialogue that occurs so that they may mediate when necessary. Asynchronous web-based discussion (eg via social media or forum) both develops and requires perspective taking to be successful (Jarvela and Hakkinen, 2003). In asynchronous discussions, perspective taking can be developed as each participant shares their own views. Selman (1980) argues that one's ability for perspective taking can be evaluated against five stages.

The starting stage is that of egocentricity, where learners are only concerned for their own views. The second stage is subjective role taking, and involves a cursory understanding of a different perspective. The third stage is reciprocal perspective taking, which involves a genuine appreciation of the uniqueness of other people's perspective, which is then reciprocated amongst learners. However, the different perspectives have yet to be completely integrated into the actions and thoughts of each learner. The fourth stage is mutual perspective taking, where dialogue is ongoing as each participant tries to understand the views of others in a more detailed manner, and see how this impacts on various issues. The fifth and last stage is the 'societal-symbolic' perspective, and this involves being able to conceptualize the different perspectives and organize them in a way that allows them to be applied in a useful manner, for example, how ethnic minorities in the UK view diversity and inclusion policies in large corporations.

In addition to asynchronous communication, wikis are also helpful tools that provide a platform for learners to collaborate with one another in co-creating knowledge. In addition to collaboration, competition is also a useful element to use in facilitating learning. Learning activities can be gamified, with learners working in teams and competing against one another. Mobile learning technologies are important to enable people to keep in touch with one another, which is crucial, as informal learning is at its best when learners are able to access information and learn on demand. Learning is also about who you learn from when you need to.

Learning from and with others is important, and technologies can genuinely enhance blends with such emphasis. However, it should always be kept in mind that technologies are just tools. Social learning is also 'organic' and therefore L&D professionals also need be dynamic and flexible, ready to change as they go with the flow. Information exchanged today is also much richer, including both factual and empathic (Van Oostendorp, 2003) and so L&D professionals need to create well-crafted social policies/protocols to facilitate social learning.

Exercise

Using Salmon's (2011) model for e-learning facilitation, provide examples for each stage of her model.

Table 6.4 Salmon's Five Stages

Salmon's 5 stages	Example of activities for this stage
Stage 1 – Access and motivation: To ensure that learners can easily access the system and materials, and are motivated to learn.	
Stage 2 – Online socialization: To help learners to get to know one another and to establish netiquette.	
Stage 3 – Information exchange: To encourage learners to exchange information and perspectives in regard to the subject matter and/or topic at hand.	
Stage 4 – Knowledge construction: To encourage learners to co-create knowledge and go beyond just information and give meaning to their discussions.	
Stage 5 – Development: To develop learners in the context of personal development, ie how does what has been discussed impact them personally?	

6 Conclusion

This chapter has presented and discussed various technologies related to learning and development. The technologies presented here are far from exhaustive, and with the development of technology advancing at great speeds, it is almost impossible to have a complete and definitive list that will remain up to date for long. What we know of present-day technologies will change in some shape or form in the near future. A caveat here is to move away from the labels and names we give technology and to better understand its functionality and features. For example, some may say VLEs are out of fashion, but it is possible that it is just the label 'VLE' that is out of fashion. The functionality and features of a VLE are still present and play an invaluable role.

Therefore, this chapter has encouraged L&D professionals to focus on the functionalities and features of technologies that provide more insight into how they may be used for learning and development. This knowledge, together with understanding the principles of digital and multimedia, enables L&D professionals to better design and develop digital and blended learning solutions. L&D professionals need to be savvy in this, and also practical. There may be times when technology can and may drive the development of L&D interventions and environments, but in some other instances it should play a supporting role. In addition, learning and development is being democratized and the learners are being empowered by technology to be more self-directed and autonomous in driving their own learning (Deloitte, 2016). In fact, many of the digital technologies here can be used by learners themselves (eg curation tools) to design and develop their own personal learning environments.

Indeed, there are inspiring stories that tell of how technologies have completely revolutionized learning experiences. Whilst this is true and possible for any organization that has such aspirations, there are certain realities that remain valid and influential in how L&D and organizations design, develop and deliver learning and development programmes. An example is cost. Many technologies are free to use, but there are also many that are costly, especially when used enterprise-wide. In addition, informal, person-to-person channels still play an important and significant role in how people learn in the workplace. Therefore, L&D professionals should always have an open mind and be pragmatic in terms of using technology as an enabler or driver of learning and development in their organizations.

Further reading

Donald H. Taylor's list of recommended blogs on learning and development: https://donaldhtaylor.wordpress.com/2013/04/30/which-blogs-to-read-in-learning-and-development/

Whiteboard example: https://awwapp.com/ or https://realtimeboard.com/

e-library example: The World Digital Library at https://www.wdl.org/en/

e-Portfolios, discussion from the University of Newcastle: http://www.eportfolios.ac.uk/

Mozilla's learning badges (http://openbadges.org/) and Badgecraft (http://www.badgecraft.eu/)

LMS providers are listed at Capterra: http://www.capterra.com/learning-management-system-software/

Screen casting and lecture capture: http://www.fresnostate.edu/academics/tilt/toolsforteaching/lecture-screen-capture/

Example of enterprise social networks: http://mashable.com/2013/06/14/enterprise-social-networks

Blackboard: http://uki.blackboard.com/sites/international/globalmaster/

MOOCs: https://www.mooc-list.com/

Minecraft is located at: https://minecraft.net/. View this story on the BBC on how Minecraft is being used in education: http://www.bbc.co.uk/news/technology-35341528

References

Ackerman, P L and Kanfer, R (2004) Cognitive, affective and conative aspects of adult intellect within a typical and maximal performance framework, in *Motivation, Emotion, and Cognition: Integrative perspectives on intellectual functioning and development*, ed. D Y Dai and R J Sternberg London: Lawrence Erlbaum, London, pp. 119–42

Campus Alberta Repository of Educational Objects (2015) [online] http://www.careo.org/

Cheetham, G and Chivers, G (2001) How professionals learn in practice: an investigation of informal learning amongst people working in professions, *Journal of European Industrial Training*, 25 (5), pp. 248–92

Clark, R C and Mayer, R E (2011) *E-Learning and the Science of Instruction: Proven guidelines for consumers and designers of multimedia learning*, 3rd edn, John Wiley & Sons, San Francisco, CA

Coughlan (2012) 'Crowd-sourcing' website to decipher ancient writing, *BBC* [online] http://www.bbc.com/news/education-20066885

Deloitte (2016) Global human capital trends 2016: The new organization: different by design, *Deloitte* [online] http://www2.deloitte.com/global/en/pages/human-capital/articles/introduction-human-capital-trends.html

Ferreira, P A and Ribeiro, J L (2001) The relationship between violent electronic games and aggression in adolescents, *Aggressive Behavior*, 27, 166–67

Goldstein, J (2003) People @ play: electronic games, in *Cognition in a Digital World*, ed. H Van Oostendorp, Lawrence Erlbaum Associate, New York, pp. 25–46

Jarvela, S and Hakkinen, P (2003) The levels of web-based discussions: using perspective-taking theory as an analytical tool, in *Cognition in a Digital World*, ed. H Van Oostendorp, Lawrence Erlbaum Associates, New York , pp. 77–96

Katz, M and Shapiro, C (1986) Technology adoption in the presence of network externalities, *Journal of Political Economy*, **94**, pp. 822–41

Landers, R N and Landers, A K (2014) An empirical test of the theory of gamified learning: the effect of leaderboards on time-on-task and academic performance, *Simulation & Gaming*, **45** (6), pp. 769–85

Lazar, J and Preece, J (2003) Social considerations in online communities: usability, sociability and success factors, in *Cognition in a Digital World*, ed. H Van Oostendorp, Lawrence Erlbaum Associate, New York, pp. 127–52

Loon, M (2014) An investigation into the use of computer-based simulation games for learning and teaching in business management courses, *Worcester Journal of Learning and Teaching* (9), pp. 108–16

Loon, M, Evans, J and Kerridge, C (2015) Learning with a strategic management simulation game: a case study, *The International Journal of Management Education*, **13** (3), pp. 227–36

Low, R and Sweller, J (2010) The modality principle in multimedia learning, in *The Cambridge Handbook of Multimedia Learning*, ed. R Mayer, Cambridge University Press, New York, NY, pp. 147–58

Manyika, J, Chui, M, Bughin, J, Dobbs, R, Bisson, P and Marrs, A (2013) Disruptive technologies: advances that will transform life, business, and the global economy, *McKinsey* [online] http://www.mckinsey.com/business-functions/business-technology/our-insights/disruptive-technologies

Marsick, V J and Watkins, K E (2001) Informal and incidental learning, *New Directions for Adult and Continuing Education*, **89** pp. 25–34

Mayer, R C and Davis, J H (1999) The effect of the performance appraisal system on trust for management: a field quasi-experiment, *Journal of Applied Psychology*, **84**, pp. 123–36

Mayer, R E (1997) Multimedia learning: are we asking the right question? *Educational Psychologist*, **32** pp. 1–19

Mayer, R E (2010) Principles for managing essential processing in multimedia learning: segmenting, pretraining, and modality principles, in *The Cambridge Handbook of Multimedia Learning*, ed. R Mayer, Cambridge University Press, New York, NY, pp. 169–82

Multimedia Educational Resource for Learning and Online Teaching (2015) [online] http://www.merlot.org/merlot/index.htm

OUP (2016) Mobile learning, *YouTube* [online] https://www.youtube.com/watch?v=3IDYXiKxv8g

Overton, L and Dixon, G (2015) Embracing change: improving performance of business, individuals and the L&D Team. 2015–16 industry benchmark report, *Towards Maturity* [online] http://www.towardsmaturity.org/article/2015/11/05/embracing-change-improving-performance-benchmark/

Paivio, A (1986) *Mental Representations: A dual coding approach*, Oxford University Press, New York

Perkins, D, Jay, E and Tishman, S (1993) Beyond abilities: a dispositional theory of thinking, *Merrill-Palmer Quarterly*, **39** (1), pp. 1–21

Perloff, R M (1999) The third person effect in mass media research, *Media Psychology*, **1** pp. 353–78

Proserpio, L and Gioia, D (2007) Teaching the virtual generation, *Academy of Management Learning & Education*, **6** (1), pp. 69–80

Sadideen, H, Weldon, S, Saadeddin, M, Loon, M and Kneebone, R (2016) Video analysis of intra- and inter-professional leadership behaviours within 'The Burns Suite': Identifying key leadership models, *Journal of Surgical Education*, **73** (1), pp. 31–39

Salmon, G (2011) *E-Moderating: The key to teaching and learning online*, 3rd edn, Routledge, Oxon, UK

Scott, D (1995) The effect of video games on feelings of aggression, *Journal of Psychology*, **129**, pp. 121–32

Selman, R (1980) *The Growth of Interpersonal Understanding: Developmental and clinical analysis*, Academic, San Diego, CA

Sweller, J (1994) Cognitive load theory, learning difficulty and instructional design, *Leanring and Instruction*, **4**, pp. 295–312

UWE (nd) SHE: Audit SIM [online] http://www1.uwe.ac.uk/aboutus/departmentsandservices/professionalservices/educationinnovationcentre/knowledgebase/shesimulationsinhighered/auditsim.aspx

Van Oostendorp, H, ed (2003) *Cognition in a Digital World*, Lawrence Erlbaum Associate, Mahwah, New Jersey

Facilitating collective and social learning

07

MICHAEL BAGSHAW

1 Introduction

We know that the world is changing fast. That's a cliché. Increasingly, we are faced with what have come to be called wicked problems (Grint, 2005). These are problems with no obvious solutions and where past learning doesn't give a good guide. Some of these problems involve profound human change and social problems, such as substance abuse, crime, pandemic diseases, mass migration, international drug trafficking, and war. But organizational problems can feel 'wicked' too. These can be issues such as developing sustainable competitive advantage when money is in short supply, losing too many good people from the pressures of merger and acquisition change, low performance, disengaged employees and dysfunctional silos, and disruptive changes in markets or technologies.

We are aware that with this type of problem, the problem-solving process needs to involve working together to get the best from different perspectives. Typically, we can't rely on the expert or the boss. No one person has the answers. There needs to be a continuous process of vigilance throughout the organization. Collectively, we need to be able to separate signals telling us that important things are changing from the general noise. These signals may be weak, so we need to develop our 'peripheral vision' and seek insights widely both inside and outside our organization. When we sense these 'shifting winds', we need to communicate our observations, share our hunches, and listen to all the stakeholders including the rank and file and of course customers, internal and external (Day and Schoemaker, 2008).

Most importantly, we need to learn together as we go. In order to do this, we need to not only absorb and analyse information, but also to develop our communication, be open with each other, and be prepared to state our assumptions and challenge others' assumptions in a spirit of learning and inquiry. This requires openness and trust. We sometimes seem incapable of collaboration and learning together. Interpersonal competition, turf politics and egos can mean that the whole is often less than the sum of the parts. We need to develop cultures that facilitate effective learning together. To help to achieve this goal, this chapter is organized around six sections, after this first introduction section:

Section 2: Learning together: the new paradigm of learning.

Section 3: Types of social and collective learning.

Section 4: Creating a culture of social and collective learning.

Section 5: Social and collective learning tools and processes.

Section 6: Social media and learning.

Section 7: Mentoring, coaching and leadership for social and collective learning.

2 Learning together: the new paradigm of learning

Requirements in the workplace are changing so rapidly that learning courses with a fixed syllabus have a short shelf life. It is far better to have continuous learning and collaboration built into the culture. We need cultures where people come into the action with their existing knowledge, build on that through sharing and collaborating, and incorporate new learning, intertwining old new experience, debating with others, and adjusting their perceptions in line with new changes, thereby building new knowledge, over and over again.

Traditional learning has separated acquiring knowledge and learning from workplace practice. As a result, a major problem in conventional training and development has been the transfer of learning from the classroom to the work setting. Lave and Wenger (1991) in particular have been in the forefront of arguing that this separation is unsound. Similarly, Brown and Duguid (1991) say that learning is becoming a practitioner, not learning about practice. They argue what managers in the workplace know intuitively, that much of what they learn is embedded in the work they do and particularly in the relationships they have with colleagues, supervisors, mentors, coaches and informal discussions with fellow professionals inside and outside their organizations.

The 'contact sport' of this kind of 'collective learning' (De Laat and Simons, 2002) takes place with other people in interaction with each other, sharing and building on each other's knowledge and experience and generating new ideas and information. This can mean with colleagues in a project group, amongst team members, within a committee or special working group, or any collection of people that functions as a unit or network of some kind. Collective learning takes place in the practice itself, ie whilst we are working. The learning can be formal or informal. It becomes formal when we decide how we are going to learn and review what we have learned. This can involve periodic learning reviews, rules and norms about how we share knowledge, and getting together to generate new learning by using specific methods such as brainstorming, presentations, action learning sets and problem-solving groups.

These knowledge-sharing social interactions produce better understanding and solutions as a result of the synthesis of different perspectives focused on the problem or challenge (Golub, 1988). Knowledge is seen as something to be expanded and used by the process of sharing insights, helping each other, finding ways to solve problems, and creating frameworks and tools, together. In other words, we learn collaboratively.

The traditional view is that knowledge acquired by individuals should be recorded in a retrievable way. This will then incrementally increase the body of knowledge across the organization, but there is increasing acceptance that this is not enough. When knowledge is shared, discussed and expanded on, and thought is given to how the new knowledge can be applied, the increase in knowledge can be transformational.

There is also less reliance on formalized training and more acceptance of learning that comes from doing the job (Bolhuis and Simons, 2003; Eraut, 2000). When somebody leaves, it is often realized that that person had a great deal of tacit knowledge, which is difficult to recapture. This informal learning, which is often high both in quality and quantity, is difficult or impossible to measure, precisely because it is informal. Nonaka and Takeuchi (1995) said that tacit knowledge is valuable in itself, and can also sow the seeds of innovation. Part of collective learning is bringing tacit knowledge to the surface, so it can be shared, discussed and expanded upon, and become part of the social learning experience.

More recently Jane Hart and Jay Cross (Hart, 2011) have provided a model of 5 stages of workplace learning, which moves from top down to bottom up control:

Stage 1: Classroom training

Stage 2: E-learning

Stage 3: Blended learning

Stage 4: Social learning

Stage 5: Collaborative learning/working

The framework also roughly parallels a move from formal to informal learning. So classroom training is very much tutor led and formal, and represents top-down control, whereas collective or collaborative learning is more informal, learner led, with bottom-up control. In her blog in 2010, Hart argued that most organizations were in Stage 3, where the learner learns through a combination of digital and online media content and instruction, face-to-face training and self-paced study. But increasingly she now sees organizations giving serious consideration to Stage 4 and even Stage 5. Hart emphasizes that the move to Stage 5 is not just about social media tools and technology. It requires a new mindset in which the organization creates and supports the climate for continuous learning and recognizes the interdependency of working and learning.

The author's model below builds on these ideas to create a more dynamic interaction of key components. This doesn't describe all the complexities of learning but it suggests a practical tool for determining a learning intervention. The decision about methodology is based around what level of learning/knowledge is required and what level of learner engagement is desirable. Practitioners are invited to adapt this model, which is akin to the situational model to be found in leadership research (Hersey and Blanchard, 1993). The levels of knowledge utilize Anderson and Krathwohl's (2001) revised version of Bloom's taxonomy. The definitions are mine:

- Factual Knowledge: The facts that we need to know to solve our problems.

- Conceptual Knowledge: The understanding of concepts and theories that help us to make sense of data/observations.

- Procedural Knowledge: How to translate our understanding into value-added actions.

- Metacognitive Knowledge: Awareness of our own ways of construing the world and being able to adjust and change our mental models in the light of feedback from the environment.

Figure 7.1 Model of workplace learning

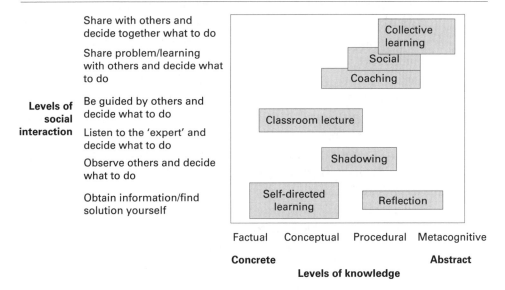

3 Types of collective and social learning

We can define social and collective learning in a number of ways. In particular, we need to differentiate between social interaction and collective learning. In social interaction there may well be individual learning outcomes, but this is not necessarily the purpose of the interaction. It becomes collective learning if the people involved intend at the outset that they will learn as a group. This is described in Table 7.1.

Table 7.1 Types of learning (based on De Laat and Simons, 2002)

	Individual learning outcomes	*Group learning outcomes*
Individual learning process	**Going solo**	**Pooling**
	Knowledge/insight/ solution gained through independent learning	Individual learning pooled to produce an agreed group product
Group or network learning process	**Interactional learning**	**Collective learning**
	Individual gains knowledge/ insight/solution through social interaction	Collaborating to learn and produce an agreed output together
		Communities of practice and learning

We can see that individuals can learn separately, without any collective outcome. This is individual learning *(going solo)*. If the learning takes place in a social situation, but without a collective outcome, it is still individual learning *(interactional learning)*. Another situation is where individual learning is used in a planned way to create a collective outcome. Everyone is assigned a relevant topic to research on their own and report back to the group. The results are then pooled in order to make a decision *(pooling)*. This is individual learning with a collective outcome. When the group intends from the outset that there will be learning outcomes from their collaboration this is *collective learning*. This is the basis for learning groups and learning organizations, which are more than the sum of their parts or the individuals learning within them.

This typology may seem theoretical but there are practical implications. It may help us to decide what kind of learning is best to solve particular problems. Going solo will be useful when the individual needs to learn about a specific topic in order to present a report or pass an exam or write a book chapter. They need to concentrate and focus on acquiring the knowledge they need through independent study. But even in this situation, we can short circuit the learning process by using the group or network. For example, we can ask for feedback on our ideas from colleagues or friends, or contact experts in the field for their views. In fact, it's probably rare just to learn alone, particularly as the problems we need to learn about often occur in a social context. In this form of 'interactional learning', for example, you could consider reading an article as a useful piece of knowledge and opinion that could help you in making some decisions. That may have some practical value. However, if you discuss it with your colleagues and seek their opinions and experience and ask how they might use the content of the article, the value can be increased significantly. The caveat to that is, of course, that your colleagues have to want to discuss the issues and be willing to share their knowledge and experience.

When a problem involves a number of stakeholders and there is agreement that no one person has the solution, then we may decide to pool our individual knowledge. Through a process of consensus building, we decide on the best way forward. This process assumes that the pooling of our individual past knowledge and learning will move us forward, but nonetheless it is often a good start for addressing complex problems.

When the problem is 'wicked' (Grint, 2005) our past knowledge and experience may not be sufficient. Then we may need not only to pool our knowledge but also to collaborate in the moment to learn something together. Collective or collaborative learning is based on the idea that knowledge can be created, or emerge from the process of sharing and building on each other's perspectives, knowledge, skills, intuitions and hunches. It takes pooling further because we need to be prepared to listen and empathize, and suspend our judgement on an individual level, but also to listen to the emerging collective voice in the group and to crystallize the emerging vision (Scharmer, 2009).

3.1 Learning in networks

Learning in networks has an individual outcome; there is a great deal of sharing. The network rarely if ever meets as an entity, but there are many groupings within it. Everyone decides the extent to which they will be involved, what outcomes they want for themselves, and what they are prepared to offer. Networks can be excellent for sharing ideas, reformulating views, adding to knowledge, and looking at things anew.

It is in the nature of business that it has to change, sometimes fundamentally, and sometimes in response to catastrophe. It often has to be recognized that the change is permanent, and there will be no 'back to normal' after a few tweaks. When change is abrupt and massive, traditional management taking charge and directing the change may not be appropriate. Using networks may be quicker and more reliable, as networks with people from several parts of the organization have more knowledge than a few people at the top. While the change is going, on normal operations have to continue.

The banking crisis of 2007–8 is an example where change was so cataclysmic that ordinary measures were inadequate and inappropriate. Existing controls had not properly regulated the processes, and rapid major changes had to be put in place. Another example of catastrophic change was the explosion at BP's refinery in Texas in 2005, which killed 15 people, injured many more, and was an ecological disaster. This situation demanded rapid learning, problem solving and risk management. It was clearly not sufficient to take a hierarchical approach where top management would instruct those on the ground.

3.2 Learning in teams

Learning in teams focuses on particular tasks or problems, and often the team is formed for a specific purpose and disbanded after that purpose is fulfilled. Teams may be learning teams (profession related) or working teams (organization related). Learning teams bring collective learning, but there needs to be an explicit intended outcome for the learning to be collaborative. Action learning is an example of team learning. This involves working with others on finding solutions to real problems in the organization.

Revans (2011) calls it 'comrades in adversity.' Engeström, Miettinen, and Punamäki (1999) have coined the word 'knotworking' to describe innovative and creative learning in working teams. Teams tie knots and untie them successively for the period of time that it is necessary to complete the task or solve the problem. There is no formal fixed responsibility assigned to anyone in the 'knots'. People whose work is connected, maybe only for a short time, work collaboratively to bring their different contributions together. It changes as it goes along, allows hunches to be followed, and for it to work, the people must be ready to embrace the ideas of others and be receptive to frequent change.

3.3 Communities of practice and learning

Community of practice

A community of practice is a collective learning process where a group of people in the same pursuit are learning from each other. The concept was coined by Etienne Wenger, who wrote:

> Communities of practice are formed by people who engage in a process of collective learning in a shared domain of human endeavor; a tribe learning to survive, a band of artists seeking new forms of expression, a group of engineers working on similar problems, a clique of pupils defining their identity in the school, a network of surgeons exploring novel techniques, a gathering of first-time managers helping each other cope (Wenger-Trayner and Wenger-Trayner, 2016).

In a nutshell: communities of practice are groups of people who share a concern or a passion for something they do and learn how to do it better as they interact regularly (Wenger-Trayner and Wenger-Trayner, 2016). In Lave and Wenger's (1991) original research, communities of practice develop naturally as a result of individuals self-organizing into groups with shared interests and concerns, who want to learn how to improve things.

According to Wenger, to be a community of practice, people need not work at the same place or at precisely the same job. They have to have the same area of knowledge, and meet regularly, actually or online, to discuss their work and ideas and new theories with each other. It could be an experimental community, for example musicians who want to depart from their usual type of music and work on something brand new. They have to be practising the area of common interest. It is not enough that someone is interested and enjoys television programmes about it. A community of practice consists of people actually doing the work, experiencing the problems and successes, and their interaction with others in the community brings ideas of how to improve their work.

Communities of practice come under many names, such as photography clubs, where photographers compare photographs, discuss problems, celebrate success and come away with more ideas. The oldest communities of practice may have been Neanderthals, working out together how to survive. If a group of people share goals, have a need to learn, and regularly discuss their efforts with each other, that is a community of practice.

Communities of practice can be informal groups, and can arise spontaneously, but it cannot be assumed that it will happen. There are strong reasons for organizations to encourage them to form. Practitioners in the same field know where the gaps in knowledge are and will have ideas that do not necessarily lead to a solution. With a community of practice, sharing those ideas will give new directions that may help. In discussion, connecting one person's experience with someone else's may lead to new insight. Then, as they are all knowledgeable about how things work in their field, they are likely to have ideas about how the new knowledge can be applied. Sharing these ideas is more likely to make it happen than a lone practitioner, or even several practitioners with the same idea but who never meet.

Bureaucracy can be a block. Communities of practice, even if started in a formal way, tend to become sociable, which becomes an advantage when discussing ideas for change. People forget the obstacles of regulations, and then there needs to be new debate about whether or not the regulation is necessary, whether it is a good brake on excess zeal, or whether it is simply preventing progress.

Since communities of practice in this modern age are not limited by geographical distance, practitioners from different cultures can be in the same community. This contact between people with a common interest and expertise, but looking from different viewpoints, can open up ideas that have been obscured because of cultural assumptions. This, of course, requires the additional factors of respect for others, openness to the unfamiliar, and general emotional intelligence. These factors are important in any debate or exploration of ideas, but more so when it's cross-cultural. And it is also true that diverse viewpoints make a rich bed for developing new ideas, as long as minds are open on all sides.

Communities of learning

De Laat and Simons (2002) make the distinction between communities of learning (profession based) or communities of practice (organization based). In their formulation, organizations are beginning to create communities of practice as a learning process within the organization, with learning processes and outcomes made explicit. Communities of learning, however, are fuelled by the expertise of the members under the banner of a particular professional grouping, and the stimulation that comes from others who have related expertise but a different set of experiences (Brown and Campione, 1994).

There is no strong explicit link to the particular organizational setting. However, it is likely that the individual members will try to convert their learning from the professional group to their specific workplace practice. For example, a clinical psychologist in the prison service may attend a conference of fellow professionals to share knowledge of ethical issues. It may be that the other clinical psychologists work in private practice or for the NHS. Nonetheless, the prison psychologist may gain inspiration from their discussions and look for ways to apply their learning in the prison context.

Exercise

Using the chart below, think of all the learning opportunities you have experienced in the last 12 months. Then decide how much those experiences involved social interaction and the sharing of information and knowledge, either in a formal or informal setting. Reflect on and/or discuss with a colleague where you have gained most learning value to enable you to work more effectively in your organization.

4 Creating a culture of collective and social learning

Social learning theory says that we learn from observing other people, and this includes behaviours we learn in childhood. In 1961, Bandura (1978) conducted an experiment where children were shown a film of a doll being treated aggressively. Those children then displayed more aggressive behaviour than children who were shown a non-aggressive film or no film at all. This suggests that there is learning by imitation. There is also a cognitive element, where children observe the consequences of someone else's behaviour, and model their own behaviour on that. A child that refuses to say

Table 7.2 Learning opportunities charting template

Learning opportunity	Sharing	Value of learning
	High – Working with others, sharing learning and generating new ideas together in open and constructive ways to produce solutions and new knowledge. **Medium** – Some sharing of information but little active working together to produce a collective outcome. **Low** – Most learning involves acquiring knowledge from sources that don't involve reciprocal sharing.	High Medium Low
Learning from instruction		
Working with colleagues in teams/projects		
Learning through independent study either through traditional (eg books) or e-learning methods and the web		
Personal learning experiences outside work such as conferences and professional networking events		

thank you is denied the toy, so the next child says thank you. This type of learning continues into adulthood.

Social learning is also joining with others to exchange ideas, share information, and to try to make sense of the unfamiliar. With global communication and social media, there is far more opportunity for this sort of learning than in the past. The technology that makes this possible is not enough on its own. E-learning with a tutor is not social learning – it is planned transfer of specific knowledge from one person to another.

In social learning, the people interacting (by whatever means) start with a certain level of knowledge and the intention of finding out more through the sharing of ideas. They need to be able to express themselves clearly and explain what they mean, but this does not ensure social learning will take place. For this to happen, there has to be a spirit of learning together, of tackling problems with joint expertise, learning from listening to the experience of others, and being ready to contribute, with an end goal of finding out more.

Informal social groups also learn; people pick up knowledge in the general process of being with other people, but this is not social learning. In social learning, there is effort involved on all sides. The social aspect means interacting with others, and is an age-old way of learning, long before it was possible to speak to people out of earshot.

Technology makes it far easier to set up social learning groups, with people in them not necessarily even on the same continent. It is easy technologically to have healthy cross-cultural debate, although the need for basic human qualities such as respect is as vital as ever. There are limitless opportunities for organizations to set up programmes for collaborative learnings of all types, with everyone in the same room, either virtually through technology, or literally within the same four walls.

Clearly, collective learning and social learning are linked. We can learn in social interactions (with and from others) but in collective learning the members of the group consciously strive for common learning and/or working outcomes. This form of learning may also be called group learning or organizational learning.

4.1 What is a learning culture?

The following two descriptions set out the attitudes to be found in organizations that have, or have not, a spirit of learning and inquiry that will lead to learning for the individual and for the organization.

Attitudes in a static culture

We select experts in their field, so that they will simply get on with it, and we assess their performance at appraisals. Once a project is finished, that's it; we don't spend time thinking about how it went. We don't have management training programmes or spend time on abstract ideas like assumptions and values. We give information to those who need to know, and they know when to keep quiet. People at all levels know what to do and get on with it, or if they're not sure, they won't try out unfamiliar things. We don't seek customer feedback and don't act on it if we get it. Motivation comes from extrinsic reward, such as profit and the bonuses that go with it.

Attitudes in a learning culture

We select people from the start who can learn and adapt and will try things out. Appraisals focus on what they have learned. We encourage training for all our employees so they can fulfil their potential. When projects are proposed, when they're going on, and after they've finished, people discuss it all the time, thinking about what went well and what could be better next time. This includes looking at the processes, trying to find beliefs and values beneath the surface that may be having an effect, positive or negative. We seek customer feedback, analyse and act it, and act on the result. Energy comes from intrinsic reward such as learning, interest, and engagement with work.

4.2 Nurturing a learning culture

A learning culture supports individual learning, and in doing that, supports organizational learning as well. Learning and improvement are not occasional events, but are built into the systems. This sets the scene for continuous improvement.

Organizations cannot be learning organizations if employees see them as immutable or are reluctant to challenge what goes on. There needs to be encouragement for people at all levels to pass comment on how things are run, both in praise and adverse criticism, to suggest alternatives, and to give ideas for development. Senge (1992) argues that the knowledge of the group is greater than the sum of the individual members' knowledge, but to capture that collective knowledge we need a learning culture comprising five disciplines:

1 **Personal mastery** – improving skills and encouraging all involved to work towards the goals of the organization.
2 **Mental models** – being aware of thoughts and assumptions, recognizing that these are not absolute truth, and challenging them if necessary.
3 **Shared vision** – the vision is not simply set from above but is the result of a common desire to take the organization forward and achieve its goals.
4 **Team learning** – building a team that wants to reach beyond the tasks required, and has learning as an inbuilt goal.
5 **Systems thinking** – looking at the whole organization and the systems in it, and how activities in one part will affect other parts.

At their core, these disciplines are saying that the organization can gain more than the aggregate contributions of all the individuals working there, by having a culture where people learn and expand their learning by sharing it with others. Individual learning merely adds to overall knowledge; shared learning multiplies it. But the change from a collection of individual learners to a fully learning organization won't just happen, and it will never be complete, as there will always be more learning to do. And there will always be a need to share and discuss, and to incorporate new knowledge into existing knowledge.

The need for collaborative business is now accepted by the British Standards Institution (BSI). There is now a BSI standard, BS11000 (BSI, 2016) for Collaborative Business Relationships (Hawkins and Little, 2011). They list the benefits as bringing successful collaboration with chosen partners, creating a neutral platform for mutual benefit, defining roles and responsibilities to improve decision making, sharing costs, risks, resources and responsibilities, increasing training opportunities, and building better relationships that lead to better results.

Learning culture to help address adaptive problems

The benefits of collaboration are clear and rarely disputed. But how do you get from a closed, untrusting, defensive culture to an open, trusting, learning organization?

Heifetz, Grashow, and Linsky (2009) describe this as an adaptive rather than a technical challenge.

Technical challenges can be solved by technicians or experienced employees. They can identify the problem and apply techniques that they already know, maybe with minor adjustments. The result is that the problem is fixed. This would also apply to practical problems like not having enough shelf space – buy more shelves. The authors say that dealing with problems in this way is akin to 'rearranging the deck chairs on a ship that may be sinking'. If applied to adaptive challenges the changes are often ineffective quick fixes that don't address underlying issues.

Adaptive problems need changes in the way people think about things, and the way they see themselves and their roles. They may change parts of the job, and involve rethinking how to do things. Values may be shaken up. The nature of the work community may change. There may be parts that are psychologically difficult to accept. If it is deemed too difficult for the organization to cope with alone, and external experts are brought in, there may be feelings of loss of ownership or resentment at the intrusion. The changes require innovative thinking and learning as we go, and need to involve all of the organization community. The type of change necessary will be trans-formational, which upsets the status quo and 'business as usual'. Resistance is to be expected.

Trust and social capital

Given the importance of knowledge sharing and mutual learning in a social context, it is not surprising that trust looms large as a major factor in a collective learning culture (Gubbins and MacCurtain, 2008). This is particu-larly true where we are dealing with the stress and uncertainty of adaptive challenges.

Trust is a valuable asset, but trust is vulnerable at times of change. Trust is too often taken for granted, and steps are not taken to build or maintain it. Sometimes trust is patchy, with small groups within the organization trusting each other absolutely. This may give a false impression that trust is high throughout the organization, when there is actually a lot of cynicism. With this comes a reluctance to share information. High levels of genuine mutual trust are essential in creating a learning organization. Those at the top need to set an example of openness as a first step.

It should be clear that the leaders see learning and development as part of company strategy, built into the system, not an add-on afterthought, nor just for high flyers. In learning organizations employees at all levels are expected, not just allowed, to take advantage of opportunities to learn, both formally and informally. Learning organizations provide training opportu-nities, including coaching and mentoring, and arrange learning events that are visibly in line with the strategy.

Success, from individuals and from teams, is noticed and celebrated. Mistakes are expected as inevitable parts of the process; not blameworthy, but a piece of added learning. Without blame, guilt feelings go away, and the lessons learned can be discussed without rancour.

In an atmosphere of low trust and high change (a commonplace situ-ation), there will be strong resistance. There may be statements that every-one is doing enough learning, thank you very much. But the point is that the learning needs to be collective, and this needs to be part of the culture. The learning culture is dependent on networks of trusting relationships. It was less important when command and control was the norm. Controls in a collective learning culture are more informal and founded on trust. People have to be empowered, which means giving them freedom to take control of themselves, and letting go of organizational power.

When there is trust, people collaborate, share information, and give others the benefit of the doubt. Without trust, you get suspicion, hostility, tension, conflict and negative politics. Both trust and mistrust can create a spiral that reinforces itself. If we don't trust, we are suspicious, we watch out for deceit, and are self-protective. If we do trust, we welcome what others say and expect to get added value. There are times when trust is misplaced, but trusting nobody is a policy that blocks any relationship. We need to have belief in others, emotional resilience if we are let down, and willingness to build more relationships of trust.

Putnam's (2001) concept of social capital is important here. Putnam defines social capital as 'features of social life – networks, norms, and trust – that enable participants to act together more effectively to pursue shared objectives. Social capital, in short, refers to social connections and the attendant norms and trust.'

Social capital is what you get when people get enthusiastic about a project, want to be involved, and want other people to join them. It comes with willingness to do what's necessary to make it work. The reward for effort comes from success in the project, rather than from others returning the favour. The favour goes around and everyone involved benefits. This is reciprocity; the feeling that everyone is ready to help as necessary. Reciprocity is essential for successful social capital.

Mutual trust is essential. This means that when members of the group say they will do something, others have the confident expectation that it will be done as promised. If some repeatedly fail to do this it affects the cohesion of the group, and may lead to different groupings where trust is honoured. Thus, social capital represents the informal networks of trust and reciprocity.

Without trust, cooperation in relationships and depth of learning are limited. A growing body of research has identified how social capital has a positive impact on the individual, the group and the community. It has a beneficial effect on health, education, crime and economic viability of organizations and the community. Collective learning requires strong social capital and therefore trust.

Putnam (2001) describes two kinds of trust – thin trust and thick trust. Thin trust is the general trust that we feel for strangers across the different groups in a community, the assumption being that others have the same basic values of honesty and truth telling. So when a group forms to start a project, there is already a basic level of trust. As long as the group consists of people who all feel this, thin trust has a high value. It is readymade and doesn't require working on. This, of course, will break down if there are some who cannot be trusted. Thick trust is found in strong personal relationships where the people have been involved in similar goals for a period of time. It is slow to grow, but is then resilient to minor lapses in loyalty.

Because thick trust is rooted in the strong ties of kin and friends the danger is that strong 'us versus them' attitudes develop. In our thick trust group, we feel safe and assume that we can be ourselves. Community cohesion relies on groups networking with each other and developing the 'thin trust'. Equally, in organizations, thick trust can lead to silo mentalities in which we only trust our part of the organization. The consequence of that is we are less likely to share our knowledge and learning or take account of the needs of other groups. Collective learning is diminished.

Exercise

The questionnaire below aims to get the debate started about the culture of learning in your organization. The scoring needs to be treated with caution, but after completing it reflect on where the gaps are in your organization for realizing your collective learning capabilities.

Table 7.3 Organization learning questionnaire

Knowledge and information are difficult to access. Processes are duplicated and the wheel is regularly re-invented.	**1 2 3 4 5**	Organized and accessible knowledge management systems so employees can contribute knowledge to a centrally stored resource, and access the knowledge acquired by others.
Organization is internally focused. Information and knowledge from outside aren't systematically collected, shared, discussed or acted upon.	**1 2 3 4 5**	Knowledge is systematically acquired from outside so that we continuously benchmark ourselves against best practice.
People tend to hoard information and knowledge. Little useable information is transferred across teams, departments, and divisions.	**1 2 3 4 5**	Creation, sharing and use of knowledge is celebrated and best practice is broadcast.
People are inadequately trained or supported in the use of social media applications, so spend too much time in aimless browsing and wasting time looking for information.	**1 2 3 4 5**	People are well trained and equipped to use tools that collaboratively and socially connect them with others to acquire, disseminate and share knowledge effectively.

Table 7.3 *continued*

Knowledge is seen as power. People don't share knowledge, either because they don't know how, or they claim they are too busy. Reward, recognition and promotion go to those who have knowledge, not to those who share it.	**1 2 3 4 5**	Sharing of knowledge is rewarded. People recognize the importance of investing time now in knowledge sharing and transfer in order to create a sustainable future.
Knowledge is locked into the hierarchical structure. There is a climate of secrecy and exclusion.	**1 2 3 4 5**	Few hierarchical differentiations. Work environment facilitates sharing of knowledge.
Many hidden agendas, blaming for mistakes and self-interested politics.	**1 2 3 4 5**	People display respect for others, are straightforward and learn from mistakes, risks and successes together.

28–35. High learning capability: committed action and collective drive to continuously learn for sustainable advantage.

21–27. Developing capability: growing realization and action to facilitate a learning community but more development required.

14–20. Locked-in capability: some learning initiatives but much valuable knowledge may remain locked up in the minds of individuals. Systems may tend to be bound by hierarchy and bureaucracy.

7–13. Rock bottom potential: knowledge in the organization is difficult to leverage. Business may be based on old formulaic processes which are resistant to change.

5 Collective and social learning processes and tools

There are many collective learning methods now surfacing in order to involve key stakeholders in solving complex problems that affect us all. Some examples are 21st-Century Town Hall Meetings, Appreciative Inquiry, Charrettes, Citizen or Constituent Assemblies Panels or Juries, Conversation Cafes, Future Search, Large Scale Forums, Open Space, Peace-Making Circles, PeerSpirit Circle, Public Conversation Projects, Real-Time Strategic

Change, Study Circles, Whole-Scale Change, Wisdom Councils, World Café, and more. According to Myrium Laberge of Breakthroughs Unlimited, the reasons for facilitating collective learning processes and outcomes come into four main categories (Laberge, 2006):

- to increase awareness of an issue;
- to build relationships, sometimes to mend after conflict;
- to make decisions after seeking a variety of options;
- to collaborate with others who have an interest in the outcome from different perspectives.

More than one purpose is usually present, and it changes over time. There are some things that stay the same. There needs to be a shared desired outcome. People must be ready to invite ideas and to listen, with the expectation that the other person has something useful to say. There should be sufficient time to explore the ideas on offer. Each person should expect to contribute and to learn, to look at many different perspectives, and to merge ideas in collective learning. This is different from negotiating, where each person gives a bit and wins a bit. It is genuine mutual involvement with a shared will to find the best solution. In short, it is depth learning communication which involves dialogue and quality advocacy and inquiry.

5.1 Dialogue and the learning circles

Circles have a long history as the best shape for egalitarian debate. King Arthur's knights had a round table for that reason. The circle is the best shape for a group to denote equal status for all, in contrast to someone being at the head of the table to direct operations. A round table is not essential, but the concept of the circle needs to apply. The beginnings of dialogue were probably found in hunter-gatherers sitting around the fire to share stories about their experiences. This type of gathering created, and still creates, a sense of belonging, and spreads tacit knowledge. The physicist David Bohm took this basic human experience and developed it as a way of exploring the individual and collective presuppositions, ideas, beliefs, and feelings that subtly control our interactions (see http://www.dbohm.com/david-bohm-videos.html).

Organizations often do not follow a dialogue path. More often people have pre-formed ideas of what the outcome ought to be, and see alternative suggestions as obstacles to be resisted and dismantled. 'Sticking to your guns' is seen as a quality, and dissent as a tiresome waste of time. People are possessive about information they hold, and exclude others because of lack of trust. They make unwarranted assumptions; people lack the interpersonal skills for open discussion, and there is not enough time anyway. There are unwritten rules about not admitting to mistakes, avoiding anything that might arouse conflict, and saying what the bosses want to hear, not what they need to know. This type of communication or miscommunication is dysfunctional; it does not get near the root of complex systemic problems.

There is a growing realization that in a fast-moving, complex, knowledge-rich world, we need sometimes to slow down, deepen our communication and use our collective brainpower. There needs to be more empowerment, team working, partnerships and alliances that cross boundaries. Good dialogue will foster this. Genuine dialogue is the antithesis of 'justify and defend'.

Dialogue has been defined as 'sustained collective inquiry into the processes, assumptions and certainties that compose everyday experiences' (Isaacs, 1993). In dialogue, people come to suspend their inner voice of judgement and defensive reactions in order to explore meanings at a deeper level. Table 7.4 below highlights some characteristics of dialogue in contrast to the 'justify and defend' routines more typical of workplace discussions and meetings.

Table 7.4 Difference between dialogue and justify-and-defend communication process

Dialogue	Justify and defend
• Invites other people's points of view	• Resists other people's points of view
• Suspends assumptions	• Protects assumptions
• Accepts assumptions could be false	• Takes assumptions to be fact
• Reflects on reasons for assumptions	• Brushes aside anything that doesn't fit
• Culture differences seen as food for thought	• Culture differences seen as clash
• Starts with looking at the problem	• Starts with looking at the solution
• Ready to give information	• Conceals information
• Inquires and reflects	• Tells and explains
• Asks: Why are we thinking as we do?	• States: We think this
• Willing to put forward risky points	• Unwilling to consider risky points
• Blends divergent viewpoints	• Protests against divergent viewpoints
• Clarifies mental models	• Confirms mental models
• Explores deep level thinking	• Stays at superficial level
• Aims for shared understanding	• Aims for victory for own wishes

In short, dialogue is about creating and sharing knowledge. The goal is to achieve transformational results not possible by one individual, ie SYNERGY – 'the sum is greater than the parts'. It is particularly powerful in situations that require collaborative effort and where the leader's knowledge is no greater than that of individual team members. It focuses on our fundamental assumptions about reality, in order to unfold shared meaning and to develop collective action.

The key distinction to be drawn out is that we need to move towards dialogue when we want to engage everyone to learn more about the problem or issue. We are more likely to use discussion when we want to decide what immediate action to take. Of course, we can have situations that involve a combination of discussion and dialogue characteristics. But even when we need an immediate solution it can still be useful to build in some time for dialogue. We often make the wrong decisions by jumping too quickly to a solution before we have had all perspectives on the problem.

Exercise

Try the checklist below to assess the level of dialogue in your team. Health warning! This is not an empirically validated questionnaire. It was designed by the author as a starting point to assess the readiness for dialogue in your team.

Table 7.5 Team readiness questionnaire

How far are the following statements true of your team? 5 = strongly agree 1 = strongly disagree					
1 Everyone agrees at the meeting, but it's different later on.	1	2	3	4	5
2 They're careful not to say anything that upsets anyone.	1	2	3	4	5
3 They do discuss things, but it's often quite superficial.	1	2	3	4	5
4 Sometimes they're fireballs of energy and commitment. Sometimes they're damp squibs.	1	2	3	4	5
5 They tend to keep quiet about disagreement for fear of rebuke.	1	2	3	4	5
6 They can be quite forceful in getting their views across, and work hard to persuade others.	1	2	3	4	5
7 They feel there's no good reason to get a dialogue going.	1	2	3	4	5

Table 7.5 *continued*

8 Once they've said what they think, they don't want to hear what the rest think.	1	2	3	4	5
9 They don't say things at the meeting unless they're completely sure of their ground.	1	2	3	4	5
10 There are some subjects that we simply do not discuss.	1	2	3	4	5
Totals					
Grand total					

Interpretation

10–20	The team is ready for dialogue. They have discussions over a wide range of topics; they listen and feel heard.
21–30	The team is defensive in some areas, but they can discuss deeper issues. They might need help from a facilitator to get into real dialogue.
31–40	There are hidden agendas that prevent productive discussion. Members are reluctant to expose their views in public, and are defensive when they do.
41–50	There is a great deal of internal politicking going on. They are protecting their turf and not communicating openly. They will resist dialogue.

5.2 Advocacy and inquiry

Collective learning requires open communication. More than that, generative learning is more likely to take place if we raise the bar of quality communication. Ross and Roberts (1994) argue that 'managers in western corporations have received a lifetime of training in being forceful, articulate "advocates" and "problem solvers".' They know how to present and argue strongly for their views. But as people rise in the organization, they are forced to deal with more complex and interdependent issues where no one individual 'knows the answer', and the only viable option is for groups of informed and committed individuals to think together to arrive at new insights. They need to learn to skillfully balance advocacy with inquiry (Ross and Roberts, nd).

Advocacy is saying what you think and feel, giving your opinion, recommending a course of action, promoting your own view and defending it.

Inquiry is asking others what they think, gaining information and ideas from other people.

In the west, managers are expected to give their views, solve problems, and use advocacy. This is getting more difficult, as frequently nobody knows the answer. It's better to form teams to think round problems, discuss matters, and find new insight. We can start to balance advocacy and inquiry by saying what we think and giving our reasons, ie advocacy. Then we need to accept challenges from other people, who will have different viewpoints and draw different conclusions, ie inquiry.

It is not easy to do this. Most people enthusiastically advocate and then try to convince others that they're right. This can turn to defensiveness or even verbal attack. It may escalate into a spiral of attack-defend, which is bad for new learning, and guards the status quo.

To get past this, it's essential that people are willing to learn from the views of others. This clearly involves giving your own views so that others can learn from them, but with a willingness to pause, listen, and take in what others are saying.

With inquiry, team members focus on the ideas that the sender is sharing, rather than trying to decide whether these ideas are good or bad. Inquiry allows a group to solve problems creatively and provides the forum for developing collaborative ideas (see Figure 7.2). For example, when a team member presents a conclusion, other team members might ask, 'What's led you to that conclusion?', 'What data are you using?', 'What's made you think that?' This inquiry is likely to be more effective than advocacy, especially at the beginning of a project.

When the team is ready to decide the best method to reach its goals, advocacy can be a useful way to push on to the next stage. At first, a climate of inquiry will help people to direct their energy towards understanding, rather than self-defence.

To get full synergy, it's not enough to balance advocacy and inquiry. Both have to be of high quality:

High-quality advocacy means giving reasons for your beliefs, and being open about any assumptions you're making.

High-quality inquiry means challenging other people's assumptions at the same time as seeking their views.

High advocacy, high inquiry gives mutual communication and learning. Each person gives their thoughts, inquires what the other person thinks, and is receptive to being questioned about the way they're thinking.

Figure 7.2 Advocacy and inquiry matrix

ADVOCACY		
	Low Advocacy – Low Inquiry	**High Inquiry – Low Advocacy**
	Positive – Observing	*Positive* – Finding out
	Listening and reflection can help to increase the quality of your contribution later.	Can be part of investing in understanding before being understood.
	Dysfunctional – Withdrawal	*Dysfunctional* – Manipulation
	Can be caused by withholding views and avoiding the 'undiscussables'.	The 'inquirer' has a hidden agenda.

LOW

INQUIRY

LOW   **HIGH**

	High Advocacy – Low Inquiry	**High Inquiry – High Advocacy**
	Positive – Explaining	*Positive* – Mutuality
	Useful for giving information. Doesn't enhance understanding of diverse perspectives.	Two-way communication and learning. I state my views and I inquire into yours.
	Dysfunctional – Imposing	*Dysfunctional* – Over-engaging
	Creates compliance or resistance.	Issues get lost in the desire to check and test. There is little quiet reflection.

Guidelines for productive advocacy and inquiry.

- Frame of mind:
  - recognize that assumptions can be a barrier to learning;
  - realize that other people will see things that you don't;
  - if someone seems to you to have odd views, recognize that it makes sense to them, and try to discover their reasons.
- Advocacy:
  - explain reasons for beliefs and actions;
  - repeat back what you understand from others, to check you've understood what they mean;
  - if you think there will be bad effects from what others are doing, tell them, without suggesting that they are foolish or that they meant harm;

- – use language that starts from yourself, which expresses how you feel, rather than starting from the other person, which can sound accusatory. 'I feel overloaded', is more likely to get a positive response than 'You've landed me with too much to do'.

- Inquiry:
  - – ask other people how they see things and ask for their reasons;
  - – if you don't understand, ask them to explain more;
  - – ask other people to tell you if they can't see the links in your reasoning;
  - – ask others how they are feeling;
  - – if other people seem unreasonable to you, ask them why they want to do what they're doing;
  - – be prepared to see how your own behaviour might contribute to the problem.

See below as an illustration of advocacy and inquiry in action.

Advocacy and inquiry in action

One famous example of a change of approach from primarily advocacy to more inquiry was President Kennedy's dealing with two major international crises – the Bay of Pigs and the Cuban Missile Crisis.

Eisenhower's administration had planned the attack on Cuba, and Kennedy was strongly advised to carry this out. Those of Kennedy's staff who disagreed decided against rocking the boat, and people from the State Department's Latin America desks were not asked their opinion. It was a case of glossing over doubts and pushing the plan through. They missed vital facts, such that the mountains where the exiles might hide were 80 miles from the landing site. The result was a hundred deaths and many more hostages being taken. The process was a dysfunctional form of *high advocacy*.

Kennedy responded to this with a review of the processes used for decision making. This led to five major changes:

1 People were encouraged to be sceptical, and to discuss issues as though they were looking from the outside, rather than being involved.

2 Two people were appointed to look for drawbacks and unwarranted assumptions.

▶

3 Formality was discouraged where it might inhibit discussion. People were encouraged to stray from the agenda and ignore rank when they had a point to make.

4 Some committees split into sub-groups to discuss matters further, so there could be more concentration, and less conformity brought on by the force of numbers.

5 Kennedy himself decided not to be present at early meetings, so that he would not unduly influence discussions, just by being there and being the president.

This radical change of approach was put to the test when Soviet nuclear missiles were found on Cuban soil. Top-level discussions took place, involving many of the same people who had been in the task force for the Bay of Pigs, but the protocol had changed.

- Other opinions were sought, and experts from different areas invited to join in discussions.

- Kennedy absented himself on occasion to ensure that his status didn't prevent debate from going in an unconventional, but possibly right direction.

- Robert Kennedy actively encouraged alternative opinions and discouraged simple dichotomies of thought.

- Assumptions were tested to see if they had validity.

This resulted in two sub-groups, one recommending an air strike, the other a blockade. These two groups were in open communication with each other, exchanging information and papers, and met to continue debate. They produced two papers, to present both options. Kennedy made the final decision for the blockade. The result was a peaceful conclusion.

This was *balancing advocacy with inquiry*.

Exercise

Use the questionnaire below to assess your contribution in the next meeting or group forum you are involved in. Total your score after completing the questionnaire and refer your score against the table and diagram that follow the questionnaire. Reflect on and/or discuss with a colleague the quality of your advocacy and inquiry communication.

Table 7.6 Advocacy and inquiry skills questionnaire

Advocacy and inquiry skills questionnaire	Never				Often
1 I sought others' help in finding a joint solution.	1	2	3	4	5
2 I helped to create an atmosphere where people felt safe giving their ideas and sharing their reasons.	1	2	3	4	5
3 I shared my thoughts and assumptions and invited others to comment on them.	1	2	3	4	5
4 I attempted to get all issues out in the open.	1	2	3	4	5
5 I gave my ideas as confidently as I could and then asked others for their ideas.	1	2	3	4	5
6 I drew on my experience to explain what I thought was the right way to do things.	1	2	3	4	5
7 I made sure everyone understood what I was saying and why.	1	2	3	4	5
8 I made an effort to make sure my meaning was clear.	1	2	3	4	5
9 I could see the best way forward, and I tried to communicate that.	1	2	3	4	5
10 I wanted to make sure everyone understood what I meant.	1	2	3	4	5
11 I went into other people's viewpoints in depth.	1	2	3	4	5
12 I checked that I understood what other people were saying.	1	2	3	4	5
13 I asked questions, to help other people to get their point across	1	2	3	4	5
14 I asked questions to understand how people had reached their conclusions.	1	2	3	4	5
15 I tried to get the full meaning behind what people were saying.	1	2	3	4	5
16 I observed others reactions and tried to see things as they were seeing them.	1	2	3	4	5
17 I made some observations about the progress we were making.	1	2	3	4	5
18 I tried to be aware of my own assumption-making thoughts.	1	2	3	4	5
19 I spent time reflecting on how we were communicating with each other.	1	2	3	4	5
20 I attended to everything that was going on throughout.	1	2	3	4	5

DIALOGUE High advocacy, high inquiry	ASSERTING High advocacy, low inquiry	QUESTIONING High inquiry, low advocacy	ATTENDING Low inquiry, low advocacy
1	6	11	16
2	7	12	17
3	8	13	18
4	9	14	19
5	10	15	20

Figure 7.3 Advocacy and inquiry map

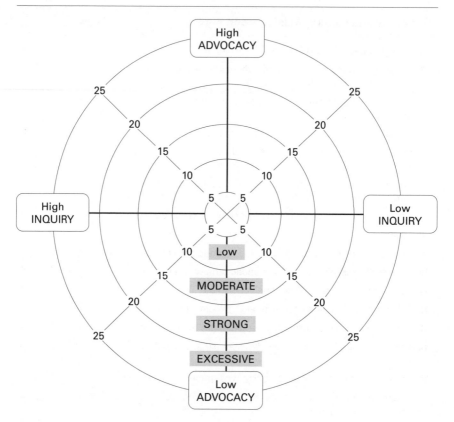

5.3 Ladder of inference

We all have assumptions based on what we have heard and what people around us also assume. These beliefs are deep rooted as assumptions, but rarely questioned, so may be quite shallow in terms of reality. These include what we were told in childhood, what people typically say in social gatherings, and what it is comfortable to accept. Assumptions may also be valid and true, but many are not. They are nevertheless very strong, and frequently block new ideas that in any way loosen the assumptions. The basis of our assumptions is: I think this is true – and it obviously is true – there is data to prove it – I select the data that is true (ie the data that confirms my assumptions).

The Ladder of Inference concept was developed by Chris Argyris (Ross, 1994) to counteract these psychological roadblocks to learning. The idea is that we deal with information by selecting and editing according to our beliefs and preconceptions. However, while our beliefs may be our truth, they aren't always The Truth. Conflict arises when two or more people of differing opinions need their truth to be recognized as The Truth. Unfortunately, we do not easily separate our beliefs and opinions from our concept of who we are, which leads us to take differences of opinion personally.

Figure 7.4 Ladder of inference

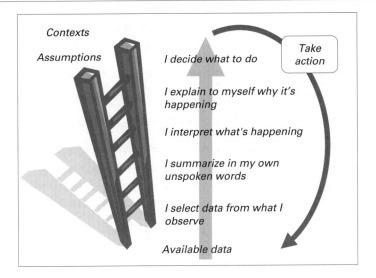

We are so skilled at thinking that we jump up the ladder without knowing it:

- we tacitly register some data and ignore others;
- we impose our own interpretations and draw conclusions;
- we lose sight of this because we don't think about our thinking;
- our conclusions feel so obvious to us that we see no need to retrace our steps through our assumptions and beliefs.

The context we are in, our assumptions, and our values channel how we jump up the ladder:

- our models of the world and our repertoire of actions affect what data we select, our interpretation and our conclusions;
- our conclusions make us act in certain ways, and usually this confirms our own assumptions.

Our skill at reasoning is both essential and gets us in trouble:

- if we thought about each inference we made, nothing would get done;

- as people see their own conclusions are obvious, they don't feel the need to analyse them;

- when people disagree, they often keep repeating the conclusions they have already drawn.

This makes it hard to resolve differences and to learn from one another.

Drawing conclusions and adding meaning to your life is important. You can't analyse every situation. But there are three ways you can use the ladder of inference to improve your communication:

1 becoming more aware of your own thinking and reasoning *(reflection)*;

2 making your thinking and reasoning more visible to others *(advocacy)*;

3 inquiring into others' thinking and reasoning *(inquiry)*.

As with the early stages of learning any new technique, at first it can feel contrived and unnatural. You need practice to embed it into the way you think. The following five rules may help you to move towards inquiry, and to explore the ladder of inference:

1 identify the conclusions someone is making;

2 ask for the data that led to the conclusion;

3 inquire into the reasoning that connects data and conclusion;

4 infer a possible belief or assumption;

5 state your inference and test it with the person.

Exercise: The left-hand column.

This is an exercise devised by Chris Argyris to check and test our assumptions and inference processes. Choose a difficult conversation (the type you would prefer to ignore) that you have had recently. Write a brief paragraph describing the situation. What are you trying to accomplish? Who or what is blocking you? What might happen?

Draw two columns in which to record the conversation:

- In the RIGHT-hand column, write out the actual conversation. Write it like a play script, with the speaker's name and the words they used. Be as accurate as your memory will allow.

- In the LEFT-hand column, describe what you were thinking and feeling but not saying.

Reflection: Using your left-hand column as a resource

You can learn a great deal just from the act of writing out a case. You can then use it to examine your own thinking, as if you were looking at the thinking of someone else. As you reflect, ask yourself:

- What really led you to think and feel this way?
- What were you trying to accomplish?
- Did you achieve the results you intended?
- How might your comments have contributed to the difficulties?
- Why didn't you say what was in your left-hand column at the time of the conversation?
- What assumptions are you making about others?
- What were the costs of operating this way? What were the payoffs?
- What prevented you from acting differently?
- How can you use your left-hand column to improve your communications?

See Senge *et al* (2004, p. 246) for an example and further explanation of the left-hand column.

5.4 Open Space Technology

Open Space Technology (see Owen, 2008), is a way of including large numbers of people for one to three days. It is very open and almost anyone can join to discuss and have activities about any issue. It is a way of bringing in large numbers of people when it is not appropriate for those at the top to make decisions without consultation. The theory is that there are solutions in there to be delved into, and a large group, given suitable direction, can organize itself into useful sub-divisions in a way that will lead to good decisions. There are no pre-booked speakers, panels, or workshops. People join at points that interest them. It begins with short meetings to spark off discussion and to start to look at the issues before going deeper. These develop into longer meetings where shared commitment grows and action planning begins. It works, but it does rely on individuals feeling a responsibility for the outcome of the whole event.

5.5 World Café

World Café (see Brown and Isaacs, 2007) starts with the assumption that people have the necessary abilities to face challenges, and that groups of people have more than the sum of their individual abilities, because through listening, sharing, and rethinking, joint knowledge will multiply. World Café is there to make that happen. Conversations start, ideas connect, people listen and add ideas, patterns emerge, themes develop, and collective learning and intelligence grow. This happens in the real world where there are communicating networks, from family networks to large corporations.

There are seven guiding principles in setting up World Café (World Café, nd):

1 Set the context – what is the purpose of the conversation, and what is its place in the larger environment?

2 Provide a safe and welcoming environment.

3 Ask questions that are important to the participants.

4 Encourage everyone to contribute, and show respect.

5 Look for connections, along with diverse views.

6 Listen out for patterns, insights, and deeper questions.

7 Gather the harvest – share collective discoveries, make them visible.

5.6 Action learning

Action learning (also discussed in Chapter 5 in the context of enhancing learner engagement) is a problem-solving approach that combines learning, action and reflection in the workplace. Revans introduced the idea of action learning in 1945 (Revans 2011). He wondered how the Titanic came to sink, when experts in shipbuilding believed it to be unsinkable. This rock-solid belief stopped people questioning what they were doing, and this lack of questioning was a substantial part of the problem.

As a physicist, Revans was trained to keep asking questions to find out why things happened, and he came up with the idea of action learning. The process of action learning is to ask questions in order to explore issues, problems, or situations at a deeper level. People thinking on their own often go in for self-confirmation, where they agree with their own early thoughts, and do not notice they are making assumptions that may cloud their thinking. Action learning replaces confirmation with questions. It is linked to 'communities of practice', given that it involves people who 'engage in a process of collective learning in a shared domain of human endeavour' (Wenger, 2000).

Members of the action learning group (called a set) decide what topic, issue, problem or situation they want to explore. One member then presents the topic as they see it, and the others ask open questions about it. One person takes on the role of facilitator, keeping the discussion on track so that it sticks to the same topic, moves forward, and keeps to the basic ground rules, including that people are treated with respect and confidentiality will be preserved. Each member takes a turn at presenting the topic as they see it, and being questioned about it by the rest of the group. This helps to bring to the surface tacit assumptions, shows where preferences or interests are influencing views, and gives people practice in presenting their case, reflecting at a deeper level, and learning from the experience of others. This has clear benefits when they return to the workplace.

Ground rules for action learning sets:

- respect confidentiality;
- be respectful of people, their views and their feelings;
- practise active listening (be attentive to what the person means);
- focus on the person presenting;
- think about the subject matter;
- at first, ask questions only – suggestions come later;
- stick to open questions, ie questions that invite thought and expansion of ideas, as opposed to closed questions, which expect specific answers that end the debate.

5.7 GROW Model for open questions

The GROW model (briefly discussed in Chapter 1), Goal, Reality, Options, Wrap up, gives a useful framework for questions in action learning:

- At the Goal stage, open questions can be about what is important now, and what would be a good result.
- At the Reality stage, open questions can be about the current situation, what is working well, and what needs work.
- At the Options stage, open questions can be about past experience and how it applies to the current situation, including the 'don't do that again' option.

- At the Wrap up stage open questions can be about what actions are to be taken, how to make sure that this happens, and how success will be measured.

5.8 TOOT – Time out of Time

Barry Oshry developed the TOOT tool to combat what he called spatial blindness (Oshry and Devane, 2009). This is when people are familiar with their own part of the system but blind to other parts, which can be a source of considerable misunderstanding and conflict.

All members, or a sufficient number to be representative, take time out of their ordinary day to meet and to convey what their part of the system is like. The meeting place is away from the normal workplace, somewhere that is neutral for everyone. Each person has a turn to describe what it is like for them. There are ground rules that everyone must listen, and recognize that the person speaking is experienced in the area they are speaking about. Everyone must stick to the truth, and this is not an arena for debate. The idea is to understand what it is like in other parts of the organization, and how the parts fit into the whole. This happens through open and non-judgmental questions.

This simple group process is linked to social collective learning processes because people learn from each other by attending to the here and now events in the group. The TOOT brings participants from all parts of the organization system together in one space, providing an opportunity for them to overcome 'spatial blindness' and learn from each other. The collective part is that the whole group starts to understand the emerging themes and changes in the organization.

6 Social media and learning

In our digital age the workplace context is changing as a result of web-based knowledge and communication systems. It is important to make a distinction these and between web activities that are essentially one-way communication, (although there may be some form of response from someone else) where there is limited participatory knowledge making. Web 1.0 activities (from the first stage of the World Wide Web, which was entirely made up of web pages connected by hyperlinks) such as chat room synchronous (or occasionally asynchronous) conversations, e-learning, podcasts, search functions, video conferencing, web forums, and webcasts do facilitate independent learning. However, interactivity is often limited. Web 2.0 tools (using the second stage of development of the internet, characterized especially by the change from static web pages to dynamic or user-generated content and the growth of social media) such as blogs, the Cloud, internet forums, social bookmarking and social networking (eg Facebook) allow the possibility of more interactivity so that two-way communication, collaboration and learning form a more dynamic, changing process.

Web-based social media (as discussed in Chapter 6) is very new compared to classroom teaching, and although used by millions, it is still regarded with some suspicion as a mode of learning. Early social media sites were simply social, devised for people to make contact and be friends. The idea of using them for learning has attracted both interest and opposition, as can be expected from something not widely tested. Socrates feared that the spread of written documents would erode people's memories. Now it is feared that informal learning will reduce 'real knowledge'. It is true that a great deal of time can be wasted on social media sites, but this can be said about classrooms too. Ways need to be found that make good use of the medium. Social media sites are not substitutes for classrooms; they are another route to learning. The social aspects bring a new dimension, made easier by technology.

When something is created purely for social purposes it can be difficult to think of it as a learning process. We know that social factors can give a boost to learning, but to use what has been simply social as a learning medium may seem like ducking out of real study. It needs an overturn in the way we look at learning, and the way we look at social activities.

In some ways, gathering together in virtual spaces on the net is the same as gathering together in a room. When people are motivated by their work, they will learn from each other through social contact, whether that is in the coffee bar at work, in the office, on the train home, or in totally different places, linked by the net. This natural learning can be augmented by setting up programmes to encourage and reinforce the learning.

Learning via social media is not the same as e-learning, which can also be excellent. Any type of course, whether aided by technology or not, has its focus on content and closely defined objectives. With learning through social media the social aspects need to be harnessed, which means thinking about how people learn. Learning by doing is the first way we learn; in our early lives, before we have language, we repeatedly perform the same acts, like dropping an object from the high chair, until we realize it will always fall. Once we are able to talk, we can find things out from others, and this gradually reduces the need for constant experimenting ourselves. In adult life, although we can grasp theories about things we have never done, we still learn best about tasks that we actually do. We add to that knowledge by talking to others, comparing and contrasting different aspects of the job. Social media makes it much easier to do this.

Social learning is open ended. There is no course to complete, and no limits are set as to what can be learned. It can include organized content that people offer, and which we can discuss to enlarge the experience. It may include highly academic debate, or may focus firmly on this week's problems. Whatever the content, the social interaction will create a supportive circle where people learn from each other. The participants are guiding the content, so it will stay relevant. Whereas a good classroom course will give useful material to take back to the workplace, learning in social media comes from the workplace, and is part of it at the time of learning.

Remember, technology provides useful tools for supporting learning, but it is the 'soft stuff' of sharing, thinking together, building knowledge, challenging, developing and solving problems together that is the real stuff that produces results.

7 Mentoring, coaching and leadership for collective and social learning

7.1 Mentoring and coaching

The theory of social learning posits that people learn from one another through observation, imitation and modelling. They learn new behaviour through observing the behaviour of others. If people see positive, desired outcomes from a behaviour, then they are more likely to model, imitate, and adopt the behaviour themselves.

Mentoring is a way of using the skills and knowledge of experienced employees to help newcomers to learn. This is good both for the individual being mentored and for the organization. The mentor is not usually directly responsible for the employee. Mentoring means discussing, focusing on skills existing and skills required and opportunities for training for personal and career development. The mentoring relationship can be described as a formalized social learning process where the mentee gains from the experience of the mentor. The process involves giving examples, showing ways to do things, asking for ideas about how the mentee might proceed, observing actions and discussing results. This social learning can be augmented by groups of mentees meeting to discuss their experiences and to learn from each other. Peer mentoring can take place between people at the same level, but with one having more experience in a specific area. It encourages learners to get involved in their own learning.

Peer mentoring is useful for people making lifestyle changes, such as recovering from a crisis. The peer mentor is someone who has had a similar experience and has learned ways of dealing with it. They are in a position to provide their own insights, to support the person going through recovery, and to challenge them if they have reached blocks that need to be confronted but are uncomfortable. The peer mentor needs to be emotionally intelligent, reliable, and to have high respect for confidentiality.

Coaching overlaps with mentoring, but is more focused on the job. The coach challenges the coachee to define their goals and to define what they need to do to reach those goals. This is done not by instructions but by a process of short open questions that enable the coachee to form their own conclusions and make plans for their progress. The coach empowers the coachee. The coach can be like a mirror, slightly changed, where the coachee sees similar processes going on, but not quite the same as their own. This gives material for thinking and encourages learning, without being told what to do.

7.2 GROW model for coaching

The GROW model described earlier in the chapter in relation to action learning is also helpful in coaching and mentoring. Learners need to define their Goals, recognize Reality, identify Opportunities, and know their Weaknesses. This is also a useful framework for self-coaching. This is a learning process that occurs day to day in our social world. We have a learning relationship with a mentor or coach and then we internalize the process (or technique) which has been useful to us and apply it to ourselves without the help of the coach or mentor. We in effect coach and mentor ourselves. We may then use the same process to help others. In that way, the dyadic learning relationship can become a collective learning process.

7.3 Leadership: direction, alignment and commitment

As discussed above, the speed of change, volatility, uncertainty and complexity mean we do not know where the best ideas will come from. Collaborative relationships are required in business and organizational boundaries need to be fluid. Self-organizing networks and universal access to information are shifting the agenda so that traditional hierarchy is giving way to more peer-like interactions. Employees at all levels and locations and a variety of external stakeholders will hold the relevant information. Shared goals and values are the basis for accountability and control, and are better motivators than carrot and stick. People want autonomy and work that is intrinsically motivating.

This requires a new form of leadership to steer collaborative interaction and learning (Ibarra and Hansen, 2011). Having formally designated leaders directing followers towards agreed goals may impose unnecessary limitations on leadership in the new digital environment. Leadership with the Facebook generation needs to value contribution, not position. It needs to be network-centric, building social capital across networks and developing quality advocacy and inquiry skills. It needs to be able to address systemic issues and be responsive to weak signals in the environment that are signalling significant changes to come. Leadership needs to become more open, transparent and inclusive, in order to connect people within and beyond organizations.

Drath *et al* (2008) argue that leadership should be viewed as a set of functions rather than a role. They posit that as the contexts calling for leadership become increasingly peer-like and collaborative, the old ontology of the lone leader influencing followers needs to be replaced by an ontology in which the essential entities are three leadership outcomes, without specifying how these outcomes are created:

- *Direction:* Widespread agreement in a collective on overall goals, aims, and mission. A shared and collective agreement on our goals and a willingness to change from the current reality towards some future state.

- *Alignment:* Organization and coordination of knowledge and work in a collective. A coordinated effort to ensure people, skills, and processes produce collective work in the service of the shared direction.

- *Commitment:* Willingness of members of a collective to subsume their own interests and benefit within the collective interest and benefit. A willingness of people to devote their time and energy in the service of the shared direction.

To realize these outcomes, leadership can take any number of forms, but typically it is likely to be some form of shared leadership. The concept of shared leadership emerged from the work of Gibb (1954), who formulated the notion of *distributed leadership*. Gibb challenged the traditional assumption that leadership should reside in a single individual and argued that such roles should be dispersed across the team. Recent trends have underscored the importance of shared leadership. The complexity of teams, coupled with frequent changes to their role and structure, reduces the likelihood that a single person has acquired the skills and competencies to fulfil the gamut of necessary leadership functions successfully. The prevalence of self-managing teams and networks underscores the importance of encouraging members to demonstrate leadership behaviour by influencing other members as well as providing direction, fostering motivation, and offering support (Carson, Tesluk, and Marrone, 2007; Pearce and Conger, 2003).

The concept of collaborative leadership seems particularly apt when addressing collective and collaborative learning. Archer and Cameron (2009) define collaborative leadership as:

> the type of leadership required to get results across internal or external organizational boundaries. And that means the leadership required to get value from the differences (in culture, experience, or skills) that lie in the organizations that sit either side of these boundaries. This means leaders investing time to build relationships, being ready to handle conflict in a constructive manner and, most importantly, being able to share control.

They define three skills of collaborative leadership:

Mediation – addressing conflict constructively and effectively as soon as it arises. This is a demanding skill. Evidence from many collaborative leadership 360-degree feedback programmes suggests that handling conflict and the associated mediation skills are often the number one leadership development priority.

Influencing – sharing control and so choosing the best approach to influencing partners. This requires an understanding of the organizational culture and personality type of partners as well as an objective analysis of the business situation to hand.

Engaging others – networking and relationship building. This means communicating with clarity, often in high-stress situations, and involving others in decision making at the right time.

In support of these three skills, collaborative leaders need the following essential attitudes:

Agility – these complex collaborative situations require a forward-looking attitude of mind, coupled with an ability to quickly assimilate facts and ask incisive questions.

Patience – managing relationships takes time and collaborative leaders need to be able to take a calm and measured approach, reflecting on new information and giving confidence to others.

Empathy – all the attributes of any collaborative leader must be under-pinned by a willingness to truly listen and be open minded to the views of others.

These attitudes are essential to developing the high degree of self-awareness necessary to accurately assess the impact of their behaviour on others.

By nature, human beings gather together, and we naturally collaborate (usually with those we regard as of our own tribe) and compete (usually with those we regard as from outside). Collaborative leaders need to create a culture where people will collaborate with those best able to help in achieving shared goals, regardless of whether or not they are like themselves:

Building relationships – relationships should be built before there is a project that needs collaboration. The trust and shared values need to be ready and waiting.

Handling conflict – recognizing conflict before it escalates gives the chance to look at the issues in a collaborative way.

Share control – leaders can't achieve the objectives alone. They need to know where they need to be aligned with others, and when they can make autonomous decisions with limited need to involve and consult others.

Exercise

Reflect on your workplace interactions over the last few months and consider any situations where you exhibited these collaborative leadership competencies. Reflect on areas you could improve and discuss these with a colleague.

8 Conclusion

In this day and age, solitary work is rare. Increasingly there are small teams up to large networks. This means that learning done by one person is useful only in the small pockets of work the same individual does, and that is a tiny portion of the work that an organization does. Moving up to small teams – a great deal of learning occurs when small teams work together, but most of this is focused on the task in hand and its application elsewhere is limited. It is broad social networks, where learning is shared, discussed and expanded, that give highest value, and increase the level of knowledge most. This also improves results.

Organizations need to invest in enabling social networks and the learning that goes on in them. The more people know about what is happening around them, nearby and at a distance, the more they are able to make accurate assessments of situations, and thereby make sound decisions. The learning that comes from social networks can cover anything from the nuts and bolts of everyday processes, to the far-reaching effects of world changes.

Technology is one part of it. It means that information can travel in every direction, for any distance in seconds. What happens to that information afterwards is a slower and more important process. We need people to see the information, think about it, interpret it, share it, take on board other interpretations, collate the data that emerges, discuss, incorporate more information, and so on, continuously.

Non-technology elements, like adaptability, openness to ideas, the ability to deduce, and willingness to change, are even more important. We need emotional intelligence to guide ourselves and others through difficult times, to be ready to reciprocate without a direct reward, to be trustworthy, and able to trust others. We need to be self-aware and know when to bring in others to help, and to trust those in a wider network than our personal circle. This departs sharply from having individuals at their own desks each performing their allotted task. The way forward will involve continuous social learning in wide networks.

Informal learning will become more and more important. Fixed-syllabus qualifications will become irrelevant shortly after the exams are passed, and people will need to learn again. Social learning is a way to bring steady updating, as new information comes in and the world changes yet again.

References

Anderson, L W and Krathwohl, D R, eds (2001) *A Taxonomy for Learning, Teaching, and Assessing: A revision of Bloom's taxonomy of educational objectives*, Longman, New York

Archer, D and Cameron, A (2009) Collaborative Leadership: How to *Succeed in an Interconnected World*, Elsevier, Burlington MA

Bandura, A (1978) Social learning theory of aggression *Journal of Communication*, **28** (3), pp. 12–29

Bolhuis, S and Simons, R J (2003) Naar een breder begrip van leren (Towards a broader understanding of learning), in *Human Resource Development: Organizeren van het leren (Human Resource Development: The Organization of Learning)*, ed. J W M Kessels and R Poell, Samsom, Groningen, pp. 37–52

BSI (2016) Getting started with BS 11000 collaborative business relationships, *BSI* [online] http://www.bsigroup.com/en-GB/bs-11000-collaborative-business-relationships/Introduction-to-BS-11000/

Brown, A L and Campione, J C (1994) *Guided Discovery in a Community of Learners*, The MIT Press, Cambridge, MA

Brown, J and Isaacs, D (2007) *The World Café: Shaping our future through conversations that matter*, Bernett-Koehler, San Francisco, CA

Brown, J S and Duguid, P (1991) Organizational learning and communities-of-practice: toward a unified view of working, learning, and innovation, *Organization Science*, **2** (1), pp. 40–57

Carson, J B, Tesluk, P E and Marrone, J A (2007) Shared leadership in teams: an investigation of antecedent conditions and performance, *Academy of Management Journal*, **50** (5), pp. 1217–34

Day, G S and Schoemaker, P J (2008) Are you a 'vigilant' leader'? *MIT Sloan Management Review*, **49** (3), pp. 43–51

De Laat, M F and Simons, P R J (2002) Collective learning: theoretical perspectives and ways to support networked learning, *European Journal for Vocational Training*, **27** (3), pp. 13–24

Drath, W H, McCauley, C D, Palus, C J, Van Velsor, E, O'Connor, P M and McGuire, J B (2008) Direction, alignment, commitment: toward a more integrative ontology of leadership, *The Leadership Quarterly*, **19** (6), pp. 635–53

Engeström, Y, Miettinen, R and Punamäki, R L (1999) *Perspectives on Activity Theory*, Cambridge University Press, Cambridge, UK

Eraut, M (2000) Non-formal learning and tacit knowledge in professional work, *British Journal of Educational Psychology*, **70** (1), pp. 113–36

Gibb, C A (1954) Leadership, in *Handbook of Social Psychology Vol. 2*, ed. G Lindzey, Addison-Wesley, Reading, MA, pp. 877–917

Golub, J (1988) *Focus on Collaborative Learning. Classroom practices in teaching English*, National Council of Teachers of English, Urbana, IL

Grint, K (2005) Problems, problems, problems: the social construction of leadership, *Human Relations*, **58** (11), pp. 1467–94

Gubbins, C and MacCurtain, S (2008) Understanding the dynamics of collective learning: the role of trust and social capital, *Advances in Developing Human Resources*, **10**, pp. 578–99

Hart, J (2010) 5 stages of workplace learning, *Jane Hart's Blog* [online] http://www.c4lpt.co.uk/blog/2010/05/07/5-stages-of-workplace-learning-2/

Hart, J (2011) 5 stages of workplace learning (revisited), *Jane Hart's Blog* [online] http://www.c4lpt.co.uk/blog/2011/12/06/5-stages-of-workplace-learning-revisited/

Hawkins, D and Little, B (2011) Embedding collaboration through standards – Part 1, *Industrial and Commercial Training*, **43** (2), pp. 106–12

Heifetz, R, Grashow, A and Linsky, M (2009) *The Practice of Adaptive Leadership*., Harvard Business School Publishing, Boston, MA

Hersey, P and Blanchard, K H (1993) *Management of Organizational Behavior: Utilizing human resources*, 6th edn, Prentice Hall, Englewood Cliffs, NJ

Ibarra, H and Hansen, M (2011) Are you a collaborative leader? *Harvard Business Review*, **89** (7/8), pp. 68–74

Isaacs, W N (1993) Taking flight: dialogue, collective thinking, and organizational learning. *Organizational Dynamics*, **22** (2), pp. 24–39

Laberge, M (2006) Collective learning for co-creative engagement, *Breakthroughs Unlimited* [online] http://www.breakthroughsunlimited.com/

Lave, J and Wenger, E (1991) *Situated Learning: Legitimate peripheral participation*, Cambridge University Press, Cambridge, UK

Nonaka, I and Takeuchi, H (1995) *The Knowledge-Creating Company: How Japanese companies create the dynamics of innovation*, Oxford University Press, New York, NY

Oshry, B and Devane, T (2009) The Change Handbook, Berrett-Koehler Publishers, San Francisco, CA

Owen, H (2008) *Open Space Technology: A user's guide*, Berrett-Koehler Publishers, San Fancisco, CA

Pearce, C. L and Conger, J A (2003) *Shared Leadership: Reframing the hows and whys of Leadership*, Sage, Thousand Oaks, CA

Putnam, R D (2001) *Bowling Alone: The collapse and revival of American community*, Simon and Schuster, New York, NY

Revans, R (2011) *The ABC of Action Learning*, Gower, London

Ross, R (1994) The ladder of inference, in *The Fifth Discipline Fieldbook: Strategies and tools for building a learning organization*, ed. P Senge, Nicholas Brealey Publishing, London, UK, pp. 242–46

Ross, R and Roberts, C (1994) Balancing inquiry and advocacy, in *The Fifth Discipline Fieldbook: Strategies and tools for building a learning organization*, ed. P Senge, Nicholas Brealey Publishing, London, UK, pp. 253–59

Ross, R and Roberts, C (nd) Balancing inquiry and advocacy, *Society for Organizational Learning, North America* [online] https://www.solonline.org/?page=Tool_InquiryAdvocacy

Scharmer, C O (2009) *Theory U: Learning from the future as it emerges*, Berrett-Koehler Publishers, San Francisco, CA

Senge, P (1992) *The Fifth Discipline: The art and practice of the learning organization*. Random House, Sydney

Senge, P, Kleiner, A, Roberts, C, Ross, R and Smith, B (1994) *The Fifth Discipline Fieldbook: Strategies and tools for building a learning organization*, Nicholas Brealey Publishing, London

Wenger-Trayner, E and Wenger-Trayner, B (2016) Introduction to communities of practice. A brief overview of the concept and its uses, *Wenger-Trayner* [online] http://wenger-trayner.com/introduction-to-communities-of-practice/

Wenger, E (2000) *Communities of Practice: Learning, meaning, and identity*, Cambridge University Press, Cambridge

World Café (nd) Design principles, *World Café* [online] http://www.theworldcafe.com/key-concepts-resources/design-principles/

Developing and delivering L&D solutions for international markets

08

SA'AD ALI AND MARK LOON

1 Introduction and background

As shown throughout this book, learning and development (L&D) is crucial due to its importance in developing organizational capability. The previous chapters have highlighted how the design, development and implementation of L&D are contingent on various factors. This is even more so when the international context is considered. The aim of this chapter is to explore some of the key factors that may impact on L&D from an international perspective. In doing so, this chapter will meet two learning outcomes:

1 Appreciate how contextual factors play a role in shaping L&D practice and expectations.

2 Be able to develop and deliver L&D solutions for international markets.

This chapter builds upon the previous chapters, in particular Chapters 5 to 7, which discussed how L&D solutions might be developed to consider enhancing learner engagement, how technology has changed the way L&D professionals develop solutions in the digital world and for blended learning, and collective and social learning. This chapter examines how the effectiveness and even appropriateness of the concepts discussed may be contingent on nation-specific factors such as culture. Our discussion also adopts the perspective of international organizations who operate across borders and have to consider more than one national context at any given time.

Theodorakopoulos, Patel and Budhwar (2012) attributed the increased interest in the practice of L&D internationally to two different but related developments that have emerged over the last 30 years: the continuing growth globalization, in particular its impact on mobility, and the increasing realization that human resources is a form of capital across different levels of economies.

The first set of developments relates to the impact of globalization, specifically involving the mobility of people, organizations and even sectors. The mobility of people can be observed from the migration of people in various directions (particularly from developing to developed countries), which has created a need for organizations to equip their workforce not only with the skills to perform in their chosen field but to be able to adapt to their new local environment (as discussed in Chapter 2), as well as to work ably with colleagues of different nationalities.

Mobility also involves organizations, as many are now able to easily cross borders to undertake their business. Technology has changed the rules of the game and now even small companies are able to internationalize quickly (albeit in modest ways). This is a major trend, and McKinsey and Co reports the growth of the micro-multinational (which could be as small as a two-person set-up) as a substantial economic force (Manyika *et al*, 2014).

'Sectors' are also more mobile, as their supply chains cross multiple nation states. The configuration of some supply chains can easily involve countries on all continents and can be changed with relative ease. For example, capital-intensive industries have 'migrated' from the developed economies of North America and Western Europe to the developing economies of South East Asia, the Indian subcontinent, and countries in Africa.

These developments have resulted in an increased perception of L&D being considered a vital function for helping people and organizations adapt to their new surroundings. Such perceptions may also be due to the influence of western education and organizational practices, which recognize individuals' continuous learning as a critical success factor for organizational success. The recognition of continuous learning continues to extend to organizations across the world, albeit to varying degrees (Awate, Larsen and Mudambi, 2014).

The second underlying reason for the growth of interest and need for L&D in an international context involves the increasing realization that human resources is a form of capital that is almost equally as important as financial capital across different types of economies (not just knowledge-intensive or service-based economies) (Theodorakopoulos, Patel and Budhwar, 2012; Zahra and George, 2002). Human capital is crucial to enhance over-all organizational capability (as discussed in Chapter 1) irrespective of the type of asset that is primarily employed in an organization or sector.

Even governments of developing countries that rely on naturally endowed resources, such as Qatar, Kuwait and Saudi Arabia in the Middle East, or manufacturing, such as China and South Korea in East Asia, recognize the importance of human capital and many have policies in place to develop their labour force by enhancing human capital-intensive sectors (eg services) in parallel with other sectors. Many governments have invested heavily in their education sectors to support this growth. For example, in India, the government has focused on developing its education system to the extent that it is expected that by the year 2020, India will have the world's largest tertiary-age population and second-largest graduate talent pipeline. The message here is that wherever we go, in most countries and places, learning and development plays a crucial role.

No organization is immune to the impact of international forces. Even local firms are impacted, as foreign organizations will ultimately affect local companies in some way or other (eg importing substitute products or services). So how do L&D professionals help their organizations address the opportunities and threats that the international domain brings with it? This chapter addresses this overarching question by examining international macro trends and national cultural differences, to help inform us of the skills and capabilities required for a global L&D professional.

The first set of challenges are the macro factors in the economic and technological environments, and those of the labour market and education systems. The impact of these macro factors on L&D strategies and practices is presented and discussed in Section 2. The second set of challenges is reflected in the differences in national culture between countries and how this relates to L&D. Despite the fact that culture can be viewed as a macro factor, the substantial impact it has on L&D warrants exploration in its own section, and we look at this through the use of Hofstede's cultural framework in Section 3. Section 4 offers insights on the capabilities required for an L&D professional to become a global practitioner. Section 5 presents a summary of the chapter and provides the reader with points to reflect on when addressing L&D in an international context. We provide a number of detailed case examples to provide real-life insights and to illustrate the potential challenges and issues that L&D professionals may face in international markets.

2 Macro factors and L&D in an international context

This section examines some key macro factors that impact L&D in an international context. It builds upon some of the discussion in Chapter 2 by focusing on the impact of macro trends across countries, for how a trend might have a different effect on two different countries. This chapter provides a 'framework' for L&D professionals to 'explore' and evaluate the international context. The discussion is not intended to be exhaustive, but examples are provided to help you, the L&D professional, to better appreciate the ideas. We present three important areas that may help broaden L&D professional's perspectives in evaluating how the global macro environment impacts on L&D in delivering for international markets. The three areas are economic development and cycles, technology infrastructure and application (including the perception of technology in L&D), and labour markets and education systems.

2.1 Economic development and cycles

There is an increasing interdependence amongst major economies and one could argue that this process is irreversible. This is evidenced in a report from McKinsey & Co that claimed global flows (eg transactions, trade) between major economies were worth US $26 trillion, or 36 per cent of the global Gross Domestic Production (GDP) – 1.5 times as large relative to GDP as they were in 1990 compared to 2012 (Manyika *et al*, 2014). The degree of interdependence amongst countries is only growing more over time, with new types of flows emerging. In fact, knowledge flow (from knowledge-intensive sectors such as research and development) has outpaced flows from all other sectors (eg the service sector) (Manyika *et al*, 2014).

The report illustrates three important points. The first relates to the growing interdependence amongst countries in almost all aspects of their economies (eg manufacturing, service and knowledge-based). The second point is that the growth of 'flows' (note: flows is a term used by McKinsey's Global Institute to refer to, for example, the sum of imports and exports of products and services, foreign direct investment, bonds and equity trading, cross-border lending for financial flows etc) of knowledge-intensive sectors serves as both a reflection and the result of the increased importance of learning and development as a crucial element for knowledge flows (for example goods and activities that have a high component of research and development or use highly skilled labour such as those in engineering and law) to take place. The third important lesson that one can draw from the report is that the economies involved are more varied than ever before, as it does not solely involve developed countries. Major economists predict China's imminent succession over the Unites States as the world's biggest economy, not only signalling the importance of the BRICS (Brazil, Russia, India, China, South Africa) nations as key sources of growth (Euromonitor International, 2014) but also that of other emerging economies.

Developed and developing economies

The focus on L&D is on the rise in both developed and developing economies; however, as mentioned, the way L&D strategies and practices are developed and diffused is dependent on whether the organization is from a developed or developing economy. Indeed, Allinson and Hayes (2000) suggest that a helpful way to classify and better understand nations is to look at their stage of industrial development. These differences are also down to the location of the organization's headquarters and subsidiaries, especially where multinationals are concerned. Awate, Larsen and Mudambe (2014) compared knowledge flows between developed and developing countries and found that organizations from the developed economies of North America and Western Europe usually have their headquarters serving as the primary source of L&D strategies and practices, which are transferred to subsidiaries operating in developing countries. Meyer (2007) argued that in some circumstances, if the parent company is from a developed economy and the subsidiary is from an emerging economy such as a Central or Eastern European country, the subsidiary tends to view parent as a reservoir of technical know-how and therefore this affects their expectations of their learning and development.

In contrast, organizations headquartered in developing economies formulate their L&D strategies and practices from their subsidiaries that operate in more advanced economies and then transfer this to the headquarters. As a result of these differing practices, any potential innovations in the L&D practices of organizations in developing economies may develop more slowly and perhaps with greater difficulty than those in developed economies; this is termed 'L&D innovation catch-up' (Awate, Larsen and Mudambe 2014). Learning and development at the international level does not just involve learning between parent and subsidiaries or subsidiaries between each other, but also with external partners (eg in joint ventures and/or strategic alliances) who may be local or from any part of the world. From an L&D perspective, learning in an international context can take on many more different forms and purposes.

Economic cycles

In addition, the economic development stages of organizations' L&D strategies and practices are also largely contingent on the resources available, which usually relates to the expansion and contraction of a country's economy. In other words, if the economy is booming it is more likely that there will be an increase in the funding and budget allocated for L&D activities. On the other hand, if the economy is in recession then it is more likely that the focus (and budget) of the organization will shift from L&D to other operational activities. This is evidenced in the CIPD's Learning and Development survey (2015), which reported that organizations operating in the UK and the United States, who have been experiencing tough economic times, are more likely to have their L&D budgets, headcount and use of external associates reduced. This was in contrast to the fortune of some organizations based in India, which was generally in a better economic position, and as a result they projected an increase in training budgets to fund external courses, technology and conferences, books, training manuals, and to hire external consultants and trainers.

There are two implications of how economic cycles impact on L&D from an international perspective. The first involves multinationals that may be operating in countries that face contrasting economic cycles in about the same period. In such situations, L&D strategies may need to be revisited to counterbalance L&D budgets from one subsidiary (in a booming economy) to another (operating in a country facing recession). The second implication concerning economic cycles relates to the focus of L&D units at global headquarters on advising local subsidiaries on lessons learned (eg from other subsidiaries that may have undergone recessions in the past) to help current subsidiaries deal with reduced budgets.

L&D units in an organization's headquarters also need to be ambidextrous (doing two different and even contrasting activities at the same time) in that they need to be able to work with different subsidiaries facing different economic cycles. However, some 'blue-chip' (also known as top-deck) organizations tend 'stay on course' and not reduce L&D budgets as a knee-jerk reaction to economic cycles, as they are innovative in doing more with less, in both good and bad times (Overton and Dixon, 2015; Towards Maturity, 2013, 2014).

Exercise

This section presented two major themes in terms of how the economic environment has a significant impact on the way an organization develops and implements its L&D strategies and practices: the stage and state of the economy. Undertake research and identify three characteristics of a 'developed economy' and a 'developing economy'. In addition to L&D, how does the stage of economic development of a country impact organizations operating in them?

2.2 Technology infrastructure and application

As highlighted in Chapters 2 and 6, technology offers many opportunities for L&D professionals to support employee learning. There are diverse sets of technologies that L&D professionals can use, such as simulations games to develop more complex skills (CIPD, 2014). Technologies also include the use of 'connectivity' tools to connect people and facilitate informal learning through conversations (Bennett, 2014). Technology also fundamentally changes how organizations operate and how work is performed, both of which ultimately necessitate a response from L&D. For example, it is envisaged that the Internet of Things, big data and advanced analytics will eventually automate many forms of knowledge work that we complete today (Loon, 2014). The use of technology, however, varies in different countries depending on several factors. The most important of these include the availability of technology, the importance ascribed to the use of technology in L&D, and the need to use technology (and how it is used) in L&D.

Availability of technology infrastructure

The availability of technology infrastructure is the most important determinant of whether technology is to be used at all in L&D; you cannot use something that is not there or supported. In developed economies, the infrastructure that enables the use of high-speed internet, which is vital to facilitate the use of technologies such as video conferencing and other tools used in L&D, is taken for granted. L&D professionals who come from developed countries need to be aware that the advanced infrastructure that they experience in their home countries is not always available in other countries.

There are many organizations operating in developing countries that are not able to make use of the technologies used by their counterparts in developed countries due to the lack of infrastructure. For example, the International Learning and Talent Development comparison survey by the

CIPD (2011) found that the availability of e-learning is higher in the UK compared to other countries surveyed; just under two-thirds of UK organizations surveyed reported that they offer e-learning to the majority of their staff, compared to just over one-quarter of responding organizations in India, whose technology infrastructure is not as advanced or uniformly developed throughout the country as that of the UK.

Need for technology

The second factor relates to the need for technology in L&D. An obvious reason for a high need can be attributed to geographical factors. For example, the need to use e-learning and communication technology in L&D activities in large countries such as Australia (which is mostly populated on coastal areas) is heightened due to the high costs of conducting these activities face to face.

The need for technology can also be attributed to cultural factors where the social practices of a country might dictate the need to use some technological tools to conduct L&D activities. For example, video conferencing is commonly used in Saudi Arabia for male trainers coaching female employees or vice-versa, due to the cultural belief that women and men who are not related should not mix.

Perceived importance of technology

The third factor considered is the importance ascribed to the use of technology in different countries. Different societies embrace the use of technology differently and attribute different levels of importance to its use in L&D activities. Most, if not all people, irrespective of where they are from, use technology; however, how much importance they place on technology can be observed from how technology is integrated into their activities. For example, the CIPD (2011) reports that the use of technology in learning was not only more pervasive in countries such as the United States and the UK, but these countries tended to be more systematic in their approach to the adoption and incorporation of technologies in L&D strategies and practices.

Whilst the use of technology may be just as intense or pervasive in other countries, this does not indicate that people in a particular country think technology is important in L&D. There are some societies that just prefer face-to-face interaction in their learning and development, and may not see the value of new methods such as the use of simulation games. People in these societies may use technology just as much as other countries but in a more ad-hoc manner.

The importance attached to the use of technology of L&D may also be observed in terms of 'where' technology is used, specifically in what areas of the business. For example, in addition to basic e-learning courses in health and safety, the use of e-learning for more mission-critical areas may suggest that the business perceives technology to be suitably effective and ascribe importance to its use.

Exercise

The use of technology in L&D in an international context is contingent on a number of factors: the availability of technology, the need to use technology in L&D and the perceived importance of technology in L&D. Undertake research on two countries, one from North America (Canada or the United States) and one from the Middle East (eg Jordan, Oman, Yemen), and identify at least three unique practices in one country that are different to the other country concerning technology.

2.3 Labour markets and education systems

In recent years there have been several social trends, which were highlighted in Chapter 2, that have substantially influenced the way organizations do business throughout the world. For example, the rapid growth of the world's population and an increase in the lifespan of the average individual has helped the growth of the working population (Glenn, Gordon and Florescu, 2014; Keys and Malnight, 2014). This section specifically looks at the labour market and educations systems.

Labour markets

The world's population is growing rapidly, with some statistics showing that there will be 9.2 billion people on Earth by 2050 (Glenn, Gordon and Florescu, 2014; Keys and Malnight, 2014). The substantial increase in the world's population is coupled with an increase in the lifespan of people, particularly those living in developed countries. This increase in population and lifespan translates to a change in the demographics of the world's workforce. A growing and aging population translates to a change in the nature of careers and learning in western countries (Loon, 2014). The impact of this is of course two-pronged, as organizations operating in developing countries also have to adjust their L&D strategies and practices to counter the 'brain drain' resulting from emigration.

L&D professionals working in developed countries will most likely face the challenges of working in the aging workforce of western countries. This workforce will need more support in developing skills to use and apply new technologies, for example. Developing cohesive teams with members from diverse generations will also become a challenge. Furthermore, in many developed economies, life-long learning is now considered essential to achieving a satisfying career that also needs to be reflected in the development of L&D strategies (as well as a retention tool).

In terms of developing countries, the main challenge they face is the brain drain resulting from the emigration of skilled workers to developed countries in search of better pay, life and working conditions. As such, it is vital for L&D professionals who are working in these countries to develop 'succession programmes' to limit the negative impact of the brain drain by continuously preparing and developing junior employees more swiftly.

L&D professionals in multinationals play a crucial role in helping recruitment professionals to 'source' and develop talent from across world (in all labour markets) for placement in both developing, and in developed countries. L&D professionals, similar to global recruitment professionals, need to develop a global mind-set that observes the entire world as its labour market, as its source for talent.

Education systems

There are now more opportunities for formal tertiary education through the liberalization of regulation in the further and higher education sectors in many countries. In addition, people now have more opportunities to access education because of the use of technology that is easily scalable, allowing more learners to participate without incurring more costs (up to a certain point of course). This has resulted in a substantial increase in the number of qualified people around the world.

However, this increase in the number of educated people has not translated into an increase in the number of qualified workers, as educational institutions are criticized for not being able to develop transferable skills for their graduates (Economist Intelligence Unit, 2014). For example, in a survey conducted in Europe, 74 per cent of education providers surveyed said they were confident that their graduates were prepared for work, but only 38 per cent of the graduates and 35 per cent of employers agreed (Economist Intelligence Unit, 2014). This indicates a challenge for L&D, as companies now act as 'surrogate education system' due to the fact that graduates may not have the suitable skills and competences for the workplace (Economist Intelligence Unit, 2014).

In addition, there are shifts in the education systems in many countries such as India, where the education system generally has a strong information technology focus. In another example, the UK government is trying to increase uptake of science, technology, engineering and mathematics (STEM) subjects in schools. Government policy on education has a significant impact on a country's workforce, which then in turn helps to shapes how attractive a country will be as a foreign–direct investment for multinationals who need to recruit capable and qualified personnel.

The impact of the developments discussed has implications for both the general workforce and L&D professionals. As it appears that both developed and developing economies may have education systems that may not be equipping their workforce with the necessary skills for employment, this then put the onus on organizations to develop their employees and provide them with the competencies and skills needed for the workplace. L&D professionals whose work goes beyond their country's boundaries should pay special attention to labour trends, as this will help inform them of the potential challenges they may face. This will also enable L&D professionals to respond to these challenges by developing and implementing the appropriate L&D strategies and practices that will help employees and organizations to function well even in the face of dynamic and constant change in international macro factors.

Exercise

On the face of it, most education systems may appear to be similar, as many start to school children about the same age, and tend to end compulsory education at about the same age. In addition, most education systems will have national examinations at the end of pupils' compulsory education, as well as intermittently in between. However, content (curriculum), pedagogy (design of instruction), and the quality of teaching vary significantly, and it is such factors that shape the 'quality' of a nation's education system. Research and reflect upon your country's education system and identify its advantages and disadvantages in terms of preparing pupils for life after education, be it for further/higher education or for work. You may want to draw comparisons with other countries that you are familiar with.

The following case example is from Flavio Vong, who is currently a manager with the Commonwealth Bank of Australia. He was previously a manager in one of the big four audit and consulting firms in Sydney and Beijing. Flavio shares some of his personal observations and views on how L&D is practised in these two office locations. This case example is interesting, as both offices are part of the same firm; therefore, they should have very similar L&D strategies and policies or at least should be underpinned by similar values. However, as Flavio shares, whilst this may be correct, differences within each country have a significant influence on how L&D strategies are perceived and translated into action.

Flavio Vong, manager, enterprise services, Commonwealth Bank of Australia (formerly a manager in one of the big four audit and consulting firms)

I worked with one of the big four audit and consulting firms in Beijing, having gone over to China from Sydney to complete an MBA. During my time in that role, one of the initiatives that I was closely supporting was to improve organizational (the firm office) capability. It had been recognized by the senior management of the firm that due to the fast growth and changing client demands in consulting services in China, there was a potential gap in meeting future client demands, especially as the L&D agenda had taken a backseat as other priorities took focus. The initiative included a review of learning and development processes and policies in an attempt to align to current and future demands from clients. This experience gave me some insights into the role of L&D in the office, and how this compared with the Sydney office, where I worked previously.

The market/business landscape in Beijing is quite different from that of Sydney. Although the core service offering was mostly the same, what the majority of consulting clients wanted was to bring in someone to help them just to undertake implementation whereby, for the most part, the solution and accountability for the success of the project remained with the clients. This meant that other crucial skills offered by consultancies, such as problem assessment and evaluation, solution development and project scoping were not as critical as I had experienced in other markets. Hence, a significant number of engagements were often referred to more of as a 'body shop', whereby it was primarily about having staff who could fulfil these implementation roles and to do the 'work'. This resulted in an emphasis on the 'now', 'doing the work' and being 'chargeable' (note: one of the main indicators of external consultants is 'chargeability', ie being engaged on a billable project to an external client), which I think may have been at the expense of long-term developmental opportunities.

Another reason was organizational, specifically regarding staff turnover rate, which was also quite high. The high staff turnover may have created a hesitance in the minds of senior managers to invest in their staff, and therefore the L&D agenda may not have been completely in the forefront of management's mind. Another organizational factor was the degree of accountability of senior personnel in the Beijing office for engaging with L&D, for example regularly meeting with the mentees or ensuring that junior staff were attending requisite training courses and engaging in other forms of development. In addition, I felt that staff were not always aware of the services and support provided by the L&D unit, and I suspect this was because the distribution of information and guidance that could have been more visible. The link between the L&D initiatives and career development was not as easily discernible as it could have been. For example, I know that some of the junior staff (three to five years' experience) who had supported me on engagements, were not aware that they should have completed a number of requisite courses by this stage of their career, for example business process improvement or coaching.

The other 'shaper' of L&D in the Beijing office is cultural. The organizational culture in the Beijing office is a lot more hierarchy oriented (which reflects the Chinese culture), whereby work is instructed and directed. The views of subordinates are not necessarily sought, nor are they expected to take a proactive approach to providing them. I believe this approach to working results in staff being more dependent on guidance from management, as they have limited opportunity to develop and exercise autonomy. Although this cannot be generalized, I had a sense that this was more common than not; I realized that on a number of occasions I had to be more prescriptive than I usually am when dealing with the local staff. As a manager, I would ideally like to see my team members to not only approach me with the problems and issues they face but also to be ready with their views on the reasons for the problem/issue, their suggestions on how to resolve it, and prepared to have a dialogue with me about it.

I think these three main issues – business realities, organizational processes and culture – combined with the relatively new and fast-changing nature of consulting in the Chinese market, have influenced how L&D is viewed and practised in the Beijing office; L&D was not a core part of the office's activities. All these reasons may be interconnected and reinforce each other. For example, the relative lack of L&D means that staff do not have the ability to be autonomous, which is reinforced by a hierarchical and directive environment, where staff are not empowered and they do not have the opportunity to participate and exercise discretion.

▶

In comparison, L&D plays a prominent role in the Sydney office, where the practice of L&D-related activities was more structured, as there was a lot emphasis on consultants' learning and development. L&D's importance was recognized by all in the Sydney office and was not viewed as competing with 'earning revenue'; rather, they saw delivery capability and L&D as complementary. For example, managers in the Sydney office were held accountable for the learning and development of their subordinates. Managers had to make sure that staff not only attended the requisite training courses and milestones but also maintained their development in other ways. The synergy between 'capability' and L&D is obvious, as learning and development is not just about knowledge and skills but also confidence building, developing self-efficacy and a belief in your own abilities, nurturing the right 'attitude', and being able to take the initiative and be a self-starter. This is not just important for the firm's performance but also for personal development and career progression in moving to more senior positions. Learning and development does require the support of management to genuinely 'work'.

As we learn from the case example, even in a global firm such as one of the big four, with standardized policies and processes in its offices across the world, there are still differences in how these policies and process are applied in practice. However, there are many reasons why L&D practice and process may differ in multinationals, much less domestic firms, ie business reasons, organizational processes and even national culture. Therefore, each country and situation must be assessed on its own merits. But as Flavio pointed out, effective L&D requires a holistic approach, which includes senior management's commitment.

Exercise

Reflect upon the case example and provide some suggestions, as an L&D professional, of what you could do to improve L&D in the Beijing office and make it a priority in senior management's minds.

3 The impact of national cultures on L&D

Whilst macro factors have a strong influence on how organizations and their workforces operate, their impact on L&D, especially the durability of this impact, is questionable; economic boom and gloom comes and goes. Culture, or specifically national culture, however, has both a significant and long-lasting impact on behaviour in organizations, including learning and development. The effects of national culture are pervasive and affect all parts of life. People establish institutions to maintain and protect the values that their culture reflects. For example, the British parliament in Westminster upholds British culture, which values democracy and rule of law, whilst the National Health Service reflects how important it is to the British people that individuals have equal access to welfare.

Culture also influences how learning and development is perceived and practiced within organizations, which may differ from one country to another (Harzing and Van Ruysseveldt, 2004). L&D practitioners working with learners who are from different cultures might find 'common ground', such as in the case of organizational culture (when working in another country but in the same organization) or occupational 'culture' (when working in different organizations/countries but in the same occupation group such as human resources or in the same sector or industry such as in banking).

Nevertheless, when national culture differs, it is a significant consideration for L&D professionals, as it can 'make or break' L&D initiatives. There are visible and tacit differences between national cultures that impact on the working environment as well as the working style of individuals (Perlow and Weeks, 2002). This section examines how national culture impacts people's learning preferences, and this in turn should lead L&D professionals to reflect on the different L&D strategies and practices that can be adopted to best suit the needs of learners from different nations and cultures.

3.1 What is national culture?

In order to identify how national culture impacts L&D practice it is important to first understand what is meant by culture. The concept of culture has several definitions that revolve around the notion of values, beliefs and practices that are shared by a group of people (Van Oudenhoven, 2001). More simply, culture refers to what a certain group of people (usually living in the same country or region) consider to be 'right' or the accepted way to do things. There are obvious or easily observable differences between cultures, such as in the way people dress, the food they eat, customary practices and their behaviour. For example, many people in India still wear traditional clothes in everyday life, and many people in Finland are usually punctual when it comes to appointments. Nonetheless, there are also implicit or tacit differences between cultures such as the shared values and assumptions about how things should be, for example British values on what is right and wrong, or Swedish shared views on what constitutes equality.

Of course, the observable part of a culture is much easier to identify and as such it is easy to refer to these aspects when designing and implementing different L&D solutions. For example, it is relatively easy to identify the cultural limitations on gender mixing in the Saudi work place. The tacit part of culture, however, is much harder to identify and, as a result, to manage. For example, it is more difficult to understand and adjust to the learning pattern of Chinese learners if the L&D professional comes from a western culture. This is because, like many East Asian countries, the Chinese adopt the Confucian model in teaching and learning, which emphasizes learning from respected others and the passing on of ideas rather than learning from two-way conversations. This is in comparison to western learners who generally prefer to have dialogue and are encouraged to have constructive debates with one another and even the instructor (Tweed and Lehman, 2002).

Understanding national culture is crucial, as people are not completely or always aware that their behaviour is guided by the implicit assumptions shaped by their own culture. Knowing the differences between cultures allows L&D professionals to be in a position to better understand learners and therefore develop more effective L&D solutions. Understanding culture helps us to, at a minimum, avoid offending learners or creating awkward situations, but more importantly helps us to enhance the individuals' learning.

Cultural theory studies rest on the assumption that the implicit differences between national cultures (the tacit or unobservable part of culture) result in the differences in organizational life, eg of management styles and beliefs, and L&D (Child, Chung and Davies, 2003). Cultural frameworks use 'cultural dimensions' (points of comparison) as a tool that enables us to compare two or more cultures and to understand how culture in a country or region impacts organizations and organizational life (Harzing and Van Ruysseveldt, 2004). Focusing on cultural dimensions provides the means for evaluating the shared experiences of people who belong to that society.

Exercise

Understanding culture helps L&D professionals to have awareness and insight as to why and how employees' cultural backgrounds vary. Reflect upon your national culture. How would you describe the key characteristics of your national culture and how it has impacted the way you learn? It may be useful if you could choose another national culture that you are familiar with to compare your own national culture against.

The most prominent of cultural frameworks is Hofstede's cultural dimensions. In his first book, *Culture's Consequences* (1980) Geert Hofstede explored the differences 'in thinking and social action' at the country level between members of 50 nations. Hofstede originally used an attitude survey completed by IBM employees around the world, generating more than 116,000 completed questionnaires (Hofstede, 2001). Based on the pattern of the answers provided in these questionnaires, Hofstede created and validated four dimensions of culture. These dimensions were termed 'Power Distance', 'Uncertainty Avoidance', 'Individualism versus Collectivism', and 'Masculinity versus Femininity'. A fifth dimension, 'Long-term versus Short-term Orientation', was subsequently developed to accommodate non-western (Confucian) orientations (Harzing and Van Ruysseveldt, 2004). A sixth dimension, 'Indulgence', was also later added, although this has not been rigorously validated. Therefore, only the four initial dimensions will be discussed here.

For each of these dimensions, Hofstede and his colleagues presented possible origins as well as predictors and consequences of organizational behaviour. They also constructed an index that enabled countries to be mapped according to their scores in order to compare different countries on this index. The score of a country in each dimension provides us with an indicator of what L&D strategies and practices will be the most effective to use with the workforce coming from this culture. Hofstede's website can be found at: http://geert-hofstede.com/

3.2 Power Distance

The first of Hofstede's dimensions, Power Distance, refers to the degree to which the less powerful members of a society (and as such the organizations reflecting this society) expect and accept that power is distributed unequally (Hofstede, 2001). In the context of organizations, it helps us understand the relationship between supervisors and subordinates. The higher the power distance in a society, the more people in lower positions accept the 'gap' between them and their superiors, and would most probably expect to be told what to do (by their superiors). In most cases, this reflects a strong (and accepted) hierarchy in the society.

In the context of L&D, this also affects the way learners and trainers (teachers) interact. In countries that are characterized by high power distance (for example Ghana, which scores 80 out of 100), learners potentially expect to be given the knowledge by their instructors. In such situations, communication is usually one way, from instructor to learner. At the other end of the spectrum, in countries characterized by low power distance (for example Finland, which scores 33), learners may expect to actively interact and discuss concepts with their trainer as part of their learning. Power distance also links with the way feedback is received. For instance, individuals in cultures that are more hierarchically structured are more hesitant to 'discuss' feedback provided by someone in a higher position (eg a supervisor) and will just take it as a command to improve or adjust their work. Sometimes in such situations there may be fears that a discussion may be viewed as disrespectful, as it amounts to 'questioning' the 'teacher'.

Exercise

Reflect upon the dimension of power distance. How would power distance impact on the design of the delivery of an L&D programme? For example, individuals in senior positions from countries that scored highly on power distance may be expected to be formally addressed in all circumstances, whilst those in lower positions may be expected to just 'take instructions' from those in more senior positions. How would such expectations of individuals in countries with higher power distance take form in formal classroom-based training events? How would interaction between the trainer and learners take place? How would you design in-class exercises?

3.3 Uncertainty Avoidance

The second dimension, Uncertainty Avoidance, is defined as the degree to which the members of a culture are comfortable with uncertain or unknown situations (Hofstede, 2001). This dimension highlights the question of whether individuals should try to control the future or just let it happen. Hofstede states that this ambiguity towards the future brings with it anxiety, and that different cultures have learned to deal with this anxiety in different ways. In countries that score highly on uncertainty avoidance, people will try to control the future through the use of rules and elaborate systems in order to 'structure' life (for example Chile with a score of 86). On the opposite end of the continuum, in countries that score low on uncertainty avoidance, people tend to be comfortable with the unknown and they just 'go with the flow' and make decisions as they go along (for example the UK, which scores 35) (Hofstede, 2001).

In the context of learning and development, uncertainty avoidance may impact on a workforce's preference for formal and informal learning and development initiatives. For example, a workforce that belongs to a high uncertainty avoidance culture may tend to prefer formal training, as it has structure that provides some sense of predictability and usually leads to some form of certification. Informal learning, on the other hand, is characterized by lack of structure and rules in terms of learning objectives, schedules and/or learning support (Marsick and Volpe, 2000). In societies characterized by strong uncertainty avoidance, employees will do their best to stay away from these kinds of 'unguided' situations (Stohl, 1993). Therefore, high uncertainty avoidance societies would prefer formal training that is structured and has clear rules, goals and guidelines (El Raheb *et al.*, 2012). Furthermore, it can also be inferred that these type of societies would value and reward workers that follow and finish the formal training programme as strictly and accurately as possible. This is in contrast with societies that have low uncertainty avoidance, where employees tend to be more comfortable with informal learning, despite the fact that the rewards reaped from such learning are not so easy to identify and quantify.

Exercise

Undertake research concerning individuals from both high and low uncertainty avoidance cultures, and identify their approach to other aspects of organizational life, eg rewards and compensation, career planning, performance appraisal, or leadership development. How would you design an L&D solution that will fit both sets of individuals?

3.4 Individualism and Collectivism

The third dimension in Hofstede's framework is Individualism and Collectivism (each is at the opposite end of the same spectrum). The fundamental issue addressed by this dimension is the degree of interdependence a society maintains among its members. It has to do with whether people's self-image is defined in terms of 'I' or 'We'. A society that scores high on this dimension (for example the United States, with the score of 91) is an individualistic society where people are expected to look after themselves and their direct family members only. On the other hand, in collectivist societies (for example Jordan, with a score of 30 – a low score on individualism means a 'high' score on collectivism) people belong 'in groups' that take care of each other in exchange for loyalty (Hofstede, 2001).

In the realm of L&D, this translates to the way employees of certain cultures approach learning. In societies that score high on the individualism spectrum, employees may usually prefer to undertake L&D activities that focus on the individual (for example one-to-one coaching). On the other end of the spectrum, in societies that score low (collectivist societies), it is potentially expected that the majority of the workforce may prefer to learn in groups and as such prefer to undertake L&D activities that focus on group learning (for example, department or profession seminars). Of course, these are generalizations and there are exceptions. For example, the UK also scores highly on the individualism scale, but many organizations and their employees see the value of collective learning (as discussed in Chapter 7). In addition, whilst Chinese learners may learn better in groups, this form of learning in their context may be more of an advocacy (eg debating who is right) rather than for co-creation of knowledge. Research has shown that the Chinese may be considered as 'realist', as they are more interested in the 'one' truth, whereas in comparison, the British are considered as 'constructionist', and recognize the validity of different and differing views.

Exercise

Individualism and collectivism reflect the notions of equity and equality. Individualism reflects equity, as it concerns what the individual deserves (eg effort put in), which may be different amongst individuals. Collectivism, on the contrary, reflects equality, as it is about uniform distribution of rewards alike to all individuals in the group, irrespective of individual performance. Both equity and equality have a role to play in organizations, and the solution is in finding the right balance between the two. How would you, as an L&D professional, balance both in ensuring that talented individuals are given special attention (eg the principle of equity in talent management programmes) but at the same being fair to all employees so that everyone has an opportunity to develop just the same (eg the principle of equality)? What L&D approach/strategy would you put in place? Being able to find the right balance may help L&D professionals to design better learning and development solutions for a group of learners from both individualistic and collectivist cultures.

3.5 Masculinity and Femininity

The final dimension is Masculinity and Femininity (which is similar to the individualistic/collectivist dimension, whereby each is at opposite end of the same spectrum). Countries that attain a high score on this dimension are described as masculine societies. In these societies, individuals will be driven by competition, achievement and success.

In such cultures, society expresses a preference for 'winners' ('high earnings', 'recognition when doing a good job', 'challenging work to do'). An example of a masculine society is Japan, which attained a score of 95. On the other hand, societies that have a low score on this dimension are feminine societies. This means that the dominant values in these societies are caring for others and their quality of life. An example of a feminine society is Sweden, with a score of 5 on this end of the spectrum. A feminine society is one where quality of life is the sign of success (Hofstede, 2001). Feminine societies tend to express preferences for the interpersonal aspect of work, for example 'working with people who cooperate well with one another', and 'having a good working relationship with your manager' (Harzing and Van Ruysseveldt, 2004). According to Hofstede (2001), masculinity and femininity are value systems that start in school and continue throughout organizational life.

In terms of L&D, masculinity/femininity reflect the way learners prefer to approach learning and receive feedback. For example, it can be said that workers in feminine societies prefer to learn from each other by providing help and sharing information, which generally fits with the informal approach to learning (Eraut, 2014; Hofstede, 1986). Competition, on the other hand, is a very masculine trait (Taras, Steel and Kirkman, 2011). Because formal training is assessed and may lead to a formal certification such as a diploma or an official reference, a competitive climate might dominate (Eraut, 2014) and as such, formal training might fit better with the needs of a masculine society (El Raheb *et al*, 2012). Similar to uncertainty avoidance, this can also be linked to the reward provided with each type of learning (masculine societies prefer 'tangible rewards' such as financial rewards linked to formal learning, while feminine societies prefer 'intangible rewards' linked to informal training).

Exercise

It appears that learning in a masculine culture requires learners to be incentivized (rewarded). However, we learned in Chapter 5 that this sometimes means that surface learning emerges (rather than deep learning), as learning is perceived to be only instrumental – a means to an end. How can L&D professionals encourage more deep learning in masculine societies?

Exercise

The use of Hofstede's cultural dimensions helps L&D professionals to better understand cultures in relation to one another when designing L&D strategies and solutions. Appreciating a culture's power distance indicates to L&D professionals the learning preferences of the workforce, such as the degree of communication and dialogue whilst learning and the importance given by learners to the source of feedback. Uncertainty avoidance and masculinity/femininity are linked to learners' inclination towards formal or informal learning, as well the type of rewards resulting from each approach. Individualism and collectivism, on the other hand, provide some insight into whether a learner favours learning using individual-based methods such as coaching, or group-based approaches.

Armed with the insight that Hofstede's cultural dimensions have provided you with, as an international L&D professional working for a multinational corporation with offices in most cities around the world, your supervisor has assigned you to design bespoke leadership programmes for senior management groups in two countries: one in South America (eg Argentina, Brazil and Chile) and the other in Scandinavia (eg Norway and Sweden). Provide some highlights of your leadership programme in consideration of cultural differences. To complete this exercise:

- Select one country from each group.

- Go to Hofstede's website (http://geert-hofstede.com/) and explore how each culture scores on each of the four cultural dimensions discussed: power distance, uncertainty avoidance, individualism/collectivism and masculinity/femininity.

- Use the following table to complete this exercise.

Table 8.1 Cultural differences that impact on designing a leadership development programme exercise template

Cultural dimension	Highlight of your leadership programme contingent on the national culture	
	1st national culture selected by you	2nd national culture selected by you
Power distance		
Uncertainty avoidance		
Individualism/collectivism		
Masculinity/femininity		

As Section 3 has discussed, differences between national cultures can be significant in terms of how they impact on behaviour within organizations. However, as with all models and frameworks, Hofstede's work tends to oversimplify culture. Many of us would acknowledge that culture is much richer than the four dimensions we have discussed. Cultural models must be applied with caution, as they tend to stereotype people. There are many other factors that influence people's behaviour, such as their personality, ethnicity (ethnic culture), religion, age/generation, occupation and situational factors.

An insightful study by Allinson and Hayes (2000) showed that the commonly held belief that individuals in the West are more analytical and individuals from the East are more intuitive is incorrect. In their research of cross-national differences in cognitive styles, they found the reverse; specifically, individuals in the West were more intuitive and those in the East tend to be more analytical. Allinson and Hayes (2000) attempt to rationalize these results by arguing that many individuals in developed western countries have learned the limits of the purely rational and analytical approach, and that other 'cognitive' forms such as creativity and lateral thinking, as well as the use of intuition, are equally necessary to address the challenging problems that many organizations face. The results of their study, of course, are relative between countries and there are exceptions. For example, the cognitive style of individuals in some countries in the East such as Singapore and Hong Kong were more similar to those in the West compared to other eastern countries, as both are heavily westernized, especially given their colonial history and education systems.

Nonetheless, Section 3 does highlight how important it is to consider national culture in learning and development. Why learning and development should be undertaken, who learners are learning from, what is involved and how L&D is delivered are questions that matter when national culture is taken into consideration. However, learning and development also plays a role, especially when organizations need to develop an effective working environment with and for a workforce made up of different nationalities. The following case example from Shawn Simpson, training project manager with Agence Iter in France, illustrates how learning and development is used to address the challenge of developing trust and teamwork in a diverse multinational workforce.

Shawn Simpson, training project manager, Agence Iter France

The Agence Iter France is located in Cadarache in the South of France. It is a French government entity created in support of the ITER Organization, an international scientific research organization whose aim is to prove that fusion power can become a sustainable source of energy for future generations. The organization is founded by seven partners: China, Europe, India, Japan, Russia, South Korea and the United States. There are approximately 700 employees and about 1,000 contractors representing 35 different nationalities, in addition to the spouses and families who have relocated to the Provence region, working together with over 60 languages spoken. More than 60 per cent of employees are expatriates who had a very limited knowledge of the French language and culture upon arrival in France, and no intercultural or linguistic preparation prior to their arrival. English is the lingua franca and thus the French language is not a pre-requisite.

The challenge of managing such a workforce is obvious. How do we cultivate an environment where people from such diverse backgrounds are able to gel and work together in an effective manner? The simple answer is training to improve the way individuals from different cultures communicate (eg learning each other's language) with one another and therefore build trust and enhance teamwork. However, given the sheer volume of the workforce and limited resources available to the learning and development professionals, this would be an almost impossible task. Structured courses, such as in classrooms, may enable someone to learn a language but not necessarily to understand the culture. Also, would what has been learned be sustainable? In addition, 'teaching' culture also tends to encourage stereotyping. Individuals belonging to the same cultural and linguistic background cannot be simply classified as being the same. Each individual is different; their age, whether they come from a rural or urban setting, whether they have travelled extensively, speak any foreign languages, have experience working in international teams, etc, makes a big difference to the way they behave.

So what is the best way to ensure that this diverse and multicultural workforce can be developed to work well with another, whilst leveraging upon the limited resources available? At Iter, the 'solution' that we adopted was to focus on creating an environment for learning (although there are structured sessions, this is just to 'get the ball rolling') that focuses on knowledge sharing, and involves two related and complementary approaches: peer-to-peer learning and learning communities.

The rationale behind peer-to-peer learning is that we believe learning a language without learning about its culture, or learning about a culture without having some basic knowledge of the language is neither effective nor efficient. In peer-to-peer learning, there is no longer one person (the 'teacher') who is the gatekeeper of knowledge. Learners are also teachers. Each individual involved in the learning process is encouraged to share their language and culture with their peers.

In terms of learning communities, we realized that it did not make sense for us to not make use of the wealth of resources available to us, ie the learners themselves. Our learning communities are often made up of individuals with varied backgrounds, such as being born in a country that is different to their nationality, having studied in another country for a substantial time, being married to someone from another culture and language, and sometimes having bilingual if not trilingual children. Members of our learning communities have lived abroad for professional reasons. The individuals in our learning communities are 'rich', as they have complex backgrounds (in a good way!), possess an abundance of experience, have many insights to share and are, surprisingly, often untapped resources. The learning communities can be described as informal groups of diverse cultures and backgrounds that share the same objective: to learn more about each other.

In the knowledge-sharing approach, instead of 'teaching' a language or how to successfully interact with specific cultures, we use the learners' knowledge by promoting it. For example, learning how to express oneself in French is done in a comparative culture and language context; when explaining the word 'baguette', the traditional French bread that is part of the French staple diet, our 'facilitators' ask the participants to first explain what the equivalent might be in their culture and what it is called. This exchange takes place using the only 'bridge' language known to all, English. Once the new French word has found a cultural and linguistic 'echo' in each learner, the acquisition of this word is all the more embedded and meaningful.

Our intercultural sessions are mainly characterized by facilitating the exchange of knowledge among the participants on such subjects as intercultural awareness, understanding and communication. This exchange of knowledge empowers the learners and creates room for the expression of 'live' cultural identities from contemporary perspectives (rather than

▶

from books or research). Our learning communities have developed over the years and the initial French language programme has now expanded to include Spanish, Chinese, Russian and Japanese courses facilitated by volunteers in the organization who are willing to devote their lunchtimes to sharing their language and culture with their colleagues. Here, individuals are in charge of their own transfer of knowledge.

A primary outcome of the programme is the creation of stronger ties among the different teams and the building of trust. The participants of these learning sessions can develop a sense of belonging and of recognition among their peers. Trust is also easier to establish for some, because in this environment, they share their personal knowledge, opinions and emotions with others, thus implicitly trusting one another. Similarities rather than differences have been observed and there is a tendency to move from culture or language specifics, with curiosity and questions prevalent at first, to larger themes such as understandings, the power of words, conflict resolution and empathy.

Working for an international organization means having teams with multiple cultural and linguistic identities and thus this is where the building of trust during the learning process is crucial; once you have shared your personal stories and found empathy in your learning group, a feeling of trust is established and allows for the forming of new groups and thus new group identities, without cultural specific or language specific limitations.

Below are some quotes from our participants:

Big international organizations need to be aware of their international workforce's constantly evolving needs and expectations in order to keep up a healthy organizational culture that is favourable to communication, information transparency and intercultural synergies. Only then does the costly hunt for talent in global labour markets have its justifying return, binding expertise as added value to the organization even after the expatriates have returned to their home countries. (30-year-old, European).

Personal development has been achieved, with greater awareness of different approaches people have. I would say that I have become more globally aware (British, five years in France).

I changed personally. I respect other cultures more and understand people better (Indian, five years in France).

Multicultural organizations are known to be more creative and more responsive to change. The challenge of a truly multicultural organization is that of time; when deadlines must be respected and deliverables ensured, cultural identities can often be forgotten in the race to be efficient. Unfortunately, this efficiency is only short term. For any organization to last and be efficient over time, its foundations must be strong and deeply embedded so that every member can recognize himself/herself in it. This, once again, takes time. The true threat to fostering a truly intercultural organization of the future and to setting an example is the short-term vision that time is of the essence.

The case example from Shawn Simpson illustrates an innovative approach in L&D, specifically by recognizing and respecting learners as a source of a wealth of knowledge and as a resource for learning and development. The L&D unit in Agence Iter adopts a facilitator role to initiate the programmes and act as a conduit to facilitate communication and interaction amongst the workforce. The approach adopted by Agence Iter is an effective L&D solution, especially in fostering intercultural understanding, and it is sustainable, as it cultivates and nurtures a learning environment that is self-reinforcing.

Exercise

Shawn's case reflects the discussion in this section and as well as that in Chapter 7, specifically in relation to the concept of learning communities. In what other areas of L&D can learning communities (or the approach adopted by Shawn's team) be 'implemented'? When would learning communities be more effective (compared to formal/classroom training)?

4 Developing the 'global' L&D professional

This chapter has so far explored how major macro factors and national culture impact L&D from an international perspective. This, in turn, helps L&D professionals to tailor their L&D solutions to best support the learning and development of employees. This section rounds up these discussions by exploring what capabilities L&D professionals working in an international context (or who are at least impacted by the international context) should develop.

In order to respond to the differences in the macro environment while working in an international context, various academics and institutions (eg the CIPD and the Institute of Employment Studies) have discussed the key capabilities required by international HR professionals to enable them to be global professionals. Building upon these studies, we identify four key capabilities: adaptive skills, technical (content) knowledge, cultural savviness and business and commercial acumen (see Figure 8.1). Each is discussed using the cultural dimensions discussed in the previous section as an example.

Figure 8.1 Competencies for successful international L&D professionals

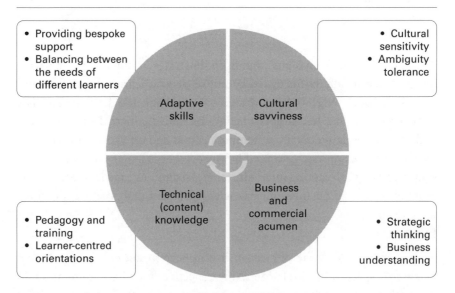

The first set of skills discussed is adaptive skills, which include the ability to provide bespoke support to employees from different backgrounds and cultures. In doing so the L&D professional should take into consideration the different needs employees might have due to the economic, technological, and social environment. For example, the general workforce in Kenya may have less access to contemporary technologies compared to their Swedish counterparts, who in turn will most likely be educated in a different education system. Furthermore, the Kenyan economy is not as developed as the German economy, relies on the agrarian sector and therefore may experience different economic cycles. As a result, from the example, it is clear that L&D professional should contextualize his/her advice and training to where the employees are, and balance their different needs. The challenges associated with the macro factors keep increasing as the population becomes more mobile, with people from different cultures working in different contexts (eg an expatriate from Kenya working in Germany for a Swedish organization). As such, the onus is on the L&D professional to know how to tailor their approach in engaging with different groups.

The next set of skills is technical (content) knowledge. This refers to not just understanding and being competent in designing L&D solutions but also to being knowledgeable of cultural differences (such as Hofstede's dimensions and the results of his research) so that L&D professionals are able to design bespoke curricula that suit learners from different cultures. This learner-centred orientation not only helps L&D professionals to develop and implement L&D solutions that are appropriate for individuals from different cultures but also to know how to combine different methods to cater for culturally diverse learners. L&D professional working internationally might need to deliver learning and coaching sessions themselves. This means that they have to develop their training delivery skills, for example, to ensure that they respond to the different learning modalities.

Another set of skills that the global L&D professional needs to develop is cultural savviness, which builds upon the previous two sets of skills. Cultural savviness is not only about being culturally sensitive, which is the ability to analyse and respond to the different needs of the members of different cultures, but also being perceptive in knowing how to leverage upon learners' inclinations due to culture to enhance their learning. Cultural savviness is about being aware of how other elements may influence learners' receptiveness to learning. for example, the use of rewards, the selection and promotion of trainers and how technology is used, if at all.

For example, when using Hofstede's culture framework to explore the cultural needs of employees from Brazil and Belgium it becomes apparent that societies in Brazil and Belgium are both generally considered high on the power distance dimension with a score of 69 and 65 respectively. This may mean employees preferring one-way communication in training (a sage-on-stage as discussed in Chapter 5) and receiving feedback from a trainer who is highly valued in the organization or society in general (somebody who is a senior manager or who holds a PhD). In another example using the same countries, Brazil scores low on the individualism dimension (which indicates it is a collectivist society) while Belgium scores the high score of 75 (meaning it is a very individualistic society). As such, L&D professional who are designing learning activities for the Brazilian workforce need to be politically savvy and design L&D exercises that occur within groups (eg action learning sets) to enhance engagement. On the other hand, Belgians prefer to focus on their own individual learning, and therefore any work related to L&D should relate to the individual, eg use of reflective learning. L&D professionals also need to be able to tolerate ambiguity, as they will have to work in situations they are not familiar with and as a result of this they need to be comfortable with being flexible and not knowing the answers all of the time.

Finally, the global L&D professional will need to develop business skills. Business and commercial acumen is crucial, as how business is done differs around the world; even the economic systems (or what drives the economy) are different. For example, the economies of Japan and South Korea reflect the notion of Keiretsu and Chaebol in the business world respectively. Keiretsu are groups of companies that have cross-shareholding in each other's companies, which therefore creates informal business groups that hold a lot of power, economically across sectors and even at times politically (Aoki and Lennerfors, 2013; Kensy, 2016). Chaebols are similar but their arrangements are more formal as they are characteristic of large conglomerates that own multiple businesses across diverse industries, and are just as powerful in their own country (Kalinowski, 2009; Lee, Ryu and Kang, 2014).

The 'arrangements' of both Keiretsu and Chaebol (and of similar forms) may not be consistent with the US and UK's view on competition and corporate governance, specifically that business organizations cannot collude with another in any way and that there are clear and genuine separations of powers in organizations. This illustrates that even countries that have a market-driven economy have their brand of capitalism, and each will have differences with others – of course much more with centrally-planned economies, by definition. Ultimately, business and commercial acumen is recognizing that different business practices in different countries may be unique (eg Australian straight talking, Japanese contemplative style of negotiation) in terms of 'what works' in different countries and 'who pulls the strings'. Not every country has business practices as transparent as those in the UK or in most western economies.

Exercise

Reflect upon the examples discussed and the challenges that L&D professionals may face from operating at an international level. What other challenges do you foresee L&D professionals confronting?

Joaquim Gonsalves, a seasoned HR professional, shares his experience in setting up an HR and L&D practice within a small airline in Cambodia. This case example draws on many of the key points discussed in this chapter, such as the impact of a country's stage of economic development on L&D, labour markets and education levels, national culture and of course capabilities required from global L&D (and HR) professionals.

Joaquim Gonsalves (MCIPD), head of HR, Bassaka Air

A global HR/ L&D professional
I am both an airline and HR/L&D professional. I spent 18 years of my work
life based in Doha with Qatar Airways. Having joined them in 1997 when
they had a strength of just four aircraft, I left Qatar Airways in 2014 with
the aircraft count having risen to 135 and a total staff strength of 45,000
employees. Besides gaining the distinction of being not only the number
one airline in the world as rated by Skytrax – an international airline rating
company – the airline had also achieved a five-star status during my time
with them. I moved to Cambodia in late 2014, as the challenge and learning
opportunity that was on offer was something I could not pass up.

The organization and human resources
Bassaka Air, based in Phnom Penh, Cambodia was a start-up airline with
two aircraft and with a total staff strength of 160. As part of the pioneering
team, my role was to set up the HR and L&D departments, and help
develop and implement strategies that were aligned with Bassaka Air's
vision. This was going to require experience, entrepreneurship and
adaptiveness. With no HR unit in place, the first step here was to develop
an appreciation and recognition across the organization of the importance
of strong HR fundamentals. Although we were operating in an emerging
market, we believed we should start with strong aspirations by adopting
higher standards and best practices, which were reflected in our HR
policies and processes.

From an HR operations perspective, our first task was to make sure we
complied with all of the country's legal requirements. For example, local
labour and commerce registrations and certifications would have to be
acquired. This was done through the Ministry of Labour and Commerce in
Cambodia. The Ministry of Labour has a requirement that all companies
operating in the country have to maintain at least 90 per cent local staff.
The ministry also required evidence of the presence of an internal HR
policies and procedures manual, and a staff handbook certified by the
ministry. We also set up a Shop Steward policy (in applying for and
acquiring work books for local staff and work permits for expatriate staff.),
which was required for companies with more than 100 employees

As all of the above was being worked on, one very important factor had
to be kept in mind, and that was our human capital. The intention here was
to avoid falling into the trap of focusing just on policies and procedures

▶

whilst forgetting who these were actually going to impact, which was our people. At an early stage, we clearly defined the values and ethos of our organization, which would be aspirational and encouraging, epitomized by our motto, 'Continuous Learning'. We encourage and nurture a climate that is conducive to continuous learning; this is reflected in both our words and our actions. We include our statement of intent in regard to continuous learning in our L&D policy and we act upon this at every opportunity as we endeavour to provide learning opportunities (formal and informal) to our workforce. I believe this clearly demonstrates our intention and commitment to articulating our employee value proposition. Having this known to prospective employees would be a crucial factor in attracting talent at an early stage in our growth.

We have concentrated on first understanding and defining the skills and behaviour we need for specific roles and then ensuring that these are practised and developed at the employees' own pace within their current work load. We have been very clear with what we expect from our employees and focused our programmes on bridging those gaps. We strive to ensure that our people grow and evolve with the business.

Cambodian labour market
L&D practices in Cambodia have tended to focus on 'hard skills' and technical abilities in support of government policies and the manufacturing sector. For example, according to the Ministry of Commerce in 2010, 320,734 people, of whom 293,664 are women, are employed in 269 garment factories in Cambodia. This sector is significant for Cambodia's economy; for example, in 2009, garment exports were valued at US \$2,385 million.

The general population census of Cambodia (for 2008) and the Ministry of Planning (in 2009) state that compulsory education completed by literate persons aged 25 years and over was approximately 47 per cent, with many not having even completed primary education. Only 1.8 per cent had completed diploma levels. Shortfalls in the labour market are accentuated in the Cambodian market by inadequate and 'unspecific' university programmes where 70 per cent of potential employees have a 'business-related' degree. It is envisaged that only 20 per cent will find a job related to their actual studies. A range of soft skill certifications are on offer, with very little valid credibility or reliability of the course offered or syllabus taught, resulting in young talent spending time and money in acquiring certificates but no placements in the job market.

From a cultural perspective, there is a strong propensity towards respecting superiors that results in employees keeping quiet at all costs to avoid conflict at the workplace, or not raising concerns until a tipping point is reached with an 'unexplained' resignation (due to frustration and job dissatisfaction). The average Cambodian business manager or employee is younger than the world average, but they are highly motivated to learn and improve.

The airline sector and L&D

Aviation is the most regulated sector after banking. Whether an airline operates with two aircraft like Bassaka Air, or with 135 aircraft, as is the case with Qatar Airways, it does not make much of a difference in meeting the threshold regulatory standards, and both will still require the same levels of effort (eg training and structures in place) in order to receive flying permissions and an international operating licence. The scale of effort in this regard can be quite substantial, and all airlines are treated equally from a technical and legal perspective. As such, size in the airline sector does help, as one can take advantage of economies of scale and economies of scope. For example, larger airlines can afford to have additional services that add to their overall brand without incurring extra technical cost. Larger airlines can offer a pick up and drop off for their First Class customers, while a smaller airline may not offer a First Class service at all.

L&D in aviation has to be clearly demarcated into certified and compulsory training as required by the International Air Transport Association (IATA), which is more technical than developmental training, which addresses competency building. IATA Certified Training at Bassaka Air is managed and delivered by our flight operations unit, with HR not having a stake in delivery or management of this training. It is specific to positions like captain, first officer and aircraft engineer. Many people outside aviation circles may not be aware that cabin crew initial training is a regulated course through the International Civil Aviation Organization (ICAO), with a set course module and requirement. Participants need to pass verbal and written examinations that are technical in nature and related to the aircraft type the cabin crew will be flying. Clearance of this course/exam, which typically takes eight weeks, results in them receiving a flying licence that has to be renewed every year through a refresher course.

▶

L&D in Bassaka Air

The L&D units work under a broader HR umbrella. The entire workforce of Bassaka Air currently stands at 160. Due to limitations in available talent, we need to retain our staff as much as possible, so L&D plays a crucial role here. Staff who feel they are developing and being challenged will tend to have higher job satisfaction and will stay. As part of the L&D process, we first focused on employee engagement, where regular sessions were conducted at a departmental, one-on-one level to understand employees' expectations (as well as each department's requirement) from a learning and development perspective.

The airline largely depends on the expertise of a few aviation professionals who have significant experience in other airlines. These professionals all have different nationalities. Whilst their experience and expertise are helpful, they also had to be provided with L&D interventions to negate the tendency to fall back on what they had learned and practised in the past rather than contextualizing their practice to their new environment (Cambodia, small airline). L&D works towards building a more cohesive organization by providing regular updates through weekly orientation sessions that help bring the staff together under one roof. At these sessions, management explain the need for certain policies to help staff understand the rationale behind them, thus leading to better acceptance.

Courses specific to language and work ethics were developed and delivered to staff at lower levels, as this was essential to create a cooperative atmosphere and address 'do's and 'don'ts' at the work place. We have also set an L&D policy in place whereby local staff of Cambodian origin are encouraged to further their managerial and leadership skills by attending training programmes in Singapore and Malaysia, as facilities there are better. These locations also provide them with an opportunity to interact with other nationalities and professionals from other industries, and expose them to new ways of thinking. This, in my opinion, allows training to have a more lasting impact. As we grow in numbers, we have plans to conduct these courses in-house, using our own staff to both design and deliver the courses. In 2016 we will be concentrating on implementing the concept of emotional intelligence in our training schedules. This will hopefully not only help staff to improve their performance at work but also enhance their personal development to be able to better manage their work–life balance.

I think our L&D initiatives are proving successful, as we currently have over 20 positions occupied by local Cambodian staff with no previous aviation experience who have, in the last 18 months, progressed from entry levels to supervisors, assistant managers and managers. As far as Bassaka Air is concerned, this is one of our great achievements; our people are empowered through training and rewarded through recognition! We now have quite a few local staff dreaming of one day flying one of our aircraft as pilots... and we in the HR/L&D team wish to keep those dreams alive and make them a reality one day! I do not see that day being too far away.

The case example illustrates some of the challenges that global L&D professionals may face. For example, Cambodia is an emerging economy and labour regulations in such countries can be very different to those in developed or developing nations. The laws in these countries can have a different focus, for example developing the indigenous workforce who may have low education attainment. In addition, the prevailing Cambodian culture discourages the indigenous workforce from questioning or even discussing frankly issues in the workplace for fear that may be perceived as being disrespectful. Such cultural differences mean that the airline requires a different approach to management and the development of its workforce.

The airline, although based in Cambodia, is also regulated by world standards that the whole industry has to meet. This, as Joaquim highlighted, is the biggest challenge, as the airline has to help develop an indigenous workforce with education attainment levels that may not be of world standards, but at the same time has to comply with regulations that are of international standard (and therefore operate at these international standards). The case example, however, indicates that the airline intends to aim higher aspires to go beyond the regulations in developing the airline's workforce. Joaquim also discusses the various training and development programmes that have been initiated for this young airline, to develop the workforce all round in both technical and soft skills. L&D in the airline is also observed to have a responsibility for employee engagement, and this not surprising, given how L&D has many 'touchpoints' with employees (given that 'normal' employee engagement channels that may be effective in the West may not be as effective in Cambodia due to the aforementioned cultural differences).

Exercise

Reflecting on the case example, how would the four key skills of global L&D professionals – adaptive skills, technical (content) knowledge, cultural savviness and business and commercial acumen – be applied?

Exercise

This exercise is to help you reflect on some important elements that may be important in developing and delivering L&D solutions for international markets. Select two countries and, using present-day information, complete the table below. Use the information in the table to guide you in designing and delivering an L&D solution involving developing the management skills of junior managers (the first column has been completed to give you an idea of what is required)

Table 8.2 Identifying important elements in developing and delivering L&D solutions for international markets exercise

Macro factors and national culture		Developing interpersonal skills	
		1st national culture selected by you (eg UK)	2nd national culture selected by you
Economic	Economic stage of development	Developed economy and highly developed standards. To include topics related to ethics, corporate social responsibility, diversity and inclusion.	
	Economic cycle	Recovering from a recession. Economic indicators are generally positive although it is still in a precarious position (may regress if the economy is not managed well). Depending on the organization, the L&D solution will need to be conscious of the costs involved.	

Table 8.2 *continued*

Macro factors and national culture		Developing interpersonal skills	
		1st national culture selected by you (eg UK)	2nd national culture selected by you
Technology	State of infrastructure	Highly developed infrastructure for technology, eg high-speed broadband and wi-fi available in most urban areas. The L&D solution can be designed involving technology without too much concern about availability.	
	Need for technology in L&D	High. Technology is pervasive. Business models, L&D curriculum are just examples of where technology is needed to help strategies and activities materialize. The use of technology may even be expected. The use of technology to be considered and incorporated into the delivery.	
	Perception of technology in L&D	Largely positive. Various technologies have evolved from being used in one function (or area) to others, eg social media for socializing to being used for work. Most people are willing to learn and experiment with new technologies. Facilitator should leverage upon learners' innovativeness in this area in the class.	

Table 8.2 *continued*

Macro factors and national culture		Developing interpersonal skills	
		1st national culture selected by you (eg UK)	**2nd national culture selected by you**
Labour	Labour market	Labour market is varied in terms of skills, reflecting the diverse sectors in the UK where the labour market for services is the largest. The labour market in the UK is considered to be highly skilled. The advancement of labour skills means that it is quite likely that the curriculum needs to reflect this sophistication. Various institutes such as CIPD and the Chartered Management Institute can be referred to for ideas.	
	Education system	The UK education system is perceived to be highly advanced. The education sector is a significant 'exporter'. An advanced education system means that L&D professionals can more easily identify the 'standard' to which they are delivering the L&D solution, eg final year undergraduate, postgraduate level. There are many benchmark statements that L&D professionals can use as reference.	

Table 8.2 *continued*

Macro factors and national culture		Developing interpersonal skills	
		1st national culture selected by you (eg UK)	**2nd national culture selected by you**
National culture	Power distance	Low power distance; people do not accept inequality. Trainers should adopt the role as facilitators. Learners' participation to be highly encouraged and designed in.	
	Uncertainty avoidance	Generally low uncertainty avoidance; people in the UK are happy to 'go with the flow'. Trainers should be receptive to learners and have some flexibility (if learners want to explore a particular topic further).	
	Individualism/ collectivism	High on individualism. Equality is important but so are the rights of the individuals (equity). Facilitators should provide more recognition to individual learners' backgrounds in designing classroom activities so that each can better contribute.	
	Masculinity/ femininity	Generally more femininity, with quality of life generally considered and appreciated. Cooperation (rather than competitive) environment for group learning.	

5 Summary and points for reflection

This chapter examined what L&D professionals have to consider in developing and delivering L&D solutions for international markets. Recent developments that have emerged over the last 30 years have led to an increased interest in the practice of L&D, namely globalization and the recent increased attention given to human capital by organizational managers. We then explored the main macro factors that impact L&D internationally: economic development and cycles, technology infrastructure and application, and labour markets and education systems.

When discussing the economy, two major themes were examined: the stage of development of an economy and the current state of the economy (economic boom or recession), and how these influence the development, adoption and implementation of L&D strategies and practices. This was followed by the exploration of the major factors that impact the use of technology for L&D purposes in different countries. Three factors were identified in this section: the availability of technology, the need to use technology in L&D, and the perceived importance of technology in L&D. The final macro factor was the discussion on labour markets and education systems, and how this shapes the skills and capabilities of a country's workforce.

The next major section involved examining the impact of culture on L&D. We used Hofstede's cultural dimensions as our lens in understanding how a nation's score on each of these dimensions helps to inform L&D professionals in designing solutions that fit best with the needs of workers in different international markets. The final section included an exploration of the different sets of skills an L&D professional should develop in order to operate at international/ global levels. The key points for reflection are:

- The macro factors identified (economic, social, technological and culture) are interconnected and ever changing. The global L&D professional should understand that these are dynamic factors and do not happen in a vacuum. As such, any change in one of these environments will impact the others and this should be taken into consideration when developing L&D strategies and solutions.

- There are several contextual factors (eg organization size, sector/industry and sub-culture of geographical region) that have been examined in other chapters (eg Chapter 2). These should also be taken into consideration by L&D professionals when designing bespoke learning and development solutions, as what works for one organization might not work for another if any of these factors differ.

- As the workforce is increasingly becoming more and more diverse and global, it is vital for the L&D professional to take into consideration not only the national culture the organization operates in but also the industry/sector and organizational culture. Multiple perspective taking should be adopted.

References

Allinson, C W and Hayes, C J (2000) Cross-national differences in cognitive style: implications for management, *International Journal of Human Resource Management*, **11** (1), pp. 161–70

Aoki, K and Lennerfors, T T (2013) Whither Japanese keiretsu? The transformation of vertical keiretsu in Toyota, Nissan and Honda 1991–2011, *Asia Pacific Business Review*, **19** (1), pp. 70–84

Awate, S, Larsen, M M and Mudambi, R (2014) Accessing vs sourcing knowledge: a comparative study of R&D internationalization between emerging and advanced economy firms, *Journal of International Business Studies*, **46** (1), pp. 63–86

Bennett, E E (2014) How an intranet provides opportunities for learning organizational culture implications for virtual HRD, *Advances in Developing Human Resources*, **16** (3), pp. 296–319

Chartered Institute of Personnel and Development (2011) International learning and talent development comparison survey 2011, *CIPD* [online] http://www.cipd.co.uk/hr-resources/survey-reports/international-learning-talent-development-comparison-survey-2011.aspx

Chartered Institute of Personnel and Development (2015) Learning and development 2015, CIPD [online] http://www.cipd.co.uk/hr-resources/survey-reports/learning-development-2015.aspx

Child, J, Chung, L and Davies, H (2003) The performance of cross-border units in China: a test of natural selection, strategic choice and contingency theories *Journal of International Business Studies*, **34** (3), pp. 242–54

Economist Intelligence Unit (2014) Evolution of work and the worker, *SHRM* [online] https://www.shrm.org/about/foundation/shapingthefuture/documents/2-14%20theme%201%20paper-final%20for%20web.pdf

El Raheb, L, Jans, I, Junior, J, Moermans, Y and Zijlstra, I (2012) The influence of L&D opportunities on highly qualified technical foreign (HQTF) workers' decision to come and stay working in the Eindhoven-Leuven- Aachen (ELAt) region, Evhoppe [online] http://evhoppe.nl/wp-content/uploads/Internationaal-FMEproject_reportfinal.pdf

Eraut, M (2014) Informal learning in the workplace, *Studies in Continuing Education*, **26** (2), pp. 247–73

Euromonitor International (2014) China overtakes the US as the world's largest economy: impact on industries and consumers worldwide, Euromonitor International [online] http://go.euromonitor.com/whitepaper-china-overtakes-us-worlds-largest-economy.html

Glenn, J C, Gordon, T J and Florescu, E (2014) 2013–14 State of the Future, The Millennium Project [online] http://millennium-project.org/millennium/201314SOF.html

Harzing, A W and Van Ruysseveldt, J, Eds (2004) *International Human Resource Management*, 2nd edn, Sage Publications, London

Hofstede, G (1980) *Culture's Consequences: International differences in work-related values*, Sage Publications, Beverly Hills, CA

Hofstede, G (1986) Cultural differences in teaching and learning, *International Journal of Intercultural Relations*, **10**, pp. 301–20

Hofstede, G (2001) *Culture's Consequences*, 2nd edn, Sage, London

Kalinowski, T (2009) The politics of market reforms: Korea's path from Chaebol Republic to market democracy and back, *Contemporary Politics*, **15** (3), pp. 287–304

Kensy, R (2016) *Keiretsu Economy–New Economy?: Japan's multinational enterprises from a postmodern perspective*, Palgrave Macmillan, Basingstoke, Hampshire

Keys, T S and Malnight, T W (2014) *The Global Trends Fieldbook: From data to insights to action*, Strategy Dynamics Global SA

Lee, J Y, Ryu, S and Kang, J (2014) Transnational HR network learning in Korean business groups and the performance of their subsidiaries, *The International Journal of Human Resource Management*, **25** (4), 588–608

Loon, M (2014) *L&D: New challenges, new approaches*, Chartered Institute of Personnel and Development, London

Manyika, J, Bughin, J, Lund, S, Nottebohm, O, Poulter, D, Jauch, S and Ramaswamy, S (2014) Global Flows in a Digital Age: How trade, finance, people, and data connect the world economy, McKinsey [online] http://www.mckinsey.com/business-functions/strategy-and-corporate-finance/our-insights/global-flows-in-a-digital-age

Marsick, V J and Volpe, M (2000) *Advances in Developing Human Resources: Informal learning on the job*, Berrett-Koehler, San Francisco

Meyer, K E (2007) Contextualising organisational learning: Lyles and Salk in the context of their research, *Journal of International Business Studies*, **38** (1), pp. 27–37

Overton, L and Dixon, G (2015) Embracing Change: Improving performance of business, individuals and the L&D team. 2015-16 Industry benchmark report, Towards Maturity [online}] http://www.towardsmaturity.org/article/2015/11/05/embracing-change-improving-performance-benchmark/

Perlow, L and Weeks, J (2002) Who's helping whom? Layers of culture and workplace behavior, *Journal of Organizational Behavior*, **23**, pp. 345–61

Stohl, C (1993) European managers' interpretations of participation: a semantic network analysis, *Human Communication Research*, **20** (1), pp. 97–117

Taras, V, Steel, P and Kirkman, B L (2011) Three decades of research on national culture in the workplace: do the differences still make a difference? *Organizational Dynamics*, **40** (3), pp. 189–98

Theodorakopoulos, N, Patel, C and Budhwar, P (2012) Knowledge flows, learning and development in an international context, *European Journal of International Management*, **6** (1), pp. 1–9

Towards Maturity (2013) The new learning agenda – talent: technology: change, *Towards Maturity* [online] http://www.towardsmaturity.org/article/2013/11/11/new-learning-agenda-talenttechnologychange/

Towards Maturity (2014) The learner voice: Part 1, *Towards Maturity* [online] http://www.towardsmaturity.org/article/2014/04/09/towards-maturity-learner-voice-part-1/

Tweed, R G and Lehman, D R (2002) Learning considered within a cultural context: Confucian and Socratic approaches, *American Psychologist*, **57** (2), pp. 89–99

Van Oudenhoven, J P (2001) Do organizations reflect national cultures? A ten nations study. *International Journal of Intercultural Relationships*, **25**, pp. 89–107

Zahra, S A and George, G (2002) Absorptive capacity: a review, reconceptualization, and extension, *Academy of Management Review*, **27** (2), pp. 185–203

Future directions

09

I hope that the eight chapters in this book have provided you with some useful knowledge and ideas of where the L&D profession is headed and how it can do its part in contributing to organizational performance through the solutions it crafts. It is also hoped that through the introduction and discussion of various frameworks, we have laid the foundations that will enable you to advance in your careers in learning and development. I would like to conclude this book by highlighting some areas that may become more prominent in the future for L&D.

There are three broad areas that play an important role in L&D's work and professional development, and therefore warrant some discussion. The first involves the development of integral qualities within L&D professionals. The second is the increasing importance of social learning (for informal learning) and work-based learning (for formal learning), and the growing use of immersive environments and role-playing interventions. Finally, the third is the configuration of L&D units in relation to other people management units within contemporary organizations.

Chapters 2, 3 and 6 have demonstrated how important it is for L&D professionals to be savvy in other areas in addition to learning and development. There are three types of savviness: business, organizational and context. Being business savvy is to understand the organization's 'business model', whilst organizational savviness is being able to work with internal processes, politics and other organizational realities. Finally, context savviness is being astute in considering the situational factors that may shape the design and development of learning and development strategy, processes and interventions that 'fit' the organization's needs, such as using the right technology for the right purposes.

The other qualities are being 'affecting and aligned'; that is, to be able to influence stakeholders and enact change to align people's capabilities through L&D strategy and activities. These qualities also provide a stronger foundation in developing relational capability to foster coalitions from a diverse set of stakeholders which, in turn, helps L&D professionals to be more effective in the role of a change agent to better facilitate change. Finally, the qualities of versatility and being ubiquitous contribute to the development of new networks, alliances and learning partnerships with business schools, unions, employer representative bodies, other educational institutions, other organizations (eg for benchmarking purposes), customers and suppliers, professional and industry bodies, government agencies, and consultancies.

In terms of the field of L&D interventions and environments, social learning will continue to play a significant role, although this may not be a surprise, as we know how important learning from peers and informal learning are to adults (as discussed in Chapters 5 and 7). From a 'formal learning' perspective, work-based learning will become more important, especially as such blends provide organizations and the workforce with the best of two worlds: gaining qualifications and authentic learning that occurs in the actual environments where performance takes place. Indeed, as L&D professionals and organizations experiment more, we may begin to see specific types of blends emerge. Blends in the future may further encompass immersive and role-playing environments (in both virtual and physical worlds).

Whilst technology is important, there are advanced L&D mechanisms that are equally effective but are technology-light. For example, although this approach has been around for some time, more and more organizations have started to recognize the benefits of real-life simulations that are authentic, and genuinely help develop skills such as leadership. Ashley Callaghan, a professional trainer, provides such services for organizations using professional actors for an array of purposes such as leadership development, developing change management skills and improving organizational performance. Ashley states that at times his team undertakes role playing covertly, so target employees do not know that they are indeed 'in training'. The impact of these training interventions is profound and insightful, as they help organizations to truly see where the gaps in their capabilities are and how they can be addressed.

Finally, how L&D professionals play a role in building organizational capability is influenced by how the L&D unit is configured with other related business units and/or integrated with other functions/activities. For example, L&D may be a stand-alone function, be part of HR, be merged with OD or may be one of OD's constituents, along with HR and change management.

How L&D is configured with other units is not an exact science and depends on how L&D is perceived within the organization compared to other functions such as talent management and organizational development

(Hird and Sparrow, 2012). There are indications that contemporary organizations are rethinking how best to organize their people operations function, which includes L&D, talent management, organizational development, performance management, and change management. From the array of combinations, Hird and Sparrow (2012) suggest that the most promising constellations that may arise in the future are:

- L&D, talent management, resourcing and leadership;
- L&D and performance management;
- L&D and organizational effectiveness;
- Collaborative L&D delivery.

In the first constellation, L&D takes the leading roles in developing change and leadership capabilities, and addressing skills gaps respectively. This configuration may suit organizations who aim to focus equally on talent as well as 'whole career' management. This constellation also uses L&D as both a motivational and retention tool. The second constellation, L&D and performance management, is premised upon the growing trend in requiring L&D to demonstrate value to the organization through increased performance of its people. This configuration pays equal attention to the talented elite and other employees who want to make the step up.

The third, L&D and organizational effectiveness, constellation, is suited for organizations that are undergoing significant changes in their business model. Hird and Sparrow (2012) claim a broad 'organizational effectiveness' label that encompasses resourcing, talent management, organizational design and development, and helps to forge a closer relationship amongst these functions, focused on organizational 'tangible' outcomes.

The fourth constellation, collaborative L&D delivery, which is a cross-organizational L&D configuration, is typically more suited for public and third-sector organizations, and for those where cost savings in this area are imperative. In this constellation, L&D provisions are decentralized and shared amongst a number of organizations such as local authorities. There is a view that it is also important to develop individuals in the extended enterprise who are part of the organization's network (Kinnie *et al*, 2012).

What the future holds for L&D professionals is not entirely known. However, as Cohen and Levinthal (1994) assert in their work involving absorptive capacity, which is about organizations' fundamental learning processes, 'fortune favours the prepared (mind and firm)'. Organizations may not know what tomorrow brings, but they can prepare themselves.

Organizations will therefore need the help of L&D professionals more than ever before, and I hope this book has, in turn, been able to help you, the L&D professional, to be well positioned to drive and enable organizational capability and performance.

References

Cohen, W M and Levinthal, D A (1994) Fortune favors the prepared firm, *Management Science*, **40** (2)

Hird, M and Sparrow, P (2012) Learning & development: seeking a renewed focus? *Centre for Performance-led HR* [online] https://www.lancaster.ac.uk/media/lancaster-university/content-assets/documents/lums/cphr/LDWP.pdf

Kinnie, N, Swart, J, Hope-Hailey, V and van Rossenberg, Y (2012) Innovative forms of organising: networked working, *CIPD* [online] https://www.cipd.co.uk/binaries/hr-and-its-role-in-innovation_2014-part-1-networked-working.pdf

INDEX

Page numbers in *italic* indicate figures or tables.